Windows Server 2012 Security from End to Edge and Beyond

Windows Server 2012 Security from End to Edge and Beyond

Architecting, Designing, Planning, and Deploying Windows Server 2012 Security Solutions

Thomas W. Shinder

Yuri Diogenes

Debra Littlejohn Shinder

Richard Hicks, Technical Editor

AMSTERDAM • BOSTON • HEIDELBERG • LONDON
NEW YORK • OXFORD • PARIS • SAN DIEGO
SAN FRANCISCO • SINGAPORE • SYDNEY • TOKYO

ELSEVIER

Syngress is an Imprint of Elsevier

SYNGRESS

Acquiring Editor:	Chris Katsaropoulos
Editorial Project Manager:	Benjamin Rearick
Project Manager:	Punithavathy Govindaradjane
Designer:	Alan Studholme

Syngress is an imprint of Elsevier
225 Wyman Street, Waltham, MA 02451, USA

Library of Congress Cataloging-in-Publication Data
Shinder, Thomas W.
  Windows server 2012 security from end to edge and beyond : architecting, designing, planning, and deploying Windows server 2012 security solutions / Thomas W Shinder, Yuri Diogenes, Debra Littlejohn Shinder.
      pages cm
  Includes bibliographical references and index.
  ISBN 978-1-59749-980-4 (alk. paper)
1. Microsoft Windows server. 2. Operating systems (Computers) 3. Computer security.
I. Diogenes, Yuri. II. Shinder, Debra Littlejohn. III. Title.
  QA76.774.M434S55 2013
  005.8–dc23
                                                                    2013005194

British Library Cataloguing-in-Publication Data
A catalogue record for this book is available from the British Library

ISBN: 978-1-59749-980-4

Printed and bound in the United States of America

13 14 15 16 17   10 9 8 7 6 5 4 3 2 1

For information on all Syngress publications, visit our website at *www.syngress.com*

Contents

Acknowledgments

After about 30 books and thousands of articles and millions of words written, you'd think the task of writing would get easier. This book was a yearlong effort shared among Yuri Diogenes, Deb Shinder, and myself. Hundreds of hours of research and testing went into this book. There are a number of people I'd like to thank and acknowledge for their efforts, encouragement, and motivation in making this book come to fruition. First, thanks to Yuri Diogenes for staying upbeat and positive in spite of long hours and multiple responsibilities—without Yuri's "Outlook," we would never have been able to complete this book. I want to thank my beautiful wife Deb Shinder for her willingness to step in and take on some of the heavy lifting while we were in midstream—without her exceptional quality input, this book would have been much less than it is today. John Dawson receives my utmost appreciation for motivating us to be all that we can be and encouraging us to reach down for that extra effort needed to bring this effort across the wire. I want to extend a special thanks for Adina Hagege for recruiting me to work for Microsoft. It's been a wild ride and there's never a boring day. The opportunities for growth and learning and pushing the boundaries make me look forward to going to work in the morning. Kudos and many thanks go to Richard Hicks for providing an amazingly helpful and actionable technical edit on this book. A big high five for Tim Rains for his gracious contribution to the foreword of this book. Thanks and gratitude go to Bill Gates, Paul Allen, and Steve Ballmer for changing the world for the better—I owe more than I can put into words. Finally, I thank God for all the blessings that He's given me, including the strength, the intelligence, and the will to complete this and all my other projects.

Tom Shinder

Every book is a new journey, and this one couldn't be different. I'm fortunate to have the full support of my wife Alexsandra Diogenes and my beautiful daughters Yanne and Ysis throughout this journey—I love you. I'm also glad that I could once more have my friend Tom Shinder sharing this project with me; this is our fourth book together, and as always it is an enormous privilege to write with such a great person. I also would like to thank Deb Shinder for joining (literally hit the ground running) this project; it was great to partner with you on that. To our technical reviewer for precisely going through each chapter and suggesting improvements, thanks Richard Hicks. To wrap up this team of great minds, I would like to thank our friend Tim Rains for writing the foreword of this book; Tim, I truly appreciate all your support, thanks.

There were many people indirectly involved on this project that I would like to thank for. Some friends keep inspiring me even after leaving the IT field to pursue a new journey. Yes, Jim Harrison, I'm talking about you, buddy. Thanks for sharing your knowledge, your experience, and your friendship. To my close friends that were able to understand the times that I couldn't meet them for a party because I was busy writing: Alexandre Hollanda, Marcelo Fartura, Wilson Souza, Jose Moreira, and Marcus Paulino. Thanks, guys! Also, to all my coworkers (new and former); they were responsible for helping shape my knowledge: Gershon Levitz, Nathan Bigman, Jess Huber, Steve Dodson, Dan Watson, Mohit Saxena, Daniel Mauser, Eddie Bowers, Andrew Davis, Dan Herzog, Thomas Detzner, Jamir Correa, Vandy Rodrigues, and Phillip Sand.

When you have great leaders at work, new challenges become easy to deal with. I'm fortunate to have great leaders that keep inspiring us to do better; thanks for Adina Hagege and John Dawson for leading us to great places.

Last, but certainly not least, I would like to thank God for guiding me daily and for enabling me to do what I love.

Yuri Diogenes

Writing a book is always a journey that takes you into unexpected places. Coauthoring a book with others makes the process easier in many ways and sometimes more challenging in others. Sometimes you get lucky and get to work with people who smooth the way. It helps when those people are not just random colleagues, but folks you know and like. So I want to extend a big "thank you" to my husband, Tom Shinder, and my good friend, Yuri Diogenes, who were my constant companions on this particular trip from outline to printed text. In addition, I thank those at Syngress for the opportunity to participate in this project, and my colleagues and readers in the IT security community, from whom I've learned so much over the years.

Deb Shinder

The authors would also like to thank Adina Hagege, John Dawson, Jose Barreto, Yigal Edery, Travis Plunk, Josh Adams, Frank Simorjay, Jose Maldonado, Cecilia Cole, Tim Springston, Ned Pyle, Joe Davis, Steve Dodson, Jim Harrison, Kim Ditto-Ehlert, Greg Marshall, Starr Anderson, Jim Dial, Jason Jones, Mohit Kumar, Pat Fetty, David Cross, Kathy Watanabe, Bryon Surace, Mike Truitt, John Morello, Ben Bernstein, Joe Davies, Bala Natarajan, Ben Ari, Pat Telford, Tam Viet Pham, Tom Roughley, Jeff Lilleskare, Dana Knipp, Shawn Aebi, and Billy Price.

About the Authors

Dr. Thomas W. Shinder is a 17-year veteran of the IT industry. Prior to entering IT, Tom graduated from the University of Illinois College of Medicine with a Doctor of Medicine degree and was a practicing neurologist with special interests in epilepsy and multiple sclerosis. Tom began his career in IT as a consultant and has worked with many large companies, including Fina Oil, Microsoft, IBM, HP, Dell, and many others. He started his writing career toward the end of the 1990s and has published over 30 books on Windows, Windows Networking, Windows Security and ISA Server/TMG, UAG, and Microsoft DirectAccess. For over a decade, ISA Server and TMG were Tom's passions, and he ran the popular Web site www.isaserver.org, in addition to writing eight books on ISA/TMG. Tom joined Microsoft in December of 2009 as a member of the UAG DirectAccess team and started the popular "Edge Man" blog that covered UAG DirectAccess. He is currently a Principal Knowledge Engineer in the Server and Cloud Division Information Experience Group Solution's Team and his primary focus now is private cloud—with special interests in private cloud infrastructure and security.

Yuri Diogenes started working in the IT field as computer operator back in 1993 using MS-DOS 5.5 and Windows 3.1. In 1998, he moved to a Microsoft Partner where he was instructor for computer classes and also wrote internal training materials on topics such as Windows NT 4 and Networking Essentials. His initial experience with security started in 1998 when he had to set up the Internet security connectivity using Microsoft Proxy 2.0 and Cisco routers. In 2001 Yuri released his first book (in Portuguese) about Cisco CCNA Certification. In 2003, Yuri accepted the offer to be a Professor in the University in Brazil where he taught operating system and computer network classes. In December 2003, he moved to United States to work for Microsoft as a contractor in the Customer Service and Support for Latin America messaging division.

In 2004, he moved to Dell Computers in Round Rock, Texas, to work as Server Advisor in the Network Operating System (NOS) Team, primarily dealing with Windows, Exchange, and ISA (2000/2004).

Yuri returned to Microsoft as a full-time employee in 2006 to work again on the Customer Service and Support for Latin America, but at this time to be dedicated to the platform division. There he was responsible for primarily supporting Windows Networking and ISA Server (200/2004/2006) for enterprise customers from Latin America. In 2007, he joined the Customer Services and Support Security Team as a Security Support Engineer where he was dedicated to work with Edge protection (ISA Server and then TMG). In 2010 Yuri cowrote the Forefront Administrator's Companion book and also three other Forefront books in partnership with Thomas W. Shinder. During this time, Yuri also wrote articles for his own blog (blogs.technet. com/yuridiogenes), *TechNet Magazine*, *ISSA Journal*, and other Security magazines in Brazil.

Nowadays, Yuri works as a senior technical writer for the Server and Cloud division Information Experience Team where he writes articles about cloud infrastructure with security functionalities baked in. In his current role, he also delivers presentations at public events such as TechED US, Europe, Brazil, and internal Microsoft conferences such as TechReady. Currently, Yuri is also working on his master degree in Cybersecurity Intelligence & Forensics at UTICA while also writing the second edition of his Security+ book (in Portuguese).

Yuri holds several industry certifications, including CISSP, E|CEH, E|CSA, CompTIA, Security+, CompTIA Cloud Essentials Certified, CompTIA Network+, CASP, MCSE, MCTS, MCT, and many other Microsoft certifications. You can follow Yuri on Twitter@yuridiogenes.

Debra Littlejohn Shinder is a technology consultant, trainer, and writer who has authored a number of books on computer operating systems, networking, and client and server security over the past 14 years. These include *Scene of the Cybercrime: Computer Forensics Handbook*, published by Syngress, and *Computer Networking Essentials*, published by Cisco Press. She is coauthor, with her husband, Dr. Thomas W. Shinder, of the best-selling *Configuring ISA Server 2000*, *Configuring ISA Server 2004*, and *ISA Server and Beyond*.

Deb has been a tech editor, developmental editor, and contributor on over 20 additional books on networking and security subjects, as well as study guides for Microsoft's MCSE exams, CompTIA's Security+ exam, and TruSecure's ICSA certification. She formerly edited the Element K *Inside Windows Server Security* journal. She authored a weekly column for TechRepublic's Windows blog, called *Microsoft Insights* and a monthly column on Cybercrime, and is a regular contributor to their Security blog, Smart Phones blog, and other TR blogs. She is the lead author on Windowsecurity. com and ISAServer.org, and her articles have appeared in print magazines such as Windows IT Pro (formerly Windows &.NET) Magazine. She has authored training material, corporate whitepapers, marketing material, webinars, and product documentation for Microsoft Corporation, Intel, HP, DigitalThink, GFI Software, Sunbelt Software, CNET, and other technology companies.

Deb specializes in security issues, cybercrime/computer forensics, and Microsoft server products; she has been awarded Microsoft's Most Valuable Professional (MVP) status in Enterprise Security for 8 years in a row. A former police officer and police academy instructor, she has taught many courses at Eastfield College in Mesquite, Texas, and sits on the board of the Criminal Justice Training Center there. She is a fourth-generation Texan and lives and works in the Dallas–Fort Worth area.

About the Technical Editor

Richard Hicks is a network and information security expert specializing in Microsoft technologies. An MCP, MCSE, MCITP Enterprise Administrator, CISSP, and four-time Microsoft Most Valuable Professional (MVP), he has traveled around the world speaking to network engineers, security administrators, and IT professionals about Microsoft edge security and remote access solutions. A former information security engineer for a Fortune 100 financial services company in the United States, he has nearly two decades of experience working in large-scale corporate computing environments. He has designed and deployed perimeter defense and secure remote access solutions for some of the largest companies in the world. Richard has served as a technical reviewer on several Windows networking and security books, and is a contributing author for http://WindowsSecurity.com and http://ISAserver.org. He's an avid fan of Major League Baseball and, in particular, the Los Angeles Angels (of Anaheim!), and also enjoys craft beer and single-malt Scotch whisky. Born and raised in Southern California, he still resides there with Anne, the love of his life and wife of 27 years, along with their four children. You can keep up with Richard by visiting http://www.richardhicks.com/.

Foreword

The threat landscape has evolved dramatically over the past 10 years in ways that have been challenging for organizations to understand, manage, and predict. In the wake of the successful mass worm attacks of 2003 (SQL Slammer and Blaster), organizations and information technology (IT) professionals began adapting to the rapidly changing threat level of the Internet. Host-based firewalls, security update deployment tools, and antivirus solutions became the primary ways in which organizations managed threats. IT professionals expanded their skill sets by learning about a whole new category of features, functionality, tools, and products that would help them manage the security of the infrastructure they were entrusted with.

For many, the new security requirements were painfully hard to understand, implement, and maintain. IT professionals were required to understand vulnerability details included in security bulletins, use this information to make thoughtful deployment decisions, and deploy security updates in large environments using rudimentary tools, all without disrupting the business they supported.

During this time, I was the technical lead on Microsoft's customer facing security incident response team. My team helped many customers get through these dark days. In times like those, an IT professional's best friend was well-written technical documentation and guidance that was accurate, authoritative, and from a trusted source. Understanding precisely how to configure, deploy, and manage security-related technologies and updates, and what to do if things didn't operate as expected, was invaluable.

Fast forward now 10 years to 2013. Things have changed dramatically. The threat landscape can no longer be characterized as a place where relatively simple worms with benign payloads run wild. Organized crime is now borrowing advanced vulnerabilities and threats reportedly developed by government espionage and cyber-warfare programs to attack organizations and governments. IT professionals, now with the aid of Chief Information Security Officers (CISOs) and professional risk managers, are defending critical infrastructures against targeted attacks perpetrated by determined adversaries who will use every dirty trick they can devise to compromise IT environments and steal information. Hacktivists focused on drawing attention to their political causes are also targeting organizations that IT professionals are expected to protect. The types of threats that IT professionals are now faced with are far more insidious than in the past, making the IT professional's job more challenging and important than ever before.

One thing that has not changed over the past 10 years is the need for well-written technical documentation and guidance that is authoritative, accurate, and from a trusted source. This is where Tom Shinder, Yuri Diogenes, and Debra Littlejohn Shinder have made some significant contributions over the years, and now in their latest book, *Windows Server 2012 Security from End to Edge and Beyond*. Within Microsoft, I have watched Tom and Yuri roll up their sleeves on a number of occasions over the past several years to become respected figures within the technical security community at Microsoft. I have seen Debra, a Microsoft Security MVP, work tirelessly to help IT professionals understand security-related technologies. Together they have produced a comprehensive book to provide IT professionals with the information they need to know about modern-day, cutting-edge security technologies. They didn't take the easy route and write about technologies that are relatively easy to understand and administer. They tackled some of the most complex security technologies that IT professionals typically look for help with, including Certificate Services, ADFS and ADRMS, and DirectAccess, to name a few. This book will help you understand the newest security technologies that are built into the latest operating systems from Microsoft that will be in IT environments for the next 5–10 years.

Tim Rains
Director, Trustworthy Computing
Microsoft Corporation

Planning Platform Security

CONTENTS

CHAPTER POINTS

- Reviewing the core Security Principles
- Planning a Secure Platform from End to Edge and Beyond
- From End to Edge and Beyond Chapter Previews

REVIEWING THE CORE SECURITY PRINCIPLES

Information security has evolved throughout the years, there is no more room for "band aid" solutions, and security must be integrated with all layers in order to better protect your data. The attacks that happened in the past years proved that investing only in technology in order to secure the data without educating the end user imposes a high security risk to the company. The most recommended formula is to keep the balance and make sure to mitigate all potential vulnerabilities, be vigilant to rapidly identify flaws, and have an incident response in place to reactive in a structured manner. But what this has to do with Windows Server 2012? Well, everything! The operating system is the main door to good and bad users to have access to your data. You might protect all other windows in your house, have a alarm system that alert you if something happens, have secure cameras all around the house, but if you fail to protect the main door, the whole investments in other security measures will not matter.

Windows 8 brings a new user experience with a radical change in the UI (User Interface) and also on the way that applications are presented to the end user. With the advent of social networks, it is clear that Windows 8 make it easier for the end user to get connected with others, share information, and socialize. While this is a natural trend for nowadays needs, the security concerns around this new era of information sharing are higher than in the past. We do not want to reinvent the wheel and we believe that the core security principles must remain intact, which means that we will focus on addressing the traditional security triad: Confidentiality, Integrity, and Availability.

In a nutshell, we believe that if you address this core security principle you will be answering the major concerns around data protection. As the operating system is the main door to access your data, we shall use the same approach to protect the operating system and how the users will use it to access the data (Figure 1.1).

Now you add to this landscape the fact that the data are not on your data center anymore, that is the way cloud computing starts introducing new challenges to data protection. The threat landscape that throughout the years companies were trying to tackle now is about to change with the adoption of cloud computing. Windows 8 is an operating system that was build with cloud computing in mind. There are many areas of improvement in this version that are related with how well Windows can be used to not only provide a great user experience while using cloud resources but also be the main platform to deploy a cloud infrastructure.

The core security principles must be applied to the whole infrastructure and that is why we have been using the phrase (which is the name of our Security Talk Show[1]): *From End* (security from endpoint) *to Edge* (regardless

User's needs	Security Concerns	Core Security Principle
I need to have access to my data while I am working from home	How can I ensure that the data are always available even when the user is remote?	Availability
I need to transmit this document to our partner and guarantee that there will be no change once I send it	How can I ensure that these data are not modified in transit?	Integrity
I need to be able to use my own device to have access to company sensitive data	How can I ensure that confidential data are preserved even when the user is using his own device to access it ?	Confidentiality

FIGURE 1.1 Evaluating user's needs while leveraging core security principles to address security concerns. (For color version of this figure, the reader is referred to the online version of this chapter.)

FIGURE 1.2 Defense in depth approach while moving to the cloud. (For color version of this figure, the reader is referred to the online version of this chapter.)

of your infrastructure edge protection is still important) *and Beyond* (beyond on-premises we mean, cloud resources). This also reinforce the use of the defense in depth approach in this new era of cloud computing. Figure 1.2 summarizes how we should use this approach while planning the overall security strategy.

---

[1]You can access the episodes of our Security Talk Show at http://blogs.technet.com/b/security_talk.

As we previously mentioned, the first step toward a better secure environment is to ensure your end users are well trained. They need to understand the risks and implications of their actions not only when they are using a corporate asset to access a resource but also when he is exposing company information in a social network. It is key to have a good security policy in place, but having a security policy without enforcing it does not really work. It is necessary to leverage technology to enforce security policy; Windows 8 provides a great flexibility and granularity on this respect. It is quite possible that your company will have some service running on the cloud while keeping others on-premises. Data will move from on-premises to the cloud and vice versa, and this imposes some risks. You cannot relax the on-premises security, because if you do, this will be your weakest point in the chain; keeping security consistent across the board is the key.

From the cloud perspective, the reality shows that many businesses will only migrate to the cloud if the cloud provider meets the compliance and regulatory requirements for the company. It is very important to be including this in the overall security plan because even knowing that is not you that will manage the compliance and regulatory needs; you are still accountable to ensure that your data are protected according to the required standards. You also need to understand the cloud provider security program. Is important to understand what this provider is doing to keep your data secure, What is security certifications do they have? Who is handling the data? We will go further on this conversation in Chapter 15, Cloud Security.

NOTE

Windows Server 2012 allows you to build your own cloud infrastructure, and this is a built-in feature in this release. Throughout the Beta timeframe, we wrote a set of documents that explains in more details how to build this cloud infrastructure.[2]

PLANNING A SECURE PLATFORM FROM END TO EDGE AND BEYOND

In order to take full advantage of the security feature set that Windows Server 2012 has built in, you should plan your security strategy in a way that security is baked in all process and procedures that exist in your company. The foundation platform that we propose is presented in Figure 1.3.

---

[2]You can access these documents from http://technet.microsoft.com/en-us/library/hh831441.aspx.

Core Elements of a Security Strategy

Phase 2
- Operating System Security
- Network Security
- Secure Software Development Strategy
- Determine Access Control

Phase 1
- Security Awareness Training
- Review Policies, Procedures, Standards and Guidelines
- Perform a Risk Analysis
- Understand Business Requirements

FIGURE 1.3 What core security elements should be addressed on each phase. (For color version of this figure, the reader is referred to the online version of this chapter.)

Before we present the foundation in which you could build your security strategy upon, it is important to emphasize that it is out of the scope of this book to provide further details on how to plan all elements of Phase 1 and Phase 2. Our core goal here is to expose those phases and as we explain and demonstrate the Windows Server 2012 security feature set, we will refer to this diagram for a better understanding of the overall security strategy. It is also important to clarify that these are core elements that should be present on the overall security strategy, which framework you will be use to implement that is also out of the scope of this book.

Understanding Business Requirements

The main goal in creating a security strategy is to address the overall business requirements regarding information security. Different company sizes will require different approaches as they will have different budget available to deal with information security. What it is really important here is that you can bring to the table a solid value proposition that will address the company's needs while stay on budget. The table below has a decision matrix sample:

As previously mentioned, this is only an example of how you can leverage the Windows 8 built in technology to address security business needs (Table 1.1).

Table 1.1

Scenario	Business Requirements	Proposed Solution
Small-medium business company with an overall limited budget without legacy applications	<ul><li>Data must be highly available for end users with a low maintenance cost</li><li>No budget for physical security</li><li>Limited budget to maintain its own IT infrastructure</li></ul>	Migrate to a public cloud infrastructure. This will address all core business needs. We will discuss more about Public Cloud in Chapter 15
Large enterprise that needs better control of the data, capability of rapid expansion and resource automation	<ul><li>Internal IT must be in control of the data</li><li>Departments should be logically isolated from each other</li><li>Reduce the amount of physical servers that are in use today</li></ul>	Migrate to a Windows Server 2012 Private cloud. This will meet all business requirements. We will discuss more about Private Cloud in Chapter 15
Large enterprise that needs to allow remote users to securely access internal resources in a transparent manner	<ul><li>Remote users should be able to access applications that are in the local network</li><li>The solution must be transparent to the user, in order words; they should have the same experience as they have when accessing the data internally</li></ul>	Migrate to Windows 8 DirectAccess Solution. This will allow users to securely access internal resources without manual intervention. We will discuss more about DirectAccess in Chapter 13
Large enterprise that has roaming users using laptops on the field and connecting to untrusted networks	<ul><li>Roaming users should be inspected for malware in all phases of a computer startup</li><li>Remediation actions should be done in order to fix potential issues</li></ul>	Migrate to Windows Server 2012 and use Platform Integrity in order to take advantage of the Trusted Boot feature. We will discuss more about Platform Integrity in Chapter 9

Perform Risk Analysis

How can you justify the security safeguards if you do not know the real risk? Well, that is what the risk analysis is for. It will be the tool that you will use to define and justify to upper management why those countermeasures should be in place. It always boils down to answering two questions:

- How much it cost if you have a breach and your data are compromised?
- How much it cost to mitigate this issue?

This is a huge subject and a deeper analysis of all variants is a book by itself. Just keep in mind that whatever you are going to propose as solution, you should have a concrete business case that was built upon a solid risk analysis.

Review Policies, Procedures, Standards, and Guidelines

No, they are not the same thing and that is why you really should understand the boundaries of each one in order to correctly plan and implement it. A company must have a security policy in place to determine the function that security will have in the organization. Different departments within the company will have different procedures in order to accomplish a specific goal. IT might have a procedure that explains how to restore a server in case of a completed failure, while HR will have a hiring process procedure that detailed explain how to hire a new employee. In both situations, there are security concerns that must be addressed. A company also needs a standard to ensure that specific needs are met before anything else. For example, a company might have a standard to always acquire hardware with at least 8 GB or RAM (for desktops), that is the standard desktop memory. Guidelines are general recommendations that the company will have for all users.

When planning your Windows Server 2012 deployment strategy, you should be aware of the overall PPSG (Policies, Procedures, Standards, and Guidelines). You should leverage technology as much as you can to assist policy enforcement. The table 1.2 exemplifies this approach:

Table 1.2		
Company Policy	**How to Enforce this Policy**	**Reference Chapters**
Users must change passwords every three months	■ Use Windows Group Policy to implement that	7
It is important to have a cleanup process during the provision/deprovision operation in order to avoid data leakage	■ Use Windows Server 2012 automation for Cloud Technologies	15
All computers must be running the latest updates no later than five days after the update was released	■ Use Windows Update Services (WSUS) role in Windows Server 2012	5
Certificates issued by the company's CA must alert the administrator that the expiration date is approaching	■ Use Certificate Lifecycle in Windows Server 2012	3

Security Awareness Training

Users must be aware of the new techniques that hackers are using to attack users by enticing them to open a malicious email or even leveraging social engineering on-premises to give them an infected USB drive. The famous RSA Attack in 2011[3] was done using a phishing e-mail that looked so legitimate that the user moved from the Junk Mail folder to the Inbox and opened the infected file. Is very important that users are well trained and upon finishing the training they should acknowledge that this training was successfully finished.

NOTE

Microsoft offers a template for security awareness training that you can use to prepare your own material. More information read this post http://blogs.technet.com/b/yuridiogenes/archive/2011/07/06/security-awareness-training-why-is-this-so-important-nowadays.aspx.

When deploying a new operating system to the users, they must be trained on how to use it and this basic training should teach security best practices so that they can securely use the features available for them. One important point about Security Awareness Training is that it can be the old passive way to teach, you cannot just send out an email with tips on how to get protected. Users should be able to learn how to differentiate from a phishing e-mail to a legitimate e-mail; they should be able to interactively practice what they learned. Most of the security awareness training focuses only on teaching terminologies instead of making the users experience a real social engineering attack. What will happen if someone walks in to the receptionist, dressing like a mail man and deliver a piece of hardware where the destination is the CEO of the company saying it is a gift from Company C but it is actually full of malware? Will this receptionist validate the package? While this might sound like tales from movies,[4] it is not, social engineering is something that will bypass most of the technologies in place because it deals with the psychological side of the human, the most vulnerable element in the enterprise chain.

Determine Access Control

The core premises here are least privilege and need to know. Each user or group should have access to only the set of documents that they need to and always assume that he doesn't needs access to it until his manager proves otherwise. It is important to use this step within Phase 2 to also determine the level of authentication and authorization that must be provided to the user. This could (and mostly will) vary between data access and application access. Not all users within the same group will need to access the same set of application.

---

[3]More information about RSA attack in 2011 can be obtained here http://blogs.rsa.com/rivner/anatomy-of-an-attack/.
[4]Read this post and you see some social engineering techniques recently used to spy individuals at http://arstechnica.com/tech-policy/2013/01/the-bizarre-tale-of-john-mcafee-spymaster/.

This is also true when you are planning your cloud infrastructure; the same person that will demand a new virtual machine might not be the same that has authorization to release it. This means that role-based access control plays a very important role in such scenario. The table 1.3 has some other sample scenarios and how you can leverage Windows Server 2012 to address those needs:

Table 1.3		
Scenario	**Solution**	**Chapters that Cover this Technology**
Users must be authenticated on-premises in order to have access to public cloud resources	■ Use ADFS on Windows Server 2012	4
Users must be part of the Cloud Operators group in order to provision a new resource	■ Use Windows Server 2012 Cloud Infrastructure	15

Secure Software Development Strategy

Most companies have their own development team to develop their custom applications that will be used internally. If security is not part of the software development strategy for those applications, chances are that all investment that was done in infrastructure and personnel training will be compromised by a security breach in the application. It is very important that security is part of the development plan.[5] The development team must be aware of how to design their solution without compromise data's confidentiality, integrity, and availability. Microsoft has its own software development strategy called SDL (Security Development Lifecycle). We encourage you to learn more about at www.microsoft.com/sdl.

Network Security

The path from end to edge and beyond always will use some sort of connection: wired or wireless. Such connection will always use a communication protocol. This means that from the security standpoint it is very important to understand your network profile. What are the protocols that are in transit in your network? Do you have a network baseline? Do you know what protocols and ports the applications that you use will leverage? Please do not tell me: everything is encrypted, so I do not care about ports. While encryption is important to avoid data leakage in transit, you should still have a clear understanding of what it is in transit within your network.

---

[5]A tangible proof that SDL pays off can be exemplified the Kaspersky's top 10 vulnerability list released in 2012 when no Microsoft Product appeared in the list. More information here http://thenextweb.com/microsoft/2012/11/02/microsofts-security-team-is-killing-it-not- one-product-on-kasperskys-top-10-vulnerabilities-list/.

It becomes vital to have this network profile done prior to deploy Windows Server 2012, mainly because of the built in firewall that Windows has. If you do not know what ports the applications will use, how can you configure a standard host firewall profile for your corporate computers? You might argue that you can do it via executable file; however if this executable file is a piece of malware that replaced the original program, then you are not in a good position. At that point, the malicious program might send request in ports that are not supposed to be authorized to use, but since it was released from the program context, it will have complete access. Sure we can mitigate that; we can use software restriction policy and only run programs that are authorized. What this really means is that you need to address the different variants of your choice (using protocol/port or using executable file name). We will discuss network vulnerabilities in more details in Chapter 11.

Operating System Security

Without a doubt, this is the main area that we will cover on this book, the Windows 8 operating system security functionality. It was very important to go over all the aspects that are part of this security foundation. You do not want to start building your house in a broken foundation, do you? Same thing applies to an operating system deployment. You do not want to deploy without planning and you do not want to plan without considering security aspects of the overall solution. Once you realize that all those pieces are part of the same puzzle is because your security maturity level has achieved the level that we want.

As explained before, Windows Server 2012 brings a new set of features that allows the operating system to be prepared for nowadays security challenges. In order to leverage the security capabilities offered by this release, you must understand that security will be used as a wrapper as shown in Figure 1.4.

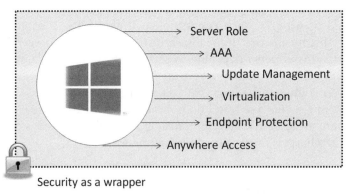

Security as a wrapper

FIGURE 1.4 Using security around the entire solution. (For color version of this figure, the reader is referred to the online version of this chapter.)

Each chapter will tackle the operating system in a different security perspective with the ultimate goal of allowing you to securely deploy and maintain a Windows Server 2012 infrastructure on-premises or in the cloud.

FROM END TO EDGE AND BEYOND CHAPTER PREVIEWS

This book takes a deep dive approach into a collection of Windows 8 platform technologies that are related to security. We focus on platform security technologies for a reason: the cloud. As cloud computing becomes ever more important in the data center, the need to bring security closer to the service and the data hosted by the service increases. This is why Microsoft is no longer investing in standalone security products. Instead of investing in standalone security products, Microsoft is working toward bringing the security protection and controls into the core Windows platform.

This book is comprised of the following chapters:

Chapter 1—Planning Platform Security
Chapter 2—Planning Server Role in Windows Server 2012
Chapter 3—Deploying Directory Services and Certificate Services
Chapter 4—Deploying AD FS and AD RMS in Windows Server 2012
Chapter 5—Patch Management with Windows Server 2012
Chapter 6—Virtualization Security
Chapter 7—Controlling Access to your Environment with Authentication and Authorization
Chapter 8—Endpoint Security
Chapter 9—Secure Client Deployment with Trusted Boot and BitLocker
Chapter 10—Mitigating Application's Vulnerabilities
Chapter 11—Mitigating Network Vulnerabilities
Chapter 12—Unified Remote Access and BranchCache
Chapter 13—DirectAccess Deployment Scenarios
Chapter 14—Protecting Legacy Remote Clients
Chapter 15—Cloud Security

Chapter 1—Planning Platform Security

Planning considerations must always take place before you being to consider the security technologies that you want to employ. What are your security requirements? What constraints to you have? What security controls do you need to apply and how do you need to apply them? How will you manage your security controls? How will you monitor them? What capabilities do you require are part of your security architecture and design? You need to be able to answer these questions before you begin your quest for finding technologies that meet your requirements. You will find that many of your security requirements will be met by the platform technologies you will learn about in this book. However, there will be other requirements that are not met by Windows 8 and you will need to look for other options. This book will provide you with an in-depth look at those technologies so that you can make an informed decision.

Chapter 2—Planning Server Role in Windows 8

Similar to Windows Server 2008 R2, Windows Server 2012 enables you to install only the server roles that you require. In order to decide which role is appropriate for the server, you need to have an understanding of the roles and features available to you. Each of the roles and features included with Windows Server 2012 are installed with default best practices security settings. However, there may be times when you want to adjust those settings. We will talk about those adjustments and how to make them in subsequent chapters. You can see a page from the Windows Server 2012 **Add Roles and Features Wizard** in Figure 1.5.

Chapter 3—Deploying Directory Services and Certificate Services

Windows Server 2012 is designed to be a comprehensive cloud operating system. One of the core requirements of any cloud-based system is identity management. The cloud introduces a number of challenges when it comes to identity, and Windows Server 2012 aims to help solve some of those challenges. Windows

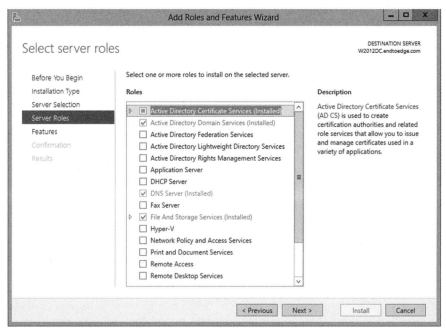

FIGURE 1.5 New Add Roles and Features Wizard in Windows Server 2012. (For color version of this figure, the reader is referred to the online version of this chapter.)

Server 2012 includes significant enhancements in a number of the Active Directory-related services and roles. The next version of Active Directory Federation Services will make it easier than ever to federate your corporate identities with partners and cloud-based identity providers. Active Directory Certificate services have also been greatly improved so that it is easier than ever to deploy and manage certificates in your private and public cloud. In this chapter, we will talk about how to deploy the Active Directory roles and features and describe how they solve problems in identity management in your next-generation data center.

Figure 1.6 shows an example from the improved Active Directory Administration Center.

Chapter 4—Deploying AD FS and AD RMS in Windows Server 2012

In the future, your private cloud datacenter will likely be connected to public cloud resources and those public cloud resources may need to be able to consume identities managed in your private cloud. How do you connect your

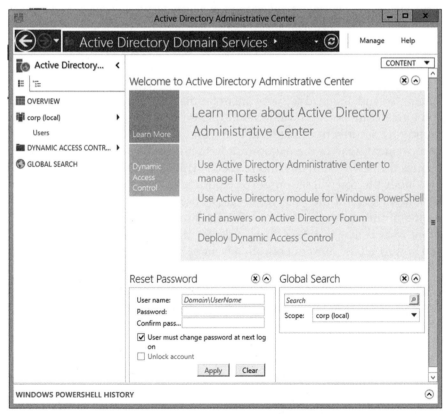

FIGURE 1.6 Set of new options available at Active Directory Administrative Center. (For color version of this figure, the reader is referred to the online version of this chapter.)

identity management system so that private and public clouds can be accessed seamlessly by your users? You can do this by taking advantage of federation services. Windows Server 2012 includes a new version of the Active Directory Federation Services (ADFS) that makes it possible for you to easily federate your corporate identities with cloud server providers and with partners.

As cloud pushes security closer to the services and the data managed by the services, it is that access controls need to also be pushed back as far as possible. The ideal security scenario is when you can protect your information, even after the network, operating system, and application has been compromised. This is where Active Directory Right Management Services comes in. With Active Directory RMS, you can apply flexible access controls over documents so that only authenticated and authorized personnel can access that information. You can also apply other policies to protected documents, such as the ability to copy or paste, or alter the document, or create an "auto destruct" time for the document.

This chapter will discuss where ADFS and ADRMS fit into your overall security architecture, how to deploy and manage these services, and how to get the most out of these critical cloud enabling security technologies.

Chapter 5—Patch Management with Windows Server 2012

Patch management is an unfortunate fact of life. No matter how well-architected and designed software might be, that software is created by humans and humans are not, and will never be, perfect. However, Microsoft continues to improve security in its platform and works on the principle of continuous improvement. One of the major improvements in the area of patch management is the new version of Windows Server Update Services (WSUS) included in Windows 8. You will see improved reporting and control of updates applied to both servers and clients in your organization. Figure 1.7 shows an example of one of the screens in the new WSUS feature. In this chapter, we will talk about what is new in WSUS, how to deploy the Windows Server 2012 WSUS, and how to get the most out of your advanced WSUS deployment (Figure 1.8).

Chapter 6—Virtualization Security

While not an essential characteristic of cloud computing, virtualization is a critical component of any cloud deployment. Virtualization enables many of the essential characteristics of cloud computing. However, as data centers continue to migrate from physical to virtual, new security challenges introduced by virtualization need to be addressed. Some of these can be solved by properly managing your virtual infrastructure, but many of them require technical solutions to enable the key security principle of isolation. Windows Server 2012 includes literally dozens of new

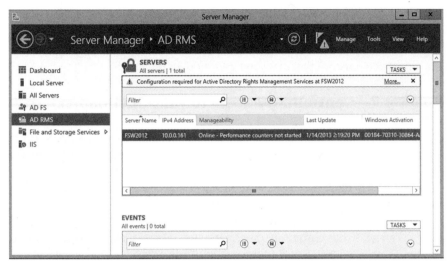

FIGURE 1.7 New look and feel for AD RMS. (For color version of this figure, the reader is referred to the online version of this chapter.)

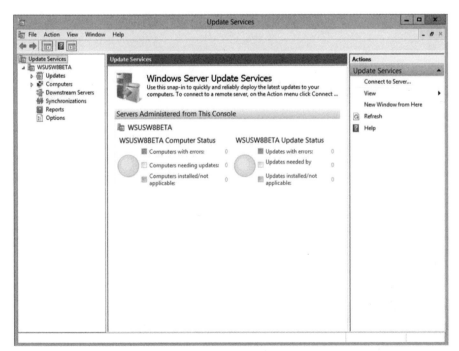

FIGURE 1.8 WSUS now fully integrated with Windows Server 2012. (For color version of this figure, the reader is referred to the online version of this chapter.)

technologies aimed at securing the compute, network, and storage components of a private cloud infrastructure. In this chapter, we will introduce you to these new technologies and explain how to deploy them so that you can reach levels of security in a virtualized environment that you never thought possible.

Chapter 7—Controlling Access to your Environment with Authentication and Authorization

Authentication and Authorization are two core elements of any security policy. While the old approach of creating groups and adding users to the groups is something that can still be used to better manage authorization of resources, there are much more variables that should be consider before authorize an user to have access to a resource. In Windows Server 2012, a new feature called Dynamic Access Control (DAC) was introduced to better reflect the diversity of scenarios that companies are facing nowadays. Active Directory Group Policy has been with us since Windows 2000 Server, and with each version of Windows, it just keeps getting better and better. The pace of improvement does not slow with Windows Server 2012. While the interface for configuring Group Policy has not changed a ton, there are a few very handy new features that help you make the most out of GPOs (Figure 1.9).

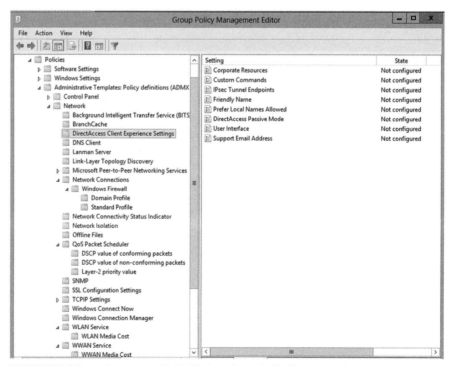

FIGURE 1.9 New policies were added in Windows Server 2012. (For color version of this figure, the reader is referred to the online version of this chapter.)

Chapter 8—Endpoint Security

As discussed earlier, this book is about security from end, to edge and beyond! The end is the endpoint—the client or server that connects to your valuable resources and interacts with other network devices. As cloud computing makes borders ever more porous, the issue of endpoint security becomes job number one for security administrators. In this chapter, we will present key questions that you will need to ask yourself about how to best secure your endpoints and help you map out these requirements to platform technologies included in Windows 8 (Figure 1.10).

Chapter 9—Secure Client Deployment with Trusted Boot and BitLocker

Mobile client systems are now the norm. This is great for employee productivity but puts your information at serious risk because of the high rate of lost or stolen mobile devices. You need to be able to prevent data leakage from these compromised devices. Windows Server 2012 includes a new feature called "Trusted Boot." The Windows Server 2012 boot process is signed and measured, helping to protect the PC from malware or viruses. Trusted Boot validates the integrity of the entire boot process, including the hardware, boot loader, kernel, boot-related system files, and drivers. Antimalware is loaded in advance of all non-critical Windows components. This means that malware, such as rootkits, is less able to hijack the boot process or hide from antimalware software.

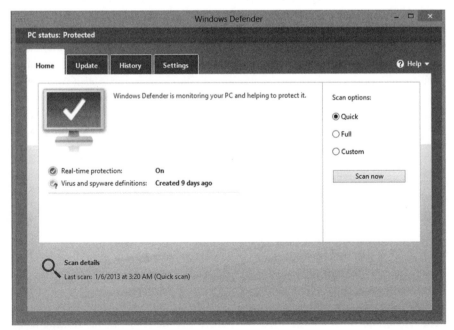

FIGURE 1.10 Windows Defender now plays a bigger role in the overall platform security. (For color version of this figure, the reader is referred to the online version of this chapter.)

BitLocker encrypts volumes using strong AES encryption. It also prevents intruders from using off-line attacks to get access to the data on the encrypted hard disk—thus keeping the data on the stolen device safe from theft. Windows Server 2012 includes a number of BitLocker improvements, such as support for encrypted hard drives (where encryption is performed on the entire disk, not just disk volumes) and network unlock. In this chapter, we will discuss how to plan and deploy these key Windows Server 2012 security features.

Chapter 10—Mitigating Application's Vulnerabilities

It does not matter how careful and assiduous you are, there are going to be flaws and weaknesses to all applications. However, this does not mean you have to put up with it and do clean up after the inevitable attacks! In this chapter, we will talk about the threat landscape that evolves as clients are getting more connected via apps and downloading them direct from Windows Store. What are the implications of this new window of opportunities and how a company can mitigate potential vulnerabilities on this space. This chapter will also cover some aspects related to security enhancements on Internet Explorer 10 and review some tools that can assist users to operate in a more safer way, some old technologies that were introduced in Windows Vista, such as User Account Control and other out of band tools such as Enhance Mitigation Experience.

Chapter 11—Mitigating Network Vulnerabilities

Whether you deploy a private cloud or run a traditional data center, you will need to have controls in place that mitigate network vulnerabilities. With the increasing openness seen in corporate network infrastructures due to the proliferation of mobile devices, the ability to protect data on the wire is just as important as protecting data during processing and at rest. Windows 8 includes a number of new enhancements that help you in your mission of protecting in-flight information. One of these new improvements is SMB 3 encryption. With little or no overhead, SMB connections to file shares can be encrypted without any special efforts required by the clients connecting to the file servers. Windows Firewall with Advanced Security is improved and can be centrally managed using Group Policy to protect the endpoints from network-based exploits. Microsoft Security Essentials also helps against network attacks by incorporate IDS/IPS components. In addition, you can use IPsec not only to encrypt data on the wire but also to make sure that only trusted computers can communicate with each other (Figure 1.11).

If you are running a private cloud, or just a virtualized data center, then Windows 8 will definitely help you secure the network components of your virtual infrastructure. New features included in the Hyper-V virtual switch include port ACLs, bandwidth control, DHCP protection, router advertisement protection, and more work together to protect your virtual infrastructure from network attacks. In this chapter, we will discuss how to make best use of these technologies and how to deploy them to enhance your network level security.

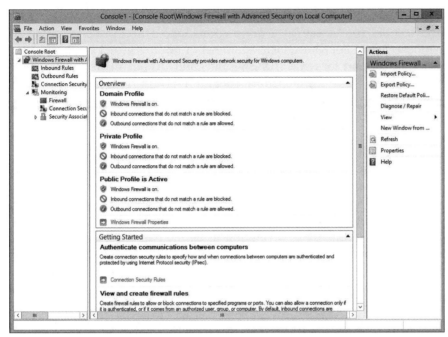

FIGURE 1.11 Windows Firewall with Advanced Security console did not change too much comparing to its predecessor. (For color version of this figure, the reader is referred to the online version of this chapter.)

Chapter 12—Unified Remote Access and BranchCache

One of the essential characteristics of cloud computing is broad network access. People need to be able to get the information they need from anywhere, and from any device. While this is often connected with the public cloud, the fact is that your users will need to access information in your private cloud, and they have the same expectations that they will be able to get to that information regardless of their current location, and regardless of type of device they are using. You will need to think about how you can provide secure remote access to your users. You will need to consider authentication and authorization, you will need to think about device state assessment, you will need to consider performance and reliability of connections, and what remote access methods work with what devices. In this chapter, we will go into the planning considerations you will need to make that will enable you to choose the right combination of Windows 8 technologies to enable the essential cloud characteristic of broad network access.

Chapter 13—DirectAccess Deployment Scenarios

Once you have put together your remote access plan and considered your options, you are ready to deploy that plan. In this chapter, we will take a look at the new and improved routing and remote access feature that integrates remote access deployment and configuration for remote access VPN client connections, site to site VPN connections, and DirectAccess connectivity. Windows Server 2012 introduces a number of improvements in DirectAccess, including support for NAT64/DNS64, the ability to put a DirectAccess server behind a NAT device, higher performance for IP-HTTPS connections and more. We will cover the deployment considerations and how to manage Windows Server 2012 DirectAccess technologies.

Chapter 14—Protecting Legacy Remote Clients

While DirectAccess is the ideal secure remote access solution for Windows 7 and Windows 8 clients, you will still need to be able to provide access to resources on your corporate network. Windows 8 includes integrated VPN services that enable legacy clients secure remote access to your network. We will discuss how to design a VPN solution using the Network Policy and Access Services role and how to perform endpoint health detection using remote access control options.

Chapter 15—Cloud Security

Windows Server 2012 is designed to be the consummate private cloud operating system. Literally hundreds of new features and capabilities have been introduced in the new operating system to make the best choice for creating the infrastructure foundation for your private cloud. However, with the advantages that you can accrue by deploying a private cloud, there are new and different security challenges that are introduced by private cloud. In this chapter, we will discuss these challenges and how you can build a framework for protecting and militating against them.

SUMMARY

In this chapter, we discussed key issues in information security and the importance of architecting and planning a secure network, server, and application infrastructure. Only after the due diligence planning is completed, you can be ready to move on to the next step, which is to investigate the products and technologies that will fulfill your security requirements. Windows Server 2012 is built from the ground up with a large collection of platform technologies that will help enable you meet many of your security requirements. We then completed the discussion with a chapter over that will help you understand what to expect as you move forward in this book.

In the next chapter, we will take a look at the Server Roles and Features available in Windows Server 2012 and focus on those that have direct and indirect impact on security issues in the Windows Server 2012 platform.

CHAPTER 2

Planning Server Role in Windows Server 2012

CONTENTS

CHAPTER POINTS

- Server Roles and Security Considerations
- Using Server Manager to Add a new Role
- Using Security Compliance Manager to Hardening Servers

SERVER ROLE AND SECURITY CONSIDERATIONS

For many years, security professionals were very focused on hardening servers and workstations to reduce the attack surface. This is without doubt a very important item to be included on your checklist. However, before hardening the server, you need to understand the role of that server in your overall infra-structure. You should ask yourself the questions below before you start any implementation:

- What role will this server play on your network (e.g., file server or domain controller)?
- Who (groups, users) will have access to this server?
- Do you have a template for this type of server role?

- What are the services that must be running on this server?
- Which protocols and ports should be open on the firewall to support the server workloads?

Random hardening templates applied to servers without defining the server's role will cause more problems than benefits. While the server might be very secure because many services were disabled and permissions and privileges were removed; the server might not be capable of providing the services that the users need. When this happens, you just broke one of the three security pillars: *availability*.

The lack of server role planning and using the wrong approach to hardening the server can lead you to other problems also. You must verify if the hardening that you are doing on the server is supported by the vendor. You cannot just come up with a series of scripts that were found on the Internet, apply them to the server, and believe that is the right way to do things because there is something called a *supportability statement*. All vendors will have different supportability statements regarding how they support to have their product hardened.

NOTE

For a real example of a hardening that broke a system and was done in a nonsupported manner, read this post http://blogs.technet.com/b/yuridiogenes/archive/2008/09/11/hardening-isa-server-in-a-supported-manner.aspx.

In Windows Server 2012, the recommended way to harden a server is by either use Security Configuration Wizard or Security Compliance Manager. The Security Configuration Wizard (SCW) enables you to create, edit, apply, or roll back a security policy on a particular server. You can use Group Policy to apply the security policy to multiple target servers that perform the same role. Security Compliance Manager (SCM) will be presented later in this chapter.

Using Security Configuration Wizard to Harden the Server

To apply a security policy to a server using SCW follow, read the scenario below and follow the steps:

SCENARIO

Tom just received a request to prepare a new file server for EndtoEdge.com International. He noticed that the company does not have a template for this type of role yet, so he decided to use this new server to do that. He gathered all the necessary information regarding who will access the server, which services should be available for those users and he is ready to deploy the server. The core requirements are

- Clients must be able to access the files while working offline.
- This server belongs to an OU (Organizational Unit) that has policy to install applications remotely.
- Administrators must be able to access this server remotely using RDP.
- Administrators must be able to administer this server using remote administrative tools (including Windows Firewall administration and Event Viewer).
- It is on the roadmap to install a new Network Interface Card (NIC) on this server to enable NLB and administrators must be able to manage that remotely.
- All successfully activities must be audited.

IMPORTANT

before running the Security Configuration Wizard to configure the server's role, you need to install the role first using Server Manager. SCW will not install a role automatically; it will only perform the necessary hardening process on top of the installed role.

Implementation steps: follow the steps below to create a new template and apply on the File Server.

1. In the **Server Manager**, click **Tools** and then click **Security Configuration Wizard** as shown in Figure 2.1.
2. The **Security Configuration Wizard** will open, click **Next** on the **Welcome to the Security Configuration Wizard page**.
3. On the **Configuration Action** page, select the option **Create a new security policy** as shown in Figure 2.2 and click **Next**.
4. On the **Select Server** page, type the name of the server that will be used as baseline to create this security policy in the **Server** field as shown in Figure 2.3 (by default it will choose the local server's name) and click **Next**.

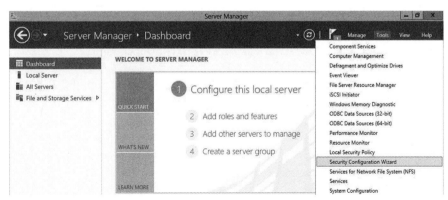

FIGURE 2.1 Launching Security Configuration Wizard. (For color version of this figure, the reader is referred to the online version of this chapter.)

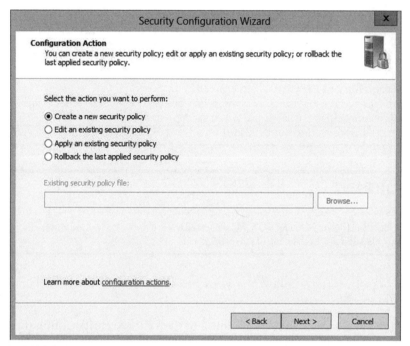

FIGURE 2.2 Creating a new security policy. (For color version of this figure, the reader is referred to the online version of this chapter.)

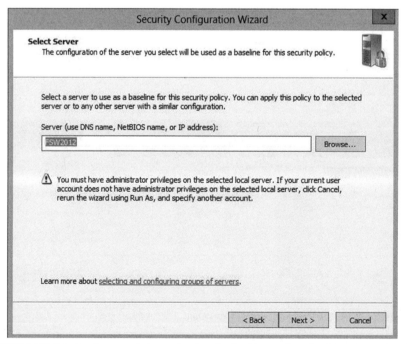

FIGURE 2.3 Selecting the server to be used as baseline for this security policy. (For color version of this figure, the reader is referred to the online version of this chapter.)

5. Depending on the configuration of the server, a gauge will appear in the **Processing Security Configuration Database** page for a moment. Once it is finished, it will allow you to view the configuration by selecting the option **View Configuration Database**. Click **View Configuration Database** to see more details. The SCW Viewer will appear, and a **Windows Security Warning** dialog box will ask if you want to enable the ActiveX Control, click **Yes**.

6. Expand **Server Roles** option and scroll down until you see **File Server** role. Expand it and read the description as shown in Figure 2.4.

NOTE

The XML files used to build these pages are located at **%Systemroot%\Security\Msscw\KBs**.

7. This description allows you to have an idea about what services must be running and also which Firewall rules should be enabled in order to allow this role to work properly. After reviewing those details close this window. On the **Processing Security Configuration Database** page, click **Next**.

8. On the **Role-Based Service Configuration** page, click **Next**.

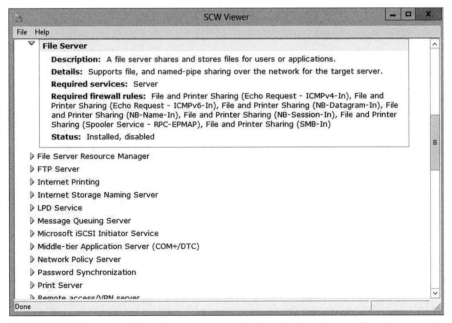

FIGURE 2.4 Explanation of the role, the services required, and the firewall rules. (For color version of this figure, the reader is referred to the online version of this chapter.)

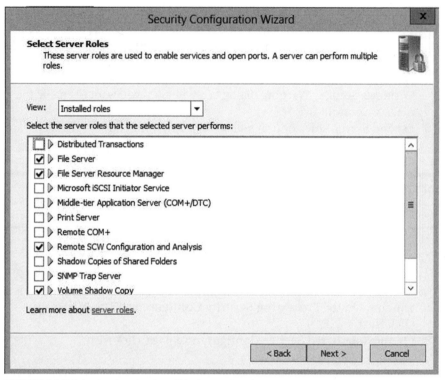

FIGURE 2.5 Selecting the roles that will be installed by this server. (For color version of this figure, the reader is referred to the online version of this chapter.)

9. On the **Select Server Roles** page, review the role selection that was done automatically by the wizard. You may select additional roles or unselect roles that are not applicable for this server. For this particular example, the selections showed in Figure 2.5 are the ones applicable for a File Server. Once you finish reviewing the selection and making possible changes, click **Next**.

10. On the **Select Client Features** page, review the feature selection that was done automatically by the wizard. You may select additional features or unselect features that are not applicable for this server. For this particular example, the selections showed in Figure 2.6 are the ones applicable for a File Server. Once you finish reviewing the selection and making possible changes, click **Next**.

11. On the **Select Administration and Other Options** page, you can select additional options that this server might be using. Here is the time where you should review your checklist to understand the server's requirement and if it needs one of those options enabled in order to work properly. The table below shows the requirements for this particular scenario and which options should be enabled on this page:

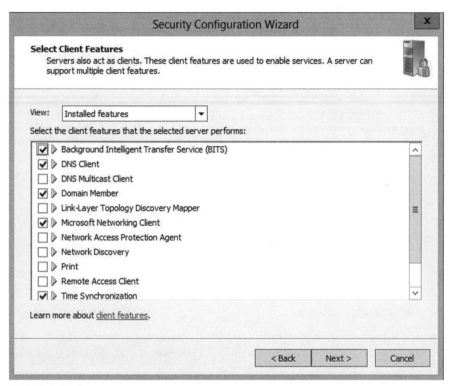

FIGURE 2.6 Selecting the client features that will be used by this server. (For color version of this figure, the reader is referred to the online version of this chapter.)

Scenario Requirement	Category	Option
Clients must be able to access the files while working offline	Microsoft Networking Client	■ Offline Files
This server belongs to an OU (Organizational Unit) that has policy to install applications remotely	Domain Member	■ Application installation from Group Policy
Administrators must be able to access this server remotely using RDP	Remote Administration	■ Remote Desktop
Administrators must be able to administer this server using remote administrative tools (including Windows Firewall administration and Event Viewer)		■ Remote Windows Administration ■ Remote Desktop ■ Remote Windows Firewall Administration
It is on the roadmap to install a new Network Interface Card on this server to enable NLB and administrators must be able to manage that remotely		■ Network Load Balancing Administration

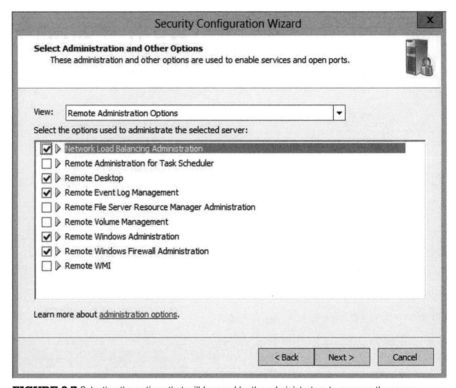

FIGURE 2.7 Selecting the options that will be used by the administrators to manage the server. (For color version of this figure, the reader is referred to the online version of this chapter.)

12. On the **Select Administration and Other Options** page, click the View drop down box and select the category (according to the table above). Once you select the correct category, make the correct selection according to the option column of the table able. Figure 2.7 shows the category Remote Administration and the selections according to the Options column. Once you finish the selections, click **Next**.

13. On the **Select Additional Services** page, ensure that all services that are necessary for this role to run properly are selected. By default, the SCW will make the selections automatically, but you may change if you want to. Once you finish confirming the selections, click **Next**.

14. On the **Handling Unspecified Services** page, you have the chance to configure how the operating system will behave when a service that was not specified by the policy is found running on the system. Although the use of this option might sound interesting, it is important to measure how this will potentially affect your environment. If the target server where this policy will be applied has already a set of services running for another reason and you do not plan to disable them, once you apply this new policy and if the option selected on this page is **disable the service**, you will face issues. By default, the selection on this page is **Do not**

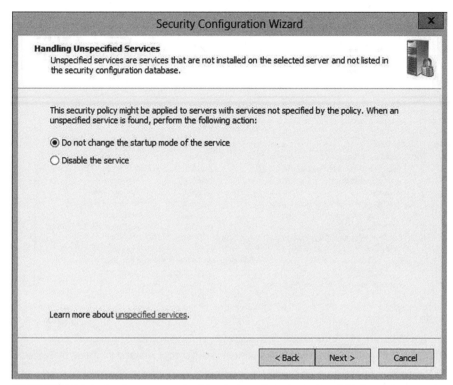

FIGURE 2.8 Selecting the startup mode of the services. (For color version of this figure, the reader is referred to the online version of this chapter.)

change the startup mode of the service as shown in Figure 2.8. Leave the default selection and click **Next**.

15. On the **Confirm Services Change** page, you have a chance to review all the changes that will be made to the services. This page has the current startup mode of the services and how the services will be after applying this new policy as shown in Figure 2.9. Once you finish reviewing the changes, click **Next**.

16. The second phase of the SCW will configure the Windows Firewall and Advanced Security settings. In the **Network Security** page, click **Next**.

17. On the **Network Security Rules** page, review the list of Windows Firewall rules that are needed for the current role as shown in Figure 2.10. If the File Server has a special need (a specific port for some specific application), you can click **Add** button and create a manual rule. Once you finish reviewing these options, click **Next**.

NOTE

You will notice that some of the rules will have a file name and a port number, for example, nlbmgr.exe, -60001. This is expected since some rules are bound to the executable file rather than the transport protocol.

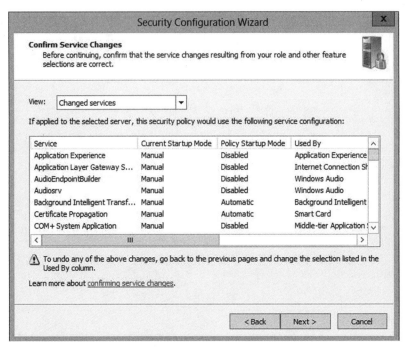

FIGURE 2.9 Reviewing and confirming service changes. (For color version of this figure, the reader is referred to the online version of this chapter.)

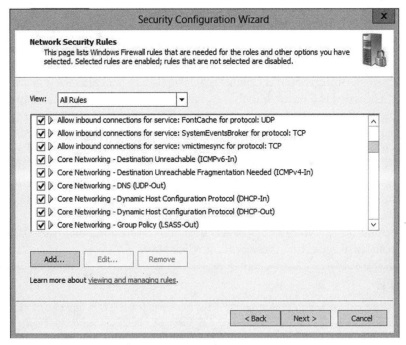

FIGURE 2.10 Controlling windows firewall rules. (For color version of this figure, the reader is referred to the online version of this chapter.)

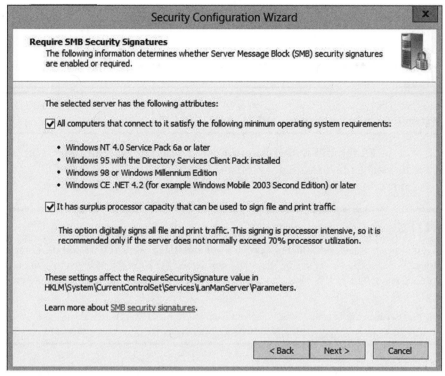

FIGURE 2.11 SMB signing selection. (For color version of this figure, the reader is referred to the online version of this chapter.)

18. On the third phase, the SCW will make changes to communications protocols and registry settings. On the **Registry Settings** page, click **Next**.

19. On the **Require SMB Security Signatures** page, you have the option to enable or disable SMB Sign SMB communication. This security setting determines whether a signed packet is required by the SMB server component. Leave the default selection as shown in Figure 2.11 and click **Next**.

NOTE

In order to take full advantage of SMB signing security feature in Windows, both client and server must be capable of signing the packet. Using the PowerShell Cmdlet *Get-SMBClientConfiguration* and *Get-SMBServerConfiguration* in Windows Server 2012, you can see if the option *EnableSecuritySignature* is set to TRUE (which is by default on Windows Server 2012 and Windows 8 Client).

20. On the **Outbound Authentication Methods**, you can specify the authentication level used by this server when it is making outbound connection. By default, the method is using domain accounts and you should preserve this option, unless this server is in a workgroup or it has connectivity with legacy Windows versions, such as Windows 9x. Leave the default selection and click **Next**.

NOTE

Changes on this page and on the next page will affect settings located in the registry key **HKLM\ System\CurrentControlSet\Control\LSA**.

21. On the **Outbound Authentication using Domain Accounts** page, you can specify the domain account authentication level for outbound connections. Leave the default selection on this page and click **Next**.

NOTE

If you select the checkbox **Clocks that are synchronized with the selected server's clock** option, another page will be presented when you click **Next** to allow you to configure the inbound authentication level and how the hashes are stored. This will be an important selection if

- Your deployment requires NTLM V2 enforcement (otherwise it will use NTLM V1).
- You have systems that require LAN Manager authentication.

22. On the **Registry Settings Summary** page, review the selections for LAN Manager Authentication, LDAP Signing, and SMB Signing as shown in Figure 2.12. Notice that since the second checkbox in step 20 was not selected, the LAN Manager authentication is using NTLMv1. Once you confirm that this selection address your requirements, click **Next**.

23. On the fourth phase, the SCW will make changes to auditing settings. In the **Audit Policy** page, click **Next**.

24. On the **System Audit Policy** page, choose the option that fits on your scenario requirement. For this particular scenario, the requirement is that all successfully activities must be audited. Leave the default selection and click **Next**.

25. On the **Audit Policy Summary** page, review the selection of what it is currently enabled on the system and how the system will look like once the template is applied. Notice that, by default, the option to include the SCWAudit.inf file is selected; this is to allow the System Access Control List (SACLS) audit the file system as shown in Figure 2.13. Once you finish reviewing, click **Next**.

26. On the **Save Security Policy** page, click **Next**.

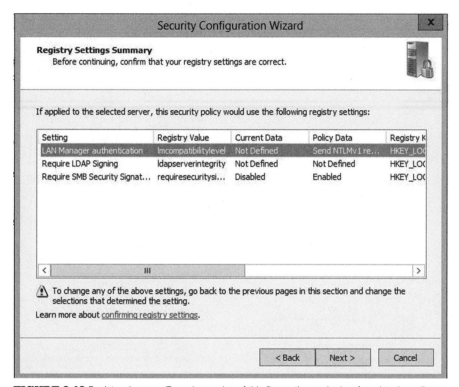

FIGURE 2.12 Registry changes. (For color version of this figure, the reader is referred to the online version of this chapter.)

27. On the **Security Policy File Name** page, type a name for this policy and optionally type a description for this template as shown in Figure 2.14. Make sure to use a name that refer to the server role rather than the server name itself since this file will be used as template in other scenarios where a new file server needs to be deployed. Click **Next** once you finish.
28. On the **Apply Security Policy** page, you can choose to apply the template now or later. For this scenario, select **Apply Now** and click **Next**.
29. On the **Applying Security Policy** page, a progress bar will appear and at this point you need to wait until the policy is fully applied on the server and the status appears as **Application complete**. Once it is finished, click **Next**.
30. On the **Complete the Security Configuration Wizard** page, take note of the location of the security policy as shown in Figure 2.15 and click **Finish** button.

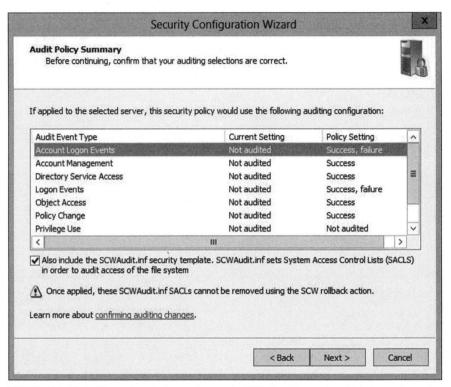

FIGURE 2.13 Auditing options that were changed by SCW. (For color version of this figure, the reader is referred to the online version of this chapter.)

If you need to review the XML file that contains all the settings that were configured throughout this wizard, you can use the command line scwcmd. For this scenario, the command line will be

scwcmd view/c:\windows\security\msscw\policies\fileserver.xml

If you want to deploy this template to other servers, you can use one of the following options:

- Use the SCW user interface, retrieve the XML file, and apply to the new server.
- Use the *swcmd* tool with *configure* parameter and use the same XML file to apply to the new server.
- Use the *swcmd* tool with the *transform* parameter to convert the XML file in a group policy compatible format and deploy it using Domain Group Policy.

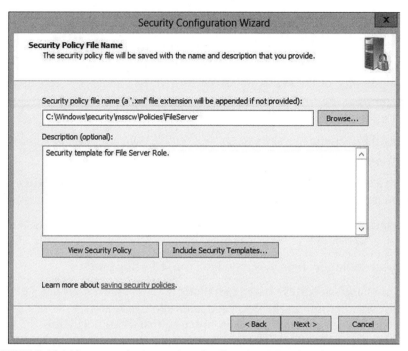

FIGURE 2.14 Adding a name for the security policy. (For color version of this figure, the reader is referred to the online version of this chapter.)

FIGURE 2.15 Confirmation page and location of template file. (For color version of this figure, the reader is referred to the online version of this chapter.)

USING SERVER MANAGER TO ADD A NEW ROLE OR FEATURE

Windows Server 2012 introduces a new and improved Server Manager. While the appearance of the Windows Server 2012 Server Manager is very different from previous versions, the approach you use to install a new Server Role or Feature is pretty much the same.

When you open the Server Manager, you will see what appears in Figure 2.16 in the upper right corner.

To add a new Role or feature, click the **Manage** menu item. There you will see the option to **Add Roles and Features** as shown in Figure 2.17. Click that option.

This opens the **Before You Begin** page in the **Add Roles and Features Wizard** as shown in Figure 2.18. Click **Next**.

On the **Installation Type** page, you have the following options:

- **Role-based or feature-based installation.** This is the traditional installation routine where you add a new Role or Feature.
- **Remote Desktop Services scenario-based installation**. Use this option to deploy a Virtual Desktop infrastructure scenario or a Session Virtualization scenario.

In this example, we will be installing the WINS Server service, so we will select the **Role-based or feature-based installation** as shown in Figure 2.19. Click **Next**.

FIGURE 2.16 Flag is raised with one item to be addressed. (For color version of this figure, the reader is referred to the online version of this chapter.)

FIGURE 2.17 Menu with options that allows you to manage servers, roles, and features. (For color version of this figure, the reader is referred to the online version of this chapter.)

FIGURE 2.18 Initial page of add roles and features wizard. (For color version of this figure, the reader is referred to the online version of this chapter.)

FIGURE 2.19 Selecting the installation type. (For color version of this figure, the reader is referred to the online version of this chapter.)

On the **Server Selection** page, you have two options:

- **Select a server from the server pool**. In Windows Server 2012, you can manage multiple servers using the new Server Manager. You add them to a "pool" of managed servers by using the **Add Servers** feature in Server Manager. When you select this option, you will see the names of the servers in your pool in the **SERVER POOL** section.
- **Select a virtual hard disk**. When select this option, you can install the Role or Feature on a running or nonrunning virtual hard disk.

In this example, we will select the **Select a server from the server pool** option and select the server you want to install; in this example, it will be **w2012DC. endtoedge.com** as shown in Figure 2.20 and then click **Next**.

On the **Server Roles** page, you will see a list of the available server roles. When you click on a role, you will see a short description of that role on the right side of the page. In this example, we are installing the WINS Server service, which oddly enough is a **Feature** and not a **Role**. Click **Next** (Figure 2.21).

On the **Features** page, you can select the Feature you want to install. When you click on a feature, you will see a description of that feature on the right side of the page. In this example, we want to install the WINS Server service, so we put a

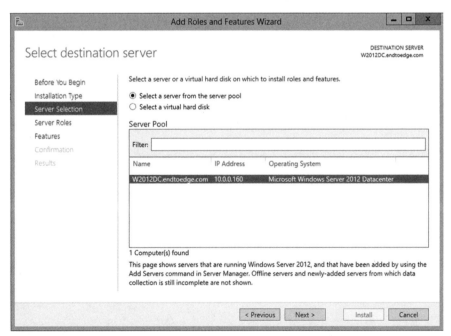

FIGURE 2.20 Selecting the target server. (For color version of this figure, the reader is referred to the online version of this chapter.)

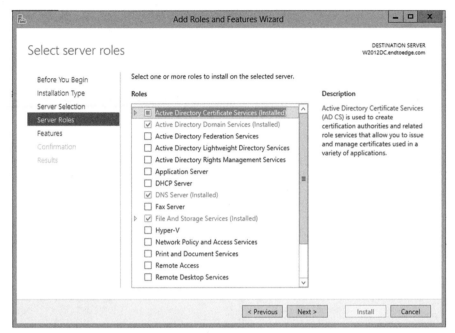

FIGURE 2.21 Selecting the roles to be installed on the server. (For color version of this figure, the reader is referred to the online version of this chapter.)

checkmark in the **WINS Server** checkbox. When we do that, an **Add Roles and Features Wizard** dialog box appears and asks if we want to install additional software to support this feature. Click **Add Features** and then click **Next** (Figure 2.22).

On the **Confirmation** page, put a checkmark in the **Restart the destination server automatically if required** so that the machine will restart if needed. When you do this, you will see a **Add Roles and Features Wizard** dialog box informing you that the machine will restart without additional notifications. Click **Yes** to confirm that you are OK with that and then click **Install** (Figure 2.23).

A progress bar will inform you about the progress of the installation (Figure 2.24).

When the installation is complete, you will see a notice that **Installation succeed on [name of computer]**. Click **Close** to close the **Add Roles and Features Wizard** (Figure 2.25).

After the installation is complete, you can see the new Role or Feature in the **Tools** list (Figure 2.26).

When you click the WINS server feature, that will bring up the WINS console (Figure 2.27).

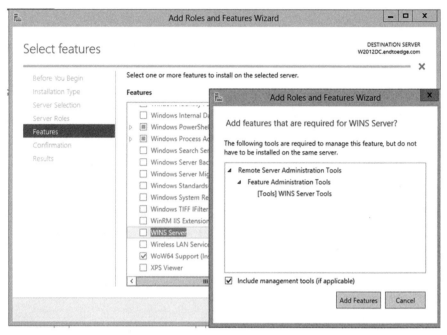

FIGURE 2.22 Selecting the appropriate features. (For color version of this figure, the reader is referred to the online version of this chapter.)

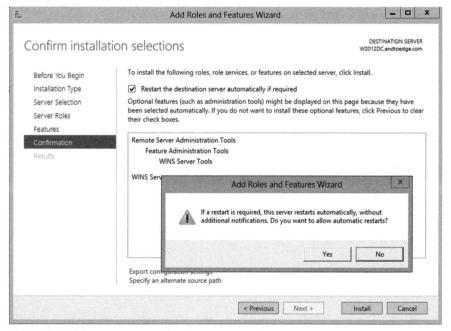

FIGURE 2.23 Restart warning dialog. (For color version of this figure, the reader is referred to the online version of this chapter.)

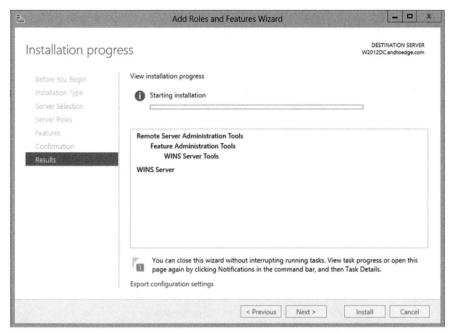

FIGURE 2.24 Installation process starting. (For color version of this figure, the reader is referred to the online version of this chapter.)

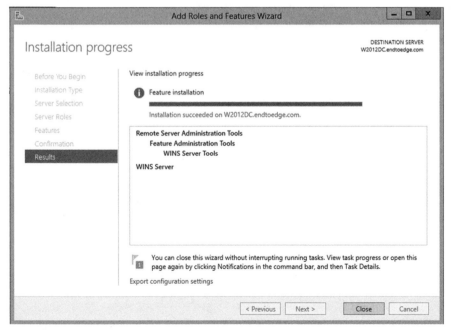

FIGURE 2.25 Installation process completed. (For color version of this figure, the reader is referred to the online version of this chapter.)

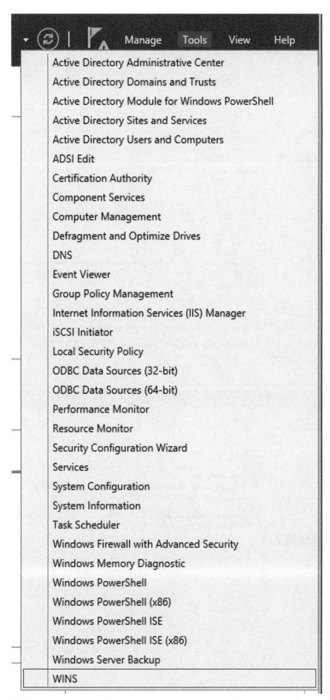

FIGURE 2.26 New role installed. (For color version of this figure, the reader is referred to the online version of this chapter.)

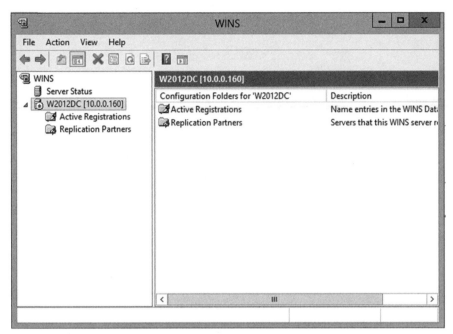

FIGURE 2.27 WINS Console after adding the role. (For color version of this figure, the reader is referred to the online version of this chapter.)

USING SECURITY COMPLIANCE MANAGER TO HARDENING SERVERS

By the time, we were reviewing this chapter to write about the Security Compliance Manager; the version available was the 3.0 Beta and it was available via Connect to download as shown in Figure 2.28.

The specific version that we used to write this section was released on 9/10/2012 and the templates used were released on 11/20/2012 (called 3.0 Beta Refresh).[1] The interface of SCM 3.0 is not very different from its predecessor as shown in Figure 2.29.

On the left pane, you have all baselines available and if you expand Windows Server 2012, you will see some templates ready to use for

- Domain Controllers
- Hyper-V
- Member Server
- Web Server

---

[1] Review Episode 22 of From End to Edge and Beyond when we talked with SCM PM about what's new in SCM 3 http://technet.microsoft.com/en-us/video/from-end-to-edge-and-beyond-episode-22.

FIGURE 2.28 Downloading SCM 3 Beta from Connect. (For color version of this figure, the reader is referred to the online version of this chapter.)

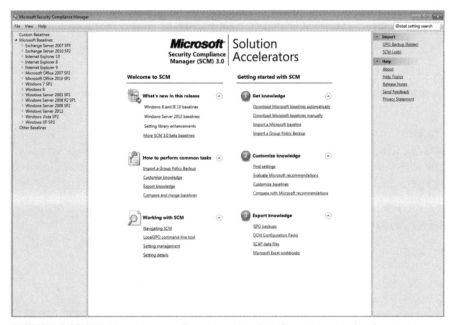

FIGURE 2.29 SCM 3.0 main screen. (For color version of this figure, the reader is referred to the online version of this chapter.)

Name	Default	Microsoft	Customized	Severity	Path
∧ **Authentication Types** 21 Setting(s)					
Interactive logon: Require Domain Controller authent	Disabled	Enabled	Enabled	Critical	Computer (
Microsoft network server: Server SPN target name va	Off	Not Defined	Not Defined	Critical	Computer (
Network Security: Restrict NTLM: Incoming NTLM tra	Not defined	Not Defined	Not Defined	Critical	Computer (
Network security: LAN Manager authentication level	Send NTLMv2 res	Send NTLMv2 res	Send NTLMv2 res	Critical	Computer (
Microsoft network client: Send unencrypted passwor	Disabled	Disabled	Disabled	Critical	Computer (
Network Security: Restrict NTLM: NTLM authenticatic	Not defined	Not Defined	Not Defined	Critical	Computer (
Network Security: Restrict NTLM: Add remote server	Not defined	Not Defined	Not Defined	Critical	Computer (
Network Security: Restrict NTLM: Audit Incoming NTI	Not defined	Not Defined	Not Defined	Critical	Computer (
Network access: Let Everyone permissions apply to a	Disabled	Disabled	Disabled	Critical	Computer (
Network Security: Allow PKU2U authentication reque	Not defined	Disabled	Disabled	Importai	Computer (
Network security: Minimum session security for NTLN	No minimum	Require NTLMv2 s	Require NTLMv2 s	Critical	Computer (
Network Security: Restrict NTLM: Outgoing NTLM tra	Not defined	Not Defined	Not Defined	Critical	Computer (
Interactive logon: Require smart card	Disabled	Not Defined	Not Defined	Importai	Computer (
Interactive logon: Smart card removal behavior	No Action	Lock Workstation	Lock Workstation	Importai	Computer (
Network security: Do not store LAN Manager hash va	Enabled	Enabled	Enabled	Critical	Computer (
Network Security: Restrict NTLM: Audit NTLM authen	Not defined	Not Defined	Not Defined	Critical	Computer (
Network Security: Restrict NTLM: Add server exceptic	Not defined	Not Defined	Not Defined	Critical	Computer (
Network security: Minimum session security for NTLN	No minimum	Require NTLMv2 s	Require NTLMv2 s	Critical	Computer (
Interactive logon: Number of previous logons to cach	10 logons	0 logon(s)	0 logon(s)	Critical	Computer (
Network security: Allow Local System to use compute	Not defined	Enabled	Enabled	Importai	Computer (
Network security: Allow LocalSystem NULL session fa	Not Defined	Disabled	Disabled	Importai	Computer (

FIGURE 2.30 Authentication types section from the Windows Server 2012 DC security compliance policy. (For color version of this figure, the reader is referred to the online version of this chapter.)

To identify what a particular baseline has, you can click on it, and on the right pane, you should observe that it will say how many unique settings are configured on this baseline. There will be a column that shows the default configuration for a particular setting and the Microsoft recommendation for the same setting as shown in Figure 2.30.

In case you need to get more familiar with a particular setting before making the change, select the setting on the right pane and click on **Settings Details**; you will notice that a description of the setting will become available as well as the potential vulnerability, the potential impact, and the countermeasure[2] as shown in Figure 2.31.

---

[2] You can download the Windows 8 Security Guide on SCM 3. Read more about this here http://blogs. technet.com/b/yuridiogenes/archive/2012/10/04/windows-8-security-guide.aspx.

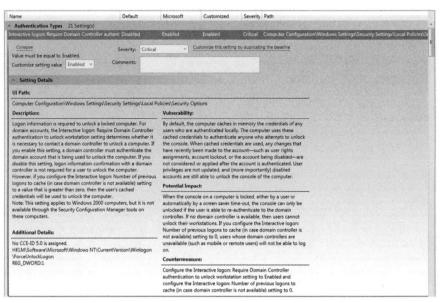

FIGURE 2.31 Important details about a particular setting with vulnerability, potential impact, and countermeasure. (For color version of this figure, the reader is referred to the online version of this chapter.)

FIGURE 2.32 Options available to export a policy. (For color version of this figure, the reader is referred to the online version of this chapter.)

FIGURE 2.33 Options available for Baseline. (For color version of this figure, the reader is referred to the online version of this chapter.)

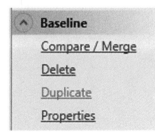

Planning Before Hardening Your Server with SCM

Although it is safe to backup the configuration, apply the template, test, and rollback if need; these are not the primary way to validate if a template is good for your environment or not. Ideally, you will have a validation lab where you can apply these templates, test them, and see if any unusual probable happens due to your environment requirements. Going a step further, even before deploying these templates in a lab environment, you should understand at least the basics of what each template is changing from the default configuration.

In the previous section, you learned how to individually see the changes that each setting represents; however, this can be quiet tedious when there are 422 unique changes that are introduced by the template. Fortunately, the tool allows you to export the whole template to an Excel spreadsheet and there you can create filters to better visualize the unique changes. To export the template, you just need to select it and then click **Excel** (.XLSM) under Export as shown in Figure 2.32.

During the planning phase, you can also create a copy of the baseline and work on this copy; it is very common that during this planning phase you identify that either a particular setting is not appropriated for your environment or that there is a particular setting that is not enabled and your environment requires that it is enabled. In this case, use the Duplicate option on the right pane to create a copy as shown in Figure 2.33.

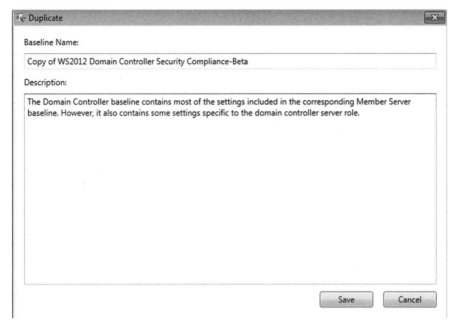

FIGURE 2.34 Duplicating a policy. (For color version of this figure, the reader is referred to the online version of this chapter.)

When you choose this option, a dialog window appears where you can add a name for this copy as shown in Figure 2.34.

When you are planning the hardening of a Domain Controller, it is not hard to realize that you just need to apply the template to maybe a couple of DCs or perhaps a dozen of DCs. However, if you are planning the hardening of member servers or even Windows 8 clients, it becomes crucial to also plan how this will be deployed. One very important option that SCM offers is the capability of exporting the template as a CAB file that can be consumed by System Center Configuration Manager (SCM). In the same Export panel on the right, you can just click **SCM** (.cab) to do that (Figure 2.35).

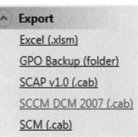

FIGURE 2.35 Exporting to SCCM DCM 2007. (For color version of this figure, the reader is referred to the online version of this chapter.)

Staying Up to Date with SCM

Since SCM is an out of band tool (does not come with Windows Server 2012) by the time that you are reading, this chapter things might have changed; therefore, we recommend you to always verify online if new resources were available for SCM. Below you have some additional links that can be useful for that:

■ SCM TechNet Wiki Getting Started Page

http://go.microsoft.com/fwlink/?LinkId=201324

■ SCM Main TechNet Page

http://go.microsoft.com/fwlink/?LinkId=113940

ADMINISTRATOR'S PUNCH LIST

- Plan Server Role before deploy
- Understand the environment needs before select the role or feature
- Plan the services that will be handled by the server
- Have a clear documentation of the traffic pattern before close doors on the server by hardening it
- Reduce the overall impact of wrong configuration or incompatibility by testing any hardening in a lab environment first
- Use only supported methods to hardening servers; SCW and SCM are your friends
- Duplicate templates on SCM before making any changes
- Plan the deployment of templates, ideally use SCM to deploy in large scale

SUMMARY

In this chapter, you learned that you need to plan carefully before you install a role or feature on a Windows Server 2012 computer or virtual machine. When considering the options for securing the server that will host a particular role or feature, you need to consider the support statement for that role or feature that server will host. The best approach for hardening the server and staying within the parameters of the role or feature support statement is to use the Windows Server 2012 Security Configuration Manager. The Security Configuration Manager includes best practices security settings for the server role or feature. You can modify the settings, but the recommendation is that you use the default settings. This chapter also presented a brief overview of the new Server Manager and how to install a new role or feature.

CHAPTER 3

Deploying Directory Services and Certificate Services

CONTENTS

CHAPTER POINTS

- The evolving threats against Certificates
- Implementing Directory Services on Windows Server 2012
- Implementing Certificate Services in Windows Server 2012

EVOLVING THREATS AGAINST CERTIFICATES

In March 2011, a major breach at Comodo[1] leads the Internet users to start wondering how secure they were even when using HTTPS to perform transactions on the Web. Probably the scariest thing was knowing that the entity that issues the certificate, trusted by all major browsers, had fraudulent certificates issued and these certificates were potentially on cybercriminals' hands. In the same month, another breach at a Comodo partner in Italy[2] happened; in May, it was time for ComodoBR in Brazil[3] to be hacked. And for you to not think that this was isolated to Comodo, in June 2011, Diginotar was hacked.[4]

These events were a wakeup call about the whole Certificate Infrastructure model, how it is used, how it is protected, and how effective it really is. With the migration to the cloud, those concerns are even bigger, mainly because of the fact that customers will have their major assets (their data) on the cloud and the communication channel (using SSL) does not seem to be bullet proof.

TIP

Read the article "Protecting your Weakest Point: On-Premise Resources" at http://blogs.technet. com/b/yuridiogenes/archive/2011/05/02/protecting-your-weakest-point-on-premise-resources. aspx to understand the risks imposed by cloud migration and what needs to be done to protect your data.

Although this incident happened on a public certificate authority, the same could potentially happen in an internal Certificate infrastructure. It is not valid to say, "but this is our internal network and nothing will happen; we know our users." Wrong, just wrong assumption! The correct assumption should be, "we trust no one and we protect everything!" One of the conclusions from the Internet Security Threat Report 2011 Trends, Volume 17, from Symantec[5] is that in 2012 the insider threat will create headlines, as the employees will continue to intentionally or unintentionally leak or steal valuable data from the company. This pretty much means that your users could put you in risk if you are not diligent to protect your assets. Encryption is not bullet proof; however, it is another layer of protection that you should implement on your

---

[1] More info at http://threatpost.com/en_us/blogs/
phony-ssl-certificates-issued-google-yahoo-skype-others-032311.
[2] More info at http://www.pcworld.com/businesscenter/article/223760/comodo_hacker_claims_
another_certificate_authority.html.
[3] More info at http://www.h-online.com/security/news/item/Another-Comodo-SSL-registrar-
hacked-1250283.html.
[4] More info at http://www.networking4all.com/en/ssl+certificates/ssl+news/time-line+for+the+
diginotar+hack/.
[5] More info at http://www.symantec.com/content/en/us/enterprise/other_resources/b-istr_main_
report_2011_21239364.en-us.pdf.

network. Defense in depth approach should still be used nowadays for internal resources, external resources, and hybrid scenarios.

The upcoming sections within this chapter cover the implementation of Directory Services on Windows Server 2012 and the Certificate Services. Assuming that you are deploying Windows Server 2012 in an enterprise, these are the core components that you should have in place to enhance your overall security.

IMPLEMENTING DIRECTORY SERVICES ON WINDOWS SERVER 2012

Identity management is a critical component of any security architecture that you build for your traditional datacenter or private cloud. A strong identity management infrastructure is especially important when you deploy a private or hybrid cloud because of the converged nature of a cloud solution. Server admins, network admins, and storage admins will often need to access the same control interfaces but must be kept from manipulating controls that are not part of their domain. In addition, the identity management system must be aware of the tenants running on the private cloud infrastructure; otherwise they may be able to break out of their security partition and impact the cloud platform itself with potentially disastrous results.

Windows Server 2012 includes the Active Directory Domain Services feature that was included in previous versions of the Windows operating system. In addition to providing an identity management solution for Windows, and through federation non-Windows networks, Active Directory provides a distributed database that can manage information about many of your network resources and application specific data for applications that are directory enabled.

There are many new and improved features pertaining to Active Directory Domain Services in Windows Server 2012. Some of these include:

- **Virtualized domain controller cloning**

In the past, the task of creating additional domain controllers was labor intensive. You have to use a sysprepped image to boot the operating system and then configure the machine to be a domain controller over that. If you tried to do this over the network, the time it took to complete the action would have been significant. In Windows Server 2012, you can clone a virtual domain controller using a single virtual domain controller image to create new domain controllers. This is great from a disaster recovery perspective because you only need a single running virtualized domain controller to recreate your forest infrastructure.

- **Virtualized DCs fully supported and safe**

While you could virtualize DCs in the past, there were a number of caveats and dangers in bringing virtualized DCs online after they have been offline for a while, such as when you bring a DC back from a snapshot. This could cause problems with inconsistent passwords and lingering objects in the Active Directory database, as well as duplicate SIDs.[6] In Windows Server 2012, the operating system can detect when snapshots are applied and when a virtual machine is copied. A virtual machine generation ID is created when snapshots are used and the Windows Server 2012 domain controllers track this ID to detect changes and protect the Active Directory database.

- **AD DS integration with Server Manager**

Previously, adding more domain controllers could be a time-consuming and difficult process. You had to use a number of Active Directory preparation tools and log in to a number of per-domain DCs to get the job done. In Windows Server 2012, you do not have to worry about the Active Directory preparation tools and wonder if you have the right version downloaded—in Windows Server 2012, they are built into the operating system. No muss, no fuss! These tools are baked into the new Server Manager. And because the new Server Manager enables you to manage multiple machines from a single location, you can create new DCs on multiple much using a single action. Nice!

- **Active Directory Federated Services (AD FS) in Windows Server 2012**

We will talk about Active Directory Federation Services in more detail in the next chapter, but here, I want to let you know that you do not have to download the latest version of ADFS because it comes in the box. It is also a lot easier to set up and manage, but we will go into those details in the next chapter.

- **Off-Premises Domain Join**

Ha! Here is one of my favorites. One of the hardest problems admins have had to deal with in the era of DirectAccess is how to get a non-domain-joined machine joined to the domain so that it can receive the Group Policy information required to get DirectAccess running. In almost all the cases, you had to do the domain joining on premises or require a VPN connection to the corpnet, which was problematic in itself, since you really do not want non-domain-joined, unmanaged client systems on your secure corpnet. Windows Server 2012 solves this problem by making domain joining possible over the Internet and does it in a secure fashion. We will go into how this works in more detail in the chapter that covers DirectAccess and other remote access technologies in Windows Server 2012.

---

[6] For a full explanation on how to virtualize domain controllers, read the article at http://blogs.technet.com/b/askpfeplat/archive/2012/10/01/virtual-domain-controller-cloning-in-windows-server-2012.aspx.

■ **Recycle Bin User Interface**

We had the Active Directory Recycle Bin in Windows Server 2008 R2, and it was great because it allowed us to recover from our mistakes. However, it was not the easiest thing in the world to work with because it lacked a good user interface. The fact is if you find that you need to use the Recycle Bin, it is probably an emergency. So you need to fix things fast. In Windows Server 2012, there is a new, intuitive, and fast user interface for the Active Directory Recycle Bin, which is part of the new Active Directory Administrative Center.

■ **Dynamic Access Control**

Dynamic Access Control is a new feature in Windows Server 2012 that allows you to extend authorization decisions so that you are not limited to just user and group membership. By using claim-based authorization, you can create your own claim statements in Active Directory and manage them centrally. This enables you to control access based on both user claims and device claims, which provides you the ability to make access control decisions using a compound identity.

■ **Windows PowerShell History Viewer**

Private clouds depend on automation to deliver on the promises of cloud computing. PowerShell is a key enabler for automating virtually and process in Windows Server 2012. However, learning PowerShell can be a difficult and gruel affair. Many people learn by example and this is where the Windows PowerShell History Viewer comes in. In Windows Server 2012, when you use the Active Directory Administrative Center, you can see the PowerShell output for the activity you performed using the graphical interface. This will help you learn PowerShell more quickly and makes the relevant Active Directory activities that you can perform in PowerShell more discoverable.

■ **Fine-Grained Password Policy User Interface**

The ability to create a fine-grained password policy was initially introduced in Windows Server 2008. However, it was not the easiest thing to configure. It was hard to determine if the manually defined policies you created actually behaved in the way you expected and wanted them to do. In Windows Server 2012, you can use the graphical interface in the Active Directory Administrative Center to easily and quickly create the Password Settings Objects and see how they are actually going to work.

■ **Active Directory Based Activation (AD BA)**

Before Windows Server 2012, you had to use a KMS server to activate your operating systems and Microsoft Office. This was a pain because there was no simple user interface available to configure the KMS. Also, you needed to provide RPC access to the KMS servers, which can be quite an impediment if you have firewalls or other network access control devices interposed between the KMS and the client systems. In Windows Server 2012, you no longer need RPC connectivity, since it supports the simple LDAP protocol. This enables all Windows 8 computers to automatically activate when joined to the domain. This even works on Read Only Domain controllers! Whoot!

- **Flexible Authentication Secure Tunneling (FAST)**

A security challenge with Active Directory passwords was that they were susceptible to offline dictionary attacks. In addition, there is a possible issue with malicious users being able to spoof Kerberos errors, which cause clients to possibly fall back to less secure authentication protocols and cause them to use weaker cryptographic key strength and ciphers. Windows Server 2012 has Flexible Authentication Secure Tunneling, which can solve some of these issues. This feature, which is sometimes referred to as "Kerberos Armoring,"[7] enables machines to establish a secure channel during authentication to protect preauthentication data for user authentication requests (computer authentication is not armored, though) and allows domain controllers to return authenticated Kerberos errors, which protects them from spoofing.

- **Kerberos Constrained Delegation across domains**

Kerberos Constrained Delegation (KCD) is a great feature that enables users to connect to the front-end of a multi-tier application and allows the front-end to impersonate the user when requesting services from the back-end. However, there was a major limitation—the front-end and back-end components needed to be in the same domain and forest. In Windows Server 2012, the front-end and back-end components of the solution can now belong to different domains and forests. In addition, you do not need to be a domain admin to configure KCD—you only need to be an administrator of the back-end service accounts.

As you can see, there have been a significant number of changes to Active Directory Domain Services that increase the overall security for your identity and access management infrastructure.

Installing the Active Directory Domain Services Role
Figure 3.1 shows the selection of the **Active Directory Domain Services** option when using the Server Manager to install the Active Directory Domain Services Role.

Active Directory Domain Services installation uses Server Manager and Windows PowerShell; Dcpromo.exe no longer installs Active Directory binaries and does not provide graphical configuration options. It is all about Server Manager now.

---

[7] For more information about Kerberos changes in Windows Server 2012, review the article at http://technet.microsoft.com/en-us/library/hh831747.aspx.

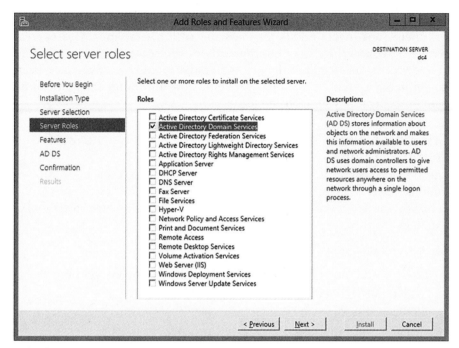

FIGURE 3.1 Selecting AD DS Role. (For color version of this figure, the reader is referred to the online version of this chapter.)

You use Server Manager or the Server Manager module for Windows PowerShell to install Active Directory DS locally or remotely from a management workstation. You can also run multiple instances of these wizards and deploy AD DS to multiple domain controllers at the same time.

Active Directory Domain Services configuration is now an operation carried out after installing the Active Directory DS role. After installing the role, you can configure the server as a domain controller using a wizard within Server Manager or using the **ADDSDeployment** Windows PowerShell module.

Dcpromo.exe remains in Windows Server 2012 for command-line unattended installations only and no longer starts the graphical installation wizard as you have seen in the previous version of Windows Server.

Domain controller configuration also performs prerequisite checking that evaluates the forest and domain prior to continuing with domain controller promotion. Tests include:

- FSMO role availability,
- User privileges,
- Extended schema compatibility,
- Other requirements.

The new approach fixes problems where domain controller promotion starts and then stops in the middle of the setup with a fatal error. This is great because it reduces the chance of orphaned domain controller forest metadata or a server that incorrectly "thinks" it is a domain controller. If you have been caught in any of those situations, you know how uncomfortable they can be (and probably ruin your weekend too!).

Creating a New Forest with the Windows Server 2012 Server Manager

Any Windows Server 2012 computers that are accessible from the computer running Server Manager can be added to a server pool. After you create the pool, you can select those servers that you want to install Active Directory DS remotely.

You can add servers by:

- Clicking **Add Other Servers to Manage** on the dashboard welcome tile
- Clicking the **Manage** menu and select **Add Servers**
- Right-clicking on **All Servers** and choose **Add Servers**

This brings up the **Add Servers** dialog box shown in Figure 3.2.

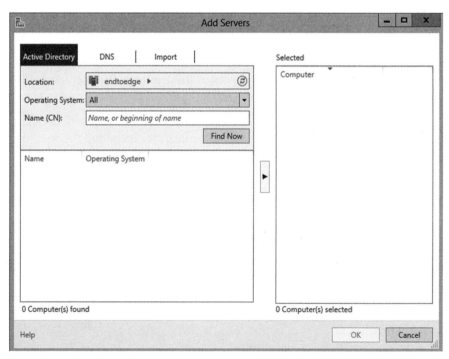

FIGURE 3.2 Adding servers to manage. (For color version of this figure, the reader is referred to the online version of this chapter.)

There are three ways to add servers to the pool:

- **Active Directory search**. This uses LDAP and requires that the computers belong to a domain; this also supports OS filtering and wildcards.
- **DNS search.** This uses DNS names or IP address using ARP, NetBIOS broadcast, or WINS lookup and does not allow OS filtering or support wildcards.
- **Import from .txt file**. This uses a text file list of servers separated by CR/LF.

Click **Find Now** to return a list of servers from Active Directory and click one or more server names from the list of servers. Then click the right pointing arrow to add the servers to the **Selected** list. Use the **Add Servers** dialog to add selected servers to dashboard role groups. Another option is to click **Manage** and then click **Create Server Group.** Or, you can click **Create Server Group** on the dashboard **Welcome to Server Manager** tile to create custom server groups.

Note that you cannot fully manage servers running any other operating system. The **Add Roles and Features** selection is running Server Manager Windows PowerShell Module **Install-WindowsFeature** in Figure 3.3.

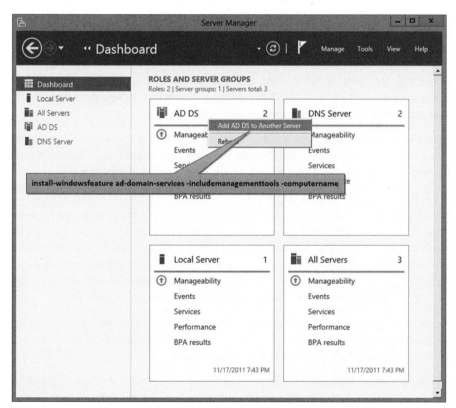

FIGURE 3.3 The UI option is also available via PowerShell. (For color version of this figure, the reader is referred to the online version of this chapter.)

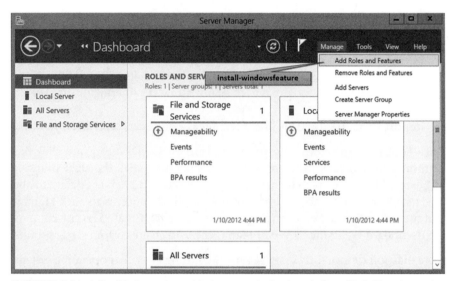

FIGURE 3.4 Installing Windows roles and features can also be done via PowerShell. (For color version of this figure, the reader is referred to the online version of this chapter.)

You can use the Server Manager on a domain controller to select remote server AD DS installation with the role already preselected by right-clicking the AD DS dashboard tile and selecting **Add AD DS to Another Server**. The computer you are running Server Manager on puts itself into a pool automatically. To install the AD DS role, click the **Manage** menu and click **Add Roles and Features**, as seen in Figure 3.4.

The **Installation Type** page gives you an option that does not support Active Directory Domain Services: the **Remote Desktop Services scenario-based installation**. That option only allows Remote Desktop Service in a multiserver distributed workload (Figure 3.5). If you select it, AD DS will not install, so do not do it!

On the **Server Selection** page, you can choose any one of the servers you added to the pool as shown in Figure 3.6. However, that server must be accessible. You also have the option to select offline Hyper-V VHD files, and the Server Manager will add the role to them directly through component servicing—is that cool or what? This is a great security option because it allows you to provision VMs with the necessary components before even turning them on.

Select the **Active Directory Domain Services** role to prepare the machine to be promoted to a DC as shown in Figure 3.7. All Active Directory administration features and required services install automatically.

Server Manager will show you a dialog box as shown in Figure 3.8 that tells you which management features this role implicitly installs; this is the **IncludeManagementTools** argument.

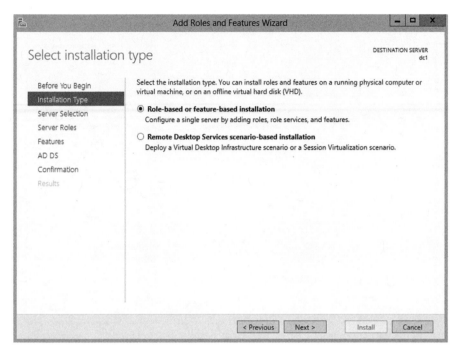

FIGURE 3.5 Selecting the installation type. (For color version of this figure, the reader is referred to the online version of this chapter.)

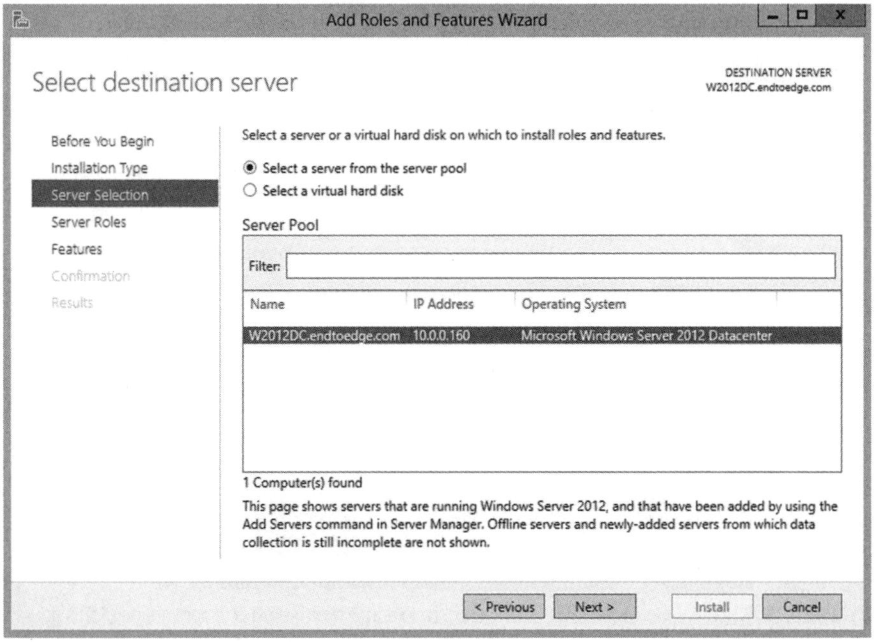

FIGURE 3.6 Selecting the target server. (For color version of this figure, the reader is referred to the online version of this chapter.)

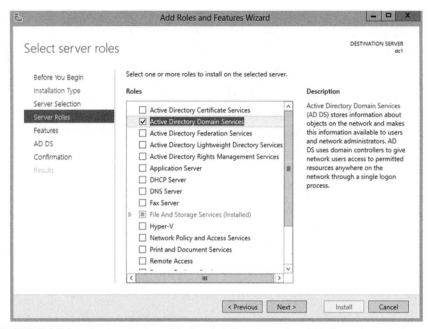

FIGURE 3.7 Selecting the roles that will be installed. (For color version of this figure, the reader is referred to the online version of this chapter.)

FIGURE 3.8 Some options on the UI have the equivalent in PowerShell. (For color version of this figure, the reader is referred to the online version of this chapter.)

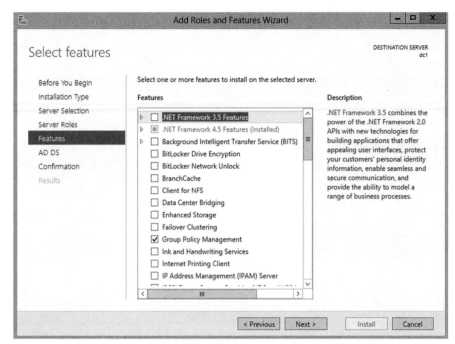

FIGURE 3.9 Selecting the features. (For color version of this figure, the reader is referred to the online version of this chapter.)

If necessary, additional **Features** can be added in the **Select features** page as shown in Figure 3.9.

The **Active Directory Domain Services** page gives you some information about Active Directory DS requirements and best practices as shown in Figure 3.10.

The **Confirmation** page provides an option to restart the computer as needed after role installation, but AD DS installation does not require a reboot. Click **Install** to begin role installation as shown in Figure 3.11.

The **Results** page shows the installation progress and the install status. Server Manager does not install the Active Directory Domain Services role. Instead, it starts **WsmProvHost.exe** which installs the role in the background. Now you know why role installation continues even if you close the Server Manager.

Verifying the installation results, shown in Figure 3.12, is still a best practice. If you close the **Results** dialog before installation completes, you can check the results using the Server Manager notification flag. Server Manager also shows a warning message for any servers that have installed the AD DS role but not been further configured as domain controllers.

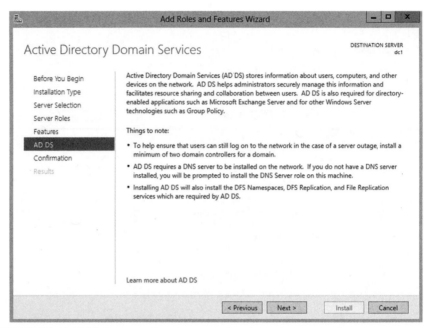

FIGURE 3.10 AD DS initial setup. (For color version of this figure, the reader is referred to the online version of this chapter.)

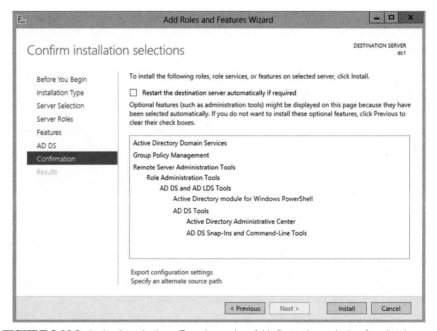

FIGURE 3.11 Reviewing the selections. (For color version of this figure, the reader is referred to the online version of this chapter.)

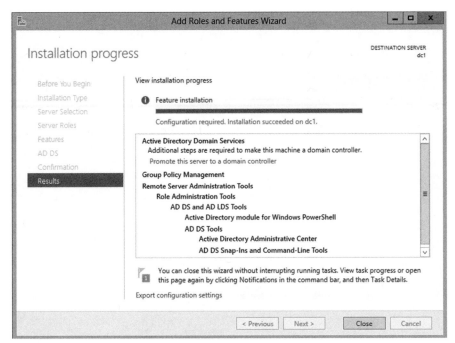

FIGURE 3.12 Installation progress allows you to view each feature that it is installing. (For color version of this figure, the reader is referred to the online version of this chapter.)

At the end of the AD DS role installation, you can continue the configuration by using the **Promote this server to a domain controller** link. While this is required to make the server a domain controller, it is not necessary to run the configuration wizard at this time. You might want to provision servers with the AD DS binaries before sending them to a branch office to be configured later. When you add the AD DS role before shipping, you make it easier for the branch office admins to complete the installation. In addition, it is a best practice to not keep a domain controller offline for days or weeks.

Server Manager begins every domain controller promotion with the **Deployment Configuration** page as seen in Figure 3.13. To create a new Active Directory forest, select the **Add a new forest** option. You must use a valid root domain name that is a fully qualified domain name—the name cannot be single labeled.

Note that you can create a new forest without being a domain admin. The domain controller promotion process uses the credentials of the built-in administrator account from the first domain controller used to create the forest root. Because the default setting is such that there is no way to disable

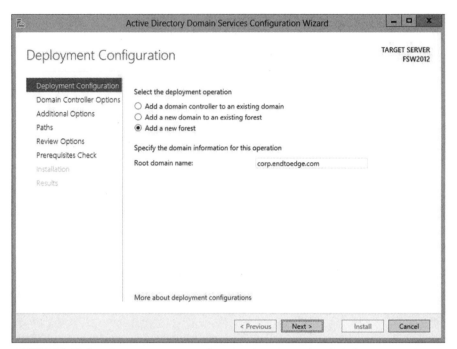

FIGURE 3.13 Choosing the deployment configuration. (For color version of this figure, the reader is referred to the online version of this chapter.)

or lock out the built-in administrator account, you can use it as the only entry point into a forest if the other administrative domain accounts are inaccessible.

The **Domain Controller Options** page, shown in Figure 3.14, gives you the options to configure the **forest functional level** and **domain functional level** for the new forest root domain. These settings are default to Windows Server 2012 in a new forest root domain. Note that In Windows Server 2012, the forest and domain functional levels *do not* provide any new functionality over Windows Server 2008 R2. Functional levels in Windows Server 2012 are used to restrict a domain controller's minimum-allowed operating system participation in that domain.

The only option you can actually configure on this page is the **Domain Name System (DNS) Server** option. All domain controllers should be able to provide DNS services for high availability in distributed environments. The first domain controller must be a GC and cannot be a read-only domain controller (RODC); that is why it is enabled by default and why you cannot change it.

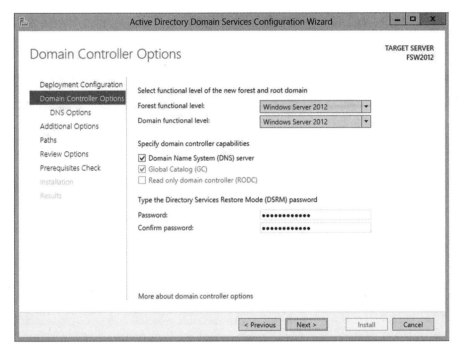

FIGURE 3.14 Selecting domain controller options. (For color version of this figure, the reader is referred to the online version of this chapter.)

The **DS Restore Mode Password** option uses the password policy applied to the server, which by default does not require a strong password. However, it cannot be blank. Always choose a strong, complex passphrase because it is critical that this account cannot be compromised.

The **DNS Options** page, shown in Figure 3.15, enables you to configure DNS delegation and provide alternate DNS administrative credentials. However, in this example, you cannot configure DNS options or delegation in the Active Directory Domain Services Configuration Wizard because we are installing a new Active Directory Forest Root Domain. The **Create DNS delegation** option is only available when you create a new forest root DNS zone in an existing DNS server infrastructure. This option enables you to provide alternate DNS administrative credentials that enable privileges to update DNS zone.

The **Additional Options** page, shown in Figure 3.16, displays the NetBIOS name of the domain and gives you the option to change it. The default setting is to use the NetBIOS name that matches the high-order (left-most) label of the FQDN on the **Deployment Configuration** page. For example, if you provided the fully qualified domain name of **corp.endtoedge.com**, the default NetBIOS domain name is **CORP**.

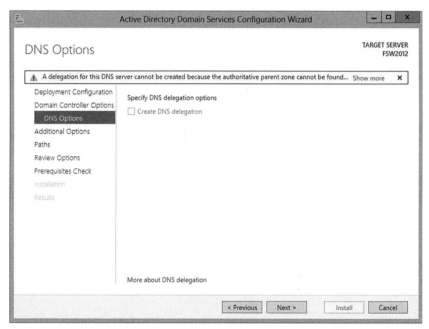

FIGURE 3.15 Configuring DNS options. (For color version of this figure, the reader is referred to the online version of this chapter.)

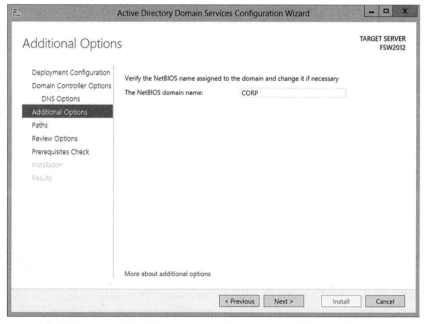

FIGURE 3.16 Choosing the NetBIOS domain name. (For color version of this figure, the reader is referred to the online version of this chapter.)

Note that this must be a valid NetBIOS name.[8] If the name is 15 characters or less and uses valid NetBIOS name characters, then it is not changed. If it is not a valid NetBIOS name, then the wizard will provide an unused, possibly truncated suggestion. The wizard then confirms that the name is not already in use by using a WINS lookup or NetBIOS broadcast. For this reason, you may wish to continue deploying WINS servers in a limited context in your production environment.

The **Paths** page, shown in Figure 3.17, gives you the opportunity to change the folder locations of the AD DS database, the database transaction logs, and the SYSVOL share. The default locations are always in %systemroot% (which is C:\Windows).

The **Review Options** page, shown in Figure 3.18, enables you to validate your settings and also includes the **View Script** button to create a text file that contains the current configuration settings you performed in the wizard as a single

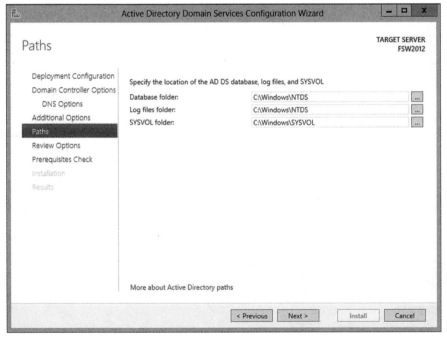

FIGURE 3.17 Choosing the database, log files, and SYSVOL location. (For color version of this figure, the reader is referred to the online version of this chapter.)

---

[8] A NetBIOS name must be 15 characters or less and cannot contain any spaces. In addition, not all special characters are supported for NetBIOS names. See http://support.microsoft.com/kb/188997 for more information.

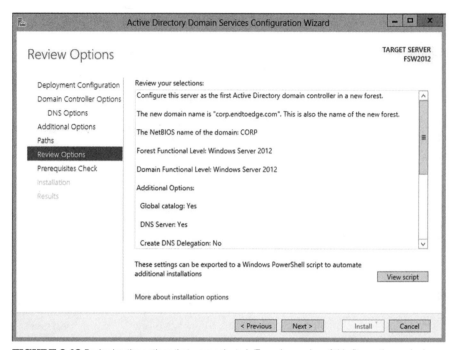

FIGURE 3.18 Reviewing the options that were selected. (For color version of this figure, the reader is referred to the online version of this chapter.)

Windows PowerShell script. You can then use the Active Directory Domain Services Configuration Wizard to configure options, export the configuration, and then cancel the wizard.

The **Prerequisites Check** page, shown in Figure 3.19, is new in Windows Server 2012. It is used to validate that the server configuration is capable of supporting a new AD DS forest. Here, the Server Manager **Active Directory Domain Services Configuration Wizard** performs a series of tests. These tests will inform you about suggested repair options. All prerequisite tests must be passed for installation to continue. The **Prerequisites Check** also provides information about security changes that affect older operating systems.

When the **Installation** page displays as shown in Figure 3.20, the domain controller configuration begins and cannot be stopped. Operations display on this page and write to logs located at:

- %systemroot%\debug\dcpromo.log
- %systemroot%\debug\dcpromoui.log

The **Results** page (Figure 3.21) shows the success or failure of the promotion and any important administrative information.

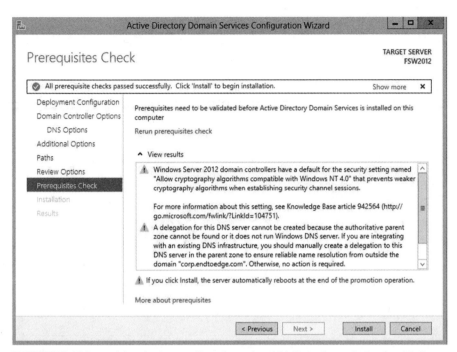

FIGURE 3.19 Prerequisites check report. (For color version of this figure, the reader is referred to the online version of this chapter.)

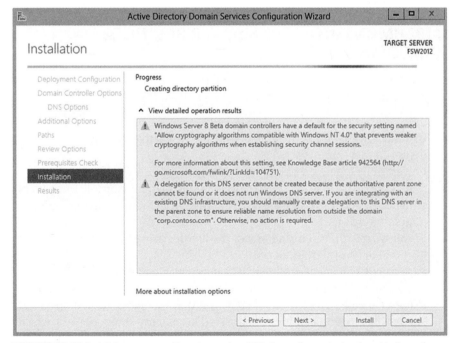

FIGURE 3.20 Installation progress. (For color version of this figure, the reader is referred to the online version of this chapter.)

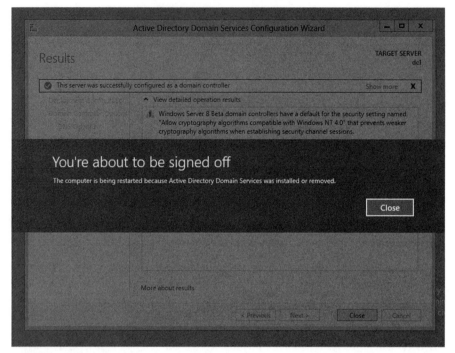

FIGURE 3.21 Notification that the user will be signed off. (For color version of this figure, the reader is referred to the online version of this chapter.)

IMPLEMENTING CERTIFICATE SERVICES ON WINDOWS SERVER 2012

Now that you learned how to implement Directory Services on Windows Server 2012, it is time to plan your Certificate Services deployment. However, before starting to plan for Certificate Services, let us see what is new in this feature:

- **Installation:** AD CS is integrated with the new Server Manager and can be deployed as a role.
- **PowerShell:** A new set of cmdlets are available for AD CS.
- **Management:** A new Template Manager Management console introduces enhancements in the administrative experience when managing multiple template versions.
- **Server Core:** You can install any of those roles using Server Core or in the Minimal Server Interface option.
- **Site-aware Certificate Enrollment**: Great improvement that allows workstations running Windows 8 and servers running Windows Server 2012 to use a CA based on their site when performing a certificate request operation. The site information in this case is retrieved from Active Directory (AD), which means that this feature will only work if the sites are correctly defined in AD.

- **Automatic Certificate Renew for non-domain joined machines**: New capability that allows non-domain-joined computers to request and retrieve certificates. This functionality is provided by the Certificate Enrollment Web Services (CES) role.
- **Internationalized Domain Names (IDN)**: Support for international domain names to remove the ASCII encoding limitation caused by some languages when enrolling for a certificate.
- **Renew with the same key:** It is now possible to configure certificate templates in order to allow Windows 8 and Windows Server 2012 to give higher priority to TPM-based KSPs for generating keys. This functionality also enables administrators to ensure that the key is still the same even after removing the TPM.
- **Increase of the default security on CA Role**: By default, the CA Role requires that all clients encrypt the RPC communication[9] while requesting a new certificate from the CA.

As part of the planning phase, you should understand what are the roles included with AD CS on Windows Server 2012. This will help you to determine which one you should install according to your company's needs. The roles are shown in Figure 3.22.

Planning AD CS Implementation

As part of your implementation planning of AD CS, you must identify which roles your Windows Server 2012 will provide when you install Certificate Services.

FIGURE 3.22 AD CS roles. (For color version of this figure, the reader is referred to the online version of this chapter.)

---

[9] If your company has Windows XP on the environment, it is recommended that you read this post before deploying Windows Server 2012 AD CS at http://blogs.technet.com/b/instan/archive/2012/11/12/xp-and-w2k3-clients-are-by-default-unable-to-enroll-from-w2k12-ca-servers.aspx.

IMPORTANT

During the planning phase, make sure to add to the plan hardening Certificate Services Server using Security Configuration Wizard. For more information about running this tool, review Chapter 2.

Certificate Authority (CA)

This is the main component of your Certificate Services Infrastructure; it is the entity responsible for issuing certificates to users, computers, or other entities, such as subordinate CAs. A CA is responsible to

- accept or reject certificate request;
- verify the requester's information and verify if the policy allows the requester to perform that operation;
- validate a certificate;
- revoke a certificate and publish it in the Certification Revocation List (CRL).

IMPORTANT

Although you can use an outside CA (public CA such as VeriSign), this book will not cover the integration of public CA with your public key infrastructure (PKI). The main focus of this chapter is to explain how to deploy an internal PKI for an Enterprise environment.

Depending on the size of your organization and on the management strategy in use, you can adopt a hierarchical mode to deploy your CAs. Assume a scenario with the following requirements:

SCENARIO

Deb is planning her PKI deployment and she has to address the following company requirements:

- The main CA (Root) should be located in the company's headquarter in Dallas, TX.
- The company has two other branches, one in Charlotte, NC, and another one in Bellevue, WA; they have their own IT Team that should be responsible for maintaining their CA.

Based on these requirements, the infrastructure shown in Figure 3.23 should be implemented:

As you can see in Figure 3.23, a root CA is the highest certificate authority of a certification hierarchy and all clients in the organization trust the root CA. Whether you use enterprise (AD integrated) or standalone CAs (more for workgroup scenarios), you need to designate a root CA. CAs that are not root CAs are considered subordinate (in this case, Bellevue and Charlotte are).

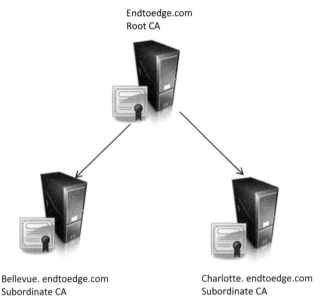

Endtoedge.com
Root CA

Bellevue. endtoedge.com
Subordinate CA

Charlotte. endtoedge.com
Subordinate CA

FIGURE 3.23 PKI using a hierarchical mode. (For color version of this figure, the reader is referred to the online version of this chapter.)

NOTE

When planning your PKI, make sure to use Microsoft best practices to distribute the servers. A good resource that you can use during this planning phase is the TechNet Wiki article at http://social. technet.microsoft.com/wiki/contents/articles/7421.ad-cs-pki-design.aspx.

Web Enrollment

One of the most common scenarios to use Web Enrollment role is to allow non-domain-joined computers to request a new certificate from the CA. Another reason to install Web Enrollment role is when you need to provide an alternative method to issue certificates, for example, for clients that are not directly connected to the corporate network or for non-Microsoft clients.

Online Certificate Status Protocol Responder (OCSP)

When a client sends a request for information about the current state of a certificate, it is the OCSP that is responsible for answering the question. OCSP is only responsible to answer to individual requests; in other words, it does not distribute any update periodically. In summary, the CryptoAPI[10] will validate the certificate by following a process similar to the one shown below:

1. The CryptoAPI determines if the certificate has the untrusted certificate store.
2. Check if the certificate has a stapled OCSP response and also if this response has a valid time. CryptoAPI will use this information to validate the revocation status.
3. Next, it will look for a matching name on the Certification Revocation List (CRL).
4. It will verify if the stapled response (or previous version of the CRL that was downloaded) is not available.
5. In this case, the CryptoAPI will attempt to retrieve the URL in order to determine the revocation status of the certificate.

The URLs used by the OCSP are built in one specific order, which is via GPO, from authority information access extension and from CDP extension.[11]

Network Device Enrollment Service (NDES)

Some network devices, such as routers and switches, will not be able to authenticate on the network in order to enroll to a X.509 certificate.[12] In order to address this problem, Microsoft uses NDES which is an implementation of the Simple Certificate Enrollment Protocol (SCEP), a communication protocol that the software running on those devices to obtain a certificate from a CA.

Certificate Enrollment Policy Web Server (CEP) and Certificate Enrollment Policy Web Services (CES)

In order to allow users and computers to receive a certificate enrollment policy via Web service, you will need to implement the AD CS Role Service called CEP. In conjunction with the Certificate Enrollment Web Service, this service enables policy-based certificate enrollment in the following scenarios:

■ When the client computer is not a domain member
■ When a domain member is not connected to the domain.

The basic functionality of this role is described in Figure 3.24.

As shown in Figure 3.24, the Certificate Enrollment Policy Web Service component uses HTTPs to talk to Client Computer and LDAP to retrieve the certificate policy from Active Directory.

---

[10] For more information about CryptoAPI, see http://msdn.microsoft.com/en-us/library/aa266944(v=vs.60).aspx.

[11] For more information on how to determine the preference between OCSP and CRL, see http://technet.microsoft.com/en-us/library/ee619754(v=ws.10).aspx#BKMK_Determining.

[12] For more information about X.509 standard, see http://en.wikipedia.org/wiki/X.509.

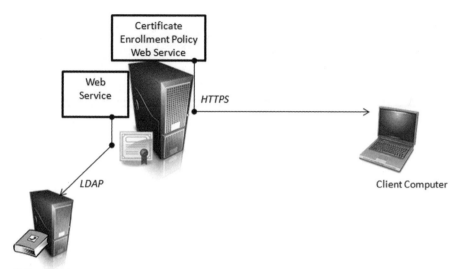

Active Directory

FIGURE 3.24 Protocols used by CEP while communicating with AD and Client. (For color version of this figure, the reader is referred to the online version of this chapter.)

NOTE

Once it obtains the information from Active Directory, it will cache to use again when the same client make the same request.

INSTALLING AD CS ROLE

You can install AD CS Role using Server Manager or PowerShell. It is recommended to perform the following actions before installing any service role in Windows Server 2012 using PowerShell:

- Verify which roles are installed by using the command *Get-WindowsFeature*.
- In the output of this command, review the Install State column to see if the role that you want to install is showing as "Available."
- When installing any role that requires a graphical user interface to manage, make sure to add the argument—*IncludeManagementTools*. If you do not add this argument, the role will be installed but the graphical management will not be available.

In this particular scenario, the result of the command *Get-WindowsFeature* will show the complete list of all roles (installed or not), so you will need to scroll down to see one by one. To avoid that, you can create a filter using the command below:

```
Get-WindowsFeature | where {$_.name -like "adcs*" -or $_.name
-like "ad-c*"}
```

FIGURE 3.25 Filtering the result of Get-WindowsFeature command. (For color version of this figure, the reader is referred to the online version of this chapter.)

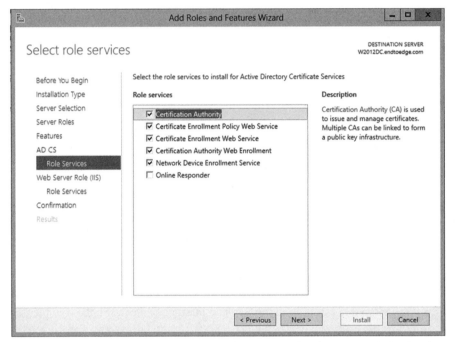

FIGURE 3.26 Selecting role services for AD CS. (For color version of this figure, the reader is referred to the online version of this chapter.)

The result (in case this, role is not installed) is shown in Figure 3.25.

You can install individual services by replacing the *argument* as shown below:

```
Install-WindowsFeature adcs-cert-authority -IncludeManagementTools
```

The argument can be replaced by any other argument from the list shown in Figure 3.26.

NOTE

You can also uninstall any of those service roles by using the command Uninstall-WindowsFeature followed by the argument (service role) that you want to uninstall.

Installing AD CS Using Server Manager

To install AD CS using Server Manager, read the scenario below and follow the steps:

SCENARIO

After a long meeting to review the overall plan for Public Key Infrastructure at EndtoEdge.com, the first part of the implementation phase was defined. The core requirements for this initial phase are:

- The Certificate Authority must be able to issue certificates for domain-joined computer as well as non-domain-joined computers.
- The Certificate Authority must be able to issue certificates to domain members that are not connected to the domain at certain point in time.
- Client computers that are not part of the domain should be able to request a certificate using a friendly Web interface.
- In this phase, the plan is to have only one Certificate Authority that should be integrated with Active Directory.
- The certificates generated by this CA should expire every 5 years.

NOTE

This scenario assumes that you already have an account member of the IIS_IUSRS group that will be used as service account for the Certificate Enrollment Web Services (CES). For this scenario, the account name is CESService. This account must have privilege to logon locally on the computer that you are installing this role service.

Implementation steps—follow the steps below to install AD CS Role and prepare the environment to meet the above requirements:

1. On the **Server Manager**, click **Dashboard** in the left pane and click **Add Roles and features**.
2. On the **Before you begin** page, click **Next**.
3. On the **Select installation type** page, ensure that **Role-based or feature-based installation** option is selected and click **Next**.
4. On the **Select destination server** page, select the target server and click **Next**.
5. On the **Select server roles** page, select **Active Directory Certificate Services** role. On the Add **Roles and Features Wizard** dialog box, click **Add Features** button and click **Next**.
6. On the **Select features** page, leave the default selection and click **Next**.
7. On the **Active Directory Certificate Services** page, click **Next**.
8. On the **Select role services** page, make sure that all options that are part of the scenario requirement are selected as shown below and then click **Next**.

NOTE

Upon selecting each one of those options, the **Add Roles and Features Wizard** dialog box is expected to appear multiple times. Make sure to click **Add Feature** button always when requested.

9. On the **Web Server Role (IIS)** page, click **Next**.

NOTE

If you already have IIS installed on this server, this page will not appear.

10. On the **Select role services** page, leave the default selection and click **Next**.
11. On the **Confirm installation** selections, leave the default selection and click **Install**.
12. On the **Installation progress** page, you have the option to wait until the installation is finished or you can click **Close** and leave the installation happening in the background. For this particular example, we will wait until the installation is successfully completed to click **Close**.
13. In the **Server Manager**, click the orange alert sign under the notification flag as shown in Figure 3.27.
14. Click **Configure Active Directory Certificate Services on the destination server** option.
15. On the **AD CS Configuration** wizard, **Credentials** page, review the installation requirements, make sure you are compliant with all requirements, and then click **Next**.
16. On the **Role Services** page, select **Certificate Authority** and **Certificate Authority Web Enrollment** as shown in Figure 3.28 and click **Next**.

FIGURE 3.27 Post deployment configuration flag. (For color version of this figure, the reader is referred to the online version of this chapter.)

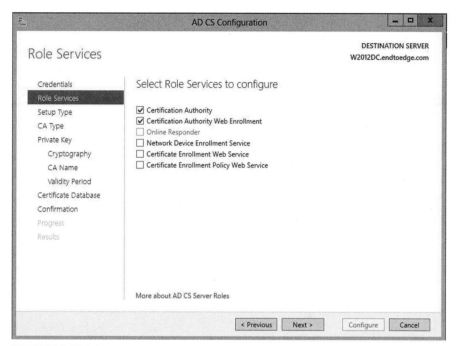

FIGURE 3.28 Role services selection. (For color version of this figure, the reader is referred to the online version of this chapter.)

NOTE

Although for this scenario we need all role services installed, you will need to install those two roles services first since they are prerequisites for the others.

17. On the **Setup Type** page, select **Enterprise CA** in order to accommodate the design requirements for this scenario and then click **Next**.
18. On the **CA Type** page, select **Root CA** since this is the first CA in this organization and then click **Next**.
19. On the **Private Key** page, select **Create a new private key** and click **Next**.

NOTE

Use the option **Use existing private key** when reinstalling a certificate authority.

20. On the **Cryptography for CA** page, select the cryptographer provider, the key length, and the hash algorithm that will be used as shown in Figure 3.29. For this particular scenario, leave the default selection and click **Next**.

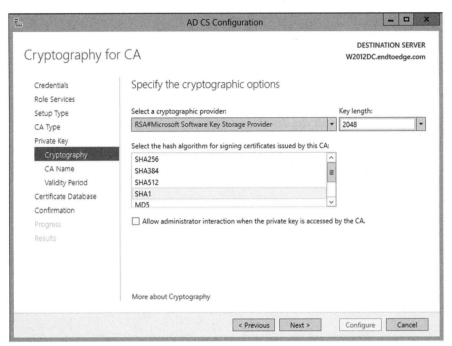

FIGURE 3.29 Choosing the hash algorithm used to signing the certificates issues by this CA. (For color version of this figure, the reader is referred to the online version of this chapter.)

NOTE

Use the option **Allow administrator interaction when the private key is accessed by the CA** if you want to prevent unapproved use of the CA and its private key. This will require that the administrator enters a password before every cryptographic operation.

---

21. On the **CA Name** page, ensure that the information is correct and click **Next**.
22. On the **Validity Period** page, leave the default selection as per scenario requirements and click **Next**.
23. On the **CA Database** page, leave the default options and click **Next**.
24. On the **Confirmation** page, review all selections as shown in Figure 3.30 and, assuming that they are all correct, click **Configure**.
25. On the **Progress** page, wait until the installation, and once it is finished, the **Results** page should appear with the confirmation that both role services were installed as shown in Figure 3.31 and then click **Close**.
26. In the **Server Manager**, click the notification flag and click **Add Roles and Features** as shown in Figure 3.32.
27. On the **Installation progress** page, click **Configure Active Directory Certificate Services on the destination server**.

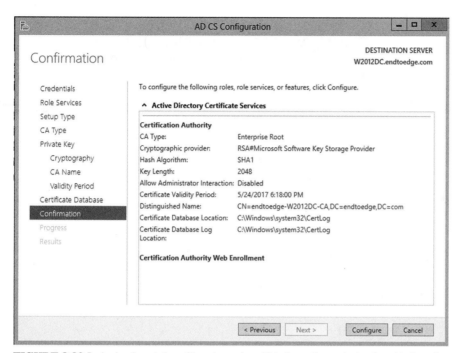

FIGURE 3.30 Reviewing the selctions. (For color version of this figure, the reader is referred to the online version of this chapter.)

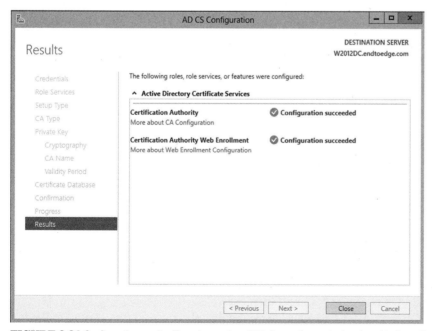

FIGURE 3.31 Configuration results. (For color version of this figure, the reader is referred to the online version of this chapter.)

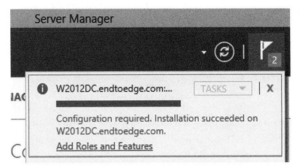

FIGURE 3.32 Post installation configuration required. (For color version of this figure, the reader is referred to the online version of this chapter.)

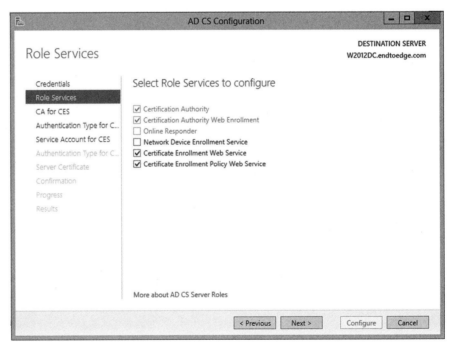

FIGURE 3.33 Selecting Certificate Web services. (For color version of this figure, the reader is referred to the online version of this chapter.)

28. On the **AD CS Configuration** wizard, on the **Credentials** page, click **Next**.
29. On the **Role Services** page, select the options required for this scenario as shown in Figure 3.33 and then click **Next**.
30. On the **CA for CES** page, leave the default selection (CA Name) and click **Next**.

FIGURE 3.34 Selecting the user account that will be used by CES. (For color version of this figure, the reader is referred to the online version of this chapter.)

31. On the **Authentication Type for CES** page, ensure that **Windows integrated authentication** is selected and click **Next**.
32. On the **Service Account for CES** page, ensure that **Specify service account (recommended)** option is selected and click **Select** button. The **Window Security** dialog box will appear for you to type the credentials of the CES Service account and click **OK**. The **Service Account for CES** page will appear as shown in Figure 3.34. Once you confirm that the account is correctly configured there, click **Next**.
33. On the **Authentication Type for CEP** page, ensure that **Windows integrated authentication** is selected and click **Next**.
34. On the **Server Certificate** page, select **Choose an existing certificate for SSL encryption (recommended)** and highlight the certificate suggested as shown in Figure 3.35 and then click **Next**.
35. On the **Confirmation** page, review the selections and click **Configure**.
36. On the **Progress** page, wait until all role services are installed. Once this process is finished, the **Results** page will appear as shown in Figure 3.36. Confirm that all roles services were installed and click **Close**, and then click **Close** again in the **Installation progress** page.

At this point, the role is installed and ready to be used.

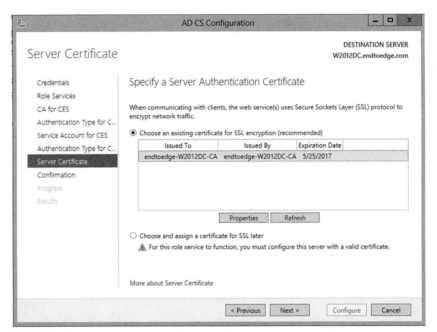

FIGURE 3.35 Server authentication certificate selection. (For color version of this figure, the reader is referred to the online version of this chapter.)

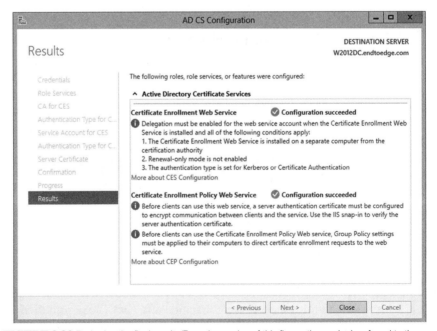

FIGURE 3.36 Reviewing the final result. (For color version of this figure, the reader is referred to the online version of this chapter.)

SITE-AWARE CERTIFICATE ENROLLMENT

As mentioned earlier in this chapter, this feature allows the administrator to control which certificate authority is used to issue a certificate request that was sent from a Windows 8 or Windows Server 2012 computer.

Here are some of the designing considerations for this feature:

- It was designed to be used with Windows 8 or Windows Server 2012 as PKI client component and Windows Server 2012 Active Directory.
- Client will select the certificate authority based on two factors: site and cost.

In order to calculate which CA it will use, the following steps (shown in Figure 3.37) are performed:

1. Windows 8 client perform the enrollment for a template-based certificate.
2. The site-aware enrollment component on the client will take over.
3. It makes a call to DsGetSiteName[13] API function in order to obtain the client's site name. The client will know which CAs are capable of using this feature because of the msPKI-Site-Name attribute.

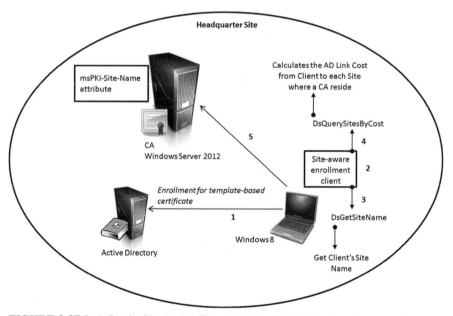

FIGURE 3.37 Basic flow for CA selection. (For color version of this figure, the reader is referred to the online version of this chapter.)

---

[13] For more information about this function, see http://msdn.microsoft.com/en-us/library/windows/desktop/ms675992(v=vs.85).aspx.

4. The site-aware enrollment component on the client will call DsQuerySitesByCost API to calculate the AD Link cost from the client to each capable CA.

5. Once the calculation is performed, the client will use the closest one.

Configuring CA Site

In order to configure CA Site information, you will need to use the Certutil command with the –SetCaSites parameter. When you first run this command with this parameter, the result is that the site information does not exist (empty) as shown in Figure 3.38.

```
C:\>certutil  -SetCaSites
set:

endtoedge-W2012DC-CA:
  Existing: msPKI-Site-Name = EMPTY
  Detected: W2012DC.endtoedge.com = Default-First-Site-Name
  Successfully updated: msPKI-Site-Name = Default-First-Site-Name
CertUtil: -SetCASites command completed successfully.
```

FIGURE 3.38 Using Certutil to obtain site information. (For color version of this figure, the reader is referred to the online version of this chapter.)

To configure the site information, you can use the following command:

Certutil-SetCaSites-f-config caDnsName\caCertCommonName [siteName]

For this scenario, the command will be:

Certutil-SetCaSites-f-config w2012dc.endtoend.com\config w2012dc Headquarter

RENEW WITH THE SAME KEY

In Windows Server 2012, the capability of renewing a certificate with the same key was introduced. This functionality will work when clients that previously received a template that are configured for renewal with the same key try to renew it. Windows Server 2012 and Windows 8 can enforce certificate renewal with the same key.

To create a template that supports the renewal with the same key, follow the steps below:

1. Open **MMC**.
2. Click **File** and then click **Add/Remove Snap In**.
3. On the **Add or Remove Snap-ins** window, select **Certificates** on the left pane and click **Add** button.
4. Click **OK**.
5. Click **Certificate Templates** on the left and highlight the Certificate that you want to duplicate in order to create the new one. The decision might vary according to the scenario's needs; a different template version[14]

---

[14] For more information about template version, see http://social.technet.microsoft.com/wiki/contents/articles/13303.certificate-template-versions-and-options.aspx.

might be required for a particular scenario. For this example, the selected certificate will be **Workstation Authentication**.

6. Right-click on this certificate and choose **Duplicate Template** as shown in Figure 3.39:

7. On the **Properties of New Template** window, **Compatibility** tab, change the **Certificate Authority** to be Windows Server 2012. The **Resulting changes** dialog appears as shown in Figure 3.40 and click **OK** to continue.

8. Under the **Certificate recipient** option, select Windows 8/Windows Server 2012. The **Resulting changes** window appears as shown in Figure 3.41 and click **OK** to continue.

9. Click **Request Handling** tab and among other options that might be appropriated for your deployment click **Renew** with the same key as shown in Figure 3.42, click **OK** to close this window once all the settings that you need besides this one are configured.

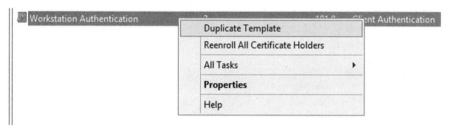

FIGURE 3.39 Duplicating a certificate. (For color version of this figure, the reader is referred to the online version of this chapter.)

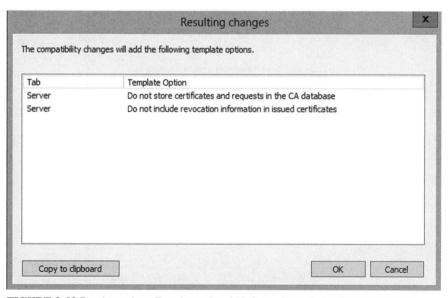

FIGURE 3.40 Template options. (For color version of this figure, the reader is referred to the online version of this chapter.)

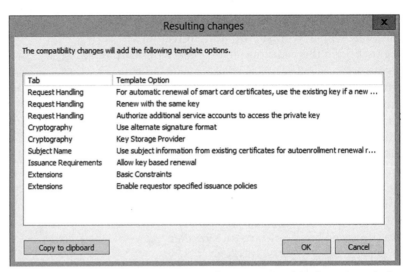

FIGURE 3.41 Compatibility changes per template. (For color version of this figure, the reader is referred to the online version of this chapter.)

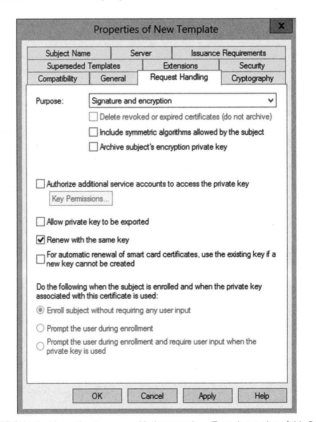

FIGURE 3.42 Selecting the option to renew with the same key. (For color version of this figure, the reader is referred to the online version of this chapter.)

VALIDATE YOUR KNOWLEDGE IN AD CS

Now that you have this understanding on how AD CS works and how to install it on Windows Server 2012, take a step further and perform the configuration yourself using the Microsoft Test Lab Guide. For this section, we recommend you to:

- Download the Windows Server 2012 Base Configuration for the Test Lab Guide from http://go.microsoft.com/fwlink/p/?LinkId=236358
- Perform the Test Lab Guide: Deploying an AD CS Two-Tier PKI Hierarchy

http://technet.microsoft.com/en-us/library/hh831348.aspx

- Perform the Test Lab Guide: Demonstrating Certificate Key-Based Renewal

http://technet.microsoft.com/en-us/library/tlg-key-based-renewal.aspx

ADMINISTRATOR'S PUNCH LIST

- Understand the threat landscape against certificate and what security methods should be in place in an end-to-end solution in order to assist mitigating this problem.
- Bake security into your AD DS planning before you implement it.
- Review the new capabilities in Windows Server 2012 AD DS and evaluate which one will be deployed. Plan ahead and validate it before you implement it. This is very critical in many of the new features, such as DC virtualization.
- Once planning is over, decide if you will deploy AD DS via Server Manager or PowerShell.
- When planning for AD CS, remember that if your environment has Windows XP, they will have problems with auto-enroll due to the new security capabilities of AD CS in Windows Server 2012.
- Plan the AD CS roles before deploying it; your company might need multiple servers.
- Once planning is over, decide if you will deploy AD CS via Server Manager or PowerShell.
- Consider deploying new templates that are capable of renewing with the same key.

SUMMARY

In this chapter, you learned about the evolving threats against certificates and the importance of deploying your own private PKI. You saw how to install a new domain controller in a new forest and how to plan and deploy Microsoft Windows Server 2012 Certificate Services. You also learned how to create a new certificate template capable of using the same key for renewal. This information sets the stage for the next chapter, where you will learn about Windows Server 2012 Rights Management Services and Active Directory Federation Services. See you on the next chapter!

CHAPTER 4

Deploying AD FS and AD RMS in Windows Server 2012

CONTENTS

CHAPTER POINTS

- Planning for Active Directory Federation Services
- Deploying Active Directory Federation Services
- Deploying Active Directory Rights Management Services

PLANNING FOR ACTIVE DIRECTORY FEDERATION SERVICES

One of the main goals of AD FS is to enable applications that are running in one domain to authenticate with user accounts that are located in another domain. The biggest complaint in scenarios like this from the user perspective is to deal with multiple authentication prompts when they try to access an application. This happens because the server that hosts the application usually requires these credentials to enable the application to take the best authorization decision. The way that AD FS will avoid this secondary credential request is by using a trust relationship mechanism. Each organization will continue to manage their own user account database as well as their own identity; AD FS will be responsible for providing a secure mechanism to enable the business-to-business (B2B) transaction. The most common scenarios to use AD FS are enumerated below:

- Access to partner's application located on the Internet with a single logon experience (see Figure 4.1).
- Maintain a single logon experience regardless of other provider's authentication schema.
- Enable SSO experience for remote employees while they are accessing Web application or services.

If you are researching about AD FS, these are the scenarios that most likely you will be implementing. However, before adding this role in your Windows Server 2012, installation is important to correctly plan how the deployment

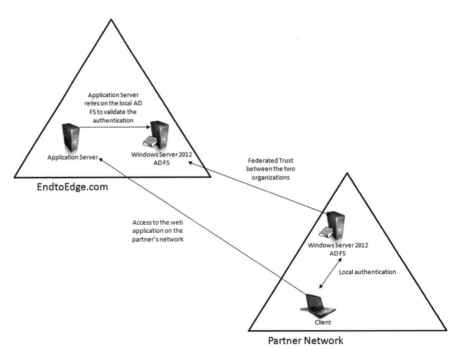

FIGURE 4.1 Topology for this scenario. (For color version of this figure, the reader is referred to the online version of this chapter.)

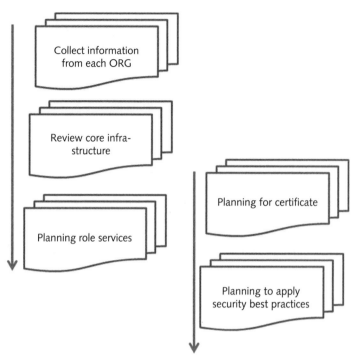

FIGURE 4.2 Proposed framework for the planning phase. (For color version of this figure, the reader is referred to the online version of this chapter.)

will be performed. The framework showed in Figure 4.2 summarizes the AD FS planning phase:

Each subphase is explained in more detail below:

- **Collect information from each organization and the business goal of this partnership**
  - This phase is important to:
    - Evaluate whether the applications will leverage AD FS
    - Identify the potential threats that must be mitigated from the partnership perspective
      - Who will have access?
      - Who will regulate the access?
      - Who will authorize?
    - Define the resource organization
      - Who will own and manage the resources?
    - Define the account organization
      - Who will own and manage the user accounts?
- **Review core infrastructure**
  - Review name resolution for the organizations involved

- DNS in the partner network must have a host (A) resource record that resolves the fully qualified domain name of the federation server to the IP address of the federation server cluster[1]
  - ■ Review PKI
    - Since certificate is part of the deployment, it will be necessary to review the current PKI used by both organizations
- ■ **Planning role services**
  - ■ Federation Service
    - Servers that share common policy and route authentication requests
      - ● Where this role will be located?
  - ■ Federation Service Proxy
    - Server that will be located in the perimeter network
      - ● Where is the perimeter network?
      - ● What is the firewall topology in this perimeter (multiple or single firewall layer)?
      - ● What ports should be opened?
  - ■ Claims-aware agent
    - Agent that will be used in a Web server that hosts claims-aware application
      - ● Where this Web server is located?
      - ● Does the organization have any Microsoft ASP. Net application that uses claims?
  - ■ Windows token-based agent
    - Agent that will be used in a Web server that hosts Windows token-based application
      - ● Where this Web server is located?
      - ● Does the organization have any application that uses Windows-based authorization?
- ■ **Planning for certificate**
  - ■ Certificates are important for secure communication and assist user authentication, mainly between Internet clients and federation servers
  - ■ Evaluate the type of certificate that will be used during the AD FS deployment
    - Token-signing certificate[2]
      - ● Used by federated server to sign all security tokens that are produced
    - Service communication certificate[3]
      - ● Used by default for Windows Communication Foundation (WCF) Message Security

---

[1] You can find additional name resolution requirements for Federation Server Proxies at http://technet. microsoft.com/en-us/library/dd807055.

[2] For more information about this type of certificate, see http://technet.microsoft.com/en-us/library/ hh341466.

[3] For more information about this type of certificate, see http://technet.microsoft.com/en-us/library/hh341473.

- SSL Certificate
  - Used by the Web server to encrypt the traffic between clients and server proxies
- Token-decryption certificate
  - Used to decrypt the token

IMPORTANT

Before deploying AD FS, make sure that you have the correct certificate installed on the federation server. Failure to install the certificate will prevent you from deploying AD FS. For more information about the type of certificate, review http://go.microsoft.com/fwlink/p/?LinkId=234887

- **Planning to apply security best practices**
  - Hardening servers that are part of the AD FS deployment
    - Use Security Configuration Wizard (SCW) to perform hardening operation as show in Figure 4.3

NOTE

For more information about Security Configuration Wizard on Windows Server 2012, read Chapter 2.

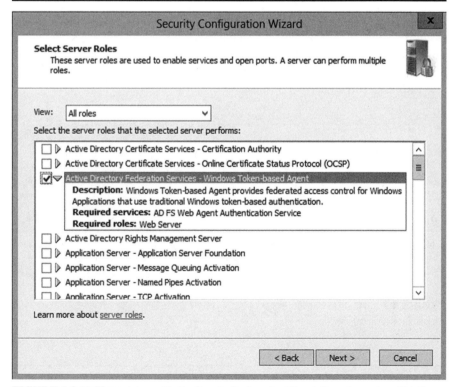

FIGURE 4.3 AD FS template provided by Security Configuration Wizard. (For color version of this figure, the reader is referred to the online version of this chapter.)

- Leverage the role extension that can be used with SCW for additional roles. Those extensions are available at %windir%\ADFS\SCW (this path will be available only when you install AD FS role)
- Perform the hardening operation using the files:
  - Farm.xml
  - SQLFarm.xml
  - StandAlone.xml
  - Proxy.xml
- Review SQL Server Security Best Practices[4]

By using this planning framework before you start deploying AD FS, chances are that you will be more successful on your deployment. The other aspect of this framework is that you can extend it; while this provides the core planning foundation for AD FS, you can still add specific steps within each subphase to better reflect particular needs of your deployment.

DEPLOYING ACTIVE DIRECTORY FEDERATION SERVICES

As previously said, companies are starting to migrate their resources to the cloud; the potential of a hybrid cloud scenario to exist during this transition phase is very high. Figure 4.4 shows a very common scenario where there are on-premise resources, cloud resources, and federation between the company and the cloud provider.

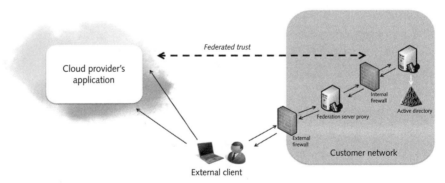

FIGURE 4.4 Hybrid cloud scenario. (For color version of this figure, the reader is referred to the online version of this chapter.)

---

[4] Review the recommendations that are used specifically for SQL Server at http://technet.microsoft.com/en-us/library/cc966456.aspx.

NOTE

In the diagram shown in Figure 4.4, the cloud provider application could be Office 365, for example. For more information on how to use AD FS with Office 365, watch this virtual lab at http://technet. microsoft.com/en-us/office365/hh744605.aspx

Windows Server 2012 Active Directory Federation Services introduces some core changes in this feature besides keeping the simplified way to secure identity federation while providing single sign-on (SSO) capabilities. The new features are as follows:

- Integration with the new Server Manager
- Integration with claims authentication for DAC (Dynamic Access Control) scenarios
- New set of Windows PowerShell cmdlets

AD FS is built on top of the claim-based identity framework called Windows Identity Foundation (WIF),[5] which was provided as an out-of-band (OOB) development kit prior to Windows Server 2012. However, WIF is now part of the. Net Framework 4.5[6] which comes built in Windows Server 2012.

Installing AD FS Role Service Using PowerShell

The installation of the AD FS Role Service and the deployment of the service happen in two different stages. The first part is the role installation, which can be done using Server Manager or PowerShell. It is recommended to perform the following actions before installing any service role in Windows Server 2012 using PowerShell:

- Verify which roles are installed by using the command *Get-WindowsFeature*.
- In the output of this command, review the Install State column to see if the role that you want to install is showing as "Available."
- When installing any role that requires a graphical user interface to manage, make sure to add the argument—*IncludeManagementTools*. If you do not add this argument, the role will be installed, but the graphical management will not be available.

---

[5] For more information about WIF, see http://social.technet.microsoft.com/wiki/contents/articles/3487. get-started-with-windows-identity-foundation-wif.aspx.
[6] Developers can review sample applications that use the new WIF at http://code.msdn.microsoft. com/vstudio/Claims-Aware-Web-d94a89ca and http://code.msdn.microsoft.com/vstudio/ Claims-Aware-Web-Service-1d55facc.

FIGURE 4.5 Using PowerShell to obtain the list of services available. (For color version of this figure, the reader is referred to the online version of this chapter.)

In this particular scenario, the result of the command *Get-WindowsFeature* will show the complete list of all roles (installed or not), so you will need to scroll down to see one by one. To avoid that, you can create a filter using the command below:

```
Get-WindowsFeature | where {$_.name -like "adfs*" -or $_.name -like "ad-fs*"}
```

The result (in case this role is not installed) is shown in Figure 4.5.

You can install individual services by replacing the **argument** as shown below:

```
Install-WindowsFeature adfs-Federation -IncludeManagementTools
```

The argument can be replaced by any other argument from the list showed in Figure 4.5.

NOTE

You can also uninstall any of those services' roles by using the command Uninstall-WindowsFeature followed by the argument (service role) that you want to uninstall.

Installing and Deploying AD FS Using Server Manager

To install AD FS using Server Manager, follow the steps below:

1. On the **Server Manager**, click **Dashboard** in the left pane and click **Add Roles and features**.
2. On the **Before you begin** page, click **Next**.
3. On the **Select installation type** page, ensure that **Role-based or feature-based installation** option is selected and click **Next**.
4. On the **Select destination server** page, select the target server and click **Next**.
5. On the **Select server roles** page, select **Active Directory Federation Services** role. On the **Add Roles and Features Wizard** dialog box, click **Add Features** button and click **Next**.
6. On the **Select features** page, leave the default selection and click **Next**.
7. On the **Active Directory Federation Services (AD FS)** page, read the description and click **Next**.

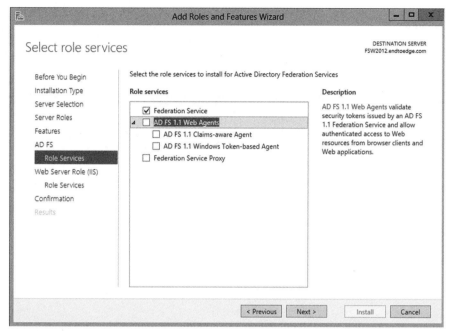

FIGURE 4.6 AD FS role service installation. (For color version of this figure, the reader is referred to the online version of this chapter.)

8. On the **Select role services** page, notice that **Federation Service** is already selected. If you plan to deploy Web Agents to validate security tokens issued by AD FS in the future, you may select the **AD FS 1.1 Web Agents** option and the type of agent that you will be using. For this example, leave the default selection as shown in Figure 4.6 and click **Next**.
9. On the **Web server Role (IIS)** page, click **Next**.
10. On the **Select role services** page, leave the default selection and click **Next**.
11. On the **Confirm installation selections** page, review the selected options as shown in Figure 4.7 and click **Install**.
12. On the **Installation progress** page, you have the option to wait until the installation is finished or you can click **Close** and leave the installation happening in the background. For this particular example, wait until the installation is successfully completed to click **Close**.
13. In the **Server Manager**, click the orange alert sign under the notification flag as shown in Figure 4.8.
14. Click **Run the AD FS Management snap-in** option, and the AD FS management console will appear as shown in Figure 4.9.
15. Click **AD FS Federation Server Configuration Wizard** (this launches %windir%\adfs\FsConfigWizard.exe).

NOTE

If you are familiar with AD FS 2.0, you will notice that the configuration at this point is very similar.

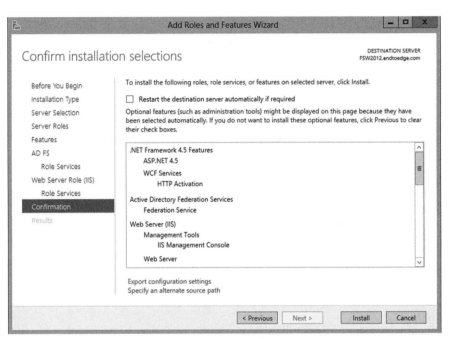

FIGURE 4.7 Summary of the options that were selected. (For color version of this figure, the reader is referred to the online version of this chapter.)

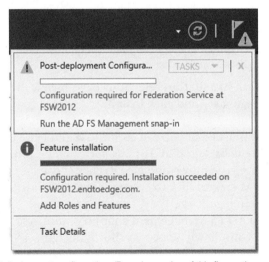

FIGURE 4.8 Post-deployment configuration. (For color version of this figure, the reader is referred to the online version of this chapter.)

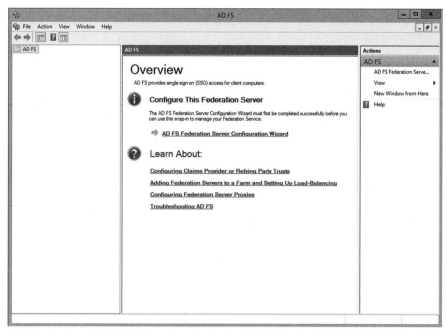

FIGURE 4.9 AD FS console. (For color version of this figure, the reader is referred to the online version of this chapter.)

16. On the **AD FS Federation Server Configuration Wizard**, on the **Welcome** page, select the appropriate option for your deployment. For the purpose of this example, the first option will be selected as shown in Figure 4.10.

17. On the **Select Stand-Alone or Farm Deployment** page, select the appropriate option for your deployment. The key decision point here is: if you are going to deploy more than one federation server, you should use the Server Farm option. For the purpose of this example, select **Stand-alone federation server** as shown in Figure 4.11 and click **Next**.

18. On the **Specify the Federation Service Name** page, the wizard should automatically search for the certificates that are installed on the Personal Certificate store of the local computer (see Figure 4.12) and use this certificate to fill the options available in this page as shown in Figure 4.13.

19. Confirm that this is the certificate that you want to use and click **Next** to proceed.

20. On the **Ready to Apply Settings** page, review the options that will be configured and once you confirm that these are the correct selections, click **Next**.

21. On the **Configuration Results** page, you will see the installation progress for each component as shown in Figure 4.14.

22. Once all components are in green and you receive a message saying that the installation was successfully completed, click **Close**.

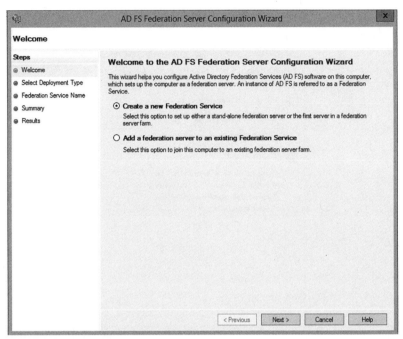

FIGURE 4.10 AD FS wizard with the initial option to create or add a federations server. (For color version of this figure, the reader is referred to the online version of this chapter.)

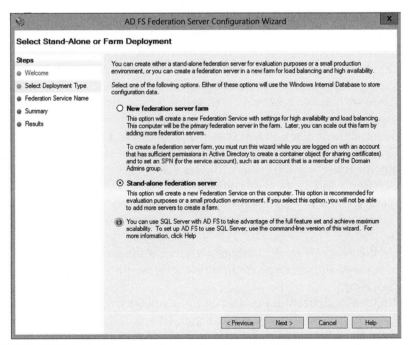

FIGURE 4.11 Selecting the type of deployment. (For color version of this figure, the reader is referred to the online version of this chapter.)

FIGURE 4.12 Certificates correctly installed on the personal store. (For color version of this figure, the reader is referred to the online version of this chapter.)

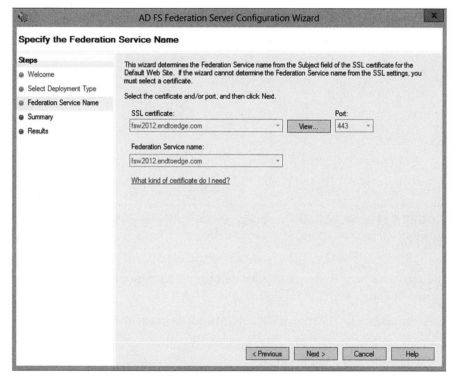

FIGURE 4.13 Selecting the federation service name according to the installed certificate. (For color version of this figure, the reader is referred to the online version of this chapter.)

This is the initial deployment of AD FS; the second part of the deployment will require you to obtain further information about the purpose of your deployment.[7] Something that should be covered during the planning phase as mentioned on the framework previously is presented in this chapter. You will notice that at the end of step 22, the AD FS Management Console

---

[7] You may find a very good example of an ADFS deployment scenario on the following article: http://technet.microsoft.com/en-us/library/adfs2-sharepoint-federated-collaboration-step-by-step-guide-01(v=ws.10).aspx. Although this is for Windows Server 2008, the steps once you install ADFS are the same in Windows Server 2012.

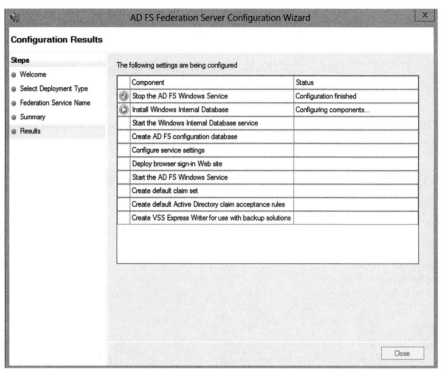

FIGURE 4.14 Configuration results according to the options that were selected. (For color version of this figure, the reader is referred to the online version of this chapter.)

changed and now it shows that an additional configuration is required as shown in Figure 4.15.

The information for the trusted relying party can be based on the following types:

- Federation metadata address (URL)
- Federation metadata file (XML)
- Manual configuration

These options will appear in the **Select Data Source** page, which is the second page of the Add Relying Party Trust Wizard as shown in Figure 4.16.

To configure a trusted relying party follow the steps below:

1. On the **Welcome** page, click **Start**.
2. On the **Select Data Source** page, click import data about the relying party published online or on a local network. In Federation metadata address (host name or URL), type the federation metadata URL or host name for the partner (e.g., https://destinationURL/App/FederationMetadata.xml) and then click **Next**.

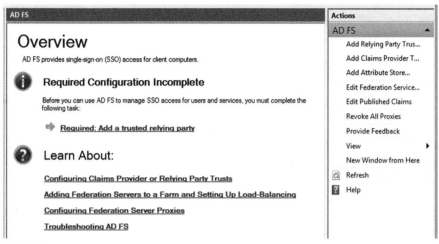

FIGURE 4.15 Initial screen with the options that are pending to complete. (For color version of this figure, the reader is referred to the online version of this chapter.)

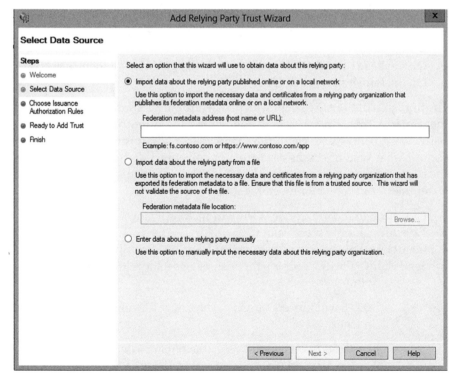

FIGURE 4.16 AD relying party trust. (For color version of this figure, the reader is referred to the online version of this chapter.)

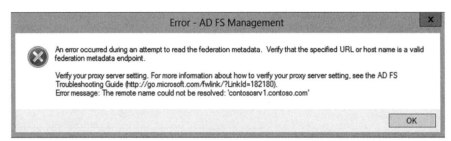

FIGURE 4.17 Error dialog that appears when a wrong URL is provided. (For color version of this figure, the reader is referred to the online version of this chapter.)

NOTE

The Wizard will perform an URL validation at this point; if you type a wrong URL, an error message shown in Figure 4.17 will appear.

3. On the **Specify Display Name** page, type a name in **Display name** and then click **Next**.
4. On the **Choose Issuance Authorization Rules** page, select either **Permit all users to access this relying party** or **Deny all users access to this relying party** and then click **Next**.
5. On the **Ready to Add Trust** page, review the options and then click **Next**.
6. On the **Finish** page, click **Close**.

The third part of the AD FS deployment will also vary according to your deployment needs. This part focuses on configuring the claim rules for the relying party. The goal to create claim rules is to enable administrators to granularly control what type of claims are issued or consumed and also to define how the claim values for each type are handled. There are many options to handle claim rules; some are mentioned below:

FIGURE 4.18 The different stages that AD FS will process. (For color version of this figure, the reader is referred to the online version of this chapter.)

- Pass through incoming values without making changes
- Pass through only some values
- Issue claims based on values extracted from LDAP attribute
- Send claim value if a user is a member of a specific Active Directory user group

AD FS will process the claim rules by following the stages showed in Figure 4.18:

- Stage 1—AD FS will verify the policy to determine what claim types are accepted from a specified authority.
- Stage 2—AD FS will verify the policy to determine what claims should be issued for a specified relying trusted party.

To configure a claims rule to use LDAP attributes (such as e-mail address), follow the steps below:

1. In the **Rules Editor**, click **Add Rule**.
2. In the **Select Rule Template** page, keep the default option **Send LDAP Attributes as Claims** selected and then click **Next**.
3. On the **Configuration Rule** page, type the name for the rule in the **Claim rule Name** field. For the **Attribute store**, select **Active Directory**. In the **LDAP Attribute column**, select **E-Mail-Addresses** for the outgoing **Name** claim, **Token-Groups—Unqualified Names** for the **Role** claim, and **E-Mail-Addresses** for the outgoing **E-mail Address** claim.
4. Once you complete this configuration, click **Finish**.
5. Click **OK** to close the **Rules Editor**.

NOTE

When you create a claim rule, what happens behind the scene is that a Claim Rule Language is used to build this request. You can click on **View Rule Language** button on the Edit Rule window to see an example of how the claim rule will look like. For more information about Claim Rule Language, review this article http://technet.microsoft.com/en-us/library/dd807118(WS.10).aspx.

TROUBLESHOOTING ACTIVE DIRECTORY FEDERATION SERVICES

When you need further information about AD FS to assist you during a troubleshooting scenario, you should first review the events trigged by AD FS. The events are stored in Event Viewer, under the AD FS node as shown in Figure 4.19.

These events are logged using Event Tracing for Windows (ETW) framework and you can control which events are logged (error, warning, or information)

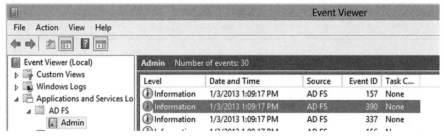

FIGURE 4.19 AD FS event location. (For color version of this figure, the reader is referred to the online version of this chapter.)

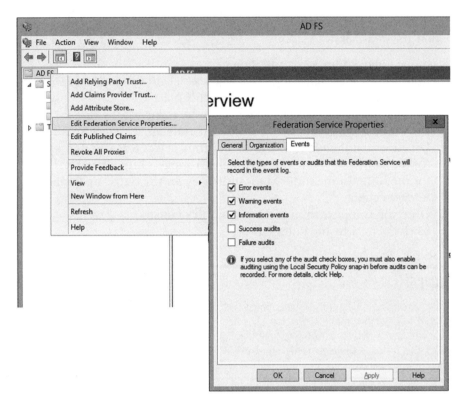

FIGURE 4.20 Selecting the type of events that will be logged. (For color version of this figure, the reader is referred to the online version of this chapter.)

via the Federation Service Properties. You can access this option using the AD FS Management Console as shown in Figure 4.20.

NOTE

You can also use this dialog box to enable auditing option for success or failure attempts. When you enable this, AD FS will write the events in the **Security Log**.

In case the troubleshooting extends to a more deep investigation and more information about the problem is necessary, you can also enable the Debug Tracing Log by enabling the option **Show Analytic and Debug Logs** in Event Viewer as shown in Figure 4.21.

This will enable the AD FS Tracing Debug node as shown in Figure 4.22.

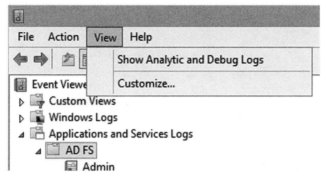

FIGURE 4.21 Selecting debug logs. (For color version of this figure, the reader is referred to the online version of this chapter.)

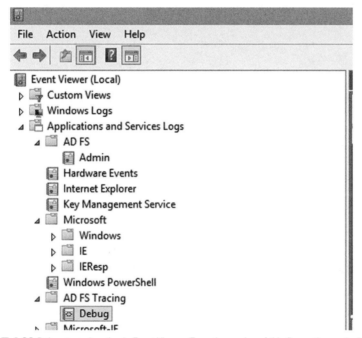

FIGURE 4.22 Debug trace location in Event Viewer. (For color version of this figure, the reader is referred to the online version of this chapter.)

The Debug Log is not enabled by default since it can cause an extra overhead of hundreds or thousands of trace messages (depending on how busy the service is) and could potentially impact the AD FS performance. It is recommended to enable the trace logging only when you need to go deeper into a trouble-shooting scenario. The ultimate goal is to enable, reproduce the issue to generate logs, and disable it. To enable the trace logging, you need to right click the **Debug** node and select **Enable Log** option as shown in Figure 4.23.

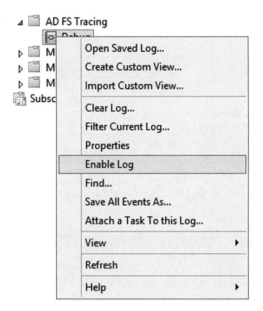

FIGURE 4.23 Enabling debug log. (For color version of this figure, the reader is referred to the online version of this chapter.)

IMPORTANT

When this log is enabled, it will only show informational messages by default, to increase the level of detail to verbose, you need to run the command wevtutil.exe sl "AD FS 2.0 Tracing/Debug" /1:5 before enabling the Debug Log.

ACTIVE DIRECTORY RIGHTS MANAGEMENT SERVICES

If you heard about Wikileaks,[8] you probably understand the reason to have a good right management protection in place to prevent sensitive or confidential documents ending up in the wrong hands. A built-in feature that comes with Windows Server 2012 that can assist some companies to mitigate data leakage caused by document disclosure is the AD RMS.

This is not a new feature in Windows Server 2012[9]; however, there are some new enhancements on this release that facilitates not only the deployment but also the management. Below, you have a list of the main changes:

[8] A very good article that brings this perspective and how AD RMS can be used on this scenario can be found at http://www.windowsitpro.com/blog/hyperbole-embellishment-and-systems-administration-blog-18/systems-management/how-ad-rms-can-stop-your-organizations-secrets-ending-up-on-wikileaks-136930.

[9] We strongly recommend you to read this post where you have more details about how AD RMS works in Windows Server 2008 http://blogs.technet.com/b/rms/archive/2012/04/16/ad-rms-infrastructure-concepts-part-1.aspx. Notice that the core functionality and concepts remains the same.

- Enhanced AD RMS deployment with Server Manager and PowerShell including:
  - Remote deployment
  - Deployment to Server Core
  - Deployment to offline VHDs
  - Local administrator privileges on SQL Server is not a requirement
- Support for stronger crypto
  - Which includes Cryptographic Mode 2
  - Supports 2048-bit RSA encryption and 256-bit SHA-2 hashing
- Simple delegation support
  - Enables assistants/delegates to have the same level of rights to RMS-protected content
- File Classification Infrastructure integration enhancement
  - No need to download additional tools (such as AD RMS Bulk Protection Tool)

These are some enhancements that you will take advantage when you have AD RMS on Windows Server 2012 on-premises. There is also the capability to leverage the Windows Azure Active Directory Rights Management Services,[10] in order to have this right management solution on the cloud. This solution enables rights management integration with Office, Exchange, and SharePoint Online.[11] Figure 4.24 shows a typical scenario of leveraging the Windows Azure RMS to protect on-premise documents.

The typical scenario above shows an internal user sending an e-mail message to a colleague; both are part of the same organization and they use Exchange Online as mail server. Tom (the sender) protected the message so that only users that are part of the same company can read. Once Deb (an user that is part of the distribution list) receives the message, the Exchange Online will leverage the RMS in the cloud to verify if the user has rights to open the message.[12] Assuming the user does have the correct permission, it will allow to open it.

General Considerations When Planning to Deploy AD RMS

If you are deploying AD RMS in a single forest, you only need to have one AD RMS root cluster; however, there are multiple forests you will need to include, at least one AD RMS per forest. You must understand that once you implement

---

[10] For more information about Windows Azure AD RMS, see http://technet.microsoft.com/en-us/library/jj585026.aspx.

[11] For more information on how to enable Windows Azure RMS with Office 365, see http://blogs.technet.com/b/rms/archive/2012/07/18/enabling-windows-azure-rights-managment-in-office-365-enterprise-preview.aspx.

[12] It is important to mention that in this diagram we are not exposing the OrgID Gateway Service that is located in the cloud. For more information about the terminologies that are used in a federated environment in the cloud using Exchange, see this article at http://technet.microsoft.com/en-us/library/gg247611(v=exchg.141).aspx.

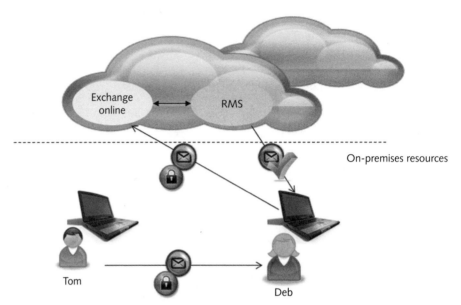

FIGURE 4.24 Leveraging Windows Azure RMS. (For color version of this figure, the reader is referred to the online version of this chapter.)

AD RMS on your environment and users start to use it, they will get used to and will demand that the service is highly available. Users would not be happy if they try to protect a document and the server is not responding, or if they are trying to read a protected message and the server is having performance[13] problems. For this reason, it is recommended that you have at least two AD RMS nodes in a cluster to provide high availability.

IMPORTANT

It is also supported to have third party load balancers performing the AD RMS load balancing (for example, F5[14]). The only caveat is that you could face issues when cookie encryption is enabled on the hardware load balancer.

It is also recommended that you do not mix roles, in order words, do not install AD RMS in conjunction with AD DS. Ideally, you will have a dedicated server exclusively for AD RMS. During the implementation later in this chapter, you will see that certificate is a very important piece of the deployment. You should use SSL certificate issued by a trusted CA in order to avoid problems with your clients (see Figure 4.33).

---

[13] Review this performance insight from Microsoft IT's implementation of AD RMS at http://technet.microsoft.com/library/dd941589(v=WS.10).aspx for more information about performance.
[14] An example of this deployment can be found at https://devcentral.f5.com/blogs/us/big-ip-and-adfs-part-1-ndash-ldquoload-balancing-the-adfs-farm-rdquo.

Installing and Deploying Active Directory Rights Management Services

In order to demonstrate how AD RMS can assist companies to protect their documents, the following scenario will be used (Figure 4.25).

The goal of this scenario is that Windows 8 client can leverage the high availability of AD RMS (which uses Windows Server 2012 NLB for fault tolerance) to protect e-mail messages that are stored on the Exchange Server. The client will also leverage AD RMS to protect documents created via Word 2010. There are some assumptions for this scenario:

- Exchange Server is already installed and functional.
- SQL Server is already installed and functional.
- Windows NLB is already installed in both nodes.

The first step is to set up the first node AD RMS node of this environment. To perform this configuration, follow the steps below:

1. On the **Server Manager**, click **Dashboard** in the left pane and click **Add Roles and features**.
2. On the **Before you begin** page, click **Next**.
3. On the **Select installation type** page, ensure that **Role-based or feature-based installation** option is selected and click **Next**.
4. On the **Select destination server** page, select the target server and click **Next**.

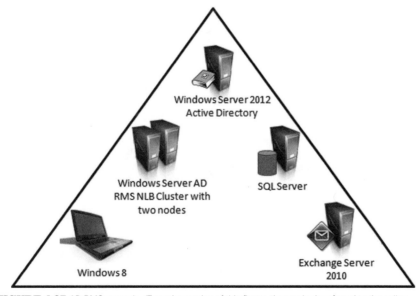

FIGURE 4.25 AD RMS scenario. (For color version of this figure, the reader is referred to the online version of this chapter.)

5. On the **Select server roles** page, select **Active Directory Rights Management Services** role. On the Add **Roles and Features Wizard** dialog box, click **Add Features** button and click **Next**.

6. On the **Select features** page, leave the default selection and click **Next**.

7. On the **Active Directory Rights Management Services** page, read the description and click **Next**.

8. On **Confirm Installation selections** page, click **Install**.

9. On the **Installation progress** page, you have the option to wait until the installation is finished or you can click **Close** and leave the installation happening in background. For this particular example, wait until the installation is successfully completed to click **Close**.

10. In the **Server Manager**, click the orange alert sign under the notification flag as shown in Figure 4.26.

11. Click **Perform additional configuration** and the **AD RMS Configuration** wizard appears. In the **AD RMS** page, click **Next**.

12. On the **AD RMS** page, select **Create a new AD RMS root cluster** as shown in Figure 4.27 and click **Next**.

13. On the **Configuration Database** page under the section **Select Configuration Database Server**, select **Specify a database server or database instance** option and enter the SQL Server name. Click **List** next to **database instance**, select the **DefaultInstance** from the drop down list and then, click **Next**.

14. On **Service Account** page, click **Specify** and type the credentials that AD RMS cluster will use and then click **Next**.

15. On **Cryptographic Mode** page under the section **Specify Cryptographic Mode**, select **Cryptographic Mode 2** as shown in Figure 4.28 and click **Next**.

16. On **Cluster Key Storage** page, leave the default selection and click **Next**.

17. On **Cluster Key Password** page, enter the password and click **Next**.

18. On **Cluster Web Site** page under the section **Specify AD RMS Cluster Web site**, select **Default Website** as shown in Figure 4.29 and click **Next**.

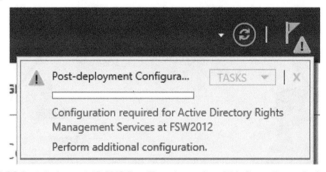

FIGURE 4.26 Post-deployment AD RMS flag. (For color version of this figure, the reader is referred to the online version of this chapter.)

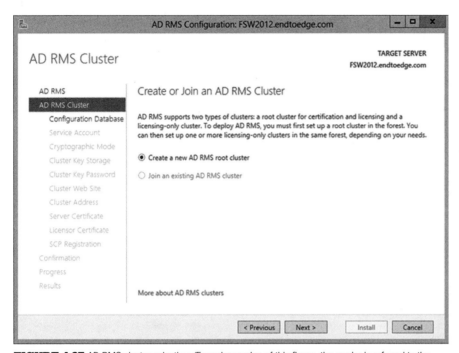

FIGURE 4.27 AD RMS cluster selection. (For color version of this figure, the reader is referred to the online version of this chapter.)

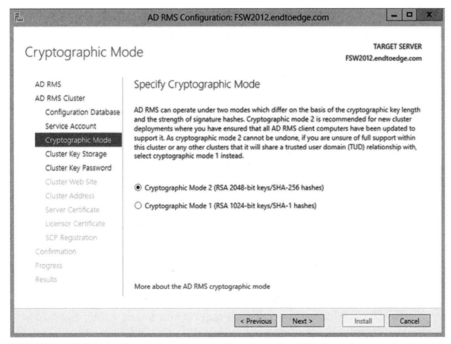

FIGURE 4.28 Selecting the cryptographic mode. (For color version of this figure, the reader is referred to the online version of this chapter.)

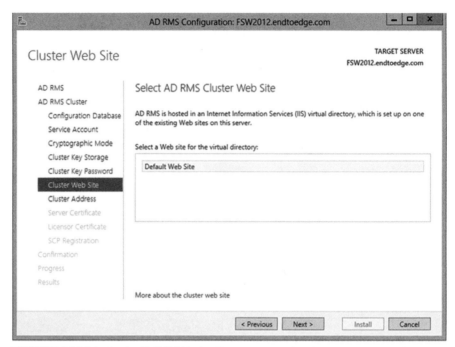

FIGURE 4.29 Selecting the AD RMS Web site. (For color version of this figure, the reader is referred to the online version of this chapter.)

19. On **Cluster address** page under the section **Specify Cluster Address**, select connection type **Use an SSL-encrypted connection**, type the Fully Qualified Domain Name and port fields of the RMS and click **Next**.
20. On **Server Certificate** page under the section **Choose a server Authentication certificate**, select **Create a self-signed certificate for SSL encryption** as shown in Figure 4.30 and click **Next**.
21. On **Licensor Certificate** page under the section **Name the server Licensor certificate**, enter the name and click **Next**.
22. On **SCP Registration** page, select **Register the SCP now** and click **Next**.
23. On the **Confirmation** page, click **Install**.
24. Verify the installation results and click **Close**.

Now that one WNLB node of the cluster is configured, you must repeat the same steps on the second node; the only difference is that you will choose to join an existing AD RMS cluster (Figure 4.27). Also, you will notice the following:

- During the database configuration (step 13), you will choose the DRMS database that was created by Node 1.
- The database information page will request you to enter the password that was used during Node 1 setup of RMS.

FIGURE 4.30 Choosing the server authentication certificate. (For color version of this figure, the reader is referred to the online version of this chapter.)

Once the configuration is over (in both AD RMS nodes), you can enable Windows NLB[15] and after that you can test the functionality using Outlook. When creating a new e-mail, you will notice under **Options** that you can select to *not forward* the message as shown in Figure 4.31.

At this point, the client (in this case, Outlook) will try to obtain information from the rights management server and the dialog box shown in Figure 4.32 will appear.

If the certificate is not trusted by the client, you will experience a dialog box similar to the one shown in Figure 4.33.

It is recommended that you ensure that the certificate is trusted by the clients to avoid this dialog box. If you want to leverage this feature to protect word documents, you can use the Protect Document[16] option and restrict who can have access to it as shown in Figure 4.34.

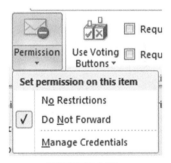

FIGURE 4.31
Controlling the permission for an e-mail message. (For color version of this figure, the reader is referred to the online version of this chapter.)

---

[15] For more information on how to configure Windows NLB in Windows Server 2012, see http://technet.microsoft.com/en-us/library/hh831698.aspx.
[16] For more information on how to protect document in Office, read http://office.microsoft.com/en-us/word-help/protect-your-document-workbook-or-presentation-with-passwords-permission-and-other-restrictions-HA010354324.aspx.

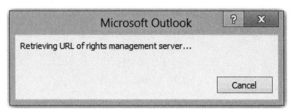

FIGURE 4.32 Outlook searching for the AD RMS Server. (For color version of this figure, the reader is referred to the online version of this chapter.)

FIGURE 4.33 Security warning that appears when the certificate was issued by an untrusted CA. (For color version of this figure, the reader is referred to the online version of this chapter.)

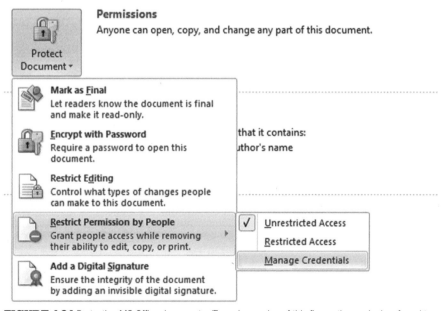

FIGURE 4.34 Protecting MS Office documents. (For color version of this figure, the reader is referred to the online version of this chapter.)

Validate Your Knowledge in AD RMS

Now that you have this understanding on how AD RMS works and how to install it on Windows Server 2012, take a step further and perform the configuration yourself using the Microsoft Test Lab Guide. For this section, we recommend you to do the following:

- Download the Windows Server 2012 Base Configuration for the Test Lab Guide from http://go.microsoft.com/fwlink/p/?LinkId=236358.
- Perform the Test Lab Guide for AD RMS using this link http://technet. microsoft.com/library/adrms-test-lab-guide-base.

SUMMARY

In this chapter, you learned the benefits of using Active Directory Federation Services to provide a better experience for end users that need to authenticate in multiple directories and want to avoid the multiple prompt for authentication problem. You learned how to install this role in Windows Server 2012 and how to deploy it. In this chapter, you also learn how to install Active Directory Rights Management Services Role and how to leverage the Microsoft Office features to protect documents that leverage the AD RMS capability.

Patch Management with Windows Server 2012

CHAPTER POINTS

- Why should you have a patch management strategy in place?
- Planning WSUS Deployment on Windows Server 2012
- Deploying and Managing WSUS on Windows Server 2012

WHY SHOULD YOU HAVE A PATCH MANAGEMENT STRATEGY IN PLACE?

The core reason why you must have a patch management strategy in place is to protect your assets against holes introduced by software vulnerabilities. We all know that software will have bugs and as long as humans develop software, security holes will exist in one way or another. Even when developers are using a security development approach, the goal is not to completely mitigate all security holes (if it was, then the software would never be released), the goal is to start writing the code with security in mind to mitigate potential vulnerabilities. This does not mean that after the product is shipped, it will be bug free or bullet proof without vulnerabilities. Chances are that sooner or later a new vulnerability will be discovered and hopefully it will be discovered by a researcher that will notify the vendor before disclosure in the wild and the vendor will fix the issue. Although this is the ideal scenario, there are situations where malicious users will discover the vulnerability and exploit it, which categorizes this vulnerability as a zero-day vulnerability.

In March 2011, I (Yuri Diogenes) wrote a post[1] on my blog called "Patch Management, the necessary evil". This post gives you some details about some of my experiences regarding companies that do not have a patch management strategy and how dangerous this is nowadays. The scenario did not change that much in the past year, matter of fact in March 2012, McAfee published a document[2] called "Risk and Compliance 2012" where it emphasizes how important it is to have a solid patch management strategy. The main phrase that I want to quote is located at page 10, where it says: "Keeping the systems patched with more frequent patch updates increase operational costs while reducing security risks". Chances are that your CEO will prefer to lower the security risk rather than to increase it, which is a side effect of not having a good patch management strategy. You may argue that operational costs are important for your company, but increasing the security risk is not the answer for that, mainly because if a known vulnerability is exploited due to the lack of patch on the target system, the likelihood that the amount of money involved closes the hole and secures the system again might be much larger. You probably remember the Sony case back in 2011, right? Read this infographic[3] to see the real cost of Sony's data hack and ask yourself if it is worth it to risk not patching your workstations, servers, and devices.

PLANNING WSUS DEPLOYMENT ON WINDOWS SERVER 2012

There are some core foundational principles that you should address before jumping into a WSUS deployment. In 2011, Microsoft released the second edition of the Microsoft Security Update Guide.[4] There you can find a very detailed

---

[1] See http://blogs.technet.com/b/yuridiogenes/archive/2011/05/05/patch-management-the-necessary-evil.aspx.

[2] See document at http://www.mcafee.com/us/resources/reports/rp-risk-compliance-outlook-2012.pdf.

[3] See infographic at http://www.prdaily.com/Main/Articles/Infographic_Cost_of_Sonys_data_hack_could_reach_24_8359.aspx.

[4] Download it from here http://www.microsoft.com/en-us/download/details.aspx?id=559.

explanation about the different stages of managing updates for Microsoft products. While all stages are very important, you should spend some time reading in more detail stage 4, which covers the six steps to deploy a security update, which are as follows:

- Planning
- Availability for download
- Obtain the files
- Create update
- Test it
- Deploy in production

This initial part of your overall planning strategy should happen regardless of software version. In other words, this initial phase is not tied to WSUS on Windows Server 2012 in particular. The overall plan needs to abstract itself from product version. You need to understand your business' needs in order to correctly plan your update management strategy. If your business does not have a validation environment where you can redeploy new updates to test for compatibility issues, the update window might increase.

Remember that from the security standpoint, the goal is to always reduce the window of vulnerability, which is the time between the vendor releases, the update, and the time that you apply the update in the production environment. According to McAfee "Risk and Compliance 2012" Report, 53% of the companies feel confident with weekly patching practice, while 43% feel confident with quarterly patching practice. Although 43% is a high number for a quarterly patching practice, this is not about how confident you are on your strategy, is about understanding that when you delay applying patches in your environment the likelihood that your system will be compromised increases.

IMPORTANT

Although this book only covers Microsoft-related products, you must understand that update management has a scope broader than Microsoft. Even hardware devices are susceptible for updates; the lack of strategy to update your hardware devices can lead you to a scenario similar to the one I (Yuri Diogenes) wrote on this post: http://blogs.technet.com/b/yuridiogenes/archive/2008/12/16/what-can-happen-when-you-think-that-only-windows-system-needs-to-be-patched.aspx.

Once you finish the overall update strategy, you should start planning the deployment of WSUS on Windows Server 2012. WSUS is a Role on Windows Server 2012, and like other roles, it can be installed using the new Server Manager. You can also automate WSUS deployment using PowerShell. The hardware prerequisites for WSUS are the same as Windows Server 2012.

The installation requirements above are for the core elements that you must have in place in the Server, where WSUS Role will be deployed. However, there are some decisions you must take before you deploy WSUS role.

Planning WSUS on Windows Server 2012

The decisions that you must take before deploying WSUS are based on the elements described in Figure 5.1.

The questions that you must answer based on this diagram are as follows:

- Does the company have or plan to have Branch Offices?
  - If it does, then follow up with the following questions:
    - Does the company want to save WAN bandwidth for updates?
    - Does the company have IT personnel to administer a remote WSUS?
    - Does the location where the WSUS Server will be located have Internet connectivity?
- Does the company want to use a separate server to store the WSUS database?
- What are the Microsoft products and languages that are used in the computers/server located in the corporate network?

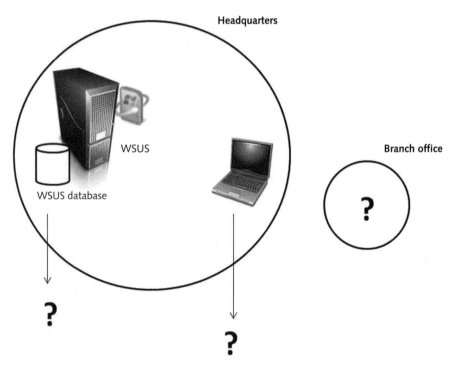

FIGURE 5.1 Knowing the environment before deploy is essential. (For color version of this figure, the reader is referred to the online version of this chapter.)

Those elements are mapped below:

Database Considerations
- Choose the database location (local server or remote server).
- Choose one of the following databases to be used by WSUS:
  - Windows Internal Database (WID) for local server's only
  - Microsoft SQL Server 2008 R2 SP1 Standard Edition
  - Microsoft SQL Server 2008 R2 SP1 Enterprise Edition
  - Microsoft SQL Server 2008 R2 SP1 Express Edition

Role Placement Consideration
- Install WSUS on a member Server. Installations of WSUS in a Domain Controller are cumbersome and not recommended by Microsoft.[5]

Deployment Model
- Choose the deployment model based on the table below:

Scenario	Deployment Model	Deployment Considerations
Company with a single location, small-mid size, and centralized management	Single WSUS Server	■ Verify if WSUS is behind a Firewall and open the appropriate ports (8530 for HTTP and 8531 for HTTPS) ■ Verify if WSUS is behind a Proxy Server to properly configure WSUS Network connections
Company with multiple locations (headquarters and branch offices), decentralized management, and aiming to reduce traffic across private WAN connection	Multiple WSUS Servers	■ Verify if WSUS is behind a Firewall and open the appropriate ports (8530 for HTTP and 8531 for HTTPS) ■ Verify if WSUS is behind a Proxy Server to properly configure WSUS Network connections ■ Install the first WSUS and configure to obtain updates from Microsoft Update. Configure the second WSUS to obtain updates from the upstream server
Highly secure and isolated facility that does not have Internet access	Disconnected WSUS Server	■ Plan the strategy to export, carry, and import the update metadata from the production WSUS Server to the disconnected WSUS Server

Notice that during this stage, there are many infrastructure questions that you should address, which means you need to know how your network is set up and ideally also to know the forecast for business growth. Abstracting yourself from business growth considerations could lead you to plan an environment that will be out of date after the first year.

---

[5] For more information about this recommendation, review this article at http://social.technet.microsoft.com/wiki/contents/articles/guidance-about-wsus-on-a-domain-controller.aspx.

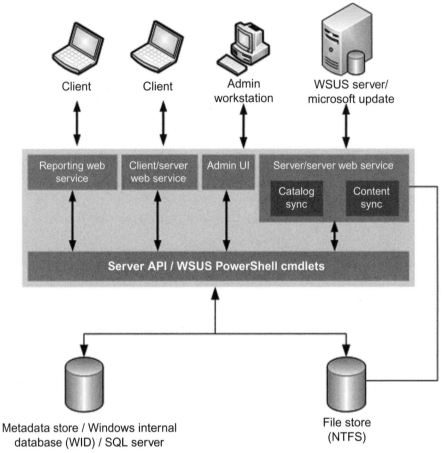

FIGURE 5.2 Diagram of the components used by WSUS. (For color version of this figure, the reader is referred to the online version of this chapter.)

Another important aspect of correctly deploying WSUS is to understand the components involved. The core architecture of WSUS is described in the diagram shown in Figure 5.2.

In this diagram, you have the different components not only from the server but also from the client perspective. The major difference in Windows Server 2012 and Windows 8 client component (Windows Update Service) was documented[6] during Beta time frame by the Windows Team. In comparison to previous versions of WSUS, the only brand new component of this diagram is the introduction of WSUS PowerShell cmdlets in the same layer as the WSUS APIs.

---

[6] Read the blog post at http://blogs.msdn.com/b/b8/archive/2011/11/14/minimizing-restarts-after-automatic-updating-in-windows-update.aspx for more information about this change.

Design Considerations for Update Options and Target Computers

Before deploying WSUS, you should also determine your strategy for other elements that are also part of the update management. If you have a multilanguage environment, you want to make sure that you know all languages that are in use within your company. It is important to make sure whether WSUS is correctly configured to download updates in multiple languages. In an environment with multiple WSUS Servers, downstream servers and client computers will not receive all updates that they might need if the language is not correctly configured for the upstream server.

In addition to the language settings, you should also collect information regarding all Microsoft products that your company is using and which ones will be updated by the WSUS Server. In some very exceptional scenarios, some companies will have some servers that will obtain updates directly from Windows Update instead of using the internal WSUS Server. This is a design decision that can vary according to the business' needs.

One very important aspect of update management is to know exactly what classification of updates you want to deploy. The available classifications[7] of the updates are as follows:

- Critical
- Definition
- Drivers
- Feature packs
- Security updates
- Service packs
- Tools
- Update rollups
- Updates

One last consideration that must be included in the plan regards target computers; will they be grouped according to department where they reside or according to roles? The ultimate goal of aggregate computers in different groups is to ensure that specific computers always get the right updates at the most convenient times; it makes the update management much easier to maintain. The available options for targeting computers are as follows:

- *Server-side targeting*: manual assignment of one or more computers to multiple groups.
- *Client-side targeting*: leverage Active Directory Group Policy (or registry settings on client computers) to assign computers to previously created computer groups in WSUS.

---

[7] The definition of each one of those classifications is available at http://technet.microsoft.com/en-us/library/dd939871(v=ws.10).aspx.

Design Considerations for Performance and High Availability

While planning for WSUS deployment, you want to make sure that all core subsystems are covered and will not impact the overall performance of the server. The last behavior that you want is to have performance issues when you most need to quickly deploy a security update. Consider the following requirements in the table below while planning for best performance and high availability:

Requirements	Best Practices
Performance	<ul><li>Use Windows Server 2012 Load Balancing and Failover (LBFO),[8] also known as NIC Teaming feature for bandwidth aggregation.</li><li>Use multiple WSUS Servers.</li><li>Use hub-and-spoke topology rather than in a hierarchical topology for WSUS.</li><li>Use DNS netmask ordering for roaming client computers.</li><li>Use Background Intelligent Transfer Service (BITS)[9] throttling.</li><li>If you use antivirus on WSUS, make sure to exclude the folders below from the real-time scanning as well as scheduled scan jobs on WSUS Server: – \WSUS\WSUSContent where \WSUS\ is the location of the WSUS content folder – %windir%\wid\data – \SoftwareDistribution\Download</li><li>Disk performance (for the Logical Disk). – When monitoring disk performance, make sure that the *Avg. Disk Queue Length* counter is not higher than two per disk spindle. – Also monitor the Avg. Disk sec/Read and Avg. Disk sec/Write counters and watch for results that exceed 25 ms.</li><li>Ideally, you should have one set of disks (with RAID 1 or 5) to store the database and a different set of disks (with RAID 1 or 5) to store the updates. This recommendation also covers high availability aspects.</li></ul>
High availability	<ul><li>Use Windows Server 2012 Load Balancing and Failover (LBFO), also known as NIC Teaming feature for fault tolerance.</li><li>Use multiple WSUS Servers with Windows Server 2012 Network Load Balancing (NLB).</li><li>Consider using at least RAID 1 or 5 technologies for the disk where the WSUS database will reside.</li></ul>

---

[8] For more information on Windows Server 2012 NIC Teaming, see http://technet.microsoft.com/en-us/library/hh831648.aspx.

[9] QueryBITS functionality has not changed; therefore, we recommend you to download this DOC file that fully explains how BIT works from the below link http://download.microsoft.com/download/b/3/d/b3d8e8ea-8c3f-4962-8a01-478b33f44e15/BITS.doc.

Table 5.1

Self-Updating Mode	Remote-Updating Mode
■ No real-time user attention ■ Update Coordinator process runs on a clustered node ■ Installs updates on a custom schedule	■ Update Coordinator process remotely connects to the cluster ■ User-initiated Updating Run ■ Rich progress updates

Notice that in the above table, we are not mentioning specific database considerations and the reason for that is because the overall performance of best practices for database will vary according to the database type and version. Refer to the best practices for performance document on Microsoft TechNet to correctly configure the database that you chose.

Design High Availability for a Cluster Environment

One new capability that was introduced in Windows Server 2012 that leverages WSUS for update management is the Cluster-Aware Updating (CAU).[10] With this new feature, cluster servers will be able to get updates with little (or none) interruption. What this feature does is to put each node that is part of a cluster into maintenance mode, fail over the roles to the other nodes (to avoid interruption of service), and apply the necessary updates. A brief comparative between the two modes that CAU can operate is shown in Table 5.1.

When planning for CAU, make sure to understand that Self-Updating mode is usually implemented when your company cannot afford real-time attention, when the cluster updating must be resilient, or when you have branch office scenarios. It is also important to add to your planning consideration for CAU that this feature only works with Windows Server 2012 clusters.

It is important to emphasize that although we are explaining CAU as part of the WSUS planning phase, this feature can work with third party patch management solution. There are APIs[11] for CAU that can be leveraged for third party vendors and samples[12] of CAU plug-ins available.

DEPLOYING WSUS

After collecting all information you need before deploying WSUS, you are ready to deploy this role. As previously mentioned, this role can be deployed using

---

[10] For a detailed explanation on how CAU works, read this post http://blogs.technet.com/b/filecab/archive/2012/05/17/starting-with-cluster-aware-updating-self-updating.aspx.

[11] Plug-in API for CAU http://msdn.microsoft.com/en-us/library/hh418084(VS.85).aspx.

[12] Samples of CAUs plug-in at http://code.msdn.microsoft.com/windowsdesktop/Cluster-Aware-Updating-6a8854c9.

the new Server Manager or using PowerShell. We will cover the Server Manager steps here and you can use the blog[13] post I (Yuri Diogenes) co-wrote, and it was published at Microsoft WSUS Team Blog that has all steps to deploy WSUS using PowerShell, including a link to a script to fully automate the process.

Follow the steps below to deploy WSUS:

1. Log on to the server where you will install the WSUS role by using an account that is a member of the Local Administrators group.
2. On **Server Manager**, click **Dashboard** and then click **Add roles and features**.
3. On the **Before you Begin** page, click **Next**.
4. In the **Select installation type** page, confirm that **Role-based or feature-based installation** option is selected as shown below and click **Next** (Figure 5.3).
5. On the **Select destination server** page, choose where the server is located as shown below and then click **Next** (Figure 5.4).
6. On the **Select server roles** page, scroll down and select **Windows Server Update Services**. The **Add Roles and Features Wizard** dialog will appear, click **Add Features** button and then click **Next**.

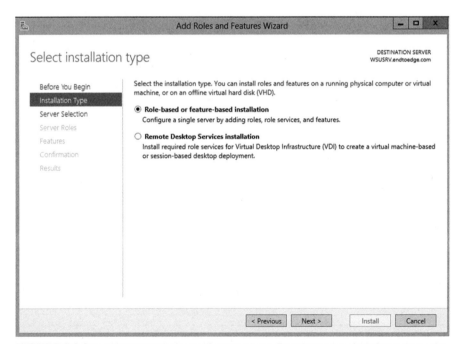

FIGURE 5.3 Server Manager add roles and features wizard. (For color version of this figure, the reader is referred to the online version of this chapter.)

---

[13] See http://blogs.technet.com/b/sus/archive/2012/03/20/installing-wsus-on-windows-server-8-beta-using-powershell.aspx.

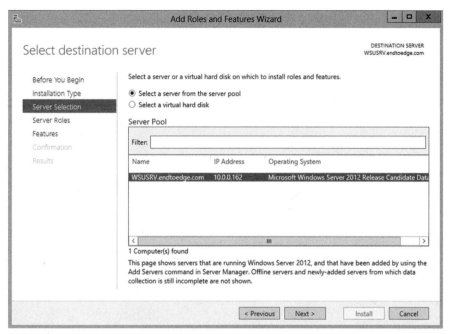

FIGURE 5.4 Selecting the server to install the WSUS role. (For color version of this figure, the reader is referred to the online version of this chapter.)

7. On the **Select features** page, leave the default selections and then click **Next**.
8. On the **Windows Server Update Services** page, click **Next**.
9. On the **Select Role Services** page, you can either leave the default selection (if your designing decision leads you to choose WID database) or select Database checkbox if you want to use SQL Server. For this example, leave the default selections as shown below and then click **Next** (Figure 5.5).
10. On the **Content location selection** page, type a valid location to store the updates. If you do not type a valid location (for example, you type C:\temp but this folder does not exist), the wizard will allow it to go through but the installation will fail at the end. The scenarios that the wizard will reject to move forward are: if you do not type a location (**Next** button will not be enabled) or if you type a wrong character in the location. For this reason, you should type a valid and existing location based on your design considerations and then click **Next** to continue.
11. If you do not have IIS installed on the server, you will see the **Web Server Role (IIS)** page and click **Next** to continue.
12. On **the Select Role Services** page, leave the default selections and click **Next**.
13. On the **Confirm installation selections** page, click **Install**.

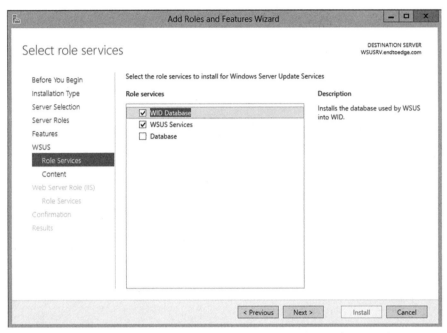

FIGURE 5.5 Selecting the WSUS services. (For color version of this figure, the reader is referred to the online version of this chapter.)

14. The **Installation progress** page appears as shown below (Figure 5.6).
15. On the **Installation progress** page, click **Launch Post-Installation tasks**, wait until the message "Configuration successfully completed" appears as shown below. Click **Close** to finish (Figure 5.7).
16. On **Server Manager**, verify if a notification appears to inform you that a restart is required. This can vary according to the installed server role. If it requires a restart, make sure to restart the server to complete the installation. If the restart is not required, you will see the notification below (Figure 5.8).

Although WSUS was added on the server as a Role, it is still not fully functional yet. There are some post deployment tasks that must be done before you start using WSUS. Follow the steps below to configure WSUS for the first time:

1. On **Server Manager**, click **Tools** menu and then click **Windows Server Update Services**.
2. The **Windows Server Update Services Wizard** appears. On the **Before you Begin** page, click **Next**.
3. Review the **Join the Microsoft Update Improvement Program** page and keep the selection or uncheck the option to join the program according to your company's needs. Once you make your choice, click **Next** to proceed.

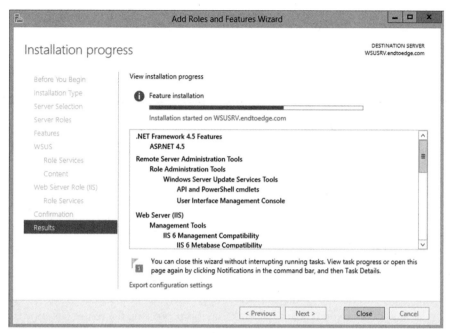

FIGURE 5.6 Installation in progress shows the selected options. (For color version of this figure, the reader is referred to the online version of this chapter.)

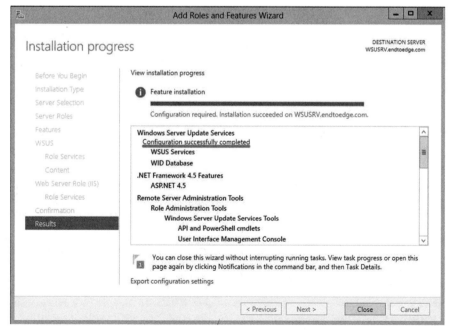

FIGURE 5.7 Installation completed. (For color version of this figure, the reader is referred to the online version of this chapter.)

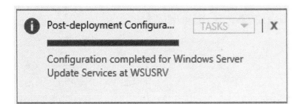

FIGURE 5.8 Post-deployment installation tasks. (For color version of this figure, the reader is referred to the online version of this chapter.)

4. The selection that you make in the **Choose Upstream Server** page will depend on your design decision. Since this is the first WSUS Server in the organization, the only correct selection is the default one. If you choose to synchronize from another WSUS server, specify the server name and the port on which this server will communicate with the upstream server. For this example, leave the default selection and click **Next**.

5. Another option that will vary according to your infrastructure is the **Specify Proxy Server** page. If WSUS is behind a proxy server, make sure to select the option **Use a proxy server when synchronizing** and then type the proxy server name and port number (port 80 by default) in the corresponding boxes. If the proxy server requires authentication, type the credentials to connect to the proxy server. Once you finish configuring these options according to your scenario, click **Next**.

6. On the **Connect to Upstream Server** page, click **Start Connecting**. The gauge will appear on the bottom showing that it is processing the request as shown in the figure below. Once it finishes, click **Next** to continue (Figure 5.9).

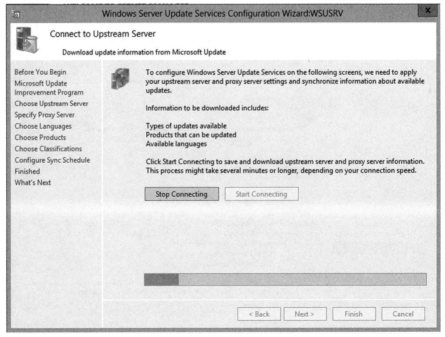

FIGURE 5.9 WSUS Wizard initial screen. (For color version of this figure, the reader is referred to the online version of this chapter.)

7. The information that you previously gathered about languages that are used on your environment, will be used in the **Choose Languages** page. Make sure to select the languages from which WSUS will receive updates. Selecting a subset of languages will save disk space, but it is important to choose all of the languages that are needed. Make the selections according to your design and click **Next** to proceed.

8. The information that you previously gathered about Microsoft products that are deployed on your environment will be used in the **Choose Products** page. In this page, select all products for which you want updates. After selecting the appropriate products according to your designing, click **Next** to continue.

9. On the **Choose Classifications** page, select the update classifications that you want to download to WSUS. The default selection covers the core types, but you should choose the options that are necessary for your environment. Once you make this selection, click **Next** to continue.

10. On the **Set Sync Schedule** page, choose whether to perform synchronization manually or automatically and then click **Next** to continue.

11. On the **Finished** page, you can force the synchronization to start by selecting the **Begin initial synchronization** check box. For this particular scenario, click **Finish**.

IMPORTANT

You can perform all those steps using PowerShell. Microsoft published a script that you can download, replace some values to meet your environment's needs, and execute on WSUS. Download the script from this link http://gallery.technet.microsoft.com/PowerShell-Script-to-37743d31.

MANAGING UPDATES WITH WSUS

There are some tasks that you should do after the initial WSUS deployment phase. The tasks are as follows:

- Synchronize WSUS
- Configure target group
- Review and approve updates

The following sections will cover in more detail how to execute each task.

Configure Synchronization

All synchronization options were first configured when you ran the Windows Server Update Services Wizard for the first time earlier in this chapter; however, the initial synchronization was not done. The synchronization options can be

Synchronization status
Status: Synchronizing...
Progress: 10%

FIGURE 5.10
Synchronization progress.
(For color version of this figure, the reader is referred to the online version of this chapter.)

configured via WSUS Management Console as well as the synchronization with Microsoft Update. Follow the steps below to force a synchronization using the WSUS Management Console:

1. On **Server Manager**, click **Tools** menu and then click **Windows Server Update Services**.
2. On **Update Services** console on the left pane, click **Synchronizations** under the WSUS Server name.
3. On the **Actions** pane, click **Synchronization Now** option. The lower pane will show the synchronization status as shown below (Figure 5.10).
4. Wait until the synchronization is over and you should see the following status (Figure 5.11).

Synchronization details
Started: 6/6/2012 6:11 PM
Finished: 6/6/2012 7:35 PM
Result: Succeeded
Type: Manual
Errors: 0
New updates: 5974
Revised updates: 0
Expired updates: 30

FIGURE 5.11 Summary of what it was synchronized. (For color version of this figure, the reader is referred to the online version of this chapter.)

To change the synchronization options from the ones that you initially configured via WSUS Wizard, follow the steps below:

1. On **Update Services** console on the left pane, click **Synchronizations** under the WSUS Server name.
2. On the **Actions** pane, click **Synchronization Options**; the available options will appear as shown below (Figure 5.12).
3. Notice that all options that were configured during the Wizard are available in this list. There are some additional options that are not directly part of the synchronization settings, such as **Server Cleanup Wizard** and **E-Mail Notifications**.

The PowerShell options to configure WSUS Synchronization are as follows:

- *Set-WsusServerSynchronization-SyncFromMU*: This command will set WSUS to synchronize with Microsoft Update.
- *Set-WsusServerSynchronization-UssServerName WSUSRV2-PortNumber 1955-UseSSL*: This command will configure WSUS to synchronize with WSUSRV2 Server using SSL on port 1955.

Configure Target Group

One of the decisions that were discussed in the beginning of this chapter was related to target group of computers. A very common approach is to create groups based on departments of your company to better manage them. Assuming that the decision is done, you should follow the steps below to configure new groups:

1. In the **Update Services** console, expand **Computers**, right click **All Computers**, and then click **Add Computer Group**.
2. In the **Add Computer Group** dialog box, type the name of the new group as shown below and then click **Add** (Figure 5.13).

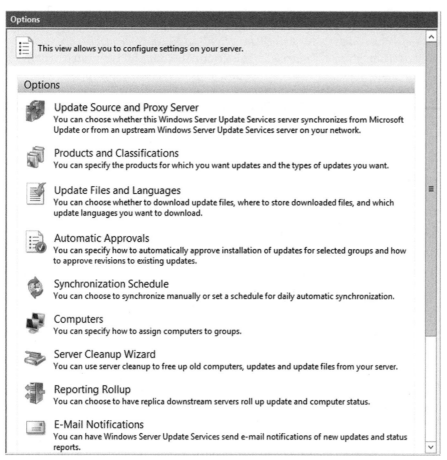

FIGURE 5.12 WSUS options. (For color version of this figure, the reader is referred to the online version of this chapter.)

FIGURE 5.13 Creating a group. (For color version of this figure, the reader is referred to the online version of this chapter.)

The PowerShell option to assign a computer to a group is as follows:

- *Get-WsusComputer-NameIncludes WIN7|Add-WsusComputer-TargetGroupName "Financial"*: This command adds all computers where the name includes WIN7 string and adds to Financial group.

At this point, you can add computers manually to this group or use Group Policy to assign computers automatically. Later in this chapter, you will see how to configure Group Policy to assign computers to a group.

Review and Approve Updates

Now that WSUS is synchronized, target groups are created; you can start reviewing the updates and approve according to the company's needs. Follow the steps below to review and approve updates:

1. In the **Update Services** console, expand **Updates** and click **Security Updates**.
2. On the middle pane, click **Approval** dropdown list and choose **Any Except Declined**. In the Status dropdown, choose **Any** and click **Refresh** as shown in Figure 5.14.
3. When you click **Refresh**, the list of all Security Updates will appear. You may click on any Security Update to view more details in the lower pane as shown in Figure 5.15.
4. You can select multiple updates by selecting the first update, holding the shift key, and selecting the last one that you want to approve. Right click on the update and choose **Approve;** the **Approve Updates** dialog will appear; select the target group; click on the arrow besides the group's name and choose **Approved for Install** as shown in Figure 5.16.
5. Click **OK** and the **Approval Progress** dialog appears as shown in Figure 5.17.
6. Click **Close** on the **Approval Progress** dialog.

The PowerShell options to review and approve updates are as follows:

- *Get-WsusUpdate-Classification Critical-Approval Unapproved-Status Any*: This command retrieves all critical and unapproved updates with *any* status (just like available in the UI).
- *Get-WsusUpdate-Classification Security*: This command lists all updates that are classified as security updates.

FIGURE 5.14 Selecting the updates to show. (For color version of this figure, the reader is referred to the online version of this chapter.)

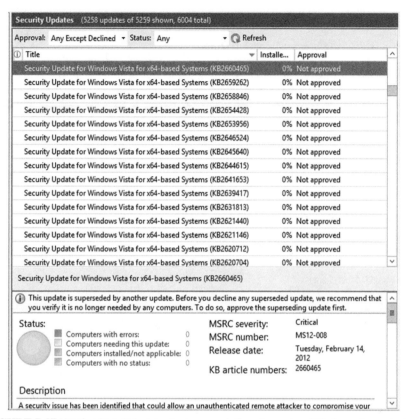

FIGURE 5.15 List of updates that were not yet approved. (For color version of this figure, the reader is referred to the online version of this chapter.)

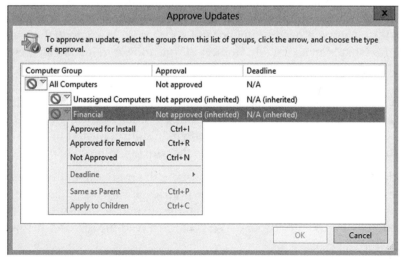

FIGURE 5.16 Approving an update to be installed. (For color version of this figure, the reader is referred to the online version of this chapter.)

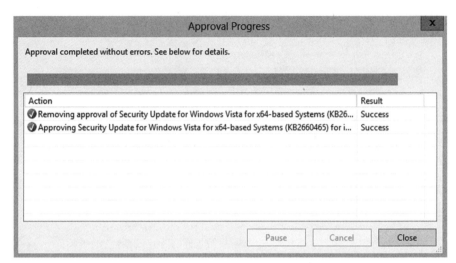

FIGURE 5.17 Approval progress window. (For color version of this figure, the reader is referred to the online version of this chapter.)

- *Get-WsusUpdate-Classification Critical-Approval Unapproved-Status FailedOrNeeded|Approve-WsusUpdate-Action Install-TargetGroupName "Financial"*: This command approves for installation of all critical updates that failed or are needed to computers located in the Financial group.

USING GROUP POLICY TO CONFIGURE WSUS

One of the biggest challenges for patch management is to ensure that you have a policy enforcement that dictates how the computers of your network will behave when new updates are available to be installed. While planning the overall strategy, you need to understand your target, the potential scenarios, and also what is an acceptable amount of time to wait to install updates after they have been released. You need to understand if there are other policies in the environment that might cause conflicts and make sure that patch management is not sacrificed by those. For example, if you have a policy that dictates that all users should shut down their computers during the night shift, then you cannot force updates to happen at night, in spite of the fact that this is the best time to update the computers since they are not in production.

Windows Server 2012 Active Directory offers the same capability as its predecessor for updating computers. The policies are the same and the configuration also has not changed. To apply an update policy to all client workstations to use the corporate WSUS Server, read the scenario below and follow the steps:

SCENARIO

Yuri just received a request to configure all computers in the "Financial" department to automatically receive updates from the new WSUS Server. All computers in the "Financial" department are already located in the "Financial" OU. The deployment for the rest of the company will occur once the validation on the "Financial" department is successfully completed. The core requirements are as follows:

- If the computers on the financial department are in sleep mode, the update management process should wake up the systems.
- Updates should be downloaded and installed automatically every day at 2 A.M.
- Obtain updates from the new WSUS Server.
- Updates should be installed immediately after the download.
- If there are users logged in the computer during the update installation, the restart of the computer should be notified and not forced.
- This update policy should not affect other computers in the organization.

Implementation steps: follow the steps below to create this new policy for all computers in the "Financial" department:

1. On **Server Manager**, click **Tools** menu and then click **Group Policy Management**.
2. Expand **Domains**, expand your domain (in this case endtoedge.com) and right click in the **Financial** OU.
3. Click **Create a GPO in this domain, and Link it here…** as shown in Figure 5.18.
4. In the **New GPO** dialog box, type **Update Policy Financial Department** and click **OK**.

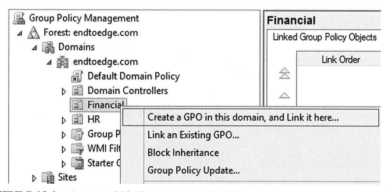

FIGURE 5.18 Creating a new GPO. (For color version of this figure, the reader is referred to the online version of this chapter.)

5. On the left pane, under **Financial OU**, click **Update Policy Financial Department**, click **OK** on the dialog box, right click on this policy and choose **Edit**.

6. Expand the following path: **Computer Configuration/Policies/ Administrative Templates/Windows Components/Windows Update**.

7. Click **Windows Update** on the left pane and the right pane will show all available options. Let us start from the top-bottom approach and review the policies that are necessary to meet this scenario's requirements. Double click on the option **Enabling Windows Update Power Management to automatically wake up the system to install scheduled updates**, click **Enabled** as shown in Figure 5.19, and click **OK**.

8. Double click **Configure Automatic Updates** and change the settings according to Figure 5.20 to accomplish what it was requested for this scenario.

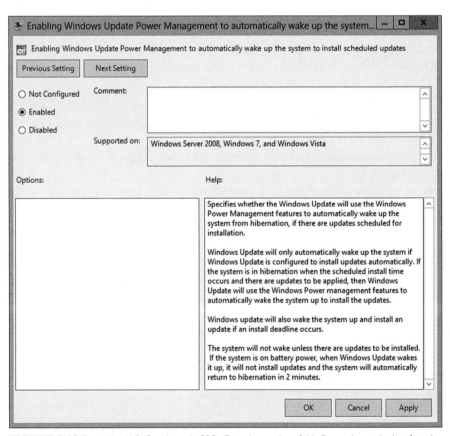

FIGURE 5.19 Controlling WSUS options via GPO. (For color version of this figure, the reader is referred to the online version of this chapter.)

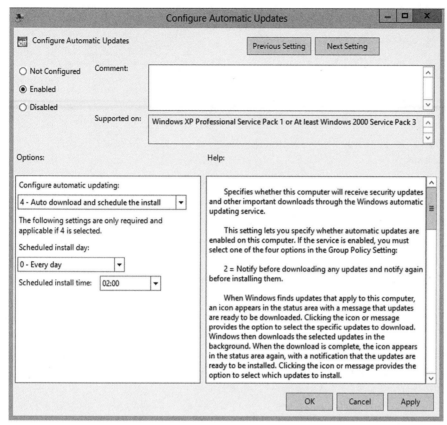

FIGURE 5.20 Enabling automatic updates. (For color version of this figure, the reader is referred to the online version of this chapter.)

9. Double click **Specify intranet Microsoft update service location**, click **Enabled** and fill the options as shown in Figure 5.21, and click **OK** once you finish configuring it.

NOTE

The name of the WSUS Server will vary according to your deployment. The port that is used in this case (8530) is the default port used by WSUS for HTTP request.

---

10. Double click **Allow Automatic Updates immediate installation**, click **Enabled,** and click **OK**.
11. Double click **No auto-restart with logged on users for scheduled automatic updates installations**, click **Enabled**, and click **OK**.

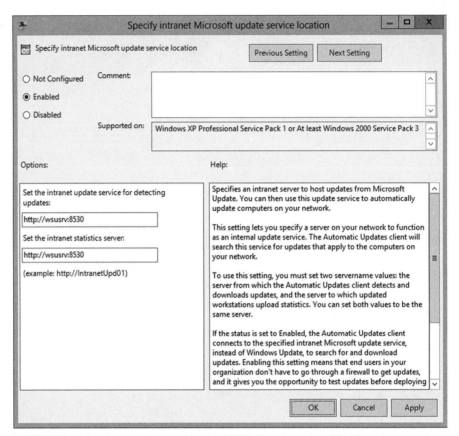

FIGURE 5.21 Specifying the intranet address for WSUS. (For color version of this figure, the reader is referred to the online version of this chapter.)

12. Double click **Enabled client-side targeting**, click **Enabled** and type **Financial** as shown in Figure 5.22. Click **OK** once you finish.
13. Close Group Policy Management Editor.

Validating the Configuration

Now that all prerequisites for this scenario are correctly configured, we can validate the configuration to make sure that the target computer is obtaining the updates from the WSUS Server and also all other settings that were configured via GPO. Follow the steps below in one of the computers from the Financial Department:

NOTE

For this example, the computer that is going to be used is a File Server, located in the Financial OU and with Windows Server 2012 installed.

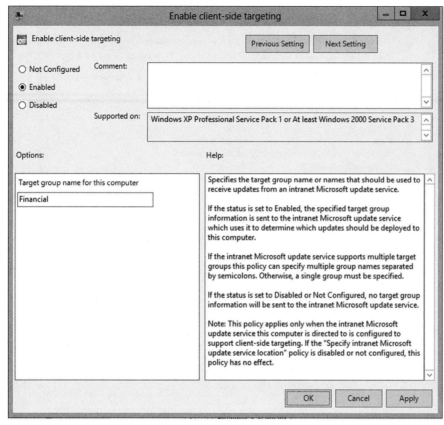

FIGURE 5.22 Enabling client-side targeting via GPO. (For color version of this figure, the reader is referred to the online version of this chapter.)

1. On the target computer, right click on the taskbar, point to **Toolbars** and click **Address**.
2. On the **Address** field, type **CMD** and press **ENTER**.
3. Type *gpupdate/force* and press **ENTER**.
4. Once it finishes, type *rsop.msc*[14] and press **ENTER**, "the Resultant Set of Policy is being processed" dialog will appear as shown in Figure 5.23.
5. When it finishes processing the Resultant Set of Policy, MMC will appear. Browse through the same location where Windows Update policies were configured before. Notice that all settings that you configured will appear as **Enabled** as shown in Figure 5.24.
6. After confirming that those policies were correctly configured, close this MMC and click **No** when it asks if you want to save it.

---

[14] You can also use gpresult for the same purpose.

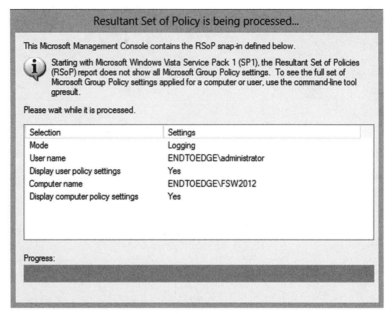

FIGURE 5.23 Validating the policy with RSOP. (For color version of this figure, the reader is referred to the online version of this chapter.)

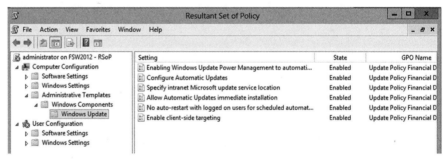

FIGURE 5.24 Confirming that the changes were correctly done. (For color version of this figure, the reader is referred to the online version of this chapter.)

7. On the command prompt window, type *net stop wuauserv* to stop Windows Update Service and press **ENTER**.

8. Once if finish stopping, type *net start wuauserv* to start Windows Update Service and press **ENTER**.

9. On the toolbar, click on the **Address** field, type **Control Panel**, and press **ENTER**.

10. On the **Control Panel**, click **System and Security**, click **Windows Update**, and click **Check for Updates**.

```
07:47:00:252    772    b48    Report   CWERReporter::Init succeeded
07:47:00:252    772    b48    Agent    *********** Agent: Initializing windows update Agent ***********
07:47:00:252    772    b48    DnldMgr  Download manager restoring 0 downloads
07:47:00:253    772    b48    AU       ########## AU: Initializing Automatic Updates ##########
07:47:00:253    772    b48    AU       AIR Mode is disabled
07:47:00:253    772    b48    AU        # Policy Driven Provider: http://wsusrv:8530
07:47:00:253    772    b48    AU        # Detection frequency: 22
07:47:00:253    772    b48    AU        # Target group: Financial
07:47:00:253    772    b48    AU        # Approval type: Scheduled (Policy)
07:47:00:253    772    b48    AU        # Auto-install minor updates: Yes (Policy)
07:47:00:253    772    b48    AU        # Will interact with non-admins (Non-admins are elevated (User preference))
```

FIGURE 5.25 Reviewing Windows update log.

At this point, if there are updates available for this computer, it should appear in the Control Panel. You can also review the Windows Update log (%windir%\ WindowsUpdate.log) to validate if this workstation is correctly reaching the WSUS Server to obtain updates. You should see the following entry on the log (Figure 5.25).

NOTE

If you need to troubleshoot[15] updates by reading the Windows Update log, make sure to review the Windows Updates error codes at http://technet.microsoft.com/en-us/library/cc720442(v=ws.10).aspx.

ADMINISTRATOR'S PUNCH LIST

- Do not allow your company to NOT have a patch management policy in place.
- Make sure that this patch management policy is effective and try to reduce as much as possible the vulnerability window.
- Have a test lab environment in place to test the updates before rolling out to production servers.
- Plan your WSUS Deployment considering the facts related to business needs, network topology, database requirement, role placement, and applications in place.
- Review the design considerations for update options and target computers.
- Review the design considerations for performance and high availability.
- Use group policy to configure WSUS on the client workstations.
- While troubleshooting issues related to WSUS, always start by reviewing the windowsupdate.log on the client workstation.
- Subscribe to www.patchmanagement.org in order to get insights and troubleshooting tips related to WSUS.

---

[15]More troubleshooting scenarios can be found at http://social.technet.microsoft.com/wiki/contents/articles/2491.wsus-troubleshooting-survival-guide.aspx.

SUMMARY

In this chapter, we look at the Windows Server 2012 Windows Server Update Service. Before installing WSUS, you need to first think about your requirements and bake those into your security update design. After the design is complete, you can use the information provided in this chapter to deploy, configure, and manage your WSUS network. We finished the chapter by describing how you can use Group Policy to configure WSUS and finally provided some steps you can use to validate the configuration.

Virtualization Security

CONTENTS

CHAPTER POINTS

- Considerations regarding Virtualization Security
- Windows Server 2012 Hyper-V Security Capabilities
- Beyond the Hypervisor
- Scenario: Virtualization Security Considerations for a Cloud Infrastructure

CONSIDERATIONS REGARDING VIRTUALIZATION SECURITY IN MICROSOFT PLATFORM

In the Private Cloud Security Architecture session that we delivered at TechED North America 2012,[1] we emphasized the Hyper-V architectural model that uses a micro-kernel hypervisor, and Hyper-V in Windows Server 2012 inherits that. These are some of the security capabilities offered by Hyper-V using this architectural model:

- It enforces an isolation boundary between partitions
- The root partition mediates all access to hypervisor
- Guests cannot write to the hypervisor
- Guests cannot perform Direct Memory Access (DMA) attacks because there are no mappings to physical devices.
- Guests cannot interfere with each other because they have dedicated worker processes and dedicated VMBus channels
- Guest communication with other guest systems are not allowed via VM interfaces
- Communication between guest and parent is isolated through a separate channel
- No address space is shared; each VM has its own address space

These capabilities are shown in Figure 6.1.

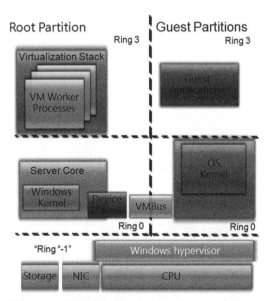

FIGURE 6.1 Hyper-V Microkernel Hypervisor

---

[1] Download the presentations from here http://blogs.technet.com/b/yuridiogenes/archive/2012/06/15/presentations-at-teched-us-2012-now-available.aspx.

NOTE

It is important to mention that technically there is no Ring −1 in the OS architecture model; the reason it is called ring −1 is to emphasize that this level has an even higher privilege mode than other kernel mode processes.

The other architectural model that you have for virtualization is called monolithic hypervisor. In this model, the virtualization stack is bigger; there are third party device drivers in the hypervisor itself. This makes that code base larger and harder to secure and test. Linus Torvalds also believes that the last place you want to see drivers is in the hypervisor[2]; at the end of the day, more codes expose more vulnerabilities, and when this happens in the hypervisor level, it can be catastrophic to the entire cloud.

The Table 6.1 describes the security enhancements in Hyper-V in Windows Server 2012:

Table 6.1 Hyper-V Feature and Security Applicability

Hyper-V Feature	Description	Security Applicability
Replica	Replicate VMs between storage systems, clusters, and data centers in two different sites	Business continuity and disaster recover
Resource metering	Allows you to track and obtain data about physical processor, memory, storage, and network usage by specific VM	Monitoring systems to identify and prevent failures
New Local Security Group	Hyper-V Administrators group is introduced in this version	Separation of duties and least privilege. Now you do not need to add Hyper-V administrators into the administrators group to allow them to manage Hyper-V
Storage Migration	Allows you to move virtual hard disks used by a VM to different physical storage	Availability. Since this process is done while the machine is running, it does not impact the production of that VM, increasing the time the VM is available to use

These are just some of the new security features in Hyper-V; however, there are a number of security enhancements in the Hyper-V Switch. The list below shows new features that are included in Hyper-V Virtual Switch and will be covered in more detail later in this chapter:

---

[2] Source http://lists.linux-foundation.org/pipermail/desktop_architects/2007-August/002446.html.

- ARP Poisoning/Spoofing protection
- DHCP Guard protection
- Port ACLs
- Network traffic monitoring
- Isolated private VLANs

There is also a new feature included in the Hyper-V called Hyper-V Extensible Switch that allows third party vendors to develop drivers that will hook directly into the Hyper-V Switch to perform actions when receiving and sending network packages. In September 2011 at the BUILD Conference in California, Microsoft demonstrated this capability in partnership with other vendors. In one of the demonstrations, Broadcom[3] showed one of their applications that were built to work with the Hyper-V Extensible Switch and it helps to prevent a denial of service attack against a VM. For a complete list of new and changed functionality in Hyper-V (not only security related), see this chapter at TechNet http://technet.microsoft.com/en-us/library/hh831410.aspx.

UNDERSTANDING AND DEPLOYING WINDOWS SERVER 2012 HYPER-V SECURITY CAPABILITIES

Windows Server 2012 was built with cloud computing in mind; the OS was designed and planned to offer you the best platform to deploy a cloud infrastructure for both private and public clouds. The security capabilities that are integrated with Windows Server 2012 Hyper-V are important to enable security for a multitenant environment, which is exactly what a cloud infrastructure needs. However, even if you are not planning to deploy a cloud infrastructure on your environment but still need to have virtualization aligned with security, these capabilities will help you to achieve that.

To allow you to accomplish that, let us start exploring some of the core security capabilities of Windows Server 2012 Hyper-V.

ARP Poisoning/Spoofing Protection

The ARP Spoofing prevention was introduced in Hyper-V 2008 R2 SP1, and there is plenty of documentation about that, including a script[4] that a Microsoft Premier Field Engineer wrote about it in 2011. However, the problem with the feature in Windows Server 2008 R2 is that it does not perform any enforcement to prevent a VM from spoofing their IP addresses. As a result, a VM could spoof its IP address and take any IP address in the network on which is connected,

---

[3] Review session SAC-559T, minute 19:32 http://channel9.msdn.com/Events/BUILD/BUILD2011/SAC-559T.
[4] Script available at http://blogs.technet.com/b/virtualpfe/archive/2011/08/02/arp-spoofing-prevention-in-hyper-v-2008-r2-sp1.aspx.

which can cause a MITM (man in the middle) attack. While this form of attack is well known in IPv4 networks, in an IPV6 network, a similar method can be used to attack ND (Neighbor Discovery) via spoofing.

When this feature is enabled and a spoof attempt is detected, the first IP spoofing attempt is logged in the system log to alert the administrator that a VM is trying to spoof the IP address. All other packets that are dropped are only logged in the diagnostic log (if it is enabled).

The following types of packets will be inspected for ARP Spoofing Prevention:

- ARP Request
- ARP Reply
- ICMP Router Advertisement
- ICMP Redirect

To implement this feature, follow the steps below:

1. On **Server Manager**, click **Tools** and then click **Hyper-V Manager**.
2. Right click on the VM that you want to enable ARP/ND Poisoning feature and click **Settings**.
3. Expand the Network Adapter option on the left pane and click **Advanced Features**.
4. On the **Advanced Features** pane on the right click **Enable router advertisement guard** as shown in Figure 6.2.
5. Click **OK**.

NOTE

This enables this feature for the virtual switch port on which this VM is connected.

The PowerShell cmdlets to enable ARP Poisoning Prevent is:

- *$vmNic = Get-VMNetworkAdapter -VMName <ServerName>*: this command will retrieve the network adapter information from VM SRV2012.
- *Set-VMNetworkAdapter -VMNetworkAdapter $vmNic -RouterGuard On*: this command will enable ARP Poisoning Protection.

Router guard
Router guard drops router advertisement and redirection messages from unauthorized virtual machines pretending to be routers.
☑ Enable router advertisement guard

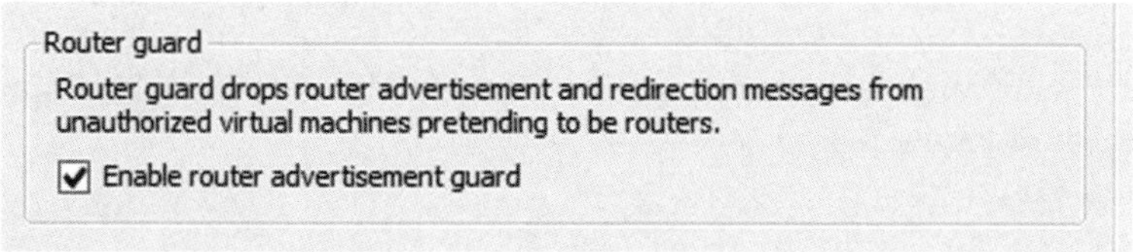

FIGURE 6.2 Enabling ARP Poisoning Protection. (For color version of this figure, the reader is referred to the online version of this chapter.)

DHCP Guard Protection

Even before virtualization was part of the equation, the problem of rogue DHCP severs on the network was already there. How many times you heard that someone brought a DHCP online while performing some lab tests and took down the whole network or the whole segment in which it was connected to? Many times and the vast majority of the times, it happens without any malicious intention. The problem is that even without malicious intent a rogue DHCP server is still able to affect a production environment.

When this happens in a cloud infrastructure, the problem can much more wide reaching effects because it can affect different tenants if the virtualization platform does not isolate traffic between tenants. The goal of this feature is to prevent issues like that from happening by dropping packets from any unauthorized guest VMs sending DHCP server traffic. To stop a VM in a Hyper-V server from distributing IP addresses as if it were a DHCP server, the Hyper-V virtual switch can discard any packet from the untrusted VM with the Operation Code (OP) equals to two (OP=2). In other words, it looks to packets like DHCP Offer, DHCP ACK, DHCP Reply, or DHCP NAK when DHCP Guard feature is enabled. This is try for IPv4, and there is a slight difference for IPv6 since it looks to the DHCP Message Type instead of the Operation Code.

NOTE

When you enable this feature on the Hyper-V virtual switch, the DHCP Guard will work for all traffic that crosses the switch. If a rogue DHCP is connected to a physical switch and there are workstations and other servers in the same physical switch, they will not take advantage of this feature.

It is important to mention that IP Source Guard and DHCP Snooping[5] are well known techniques provided by network switches which are used to secure a network by preventing traffic from untrusted clients. The Hyper-V virtual switch thus provides at a virtual network level what these other technologies provide at a physical level.

To implement this feature, follow the steps below:

1. On **Server Manager**, click **Tools** and then click **Hyper-V Manager**.
2. Right click on the VM that you want to enable DHCP Guard feature and click **Settings**.
3. Expand the Network Adapter option on the left pane and click **Advanced Features**.
4. On the **Advanced Features** pane on the right click **Enable DHCP guard** as shown in Figure 6.3.
5. Click **OK**.

---

[5] Other vendors such as Cisco also have this functionality built into their switch. Here, it is how Cisco implements this functionality in a Catalyst 4500 switch http://www.cisco.com/en/US/docs/switches/lan/catalyst4500/12.1/20ew/configuration/guide/dhcp.pdf.

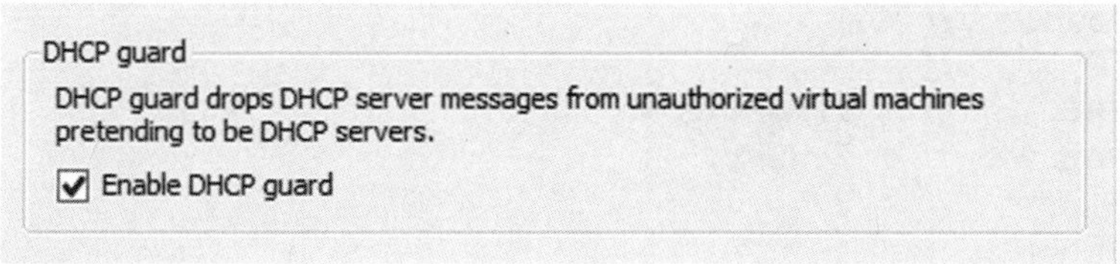

DHCP guard

DHCP guard drops DHCP server messages from unauthorized virtual machines
pretending to be DHCP servers.

☑ Enable DHCP guard

FIGURE 6.3 Enabling DHCP Guard. (For color version of this figure, the reader is referred to the online version of this chapter.)

NOTE

This enables this feature for the virtual switch port on which this VM is connected.

The PowerShell cmdlets to enable ARP Poisoning Prevent is:

- *$vmNic = Get-VMNetworkAdapter -VMName <ServerName>*: this command will retrieve the network adapter information from VM SRV2012.
- *Set-VMNetworkAdapter -VMNetworkAdapter $vmNic -DHCPGuard On*: this command will enable DHCP Guard.

TROUBLESHOOTING TIP

Packets that are dropped because of this feature will report the drop reason in the event viewer (Event ID 101—Warning).

Port ACLs

This feature provides traffic control based on filtering capability. Using this feature, you can enable virtual network isolation by creating lists of control (for example, white lists and black lists). The port ACL types are:

- MAC port ACL (Layer2): each entry contains a MAC address.
- IPv4 port ACL (Layer3): each entry contains an IPv4 address or an IPv4 prefix.
- IPv6 port ACL (Layer3): each entry contains an IPv6 address or an IPv6 prefix.

A network port ACL consists of one or more entries that contain a network address and a specific permission (permit, deny, or meter action). When a packet arrives in the virtual switch, it starts to evaluate it. Once it finds a match to in the network ACL, it will take the corresponding action is taken. The default ACL behavior is based on a preexistent rule that accepts any traffic. Each port ACL must have an explicit action defined that occurs based on the longest match. If a packet does not match any preceding ACL, then the default rule will be executed. Figure 6.4 summarizes the process for this feature.

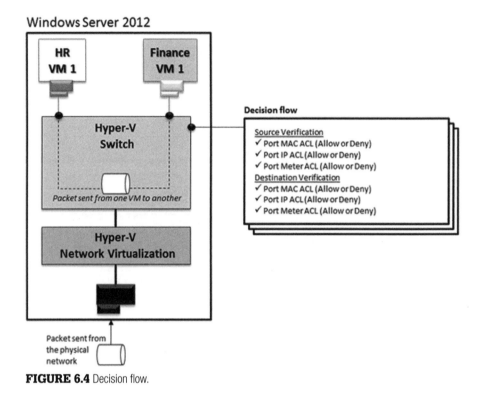

FIGURE 6.4 Decision flow.

IMPORTANT

Administrators can set the default ACL action using wildcards to match any pattern.

Another important capability of this feature is the traffic measurement of metering. This capability allows administrators to configure meter port ACLs to measure network traffic. When performing this measurement, you need to understand that measurement counters are an addition to the total incoming and outgoing traffic counters associated with each port. For a cloud infrastructure scenario, this capability can be used to measure the amount of traffic that a particular virtual machine sends to the Internet. This can later be used by the cloud provider to charge a tenant for Internet network traffic.

This capability can also be used while performing a security investigation for malicious activities. You can review the counters associated with Deny ACLs to potentially identify what's happening. Since the default rule allows, the Deny ACLs should be an exception, which means that if you see a lot of Deny it might indicate either a wrong configuration or a malicious activity.

Unfortunately, there is no user interface to assist you with configuring Port ACLs. To implement Hyper-V Port ACLs, you must use the *Add-VMNetworkAdapterAcl PowerShell* cmdlet. This cmdlet creates an ACL to apply to the traffic through a virtual machine network adapter. The example below shows how to deny all the traffic coming from a VM called "DC" to a particular subnet:

```
PS C:\Users\Administrator> Add-VMNetworkAdapterAcl -VMName
<ServerName> -RemoteIpAddress 10.30.30.0/24 -Direction Both
-Action deny -passthru

VMName: DC
VMId: c7abaeb2-9bb6-4b70-a3ec-1627673b2eda
AdapterName: Network Adapter
AdapterId: Microsoft:C7ABAEB2-9BB6-4B70-A3EC-1627673B2EDA\
D8DEB03E-A2F3-4DF8-BDA7-54F2989A684D

Direction          Address                  Action
---------          -------                  ------
Inbound            Remote 10.30.30.0/24     Deny
Outbound           Remote 10.30.30.0/24     Deny
```

TROUBLESHOOTING TIP

If the command fails to add or remove an ACL entry, it will report the details on Event Viewer (Event ID 109—Warning).

Once you apply the ACL, you can visualize all ACLs using the Get-VMNetworkAdapterAcl cmdlet as shown below:

```
PS C:\Users\Administrator> Get-VMNetworkAdapterAcl

VMName: DC
VMId: c7abaeb2-9bb6-4b70-a3ec-1627673b2eda
AdapterName: Network Adapter
AdapterId: Microsoft:C7ABAEB2-9BB6-4B70-A3EC-1627673B2EDA\
D8DEB03E-A2F3-4DF8-BDA7-54F2989A684D

Direction          Address                  Action
---------          -------                  ------
Inbound            Remote 10.30.30.0/24     Deny
Outbound           Remote 10.30.30.0/24     Deny
```

To remove an entry, you must use the Remove-*VMNetworkAdapterAcl* and then you can visualize again confirming it was removed as shown the sequence below:

```
PS C:\Users\Administrator> Remove-VMNetworkAdapterAcl -VMName
DC -RemoteIpAddress 10.30.30.0/24 -Direction Both -Action deny -
passthru
```

```
VMName: DC
VMId: c7abaeb2-9bb6-4b70-a3ec-1627673b2eda
AdapterName: Network Adapter
AdapterId: Microsoft:C7ABAEB2-9BB6-4B70-A3EC-1627673B2EDA\
D8DEB03E-A2F3-4DF8-BDA7-54F2989A684D

Direction          Address                         Action
---------          -------                         ------
Inbound            Remote 10.30.30.0/24            Deny
Outbound           Remote 10.30.30.0/24            Deny

PS C:\Users\Administrator> Get-VMNetworkAdapterAcl
PS C:\Users\Administrator>
```

You can also use IPv6 in the command syntax; the command below allows the VM "DC" to send and receive traffic from and to anywhere:

```
PS C:\Users\Administrator> Add-VMNetworkAdapterAcl -VMName DC -
RemoteIpAddress::/0 -Direction Both -Action Allow
```

If you want to implement a layer two filter by MAC Address, you can also do it. The command below denies the VM "DC" to send and receive traffic from a device that has the MAC address specified in the command:

```
PS C:\Users\Administrator> Add-VMNetworkAdapterAcl -VMName DC -
RemoteMacAddress 58-6d-8f-c3-e3-ec -Direction Both -Action Deny
```

The metering option that was previously explained can be enabled using the *-Action Meter* parameter. The command below will measure all the traffic that leaves VM "DC" to the remote subnet 10.30.30.0/24:

```
PS C:\Users\Administrator> Add-VMNetworkAdapterAcl -VMName DC -
RemoteIpAddress 10.30.30.0/24 -Direction Outbound -Action Meter
```

TROUBLESHOOTING TIP

Packets that are dropped because of this feature will report the drop reason in the event viewer (Event ID 107—Warning).

Keep in mind in a private cloud environment that port ACLs are most likely to be useful when using them with other approaches to segregate tenant and cloud infrastructure traffic. Depending on the nature of your tenants, you may want to configure tenants so that they can only communicate with the Internet. In other cases, a private cloud infrastructure will want to enable tenants to communicate with the rest of the corporate network, with the exclusion being the networks being used by the cloud infrastructure itself.

Network Traffic Monitoring

One of the drawbacks of previous versions of the Hyper-V switch is that there was no way you could enable a network monitoring device in the virtual network to see the traffic delivered to all virtual machines connected to a virtual switch. This essentially made it impossible for virtualization administrators to take advantage of network IDS/IPS.

The situation is improved with Windows Server 2012. Hyper-V administrators that are interested in reviewing the traffic that traverses the Hyper-V Switch can enable port mirroring in the advanced features settings for the virtual machine. In general, there are three types of traffic that port mirroring will be able to replicate, they are:

- VM to the physical network
- VM to VM
- Physical network to VM

IMPORTANT

For security reasons, port mirroring should not be enabled for a port that can offload IPsec processing (IPsec Task Offload [IPSecTOV2] in Hyper-V).

To implement this feature, follow the steps below:

1. On **Server Manager**, click **Tools** and then click **Hyper-V Manager**.
2. Right click on the VM that you want to enable Port mirroring feature and click **Settings**.
3. Expand the Network Adapter option on the left pane and click **Advanced Features**.
4. On the **Advanced Features** pane on the right click **Mirroring Mode** and choose **Source** if this is the port that you want to replicate or **Destination** if this is the port on which will receive a replica of the traffic as shown in Figure 6.5.
5. Once the selection is done, click **OK**.

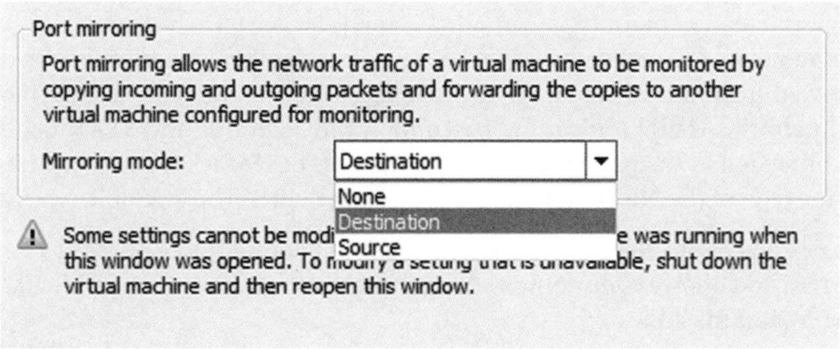

FIGURE 6.5 Enabling Port mirroring. (For color version of this figure, the reader is referred to the online version of this chapter.)

NOTE

In the destination workstation, you must have installed a piece of software that will collect the traffic, such as Network Monitor or some other solution that takes advantage of a network analyzer, such as an IDS/IPS solution.

The PowerShell cmdlets to enable ARP Poisoning Prevent is:

- *$vmNic = Get-VMNetworkAdapter -VMName <ServerName>*: this command will retrieve the network adapter information from VM SRV2012.
- *Set-VMNetworkAdapter $vmNic -PortMirroring Source*: this command will enable Port mirroring capability on this port as source. For the VM that will collect the replica of the data you must change the parameter for *Destination*.

Monitoring the Hyper-V Switch

You can use Performance Monitor counters to better understand the traffic flow on the Hyper-V Switch. Just like any other physical switch, many questions will come up once the environment is in production, such as:

- What are the characteristics of the traffic on this port?
- Do we have any problems on this port?
- Is any packet getting denied in the switch port level?

In some cases, you will deal with some of those questions built into a broader scenario, such as the example below:

SCENARIO

Chris is a Private Cloud administrator that needs to understand the amount of traffic generated by one particular VM from one of his tenant. Chris also needs to understand if there are incoming or outgoing packets that are getting dropped.

Before understanding how to resolve this scenario, it is important to understand the basic components of a Hyper-V Switch. The Hyper-V Switch (vmSwitch) supports creation of multiple virtual switches (vSwitch). Each vSwitch can have any number of virtual ports (vPort). These ports can be dynamically added or removed from the switch. Each vSwitch keeps its own FT (Forwarding Table) and performs traffic forwarding based on a MAC address and VLAN tag that are presented in the packet. There are three types of vSwitches which are based on the type of the NIC that is connected to the switch. The available types are:

- External Switch: is connected (think of it as "bound") to a physical NIC and allows communication with the external networks outside the physical machine.
- Internal Switch: is not connected to (or "bound to") a physical NIC, but it is connected to at least one virtual NIC in the root partition and zero

or more virtual NIC in the child partitions. The configuration enables the host operating system to communicate with the virtual machines connected to the virtual switch and the virtual machines to communicate with other virtual machines connected to the same virtual switch. However, the virtual machines do not have a direct connection to a physical network. It is possible to configure the host operating system to enable access to physical networks so that it can provide a bridge from the Internal virtual switch to external networks.

- Private Switch: is only connected to virtual NIC in the child partitions and it only provides communication between child partitions. What this means is that all virtual machines connected to the Internal switch are able to communicate with one another but are not able to communicate with hosts not connected to the virtual switch unless there is another virtual device that bridges/routes connections between the private virtual switch and a destination that is not connected to the virtual switch. Note the with the Private virtual switch you do not have direct connective between the host operating system and the guests; any such communications would have to take place over the aforementioned bridging gateway.

It is important to keep in mind that when you create a virtual machine and connect it to a Hyper-V virtual switch, that virtual machine is connected using a default virtual NIC that connects to a port on the virtual switch. It is possible to add more virtual NICs to a virtual machine using the user interface in the Hyper-V console. You can also use PowerShell to add virtual NICs. This is important in the event that you want to connect the host operating system to the virtual switch. In this case, you can use PowerShell to create virtual NICs that attach the host operating system to the switch. When you do this, the host operating system can take advantage of the security, performance, and availability features you obtain when using the Hyper-V switches capabilities in these areas.

When designing your virtualization security, it is very important to use the correct switch type so as to prevent VMs from sending traffic to locations that they are not supposed to. You can obtain more information about the Hyper-V Switch you can use the Get-VMSwitch PowerShell cmdlet as shown in the example below:

```
PS C:\Users\Administrator> Get-VMSwitch "Private VSwitch" |
Get-VMSwitchExtension

Id                    : EA24CD6C-D17A-4348-9190-09F0D5BE83DD
Name                  : Microsoft NDIS Capture
Vendor                : Microsoft
Version               : 6.2.8250.0
ExtensionType         : Capture
ParentExtensionId     :
```

```
ParentExtensionName  :
SwitchId             : 73679314-AC82-4BB8-9321-7F74C7CE1E91
SwitchName           : Private VSwitch
Enabled              : False
Running              : False
ComputerName         : W8HV2012
IsDeleted            : False

Id                   : E7C3B2F0-F3C5-48DF-AF2B-10FED6D72E7A
Name                 : Microsoft Windows Filtering Platform
Vendor               : Microsoft
Version              : 1.0
ExtensionType        : Filter
ParentExtensionId    :
ParentExtensionName  :
SwitchId             : 73679314-AC82-4BB8-9321-7F74C7CE1E91
SwitchName           : Private VSwitch
Enabled              : True
Running              : True
ComputerName         : W8HV2012
IsDeleted            : False
```

IMPORTANT

Among other options, the *SwitchID* might be very important when performing queries against the switch itself.

In order to monitor the Hyper-V Switch and its ports, you can use the following Performance Monitor Counters:

- Hyper-V Virtual Switch
- Hyper-V Virtual Switch Port

For the scenario that was presented in the beginning of this section, the counters that should be used are:

- Hyper-V Virtual Switch Port
  - Bytes Sent/sec
  - Dropped Packets Incoming/sec
  - Dropped Packets Outgoing/sec

NOTE

During the perfmon configuration, you will need the Switch ID to identify which switch you want to monitor; that is why it is important to use the Get-VMSwitch cmdlet.

Isolated Private VLAN (PVLAN)

Isolated VLANs or Private VLANs is a new capability built in Hyper-V Switch that allows administrators to segregate traffic on multiple VLANs. This can assist to isolate tenants in a cloud infrastructure scenario. A PVLAN involves two types of VLANs:

- Primary VLAN: All ports can receive traffic on a specific VLAN. The primary VLAN is composed by the entire VLAN Domain.
- Secondary VLAN: it is formed by the community and promiscuous ports. They can receive traffic on the secondary VLAN which they belong to (see Figure 6.6 for an example of this).

In a Hyper-V Switch, the ports can be configured as PVLAN ports or non-PVLAN ports. If a port is configured to be a PVLAN port, it has two VLAN ids: the primary VLAN id and the secondary VLAN id. PVLAN ports have different types:

- Isolated: only receive traffic on the primary VLAN and sends traffic on the secondary VLAN.
- Community: receive traffic on the primary VLAN and the secondary VLAN that it belongs to. Sends traffic on the secondary VLAN that it belongs to.
- Promiscuous: receive traffic on a defined list of VLANs (including primary VLAN and its secondary VLANs) and sends traffic on the primary VLAN.

The diagram below summarizes the types of VLANs and the different ports:

Notice that all VMs are part of the same Primary VLAN, but VM2 and VM3 are fully isolated and can only exchange traffic with the VM1 that it is running in a port configured as promiscuous mode. VM4 and VM5 can talk to each

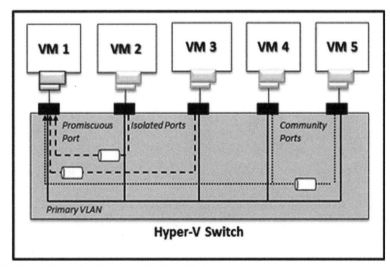

FIGURE 6.6 The different types of PVLAN and Ports.

other since they belong to the same community and also with VM1, since it is running in promiscuous mode.

To configure a PVLAN, you must use the *Set-VMNetworkAdapterVlan* cmdlet. Let us use as an example the scenario below:

SCENARIO

Deb has an environment where storage and live migration are located on their own subnets. Deb needs to configure the vNICs to its corresponding VLAN.

Solution: Following commands should be executed in the Hyper-V Server:

```
Set-VMNetworkAdapterVlan -ManagementOS -VMNetworkAdapterName
"Stora" -Access -VlanId 2
Set-VMNetworkAdapterVlan -ManagementOS -VMNetworkAdapterName
"LiveM" -Access -VlanId 8
```

TROUBLESHOOTING TIP

Packets that are dropped because of this feature will report the drop reason in the event viewer (Event ID 101—Warning).

HIGH AVAILABILITY FOR VIRTUALIZATION SECURITY

Another very important aspect of the virtualization security is the availability of the service. It does not really matter if you have the most secure virtualization infrastructure if an interruption of the infrastructure will affect the whole environment. One new feature included in Hyper-V in Windows Server 2012 is called Hyper-V Replica. This feature enables enterprises to implement an affordable Business Continuity and Disaster Recovery (BCDR) solution for their virtual infrastructure.

This feature leverages the Hyper-V security by using simple authorization model, where groups that will administer Hyper-V are created locally on each Hyper-V Server. Besides that it also uses the following components:

- Uses Windows Firewall predefined (disabled by default) rule to allow incoming replication traffic.
- Allows the communication to be encrypted using SSL Certificate.
- Allows administrators to configure mutual authentication by using Authorization Tags.[6]

---

[6] For more information about Authorization Tags, read this blog post http://blogs.technet.com/b/virtualization/archive/2012/07/08/hyper-v-replica-authorization-entries-windows-server-2012-rc.aspx.

Follow the steps below to configure Hyper-V Replica on Windows Server 2012:

NOTE

Steps 1–9 must be implemented o each Hyper-V Server

1. In **Server Manager**, on the **Tools** menu, click **Windows Firewall** with Advanced Security as shown Figure 6.7
2. In the Console Tree pane, click **Inbound Rules**, right click the **Hyper-V replica HTTP listener (TCP-In)** rule, and then click **Enable Rule** as shown in Figure 6.8

IMPORTANT

This setting is not the most secure settings for Hyper-V replica. Only use this setting in a lab environment when you are validating this feature. For a production environment, it is recommended to use HTTPS.

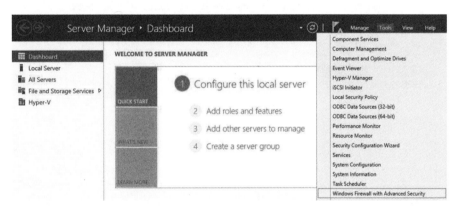

FIGURE 6.7 Accessing Windows Firewall with Advanced Security via Server Manager. (For color version of this figure, the reader is referred to the online version of this chapter.)

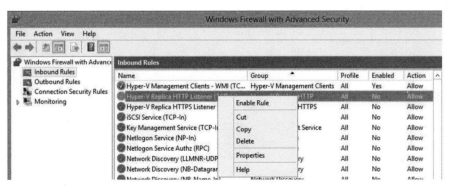

FIGURE 6.8 Enabling Hyper-V Replica built in rule. (For color version of this figure, the reader is referred to the online version of this chapter.)

3. Close the Windows Firewall with Advanced Security console.
4. Back to **Server Manager**, click **Tools** menu and then click **Hyper-V Manager**.
5. Click on the server name on **Hyper-V Manager**.
6. Right click the server name and then click **Virtual Switch Manager**.
7. Ensure External is selected, and then click **Create Virtual Switch** as shown in Figure 6.9
8. In Name, type **ReplicaNet** and then click **OK** as shown in Figure 6.10
9. In the **Apply Networking Changes** dialog box that appears as shown in Figure 6.11, click **Yes**.
10. Since Hyper-V replica is a setting that must be enabled in one VM at a time, open Hyper-V manager in one of the Hyper-V Server and select the VM that you will use for this test.
11. Right click on the VM and select Enable Replication as shown in Figure 6.12.
12. On the **Before you Begin** page of **Enable Replication for [VirtualMachineName]** Wizard, click **Next**.
13. On the **Specify Replica Server** page shown in Figure 6.13, type the name of the Hyper-V Server that will receive the replica and click **Next**.

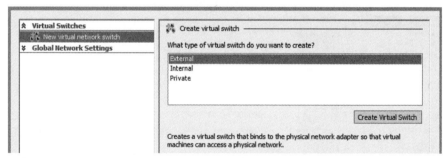

FIGURE 6.9 Creating a new virtual switch. (For color version of this figure, the reader is referred to the online version of this chapter.)

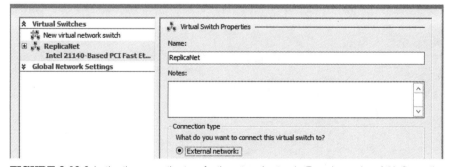

FIGURE 6.10 Selecting the connection type for the external network. (For color version of this figure, the reader is referred to the online version of this chapter.)

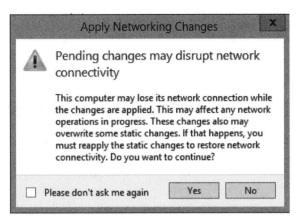

FIGURE 6.11 Warning advising that this change may disrupt network connectivity. (For color version of this figure, the reader is referred to the online version of this chapter.)

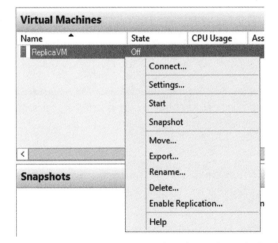

FIGURE 6.12 Enabling replication. (For color version of this figure, the reader is referred to the online version of this chapter.)

14. When you click **Next**, the error message shown in Figure 6.14 will appear; click **Configure Server**.

15. On the Hyper-V Settings for [DestinationHyperVServerName], click **Enable this computer as Replica Server**, select **Use Kerberos (HTTP)**, select **Allow replication from any authenticated server** option as shown in Figure 6.15, and click **OK**.

IMPORTANT

These settings are not the most secure settings for Hyper-V replica. Only use those settings in a lab environment when you are validating this feature. For a production environment is recommended to use HTTPS as authentication type and only allow replication to trusted servers.

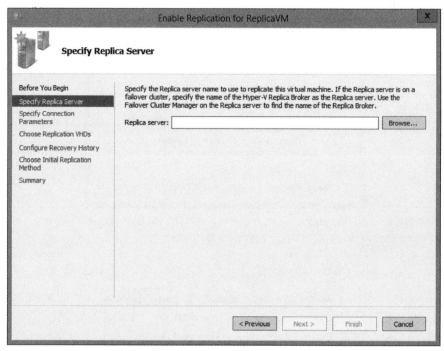

FIGURE 6.13 Specifying the replica server. (For color version of this figure, the reader is referred to the online version of this chapter.)

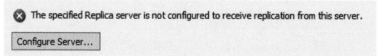

FIGURE 6.14 Error that happens when the replica server is not correctly configured. (For color version of this figure, the reader is referred to the online version of this chapter.)

16. The Settings dialog box will appear as shown in Figure 6.16; click OK.
17. On the **Specify Replica Server** page, click **Next**.
18. On the **Specify Connection Parameters** page, confirm that the settings that were configured previously (authentication type and port) are correct and click **Next**.
19. On the **Choose Replication VHDs** page, you have the chance to clear the check box of any VHD that you do not want to replicate as shown in Figure 6.17. Once you do that, click **Next** to continue.
20. On the **Configure Recovery History** page, leave the default selection as shown in Figure 6.18 and click **Next**.
21. On the **Choose Initial Replication** Method page, leave the default selection as shown in Figure 6.19 and click **Next**.

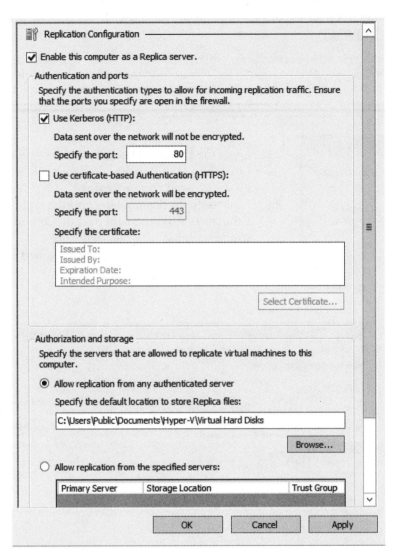

FIGURE 6.15 Enabling the server to replicate. (For color version of this figure, the reader is referred to the online version of this chapter.)

IMPORTANT

In a production environment, it is recommended to schedule the initial replication to out of business hours to not cause any impact on the environment. This recommendation should be applicable unless the replication network is isolated from the production environment.

22. On the **Completing the Enable Replication** page, click **Finish**.

IMPORTANT

At this point in time the Replication is enabled only in one Hyper-V Server, you must open Hyper-V Manager on the other Hyper-V Server (or connect remotely), right click on the server name, choose Hyper-V Settings option, and enable replication using the same settings that were configured on the other server.

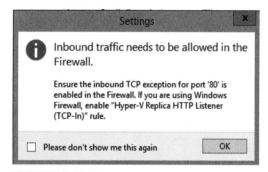

Settings [x]

ⓘ Inbound traffic needs to be allowed in the Firewall.

Ensure the inbound TCP exception for port '80' is enabled in the Firewall. If you are using Windows Firewall, enable "Hyper-V Replica HTTP Listener (TCP-In)" rule.

☐ Please don't show me this again   OK

FIGURE 6.16 Dialog box that appears to remind that inbound traffic needs to be allowed in the firewall. (For color version of this figure, the reader is referred to the online version of this chapter.)

23. Open the **Hyper-V Manager** on the server that hosts the VM that will be replicated. Right click on the VM and choose **Settings**.
24. Expand the Network Adapter option and click **Failover TCP/IP**; the right page of the Settings window should look like Figure 6.20.
25. Type the IP configuration that will be used for the failover[7] and click **Apply**.

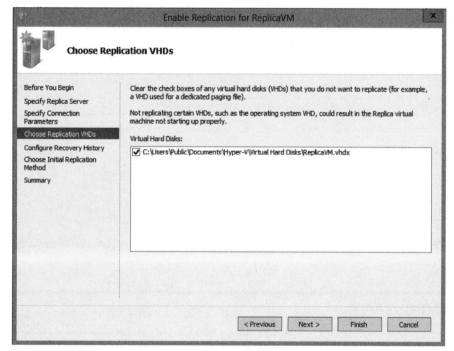

Enable Replication for ReplicaVM   [x]

Choose Replication VHDs

Before You Begin
Specify Replica Server
Specify Connection Parameters
Choose Replication VHDs
Configure Recovery History
Choose Initial Replication Method
Summary

Clear the check boxes of any virtual hard disks (VHDs) that you do not want to replicate (for example, a VHD used for a dedicated paging file).

Not replicating certain VHDs, such as the operating system VHD, could result in the Replica virtual machine not starting up properly.

Virtual Hard Disks:

☑ C:\Users\Public\Documents\Hyper-V\Virtual Hard Disks\ReplicaVM.vhdx

< Previous   Next >   Finish   Cancel

FIGURE 6.17 Choosing the VHD. (For color version of this figure, the reader is referred to the online version of this chapter.)

---

[7] When a VM is replicated from a primary Hyper-V server to a replica server, all the VM properties (including its IP address) are replicated. However, Hyper-V enables the administrator to place a new IP address on the replica of the VM to be used during the startup. DHCP is not an option available for this setting.

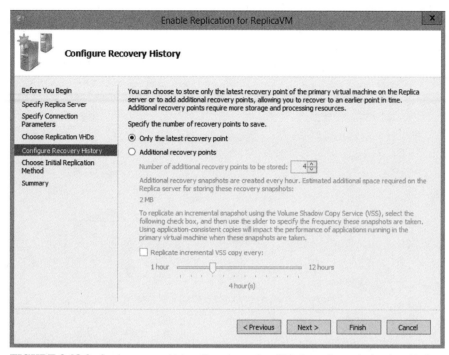

FIGURE 6.18 Configuring recovery history. (For color version of this figure, the reader is referred to the online version of this chapter.)

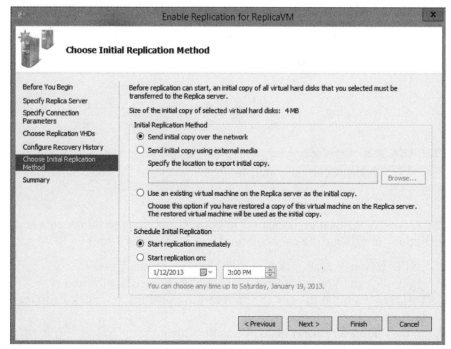

FIGURE 6.19 Choosing initial replication method. (For color version of this figure, the reader is referred to the online version of this chapter.)

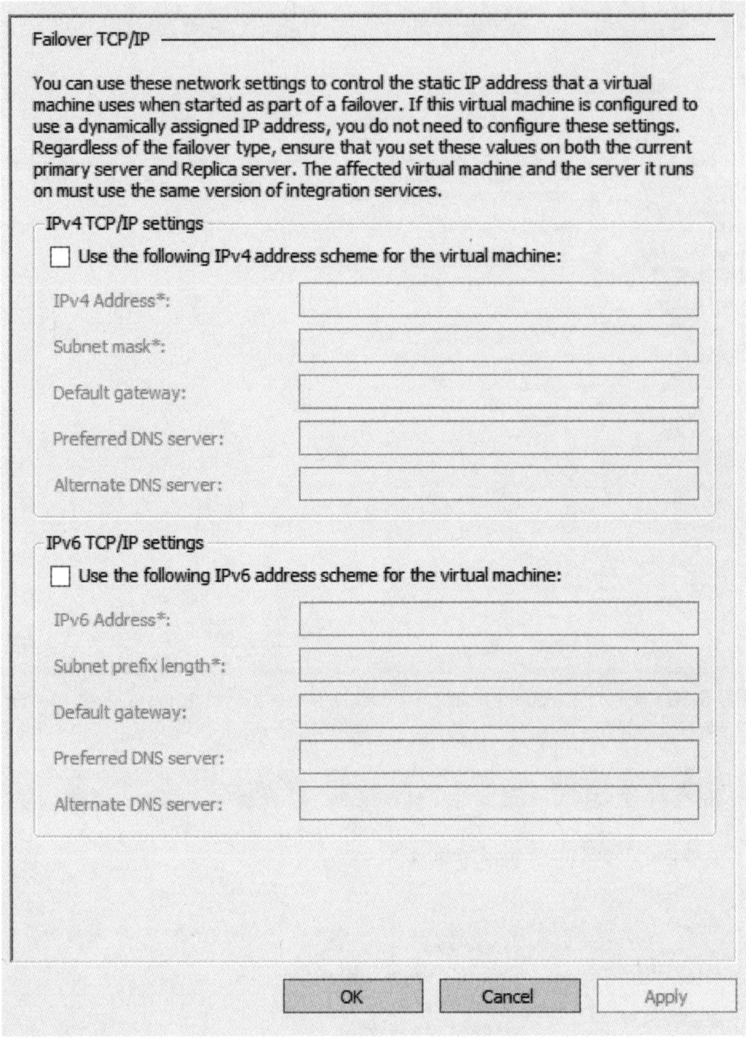

FIGURE 6.20 TCP failover settings. (For color version of this figure, the reader is referred to the online version of this chapter.)

Once Hyper-V Replication is enabled in both servers, you can validate the configuration. To validate the configuration, follow the steps below:

1. In the **Hyper-V Manager** that host the VM, on the Details pane, right click the VM, click **Replication**, and then click **Planned Failover**. Figure 6.21 will appear, read the options and click **Fail Over** button.
2. In the **Planned Failover** dialog box, click **Close**.

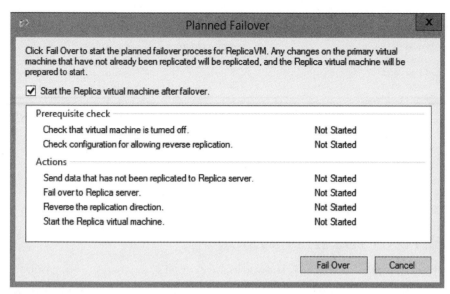

FIGURE 6.21 Planned failover window. (For color version of this figure, the reader is referred to the online version of this chapter.)

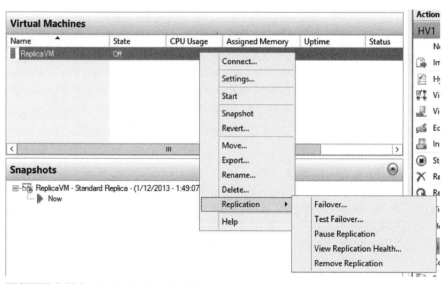

FIGURE 6.22 Replication health option. (For color version of this figure, the reader is referred to the online version of this chapter.)

The actual moving process might vary according to the amount of data that resides on the VM. You can view Replication Health option to get some statistics about the replication (Figure 6.22).

Some of the statistics available are shown in Figure 6.23.

Statistics for past 3 Minutes

From time:	1/12/2013 1:49:07 PM
To time:	1/12/2013 1:53:01 PM
Average size:	0 KB
Maximum size:	0 KB
Average latency:	0:00:00
Errors encountered:	0
Successful replication cycles:	0

Pending replication

Last synchronized at:	1/12/2013 1:49:06 PM (Less than 5 minutes ago)

Test Failover

Test failover status:	Not Running
Last test failover initiated at:	Not Applicable

FIGURE 6.23 Replication health options output.

BEYOND THE HYPERVISOR

Beyond the features that were showed in this chapter so far, there are other important considerations that you should take while planning the virtualization of your environment. Defense in depth should be employed to mitigate potential threats. Threats around virtualization are getting discovered every day, while we were writing this chapter, a new malware called Crisis was discovered. This malware was searching for VMWare virtual machine image on the server that it was able to compromise. The ultimate goal to mount the VM, inject itself into the image (by leveraging the VMWare Player Tool), and once the VM fires up, it will be already compromised.[8] This is just the beginning of a new era of attacks against virtual environments. Notice that such malware was acting in the server itself and that is another reason you want to protect your host.

The components that you want to make sure are protected in the Host environment are:

- Networking
    - Make sure that the physical network that the host connects to is redundant. You do not want to invest hundreds of dollars in an infrastructure that is compromised because the physical network has only one single path to allow access to public resource (such as a public cloud)
    - Ensure isolation and encryption in the main network, use IPSec always that possible
    - Leverage the new NIC Teaming capability of Windows Server 2012 to provide better bandwidth and high availability. We will discuss more about this feature in Chapter 11

---

[8] More details on this report at http://www.symantec.com/connect/blogs/crisis-windows-sneaks-virtual-machines.

- Leverage the built in Windows Firewall to hardening access to the Hyper-V Host
- Core Operating System
  - Use in-box delegation for the Hyper-V administrators[9] with Authorization Manager
  - Use Security Compliance Manager[10] to create security templates for the Hyper-V Role
  - To reduce the attack surface and reduce the numbers of patches consider using Windows Server Core[11] installation
- Storage
  - Use BitLocker Drive Encryption to help protect virtual machines and data at rest. Review Chapter 9 for more information about Bitlocker.

In addition to the new features and capabilities of Hyper-V in Windows Server 2012 that were presented in this chapter, all previous recommendations about securing Hyper-V and its infrastructure are still applicable. You can find more information about those recommendations at http://social.technet.microsoft.com/wiki/contents/articles/13014.virtualization-security-survival-guide.aspx.

SCENARIO: VIRTUALIZATION SECURITY CONSIDERATIONS FOR A CLOUD INFRASTRUCTURE

So far in this chapter, we have discussed virtualization security within the context of Hyper-V itself. Hyper-V can provide the virtualization platform for simple to complex virtualized infrastructures. Small organizations can deploy one or more standalone Hyper-V servers and manage them separately and get a level of high availability made possible with features such as Hyper-V Replica. For organizations that seek a higher level of availability, Hyper-V can be configured to work with the Windows Server 2012 failover clustering feature. When you take advantage of failover clustering, you can provide high availability for both your Hyper-V server virtualization infrastructure and the virtual machine workloads running within that infrastructure. And this level of availability is something that organizations of all sizes can take advantage of, since in Windows Server 2012 failover clustering is available for both the Standard and Data Center editions of the product.

---

[9] The procedure to perform delegation using Authorization Manager is similar to Windows Server 2008 documented here http://blogs.msdn.com/virtual_pc_guy/archive/2008/01/17/allowing-non-administrators-to-control-hyper-v.aspx.

[10] By the time we were writing this chapter, there was no version of the SCM available for Windows Server 2012. We encourage you to visit the Solution Accelerators Security & Compliance Blog for any announcement at http://blogs.technet.com/b/secguide/.

[11] Assuming that your Windows Server 2012 Server Core is already installed and configure you can use the command *dism /online /enable-feature /FeatureName:Microsoft-Hyper-V* to install Hyper-V.

There is a lot of discussion around the difference between cloud and noncloud virtualization projects. Many people that we talk to say that cloud is no different than a highly virtualized infrastructure. There is a good for why so many people have this impression, since conversations around cloud always seem to resolve around a particular hypervisor and the management infrastructure used to manage both the cloud infrastructure and the tenant workloads running on that infrastructure.

We believe there is a lot to be said regarding the benefits of a highly virtualized infrastructure. The performance, availability, scalability, flexibility, reliability, and stability conferred by a highly virtualized infrastructure are hard to come by in a purely physical infrastructure, and if you could get the same levels of these attributes in a physical infrastructure (and you could), the cost would be so high that most firms could not absorb it. This is why virtualization literally "sells itself"—provides so much value for the workload administrator that the explosion of virtualization projects were driven not from the top down, but from the bottom up—by virtue of the many inherent advantages conferred by virtualization.

But what about cloud? How many people have you encountered who said "cloud provides answers to all the problems that I have encountered in the past and still suffer with today?" Many people we have talked to are somewhat bewildered by why cloud computer is "such a big deal." What are the problems that cloud solves? What are the pain points that have driven the march toward cloud computing? Why is it that vendors conflate the terms cloud and virtualization so as to make us think that they are the same thing?

And then there is the issue of private cloud versus public cloud versus hybrid cloud. Are they different animals? Is the definition of "cloud" different depending on whether that cloud deployed using a private or public or hybrid deployment model? If so, are there security differences based on the different deployment models?

While we would like to go into all the details and the reasons for cloud computing and why cloud computing is different than a highly virtualized infrastructure, we will not do that since this is a security book and not a cloud computing book. We highly recommend the following resources to help you better understand what cloud computing is and how it differs from a highly virtualized infrastructure:

- Private Cloud Principles, Concepts, and Patterns http://social.technet. microsoft.com/wiki/contents/articles/4346.private-cloud-principles- patterns-and-concepts.aspx
- What is Infrastructure as a Service? http://social.technet.microsoft.com/ wiki/contents/articles/4633.what-is-infrastructure-as-a-service.aspx

- Private Cloud Reference Model http://social.technet.microsoft.com/wiki/contents/articles/4399.private-cloud-reference-model.aspx
- A Solution for Private Cloud Security http://social.technet.microsoft.com/wiki/contents/articles/6642.a-solution-for-private-cloud-security.aspx

One thing we want to make clear at this point is that cloud computing always cloud computing. That means that a cloud has a collection of attributes that make it a cloud and those attributes must be enabled by the cloud infrastructure. If those defining attributes are not present, then it is not a cloud. That is neither a good or bad thing—it just means that if those attributes that define a cloud are not present, then it is not a cloud and it is something else, like a highly virtualized infrastructure.

In general, cloud infrastructures are really ahead of their time because they are designed to enable cloud applications to take advantage of the core attributes of cloud computing. Unfortunately, these cloud applications are designed to be stateless applications, where the service and the hardware that supports the service are loosely coupled (we cannot say decoupled since a complete decoupling would make them unable to communicate with one another). The problem is that the applications we want to run today are stateful applications, many of which were initially designed in the 1990s or early 2000s, where there was a tight coupling between the services and the infrastructure. This makes them poor candidates for cloud infrastructure and much better suited for highly virtualized data centers. These highly virtualized data centers can then be provisioned with a number of technologies that address the stateful characteristics and requirements of what will in the future be considered legacy noncloud applications.

Now let us get into some security considerations for a private cloud.[12]

Private Cloud Security

OK, why private cloud security? Why did not we name this section "cloud security"? That is a good question. The answer is that you are right! We could have named this section cloud security and it would essentially be the same. The reason for that is that when it comes to security, almost everything you need to consider for a public cloud also applies to a private cloud.

The reason for this is that the core tenant of cloud security revolves around *isolation*. Isolation, isolation, isolation! We say that isolation is the core tenant

---

[12] As an introduction to this section, you can also listen to Tom Shinder and Yuri Diogenes's interview at Microsoft TechNet Radio at http://blogs.technet.com/b/yuridiogenes/archive/2012/11/14/microsoft-private-cloud-solutions-for-it-managers-series-episode-2-at-technet-radio.aspx.

of cloud security because cloud security does not change the security playing field—everything that you needed to do in a traditional datacenter needs to be addressed in a cloud data center. The big difference between the traditional and cloud datacenter security landscapes is that in a cloud you are dealing with a shared infrastructure. In a traditional datacenter, the very fact that each workload or department would have its own infrastructure conferred a level of security of its own due to the fact that it was relatively easy to prevent these dedicated or "siloed" infrastructures from interacting with each other's networking, compute, and storage components.

Now if we contrast the traditional datacenter with the cloud infrastructure, we no longer have a siloed approach. All workloads running in the private cloud share the same infrastructure. All workloads (and these workloads are running on virtual machines) will be using the same server infrastructure (compute), the same storage infrastructure/arrays (storage), and the same networking infrastructure. The challenge for the cloud security administrator is to enable the same or better level of isolation between the workloads in the cloud infrastructure that we had in the old traditional datacenter environment.

In the traditional data center, we could use physical separation of the storage, network, and compute components to provide the isolation required. In the cloud infrastructure, we are going to need to take advantage of software constructs to create logical isolation. And this is where your first confrontation with cloud security comes to fore: what is your relative level of trust between physical isolation and logical isolation?

When we talk to many of you at conferences, the first reaction is "logical isolation cannot be trusted!" and that seems to bring to an end of the private cloud security discussion. But can logical isolation really not be trusted? How many organizations take advantage of VLANs to logically isolate networks from one another? Do not switches use software to create the logical isolation? What about going up another level of abstraction and using IPsec domain isolation to logically separate networks? Or what about Network Access Control? In each of these cases, there is a shared physical infrastructure on which we layer on a software-based logical infrastructure, and in all these cases, we have virtually implicit trust in the security of the solutions.

Therefore, we believe that we can extend that level of trust to a cloud infrastructure that takes advantage of a shared resource pool. Or course, we are looking a security only from the infrastructure point of view at this time with that infrastructure defined as the core compute, network, and storage that supports the cloud solution being offered. Windows Server 2012 platform capabilities are designed to provide the level of security and isolation required for the security of the cloud infrastructure. But when you move to other areas of the private cloud reference model, there will be other considerations you will have to make.

So when thinking about private cloud infrastructure security, let us look at it from the perspectives of compute, network, and storage.

Compute Security

In the private cloud when we speak of compute security, what we are really talking about is security around the sever virtualization infrastructure. That said, it is difficult to tease out the pure "compute" from the networking and storage components of the virtualization infrastructure that drives the private cloud. The reason for this is that a virtualized environment consolidates compute, networking, and storage in a way that sometimes it is difficult to talk about one without taking others into consideration.

From the compute perspective, some things you need to consider include:

- Using a hypervisor with a minimum trusted computing base so that no virtual machine or process running on the host can compromise the hypervisor
- Providing high availability for the virtual machines running on the private cloud infrastructure
- Enabling some mechanism that prevent virtual machines with mutually incompatible security workloads from ever being colocated
- Securing the compute hosts using industry and product standard methods as well as ensuring that the compute hosts are updated as quickly as possible

We can solve the first problem by using Windows Server 2012 Hyper-V, which as we discussed earlier in this chapter, it takes advantage of the security benefits of a microkernel architecture. The microkernel architecture makes sure that only a minimum amount of code is included in the Hypervisor that runs at the virtual "ring −1" and does not expose the entire compute infrastructure from being compromised by buggy drivers and other code that is more liable to security flaws.

To provide high availability for the virtual machines and the services running on those virtual machines, we can take advantage of the Windows Server 2012 Failover Cluster feature. The new Windows Server 2012 failover cluster feature is now tightly integrated with Windows Server 2012 Hyper-V and provides much of the "cloud" functionality required to support the stateful workloads of today. You can deploy a Windows Server 2012 failover cluster running Windows Server 2012 Hyper-V and put the virtual machines on the cluster. Should the cluster node that the virtual machine is running on fail, that virtual machine is automatically moved to a surviving member of the cluster with zero downtime?

In addition to clustering the virtual machines on the virtualization host infrastructure, you can also perform what is known as "guest clustering." Guest clustering is a little different in that with the guest cluster we are more concerned about keeping the service alive rather than keeping the virtual machine running. For example, in a guest cluster, a key service might fail on one of the virtual machines, but as long as the virtual machine is running, the host cluster does not detect a fault. In contrast, the application in the guest cluster is able to detect a fault and makes the appropriate changes to recover from the fault.

The third issue is directly related to the core requirement for isolation. In this example, the need for isolation has to do with the security zoning you define. Some workloads may be in a completely different security zone than other workloads. Owners of very highly sensitive workloads may require that their virtual machines never be colocated on host servers that run workloads of lower security ratings. In that case, you can create affinity and antiaffinity groups within a Windows Server 2012 failover cluster to assure that no two workloads are ever colocated on the same host server.

Finally, you need to make sure that the host servers are hardened to the greatest extent possible. This brings in concepts related to traditional data center security as well as well-defined concepts in securely configuring Hyper-V. As mentioned earlier in this chapter, you can use the same principles used in the Windows Server 2008 R2 Security Guide to secure your Windows Server 2012 Hyper-V infrastructure. In addition, make sure you run the security configuration analyzer on all machines in which the Hyper-V cluster can take action on its recommendations. Finally, make sure that you enable Cluster Aware Updating (CAU) on the failover cluster so that you can update the cluster on a timely basis without interrupting any services running on the cluster.

Networking Security

Similar to the compute security considerations, many of the same principles that you use to secure the traditional datacenter network can be used when securing the virtualization infrastructure in your cloud. Some key considerations to consider when designing networks security in your private cloud include:

- Isolate tenant traffic from cloud infrastructure traffic
- Isolate tenant traffic from other tenant traffic
- Prevent one tenant from using up all bandwidth on the shared network connection
- Securing the different infrastructure traffic profiles
- Protect against common network attacks such as ARP spoofing and rogue DHCP servers
- Enable network IDS/IPS for the virtual switch

It is critical that tenant and infrastructure traffic are isolated from one another. No tenant should ever be able to connect to a host node in the Hyper-V cluster that forms the basis of the cloud infrastructure. When we speak of infrastructure traffic, we are referring specifically to cluster/CSV traffic, Live Migration traffic, management traffic, and storage traffic. There are several approaches you can take to isolating these various traffic profiles:

- Use the Windows Server 2008 R2 approach, where each traffic profile has a physical NIC dedicated to it. The problem with this approach is that it consumes a lot of PCI slots and complicates the networking in terms of cabling, switch port consumption, and switch port configuration. In general, we do not recommend this approach when securing the virtualization infrastructure for a Windows Server 2012-based cloud.
- Use two separate networks—one for the infrastructure traffic and one for the tenant traffic. For example, you can create one NIC team for the infrastructure traffic and one NIC team for the tenant traffic. You can then place each of these teams on different VLANs. The infrastructure NIC team can then handle all the infrastructure traffic profiles and the tenant team handles all of the traffic to and from the tenants. This gives us the critical isolation we require between the infrastructure and tenant networks. You can take advantage of Windows QoS to make sure each of the infrastructure traffic profiles gets the bandwidth it requires.
- Use a single network and run both tenant and infrastructure traffic through the Hyper-V virtual switch. In this network security design pattern, you have simplified the physical port configuration and the cabling significantly, since you are dealing with a single NIC team for all traffic profiles. In this case you take advantage of Port ACLs, 802.1q VLAN tagging, Private VLANs, and Hyper-V QoS to make sure that all traffic profiles are isolated from each other and have the bandwidth allotment they require.

Tenants need to be protected from each other. The reason for this is that in the best of all possible worlds the cloud infrastructure administrators and the cloud service provide (which would be corporate IT in the example of the private cloud) only the infrastructure on which users can deploy their services (at least in the example of Infrastructure as a Service). In that case, you provide the consumers of your cloud service with the virtual machines they need to stand up their services, but what they do with those services is up to them. If they do not want to deploy security best practices or do not want to update their machines with monthly security update, then that is up to the consumer of the service. What is not up to the consumer is making sure that rogue or compromised virtual machines cannot compromise other tenants or the cloud infrastructure. In Windows Server 2012 Hyper-V, you can use port ACLs and Hyper-V QoS to make sure that tenants are not able to communicate with one another or the infrastructure and apply QoS policies to make sure that no tenant is able to execute a network flood-based denial of service attack. In addition, you might consider using IPsec to isolate the tenants from each other or from the infrastructure network—in which case you can take advantage of the new Windows Server 2012 IPsec Task Offload feature (IPsecTO). This enables the virtual machines to offload IPsec processing from the main processor and put that processing on to a NIC that can perform this offload function.

In addition, you might want to enable more sophisticated firewalling on the Hyper-V virtual switch than just port ACLs. In that case, you can introduce third-party add-ins that can provide this functionality. We imagine in most cases virtualization infrastructure admins for private cloud will want to introduce these virtual firewalls and network security management devices to make sure that tenants are protected from each other and that the infrastructure is protected from the tenants.

Securing the various forms of infrastructure traffic is important. Consider the traffic profiles:

- Live Migration traffic. Live Migration traffic contains whatever is running in host memory on a particular node in the Hyper-V cluster. When you move that information from one node to another, that information must go over the network. You can rest assured that there is a lot of information in that data stream that your cloud consumers do not want available to anyone, including the administrators of the cloud infrastructure and whatever network IDS systems might be running on the network. Because of the potentially sensitive nature of the information moving over the Live Migration path, you will want to secure that with IPsec. While we do not have hard coded information on the performance impact of using IPsec to protect the Live Migration traffic, with the advent of modern main processors that have IPsec processing code in them and IPsec task offload NICs, it is expected that the performance impact should be nominal.
- Cluster/CSV traffic. Without going into the details of Hyper-V clustering, it is important to note that a lot of traffic moving over the infrastructure network will be redirected I/O traffic from one cluster node to another, depending on which node is the coordinate or "owner" of the storage that contains the virtual machine files. Similar to Live Migration traffic, there is a significant chance that this data steam will contain propriety information that the consumer of the cloud service would prefer not accessible to anyone. In this case, you will also want to consider using IPsec to isolate this traffic from network analyzers run by both legitimate and illegitimate users.

- Storage traffic. Approaches to securing storage traffic vary with the storage protocols and infrastructures you plan to use. For example, if you are using Fibre Channel, that fibre channel infrastructure is going to be isolated from your Ethernet network, thus creating a physical segmentation similar to what you see in the traditional datacenter. Similarly, if you choose to use an Infiniband infrastructure to connect to storage, you get physical isolation. But if you choose iSCSI, that traffic is going to be running over your Ethernet network and over IP. However, it is not a simple task to sniff iSCSI traffic and determine the contents of the communications; therefore, encryption of this traffic over the wire may not be a strong requirement. Windows Server 2012 introduces the new SMB 3 protocol where you can store virtual machine files in a storage cluster and have that storage be continuously available. This SMB traffic should be secured. However, you will not need to use IPsec in this scenario because SMB 3 supports, out of the box, SMB encryption. Enabling SMB encryption is as easy as putting a checkmark in a checkbox when you enable the scale-out file server for applications role in your file server cluster.
- Management traffic. In general, management traffic does not contain highly sensitive information and the information that is contained within it is accessible only to infrastructure administrators and thus does not need to be isolated or protected from the administrators, which is a different proposition compared to the tenant related traffic (Live Migration and CSV), where the consumers of the service do NOT want infrastructure admins to have access to their traffic. In this case, it is up to you where you think that your management traffic should be secured on the wire.

You do want to be able to secure the tenants from common network attacks such as ARP spoofing and rogue DHCP servers. As discussed earlier in this chapter, you can do that with the new Windows Server 2012 Hyper-V ARP spoof protection and DHCP authorization features.

Finally, you will want to be able to make sure that you can deploy the same network security and analysis tools on the Hyper-V virtual network that you deploy on your physical networks. This means that you will want to be able to hook up IDS/IPS systems, sophisticated bandwidth management and control systems, and other network systems that need visibility into all the traffic traversing the Hyper-V virtual switch. You can do this by enabling the port mirroring feature now available in the Windows Server 2012 Hyper-V virtual switch.

Storage Security
The issue of storage security is interesting in a cloud deployment. In a private cloud, storage is just another of the pooled resources that is shared among all

consumers of the cloud service. In a traditional data center, storage security is not so much of an issue when services are siloed into separate infrastructures that are dedicated to a particular application or service. It is only when the entire organizations computing resources are part of the cloud or at least the majority of the organizations applications and services are running in the cloud that we begin to think about isolation of storage resources.

Some issues to consider when designing storage security for a private cloud include:

■ Deprovisioning of information contained on storage
■ Segregating pooled resources based on security zones
■ Encrypting disks to prevent offline attacks
■ Securing the link between the compute and storage infrastructures

Another important problem you face in a shared storage infrastructure is the deprovisioning of cloud storage resources. In a well-run private cloud, consumers of the cloud service will obtain compute, networking, and storage resources for a period of time and when they no longer require those service, they return them to the shared pool where they can be then be obtained by other consumers. If there is no well-defined deprovisioning process, there will be a risk that subsequent consumers of the cloud service will be able to access data generated from previous consumers.

Isolation is still an important consideration when considering storage security. Similar to the situation when dealing with isolation issues in the compute infrastructure, there will be times when workloads running on the shared infrastructure should not be colocated with other workloads that are classified in a lower security zone. In this case, you may need to define separate storage pools that are dedicated to the higher security assets contained within the shared pool. You can do this with traditional SANs and also with the new Storage Spaces feature in Windows Server 2012. In Storage Spaces, you can create separate pools that have specific coordinator nodes in a storage cluster and then make it possible for consumers of the cloud service to select a high security storage option through your service menu or catalog.

While not specific for private cloud storage infrastructure, disk encryption is an important storage security consideration. With Windows Server 2012 it is now possible to apply BitLocker whole volume encryption to Cluster Shared Volumes, a major advance in storage security.

Finally, while it is important to protect the data at rest, it is equally important to protect it while in flight. For that reason, you will need to secure the information as it travels between the compute cluster and the storage cluster. We discussed this issue in detail earlier in this chapter.

In Chapter 15, we will discuss in more details how to implement security in a cloud infrastructure.

ADMINISTRATOR'S PUNCH LIST

- When starting to plan for your virtualization security, make sure to abstract from vendors and first have a clear understanding on the virtualization threat landscape following by general virtualization security best practices published by NIST.
- Evaluate each vendor based not only on price but also on feature set and built in security features.
- Once you identify which vendor you will work with for your virtualization infrastructure, make sure that you are fully up to date on the platform itself. Hypervisor vulnerabilities[13] are real and documented; you must be fully patched even when testing the platform.
- For Microsoft Virtualization platform is important to identify which features will assist you to implement the needs for your virtualization platform be as safe as possible.
- Make sure that ARP Poisoning and DHCP Guard are enabled on Hyper-V.
- Plan ahead before start creating port ACLs. It is very important to test it before put in production to avoid that valid applications are affected by this feature.
- When monitoring suspicious traffic on Hyper-V, ensure that port mirroring is enabled.
- Create isolations on your virtual LAN using PVLAN.
- Use SSL Certificate for Hyper-V Replica and only replicate to trusted servers.
- Plan the core aspects of virtualization security to be used on your private cloud environment.

SUMMARY

In this chapter, you learned some of the elements of the virtualization security in Windows Server 2012. The core security considerations while planning your virtualized environment and the new capabilities offered by Windows Server 2012 to enhance the overall security strategy of the environment. You learned the considerations regarding the virtualization beyond the hypervisor, and last, you learned how the components that should be present when planning a virtualization security for a cloud environment.

---

[13] An example of hypervisor vulnerability can be found at http://www.coresecurity.com/content/vmware-esx-input-validation-error.

CHAPTER 7

Controlling Access to Your Environment with Authentication and Authorization

CONTENTS

CHAPTER POINTS

- Planning authentication, authorization, and access control
- Understanding Dynamic Access Control
- Planning authentication
- Configuring Dynamic Access Control
- Understanding and configuring Picture Password

PLANNING AUTHENTICATION, AUTHORIZATION, AND ACCESS CONTROL

From Chapters 1–6 of this book, your core reading was about server roles, how to secure the server, and its services. However, there is one very important point that must be present in your security planning, which is how to control access, authentication, and authorization. It might sound simplistic and trivial, but these three elements (also known as "Triple A") can be the source of your security strength or the exposure of your security weaknesses. You should step back and understand that basically this approach helps you to identify who should have access to a resource, what level of access should be given, and how to deal with multiple levels of requirements (group membership, department membership, and other potential conflicts).

While it is important to plan authentication, authorization, and access control, there are also other parts of data governance that must be taken into consideration, such as:

- Data classification
- Data control
- Auditing

The need to address these requirements is growing nowadays where the environments are expanding beyond the perimeter with cloud computing and also data governance in the "big data era." There are new enhancements in Windows Server 2012 that will help you to address these requirements.

Data Classification

While File Classification Infrastructure (FCI), introduced in Windows Server 2008 R2, was a step in the right direction, it did not cover the claims scenario. With Windows Server 2012, the FCI is claims aware, which enhances the FCI feature by allowing resource properties classification.

Data Control

It is vital to understand how users access information and how to govern these parameters across many servers in the environment. In Windows Server 2012, Dynamic Access Control (DAC) allows you to perform data classification manually or automatically, and it offers a central access policy store for the organization.

Auditing

We know administrators love to enable logs, increase the auditing level, but honestly, who really reviews the logs and the auditing information?

Oh, maybe auditors will do that, right? Well, it should be that way. As a security professional, you need to guide IT PROs and system administrators to review these components. Now with Windows Server 2012, you have central audit policies for compliance reporting, which can also be used for forensic analysis.

UNDERSTANDING DYNAMIC ACCESS CONTROL

Dynamic Access Control (DAC) allows the enterprise administrator to easily apply and manage access and auditing to domain-based file servers. To accomplish this task, DAC leverages the following features:

- Claims: authentication token
- Resource properties: for the resource itself
- Conditional expressions: expressions embedded in the permissions and auditing entries

While DAC is perceived as one of the biggest enhancements in Windows Server 2012 from the authentication perspective, it does not do all that by itself. DAC leverages both the Kerberos protocol and claims, where claims represent a piece of information that a trusted source makes about a specific entity.

The advantage of this feature is that now you can grant access to file and folders based on Active Directory *attributes*. The goal is to offer the capability to go beyond a traditional allow/deny based on user or group. Now you can leverage this feature to be compliant with business requirements that tie into conditions that will vary according to a series of parameters.

The core components of Dynamic Access Control are

- Central Access Policy
- Central Access Rule
- Permissions Entries

Each Central Access Policy object can include one or more Central Access Rule objects, and each Central Access Rule object contains one or more permission entries as shown in Figure 7.1.

DAC Requirements

Although many administrators think that you need a Windows Server 2012-only environment to implement DAC, the fact is that this is not true. It is possible to leverage DAC capabilities in a mixed scenario, even when you have Windows XP. In this case, you will need to deploy the *Windows Settings/Security Settings/Local Policies/Security Options/Microsoft network server: Attempt S4U2Self to obtain claim information* policy, as shown in Figure 7.2, in order to allow

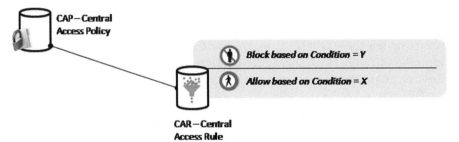

FIGURE 7.1 CAP policies. (For color version of this figure, the reader is referred to the online version of this chapter.)

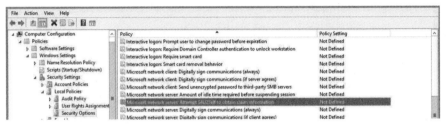

FIGURE 7.2 MMC console. (For color version of this figure, the reader is referred to the online version of this chapter.)

the file server to obtain a network client principal's claims from the client's account domain.[1]

In a nutshell, the requirements to deploy DAC on your environment are

- From the Domain perspective
  - Extend the Active Directory schema
  - Windows Server 2012 Kerberos Distribution Center (KDC)[2]
    - Enable *KDC support for claims, compound authentication, and Kerberos armoring* policy.
    - For the client you will need to enable *Kerberos client support for claims, compound authentication, and Kerberos armoring* policy
- From the File Server perspective
  - Windows Server 2012 File Server Role
- From the Client perspective, when using Device Claim
  - Windows 8

---

[1] Watch Episode 21 of From End to Edge and Beyond for more information about this http://technet.microsoft.com/en-us/video/from-end-to-edge-and-beyond-episode-21.

[2] The Windows Server 2012 KDC requirement only applies if your environment requires authorization decisions based on claims that are sourced from Active Directory attributes or certificates. If authorization decisions are based on group memberships, this is not necessary.

Planning for DAC

One very important aspect of planning for DAC deployment in a scenario where servers are running Windows Server 2012 and clients are running Windows 8 is the DC placement. When claims support is enabled, Windows Server 2012 and Windows 8 will always use a Windows Server 2012 DC to authenticate. If your environment was not sized correctly, you can have an authentication bottleneck, and this can have a negative impact in scenarios where you have remote computers in a branch office that were authenticating to a local Windows Server 2008 R2 and after enabling claims, they will look for a remote Windows Server 2012 DC over a potential congested WAN link.

PLANNING AUTHENTICATION

The core authentication protocol for Windows Server 2012 is still Kerberos, that is why features such as DAC leverage this protocol. There is no change to the core functionality of Kerberos, and for that reason, we will not cover how this protocol works.[3] However, it is important to mention some of the new enhancements of Windows Server 2012 Kerberos.

KDC Proxy

One of the main scenarios to use KDC Proxy is for DirectAccess (see more details about DA in Chapter 13). KDC Proxy allows client computers running Windows 8 to authenticate to corporate domains even when they are outside the network (Internet). KDC Proxy uses TLS and HTTP to transport Kerberos Authentication Server (AS) and Ticket Granting Ticket (TGS) requests to and from a computer residing on the Internet. There are two parts of the KDC Proxy that must work in conjunction to allow this feature to work: Kerberos Proxy Client (KPC) and the KDC Proxy Server (KPS). The basic communication flow between KPC and KPS is shown in Figure 7.3.

IMPORTANT

For more information regarding KDC Protocol Specification, review http://msdn.microsoft.com/en-us/library/hh553774(v=prot.13).aspx

---

As shown in the previous picture, the KPS listen to requests on https://address:433/KdcProxy, which means that if you have an edge firewall in between the KPC and KPS, you will need to open this port and also restrict the path to /KdcProxy. This feature is implemented in Windows Server 2012 by the service called KDC Proxy Server service (KPS) as shown in Figure 7.4.

---

[3] An excellent resource (one stop shop) for Kerberos is the TechNet Wiki Kerberos Survival Guide http://social.technet.microsoft.com/wiki/contents/articles/4209.kerberos-survival-guide-en-us.aspx; if you believe there are more things to include in this guide feel free to add them, it is a Wiki!

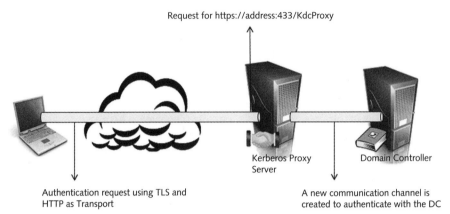

Request for https://address:433/KdcProxy

Kerberos Proxy Server

Domain Controller

Authentication request using TLS and HTTP as Transport

A new communication channel is created to authenticate with the DC

FIGURE 7.3 Kerbero proxy. (For color version of this figure, the reader is referred to the online version of this chapter.)

Name	Description	Status	Startup Type	Log On As
KDC Proxy Server service (KPS)	KDC Proxy S...		Manual	Network Service

FIGURE 7.4 KDC Proxy Service. (For color version of this figure, the reader is referred to the online version of this chapter.)

IMPORTANT

There is no service console to manage this feature; all configurations are stored in the registry under HKLM\System\CurrentControlSet\Services\KPSSVC.

Resource-Based Constrained Delegation

If you have followed our blogs from the ISA Server/Forefront Threat Management Gateway (TMG) days, you will remember the painful task of dealing with Kerberos Constrained Delegation[4] while publishing Exchange or SharePoint via ISA or TMG. The problem with the previous approach was the amount of hops to configure KCD. You basically have to add the list of service principal names to which the front-end server is allowed to request tickets on behalf of the user to the *ms-DS-Allowed-To-Delegate-To* attribute. This was done in the middle tier server and the troubleshooting aspect of this configuration involved pretty much three computers: client, middle-tier (DC), and resource (published server).

The basic flow for this feature is shown in Figure 7.5.

---

[4] A great resource that has lots of insights on how KCD works can be found here http://technet.microsoft.com/library/cc752953.aspx.

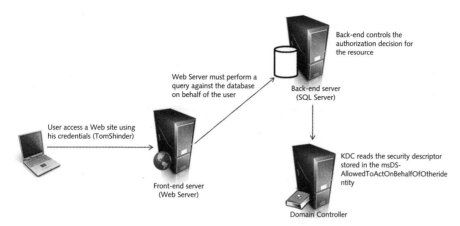

FIGURE 7.5 Solution architecture. (For color version of this figure, the reader is referred to the online version of this chapter.)

Despite the fact that we do not have TMG[5] anymore, there are other scenarios where you will have to use KCD, for example, during a cloud infrastructure configuration with Windows Server 2012.[6] Some enhancements introduced by Resource-based Constrained Delegation are listed below.

- **No dependencies on SPN for delegation configuration:** the new feature enforces constrained delegation using a security descriptor.
- **No need to have domain administrative privileges:** it uses the attribute *msDS-AllowedToActOnBehalfOfOtherIdentity* [7] which is a normal attribute for the user.
- **Delegation experience owned by the resource administrator:** delegation is managed on the back-end and not in the middle tier.

With those enhancements, the scope of delegation is much larger in Windows Server 2012 as it now goes beyond the domain; it can also be used across forest trusts.

Requirements
To take advantage of this feature, you will need to have a Windows Server 2012 KDC that resides in the front-end account domain and one that resides in the back-end account domain. When using this in a mixed environment with Windows Server 2008 R2, you will need to apply the hotfix available in KB 2665790 to all DCs running Windows Server 2008 R2 in the user account domains between the front-end and back-end domains.

---

[5] More information here http://www.zdnet.com/microsoft-axes-many-of-its-forefront-enterprise-security-products-7000004166/.

[6] See step 6 on this cloud infrastructure document http://technet.microsoft.com/en-us/library/hh831738.aspx.

[7] More information about this attribute can be found here http://msdn.microsoft.com/en-us/library/hh554126(v=prot.13).aspx.

Deployment

To configure resource-based constrained delegation, you will use the following Windows PowerShell cmdlets:

- Set-ADComputer computerName-PrincipalsAllowedToDelegateToAccount principal1, principal2, …
- Set-ADUser userName-PrincipalsAllowedToDelegateToAccount principal1, principal2, …
- Set-ADServiceAccount serviceAccountName-PrincipalsAllowedToDelegate ToAccount principal1, principal2, …
- Get-ADComputer computerName-Property PrincipalsAllowedToDelegateToAccount
- Get-ADUser userName-Property PrincipalsAllowedToDelegateToAccount
- Get-ADServiceAccount serviceName-Property PrincipalsAllowedToDelegateToAccount

Troubleshooting

When troubleshooting Kerberos in Windows Server 2012, the main source of information is the event viewer (KDC Operational Log).

IMPORTANT

A summary of what is new in Kerberos can be found in this chapter http://technet.microsoft.com/en-us/library/hh831747.aspx.

Picture Password

In Windows 8 (and in Windows Server 2012), there is a new method you can use to log on to the computer called "Picture Password." This new feature enables you to select a picture of your choice and then use your finger or your mouse to "draw" gestures on the picture. When you want to log on, you will be presented with the picture and then you just repeat the gestures you made when you enrolled for Picture Password (Figures 7.6–7.8).

Picture Password makes it easier and more fun to log in to Windows 8 and Windows Server 2012. However, Picture Password is not a new authentication protocol. Instead, it takes existing credentials and packages those credentials with an existing password. When you are presented with the picture, you repeat the gestures you made when you enrolled the picture and if they are the same, the system will send your actual credentials (user name and password).

Picture Password is a feature made available through the Desktop Experience feature in Windows 8 and Windows Server 2012. Desktop Experience is enabled by default in Windows 8, but not in Windows Server 2012. If you want to enable

FIGURE 7.6 Entering password. (For color version of this figure, the reader is referred to the online version of this chapter.)

FIGURE 7.7 Picture password. (For color version of this figure, the reader is referred to the online version of this chapter.)

Picture Password in Windows Server 2012, then you need to enable Desktop Experience using the **Server Manager** or the PowerShell command **Install-WindowsFeature**. Note that Picture Password does not work over an RDP connection and that while designed for touch interfaces, you can also use Picture Password on nontouch interfaces by using a mouse to create the gesture.

FIGURE 7.8 Picture password. (For color version of this figure, the reader is referred to the online version of this chapter.)

Setting Up Picture Password

Before you set up Picture Password, you have to first have a user account on the machine that you are going to assign the password. It can be a local, a domain account, or a Microsoft account (like Live Account), but you must have an account. After that, you can then create a Picture Password that is unique to the machine. It is important to note that there is no central management capability for Picture Password—it has to be set up on each machine, even in a domain environment.

You can enroll a Picture Password by using the **PC Settings** application in the Modern Windows Interface.

1. Hold the mouse in the lower-right corner of the screen until the **Charms bar** appears on the right side.
2. In the **Charms bar**, click **Settings**.
3. In the **Settings bar**, click **More PC settings** (this is at the bottom of the bar).
4. In the **PC Settings** application, click **Users**. Click **Create a picture password** under **Sign-in options**.

The first thing you need to do in Picture Password enrollment is to confirm your current password. This password is the password you will use to sign in to this computer and is not available to any other computer. If you have other computers, you will need to set up the Picture Password separate on each machine.

Now, you need to choose a picture. Click **Choose Picture**. By default, the Picture Password shows you the pictures folder. However, you are not limited to that folder. You can choose pictures from

- Desktop
- Downloads
- My Documents
- My Music
- My Pictures
- My Videos
- Saved Games

Select the picture that you want to use. You can also adjust the position of the picture, which is something you will want to do since the picture's position is important when sampling gestures. After you select the picture, click **Use this picture**.

Now you need to provide three gestures that will be used to package your credentials. The enrollment application samples these gestures and then securely stores the sample along with the securely packaged credentials.

Now you need to perform three gestures on the picture. A gesture starts when you put your finger on a touch-enabled screen or when you click and hold the left mouse button if you do not have a touch screen. The gesture ends either when your finger is removed from the screen or when you let go of the left mouse button. Gestures can include

- Circles
- Straight lines
- Mouse clicks or taps on touch screens

Note that the gesture is not just the circles, lines, or taps; it also includes *how* you made the gesture. Size, direction, and order are all part of the sample. For example, if you draw an "X" around your ex-spouse's face in a picture, the *size* of the circle and whether the circle was created clockwise or counter-clockwise are included in the sample.

If you do not like the gestures you used, you can always use the **Start Over** button to try again.

You complete the process by confirming your gestures. This is like when you have to enter your password a second time when working with an account security dialog box. Provide the same gestures to the enrollment application to confirm your gestures and then click **Finish** as shown in the left corner of Figure 7.9.

Logging on with Picture Password

When you are ready to sign in, you will see the credentials bar on the left side of the screen. You will see your name and also your user name. Under this is the **Switch to Password** button that you can use if you do not want to log on using a Picture Password.

FIGURE 7.9 Picture password. (For color version of this figure, the reader is referred to the online version of this chapter.)

If you choose to log on with a Picture Password, just repeat the gestures you used during enrollment. However, make sure you do the same, as you only get five tries and then you will have to log on with a user name and password. Not only that, but you will be blocked from using Picture Password again until you sign in. This block on using Picture Password means that if someone tries to use Picture Password and does not get it in five tries, and then reboots the computer, they still will not be able to use Picture Password, they will have to enter a user name and password.

What about password changes? When you enroll your picture, your current password is packaged with the picture and the gestures. The problem comes in when you change your password. What happens then? If you do a local password change, you are OK. Picture Password will look for the password change notification from Windows. But if it is not a local password change (such as when an administrator changes your domain user account), the Picture Password feature is not aware of the password change.

In this domain account situation, there are two scenarios:

- Log on without a domain controller available
- Log on with a domain controller available

If there is no domain controller available, the user will be able to log on using cached credentials. So, even if the password was reset by an administrator, the user would be able to log on with the Picture Password since the machine is unaware of the password change and can continue to use the cached credentials. However, if the machine is able to contact a domain controller, the user will receive a notification

Your picture password enrollment contains an old password. Please sign in with your new password. After the user logs in, Picture Password becomes aware of the new password and repackages the new credentials with the picture and the gestures.

Picture Password Management Issues

Remember that you can only use Picture Password for local log on. That means you cannot use it over an RDP session.

If you do not want users to use Picture Password, you can use a Group Policy setting to block this feature. Use the computer group policy setting **Turn off picture password sign-in**, which is under the **Administrative Templates\ System\Logon** node of the **Group Policy Management Editor**. This is the only Picture Password Group Policy option available and you cannot use Group Policy to change how Picture Password works outside this option.

There is no logging of the specifics of the Picture Password. There is no log information that contains the name of the picture file or that gives any indication of the gestures that were used with the picture file.

What if your users forget their gestures? They can sign in using a user name and password and then go back into the Picture Password enrollment application. From there, they can click the **Replay** button. At that point, the user will be shown the password and will be asked to confirm the existing gestures. They also have the option to resample the gestures, which gives them a new Picture Password as shown in Figure 7.10.

FIGURE 7.10 Picture password. (For color version of this figure, the reader is referred to the online version of this chapter.)

CONFIGURING DYNAMIC ACCESS CONTROL

The Dynamic Access Control configuration is performed in different locations as shown in Figure 7.11.

To demonstrate the use of this feature, we will use the following scenario

SCENARIO

EndtoEdge.com administrator received a request to create access rules on the environment based on the user's department and the country where the user is located. The goal is to set different level of access depending on the end result of this combination. One example would be: if the user is located in the United States and belongs to the Financial department, he will have certain level of access, while another user from the same department from another country might have a different access.

As mentioned in Figure 7.11, the base configuration for Dynamic Access Control will be done on the Domain Controller and on the File Server. For this scenario, there is no difference; those are the servers that you will need in order to address the scenario's requirement. To achieve the desired scenario, the steps will be grouped into three parts:

- Part 1: Domain Controller configuration
- Part 2: File Server configuration
- Part 3: Validation

Follow the steps below to configure the environment for this scenario:

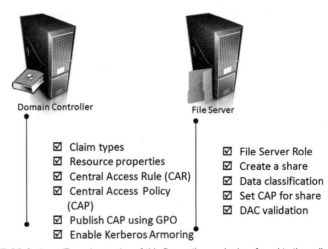

FIGURE 7.11 Options. (For color version of this figure, the reader is referred to the online version of this chapter.)

Part 1—Steps that must be done in the Domain Controller

1. In the **Server Manager** console, click the **Tools** menu, and click **Active Directory Administrative Center**.
2. In the left pane of the console, click **Tree View** icon as shown in Figure 7.12. This will facilitate the navigation throughout the steps.
3. In the **Active Directory Administrative Center**, expand **Dynamic Access Control** and then click **Claim Types**.
4. In the **Tasks** pane, click **New** and then click **Claim Type**.
5. The **Create Claim Type** window will open. In the **Source Attribute** list, in the **Filter** field, enter **Country** and select the attribute where the display name is *C* as shown in Figure 7.13.
6. Click **OK**.
7. In the **Active Directory Administrative Center**, click **Resource Properties**.
8. In the **Tasks** pane, click **New** and then click **Resource Property**.
9. In **Display name** text box, enter **Country** and click **Add**.
10. In the **Add a suggested value** dialog box, enter the values showed in Figure 7.14 and click **OK**.

FIGURE 7.12 Selecting the option. (For color version of this figure, the reader is referred to the online version of this chapter.)

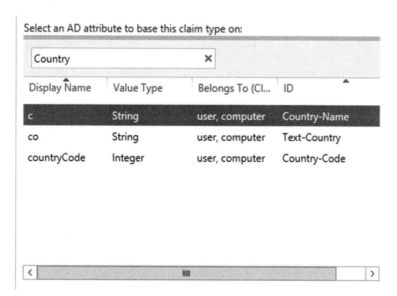

FIGURE 7.13 Configuring the attribute. (For color version of this figure, the reader is referred to the online version of this chapter.)

FIGURE 7.14 Add a value. (For color version of this figure, the reader is referred to the online version of this chapter.)

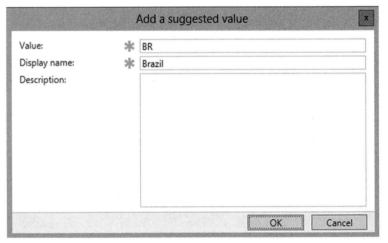

FIGURE 7.15 Adding Brazil. (For color version of this figure, the reader is referred to the online version of this chapter.)

11. Under **Suggested Value**, click **Add** button again and enter the values as shown in Figure 7.15, and then **OK**.
12. Confirm that the **Suggested Values** section looks like Figure 7.16 and then click **OK**.
13. In the **Resource Properties** filter field, enter **Department_MS** as shown in Figure 7.17.
14. In the **Tasks** pane, click **Enable**.
15. In the **Active Directory Administrative Center**, click **Resource Property Lists**.

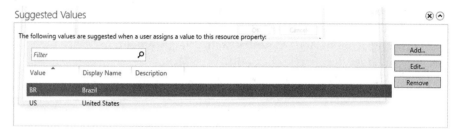

FIGURE 7.16 Configuring. (For color version of this figure, the reader is referred to the online version of this chapter.)

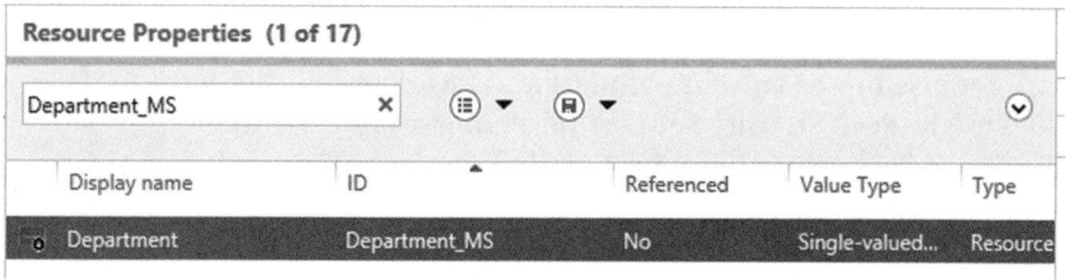

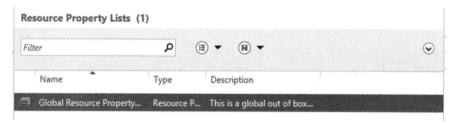

FIGURE 7.17 (For color version of this figure, the reader is referred to the online version of this chapter.)

FIGURE 7.18 Resource properties. (For color version of this figure, the reader is referred to the online version of this chapter.)

16. In the **Tasks** pane, click **New** and then click **Resource Property List**. Make sure that the Resource Property List shows the *Global Resource Property* as shown in Figure 7.18.

NOTE

If it does not show, make sure to clear the filter field (previously populated in step 13).

---

17. In the **Tasks** pane, click **Add resource properties**.
18. In the left pane, in the **Display Name** column, select **Country** and click the **Add** button.
19. Repeat the previous step but now choosing **Department** and then click **OK**.
20. In the **Active Directory Administrative Center**, click **Central Access Rules**.

21. In the **Tasks** pane, click **Central Access Rule**.

22. In the **Create Central Access Rule** dialog box, under **General** section, enter **Department-AND-Country-Match-Requirement**.

23. Under **Target Resources**, click **Edit**.

24. In the **Central Access Rule** dialog box, click **Add a condition**.

25. The first condition should look like Figure 7.19.

26. Click **Add a condition** and configure the second condition to look like Figure 7.20.

27. At the end, the access rule should have both conditions with an AND operator as shown in Figure 7.21.

28. Once you confirm the configuration is correct, click **OK**.

29. Under **Permissions** section, make sure that the option **Use the following permissions as current permissions** is selected and click **Edit**.

30. In **Advanced Security Settings for Permissions**, click **Add**.

31. In the **Permission Entry for Permissions** dialog box, click **Select Principal**.

32. In the **Select User, Computer, Service Account, or Group** dialog box, enter **Authenticated**, click **Check Names**, confirm it resolves to *Authenticated Users* and click **OK**.

33. Under the **Basic Permission** section, select **Full Control** and click **Add a condition**.

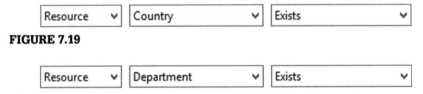

FIGURE 7.19

FIGURE 7.20

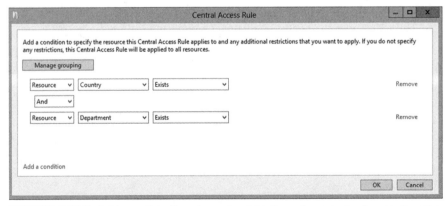

FIGURE 7.21 Central Access Rule. (For color version of this figure, the reader is referred to the online version of this chapter.)

FIGURE 7.22 Grouping. (For color version of this figure, the reader is referred to the online version of this chapter.)

34. You will add two conditions (use **Add a condition** option once you finish configuring the first one) that should look like Figure 7.22.
35. Once you finish, click **OK** three times to return to **Active Directory Administrative Center**.
36. In the **Active Directory Administrative Center**, click **Central Access Policies**.
37. In the **Tasks** pane, click **New**, and then click **Central Access Policy**.
38. In the **Create Central Access Policy** dialog box, enter **EndToEdge File Server Policy** and then click **Add**.
39. On **Add Central Access Rules** window, click **Department-AND-Country-Match-Requirement**, click the **Add** button, click **OK**, and then **OK** again.
40. Close the **Active Directory Administrative Center** and open **Server Manager**, and on **Tools** menu, click **Group Policy Management**.
41. Under **Domains**, click your domain name (in this case, **EndToEdge.com**), click **Action** and then click **Create a GPO in this domain and link it here**.
42. In the **New GPO** dialog box, enter **DAC Policy** and then click **OK**.
43. Expand your domain name (in this case, **EndToEdge.com**), click **DAC Policy**, and then click **OK**.
44. Under the **Security Filtering** section, click **Authenticated Users**, click **Remove**, and then click **OK**.
45. Under the **Security Filtering** section, click **Add**.
46. Click **Object Types**, check **Computers**, and then click **OK**.
47. In order to limit the GPO only to the file server, type the file server's name and then click **OK**.
48. In the left pane, right-click **DAC Policy** and then click **Edit**.
49. Navigate to **Computer Configuration/Policies/Windows Settings/Security Settings/File System**[8] and then click **Central Access Policy**.
50. In the **Action** menu, click **Manage Central Access Policies**.
51. Click **EndToEdge File Server Policy** and then click **Add** to make this policy applicable as shown in Figure 7.23.
52. Click **OK** and close **Group Policy Management Editor**.

---

[8] For a complete list of new Group Policies in Windows Server 2012, download the Group Policy Settings Reference http://www.microsoft.com/en-us/download/details.aspx?id=25250.

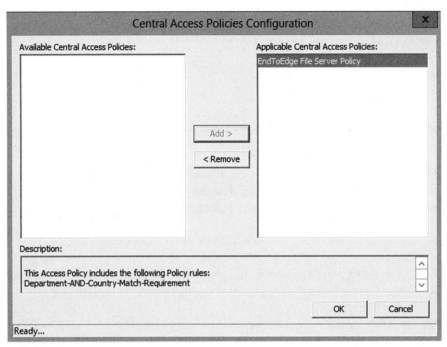

FIGURE 7.23 CAP Configuration. (For color version of this figure, the reader is referred to the online version of this chapter.)

53. In the **Group Policy Management** console, navigate to **Domain Controllers** and then click **Default Domain Controllers Policy**.
54. Click **OK**.
55. On the **Action** menu, click **Edit**.
56. Navigate to **Computer Configuration/Policies/Administrative Templates/System/KDC**.
57. Double-click **KDC Support for claims, compound authentication, and Kerberos armoring**.
58. On the **KDC Support for claims, compound authentication, and Kerberos armoring** dialog box, click **Enabled** and then click **OK**.
59. Navigate to **Computer Configuration/Policies/Administrative Templates/System/Kerberos**.
60. Double-click **Kerberos client support for claims, compound authentication, and Kerberos armoring**.
61. On the **Kerberos client support for claims, compound authentication, and Kerberos armoring** dialog box, click **Enabled** and then click **OK**.
62. Close **Group Policy Management Editor**.
63. Close **Group Policy Management** console.
64. Open **Windows PowerShell**, type **gpupdate/force**, and then press **ENTER**.

Part 2—Steps that must be done in the File Server

IMPORTANT

The steps that it follows assume that the File Server already has the File Server Role installed.

1. In the **Server Manager**, click **Add Roles and Features**.
2. Click **Next** at each step of the wizard until you reach the **Select server roles page**.
3. Expand **File and Storage Services (Installed)**, check **File and iSCSI Services**, expand **File and iSCSI Services**, and then check **File Server Resource Manager**.
4. In the **Add Roles and Features Wizard** dialog box, click **Add Features**.
5. Click **Next** at each step of the wizard until you reach the **Confirm installation** selections page.
6. Click **Install**, and then when the installation finishes, click **Close**.
7. In the **Server Manager**, click **File and Storage Services**.
8. In the left pane, click **Shares** and then click **New Share** under **Tasks** in the right pane.
9. In the **Select the profile for this share** page in the **New Share Wizard**, click **Next**.
10. In the **Select the server and path for this share** page in the **New Share Wizard**, click **Next**.
11. In the **Specify share name** page in the **New Share Wizard**, type **DataShareCorp** under share name field and then click **Next**.
12. Continue clicking **Next** at each step in the wizard and then click **Create**.
13. In the **View results** page in the **New Share Wizard,** click **Close**.
14. Open **Windows Explorer** and navigate to **C:\Shares**.
15. Right-click **DataShareCorp** and then click **Properties**.
16. Click the **Classification** tab.

NOTE

If you do not see Country and Department in the Classification field, cancel this dialog box, open Windows PowerShell, and run the command Update-FSRMClassificationPropertyDefinition. This will force the update to occur.

17. In the **DataShareCorp Properties** dialog box, click **Country** and select **Brazil** in the Value field.
18. Click Department and then click Finance. At this point, the DataShareCorp Properties should look like Figure 7.24.
19. Click **Apply** and leave the window open.

FIGURE 7.24 Properties. (For color version of this figure, the reader is referred to the online version of this chapter.)

20. Open **Windows PowerShell**, type **gpupdate/force**, and then press **ENTER**.
21. Once the group policy finishes updating it, switch to **DataShareCorp** Properties window.
22. On the **Security** tab, click **Advanced**.
23. Click **Central Policy** and then click **Change**.
24. Select **EndtoEdge File Server Policy** and then click **Apply**. At this point, the **Advanced Security Settings for DataShareCorp** window should look like Figure 7.25.

Leave this window open and then proceed to the last part.

Part 3—Validation

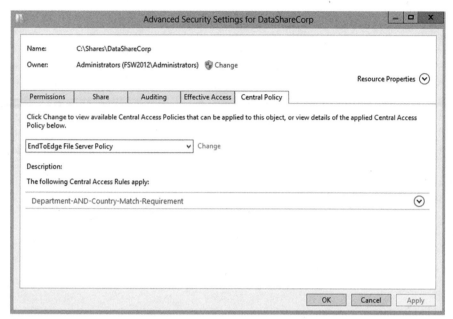

FIGURE 7.25 Account Security Settings. (For color version of this figure, the reader is referred to the online version of this chapter.)

IMPORTANT

The steps that it follows assume that there are two users created in this Domain. One user is member of the Financial Group but works in the United States (in this case, Tom) and the other works in Brazil (in this case, Yuri).

1. Click the **Effective Access** tab.
2. Click **Select a user**, type the user name (in this case, Tom), and then click **OK**.
3. Click **View Effective Access** and review the access for this user when he is not leveraging the claims capability.
4. Click **Include a user claim**.
5. Select C and type **Brazil**.
6. Click **Include a user claim**.
7. Select **Department** and then type **Finance**.
8. Click **View Effective Access** and notice the difference when using claims.
9. Repeat the validation for the user that meets both criteria and notice the difference.

SUMMARY

In this chapter, we took a look at some planning considerations you can take when using the new Windows Server 2012 authentication and authorization systems. New to Windows Server 2012 is the ability to take advantage of claims-based authorization for access to file servers. The new feature, called Dynamic Access Control or DAC, makes it possible to extend your authorization system for file share access past what was possible with traditional user/group-based authorization and access control. We also covered some new technologies in Windows Server 2012 that make DAC possible, such as the new Kerberos proxy feature set. In addition, we took a brief look at the new Picture Password feature and how you can use it to make systems more secure.

Endpoint Security

CONTENTS

CHAPTER POINTS

- Considerations regarding Endpoint Security
- Windows 8 Security Enhancements

CONSIDERATIONS REGARDING ENDPOINT SECURITY

There are many new terminologies going on today: Bring Your Own Device (BYOD), Consumerization of IT, Big Data, etc., the question is, what really matters to me and my overall security strategy? The answer is endpoint security! The reason that we affirm that is because it all starts with the weakest point in the security chain: the user. We all know that the user is the most vulnerable in the whole chain because it can bypass policies, rules, procedures, and take an action based on emotions, feelings, and perception. No matter how strict your policy is, the user always can think of ways to work around it and do what he wants to do. He might not succeed in all scenarios, but he just needs one to compromise the whole company. The most classic example of that is the RSA breach that was caused by a user action (moving the phishing e-mail from the Junk Mail folder to the Inbox and opening it).[1]

You might ask, well, if the user always makes mistakes and compromises the system, why should I spend time and money to protect my system? This is because the goal is to reduce the likelihood that such scenario happens. At the end of the day, you want to make sure that you were diligent protecting your company's assets with the technology available. Ok, so where the endpoint plays on that? It plays a key role because the endpoint device (PC, tablet, phone, etc.) is where the user will primarily work and take his actions.

Planning Endpoint Security

Now that you understand how important it is to protect the endpoint and that the ecosystem that it is upon is beyond the PC, you need to plan your endpoint security accordingly.

Understand the Company's Priorities

If 95% of your company workforce will use PC to connect to the company's network and perform their job, then this is your number one priority: immediately draw a plan to protect those assets. Once you have a plan to protect this 95%, you will start working with the remaining 5% and categorize them. It could be that from this remaining is composed by 3% of smartphones and 2% of tablets. Whatever your number, you must address them all in a priority order. The reason we are emphasizing the word "priority" is because of the budget. Sometimes, companies will need to obtain different solutions to protect the other assets. Although Windows Phone 8 is considered an Enterprise Ready Phone[2] and you can leverage some of its security capabilities without spending money with extra

---

[1] Read more about this case here http://blogs.rsa.com/rivner/anatomy-of-an-attack/.
[2] More about Windows Phone 8 Enterprise ready features here http://www.eweek.com/c/a/Mobile-and-Wireless/Windows-Phone-8-Changes-Aim-to-Ease-Pain-of-BYOD-Management-234691/.

software to fully manage and protect Windows Phone 8 and Windows 8 running on a tablet, you will need System Center 2012.[3] When you prioritize your action plan based on the company's needs, you will ensure that the right assets are immediately protected using the resources that you have out of the box.

Understand the Company's Goals

Understanding the company's goal is essential to succeed during this planning phase. If you do not know what needs to be protected, chances are that you will make wrong investments and end up with breaches where you did not realize it was important to protect. In Figure 8.1, we showed the whole spectrum of components that your company might be using: desktop, cloud computing, smartphone, laptop, and tablets. What really matters is that all those devices will be touching the company's most important assets: the data. Clearly, the company's data is the most important thing to protect; therefore, you need to include on your plan how you will protect this data. Very often we see reports

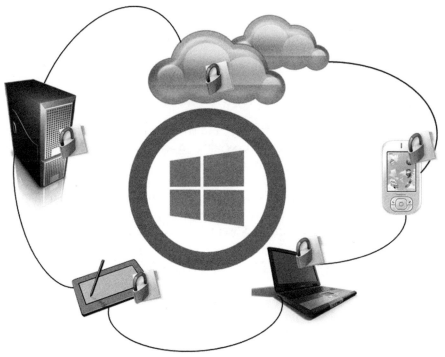

FIGURE 8.1 Windows 8 should be used as a security enabler across all devices. (For color version of this figure, the reader is referred to the online version of this chapter.)

---

[3] An excellent article that explains how System Center 2012 can help with that is available here http://blogs.technet.com/b/server-cloud/archive/2011/10/05/let-system-center-2012-configuration-manager-help-you-enable-consumerization-of-it.aspx.

in the media that companies lost billions of dollars due data leakage, and most of the time this happens on the endpoint.[4] Some Windows 8 features that can help you with that are listed below:

- **BitLocker:** drive encryption is not optional today; you must implement this across all devices that allow this capability to be used. For more information about BitLocker, read Chapter 9.
- **Right Managements Services:** protecting documents to avoid leakage is also an important part of this plan. By default, Windows 8 includes a built-in RMS Client. For more information about RMS, read Chapter 4.
- **Encryption File System:** leverage Windows 8 EFS capabilities to encrypt files and folders to protect against unauthorized access. Next section in this chapter will include more information about EFS enhancements in Windows 8.

Policy Enforcement

As part of the planning phase, you should map all priorities and goals to a policy-based approach. At the end, what you want to answer is, how can I implement my company's needs in the correct priority, leveraging Windows 8 security capabilities out of the box to achieve my company's goals? All granularities that you need are available in the built-in group policy. In Windows 8 and Windows Server 2012, you have 350 new group policy settings that can assist you through that process.[5]

Consumerization of IT

With this new paradigm the users can and should be able to bring their own device to work and use them to access company's network, sensitive data, and not be part of the IT's approved list of devices; a new era of headache might also come together. At a glance, this might sound tragic, but remember, every challenge brings an opportunity to do it better. What you really need to plan is how to take advantage of your endpoint operating system capabilities to provide a better experience for the end user while keeping company's data secure.

WINDOWS 8 SECURITY ENHANCEMENTS

We can summarize the security investments in security Windows 8 in three main areas:

- Protect and Manage Threats: by protecting client, data, and corporate resources. This was accomplished by change in the operating system to inherit security functionalities which reduces the amount of vulnerabilities that can be exploited by malicious software (malware).

---

[4] A great example of that can be found in this article http://www.eweek.com/c/a/Security/
Lost-Stolen-Laptops-Cost-Companies-Billions-in-2010-574365/.

[5] Download the Group Policy Settings Reference from http://www.microsoft.com/en-us/download/
details.aspx?id=25250 for more details.

- Protect Sensitive Data: by simplifying provisioning and compliance management of encrypted drives in a heterogeneous ecosystem and regard the form factors.
- Protect Access to Resources: by enhancing access control and data management while increasing data security in an enterprise environment.

Some of these features are listed in the table below:

Table 8.1 Technology Table

Technology	Security Category	More Information
Software Development Life Cycle (SDL)	Source Code	www.microsoft.com/sdl
Secure Boot	Endpoint	Chapter 9
Windows Defender	Endpoint	This chapter
Windows Firewall	Endpoint	This chapter
UAC	Endpoint	Chapter 10
DirectAccess	Connection	Chapter 11
AppLocker	Endpoint	Chapter 10
Internet Explorer Smart Screen	Endpoint	Chapter 10
BitLocker	Endpoint	Chapter 9
IPsec	Connection	Chapter 11
Dynamic Access Control	Resources	Chapter 7
Update Management	Resources	Chapter 5
Active Directory	Resources	Chapter 3
Windows Firewall	Endpoint	Chapter 10
Encrypted File System (EFS)	Endpoint	This chapter

While some of these features were already covered in this book at this point from the Windows Server 2012 perspective, they are still the same from the core security perspective when compared to Windows 8.

Windows Defender

Windows Defender is a technology that provides real-time protection against malware and spyware as well as other known software that is aimed at attacking the operating system. Windows Defender is able to scan a system at boot up and also while the system is running and is able to remove the offending malware.

The question often comes up regarding the difference between Windows Defender and Windows Security essentials, and that is a good question. I remember asking this question myself. Prior to Windows 8, including Windows XP, Vista and Windows 7, Windows Defender detected and removed spyware only. That meant that it looked only for a specific subset of malware and did not look across the entire spectrum of viruses, Trojans, and other types of malware that may be harbored on your system.

If you ran Microsoft Security Essentials on your older operating systems, you did not need Windows Defender because Microsoft Security Essentials had all the capabilities of Windows Defender and more. In fact, when you installed Windows Security Essentials on these older operating systems, it would disable Windows Defender.

This all changes with Windows 8 clients. For Windows 8 clients, Windows Defender is installed automatically and is enabled out of the box, similar to what you see with Microsoft Security Essentials in the older operating systems. Note that you can install third-party security products on Windows 8 clients, but make sure that the security solution you choose is certified to work with Windows 8. The main reason for this is that you want to make sure that the third-party security product will not contend with Windows Defender, because if it does, it can lead to system stability issues.

Note that you cannot install Microsoft Security Essentials on Windows 8 clients. The reason for that is that you do not need to—Microsoft Security Essentials is "essentially" installed by default, but on Windows 8, it is called Windows Defender.

Other improvements in Windows Defender in Windows 8 include the following:

- Real-time protection against malware using a file system filter
- Interface with Windows 8 Secure Boot—helps insure that the entire Windows boot path up to the antimalware has not been tampered with
- Improved performance—adding only 4% to boot time

There are three main components to Windows Defender:

- The Microsoft Antimalware Engine
- Windows Defender real-time protection
- Windows Defender Definitions

The Microsoft Antimalware Engine

The Microsoft Antimalware Engine is able to check files during startup and after the machine has started up to determine if there is malicious software on the computer. The Microsoft Antimalware Engine uses a definition database to determine what files are malware and which ones are not malware.

The Microsoft Antimalware Engine capabilities include the following:

- The Microsoft Antimalware Engine Scan
- The Microsoft Antimalware Engine Spyware Removal
- The Microsoft Antimalware Engine Update

The Microsoft Antimalware Engine Scan

The Microsoft Antimalware Engine Scan is the process of scanning the system for unwanted software. During the scan, you can perform one of three types of scans.

The types of scans that you can perform include the following:

- Quick Scan
- Full Scan
- Customized Scan

A Quick Scan does not scan the entire system. Instead, the Quick Scan only scans areas of the system that are most commonly affected by malware. A Quick Scan completes much more quickly than a full scan.

A Full Scan, on the other hand, scans the entire system and can take hours or days to run. The reason for this is that when you perform a Full Scan, the Microsoft Antimalware Engine scans all the files on the computer and also scans all running programs.

A Customized Scan allows you to take a very targeted approach to system scanning. When you perform a customized scan, you can tell Windows Defender to scan a subset of files. The time to complete a Customized Scan is based on the number of files you wish to scan.

Microsoft Antimalware Engine Spyware Removal

After performing a scan, the Microsoft Antimalware Engine may find malicious or potentially malicious software. If the Microsoft Antimalware Engine does find such software, it will either delete it or put it into quarantine. The quarantined software is put in an isolated folder with special permissions so that the software is unable to "break out" of quarantine and also that users or applications cannot access this folder.

An interesting aspect of the quarantine process is that software is not just put there and left to die. Files in quarantine can "time out" of quarantine, meaning that after a certain number of days, the files in quarantine will be deleted. You also have an option to manually delete these files through the Windows Defender interface.

In addition, when new definition updates are installed, all the files in quarantine will be checked again against the new definitions. The new definitions may find new attributes of the files in quarantine and can clean or immediately delete files that are in quarantine, depending on the policies configured in the Windows Defender interface.

Microsoft Antimalware Engine Update

Security products like Windows Defender are only as good as the definition updates they have. Outdated updates can put your computer at risk since new malware is constantly released. The Microsoft Antimalware Engine is updated on at least a daily basis, and this is configurable to use either Windows Update or Window Server Update Services (WSUS).

For more information on the Microsoft Antimalware Engine, please see http://www.microsoft.com/en-us/download/details.aspx?id=26643.

Windows Defender Real-Time Protection

The real-time protection feature of Windows Defender allows it to continuously scan both the Registry and the file system to determine the existence of malware. Real-time protection is run in the context of the logged-on user. It is able to do this by using a number of agents that look at what are called "auto-start extensibility points." There are a number of these auto-start extensibility points that Windows Defender looks at. These include the following:

- Programs that start automatically with Windows
- System configuration settings
- Add-on applications or helper applications for Windows Explorer and Internet Explorer
- Configuration settings for Internet Explorer
- System Services
- Installed drivers
- Registered applications and application registration events
- And various other Windows system add-ons

Windows Defender real-time protection includes the following capabilities:

- Real-time protection Availability
- Real-time protection Detection
- Real-Time Spyware Removal

Real-Time Protection Availability

Real-time protection means that you need to be protected when you are using the computer at any time. You cannot wait for the scan to take place automatically and you cannot depend on manual scans. If malware hits your system, Windows Defender needs to be aware that a malware event is taking place and take action. Real-time protection makes sure that it is running and working properly. If it is not, an event is triggered and the user is made aware of the condition and is instructed to take corrective actions.

Real-Time Protection Detection

As mentioned earlier, real-time protection works by checking a number of auto-start extensibility points where malware tends to install itself. When real-time Detection finds suspected malware, it will trigger an alert to inform the user of the potential compromise. At this point, the user is offered the option to allow Windows Defender to carry out its default action (which might be to quarantine or delete the suspected malware) or to allow the user to enable the file to run (which is useful in the event that Windows Defender caught a false positive). It can be tricky to allow users to make this kind of decision. You can use Group Policy settings to prevent users from being able to make these kinds of executive decisions and force the file to be quarantined so that it can be retrieved in the event of a false positive.

Real-Time Protection Spyware Removal

When the real-time protection system finds suspected malware, it needs to make a decision on what to do with it. The choices are to either quarantine or delete the file. This decision is made based on information in the signature file. The signature file will provide the suggested course of action to the user—quarantine, delete, or let the file run. An alert provides the user with these options. These are configurable through Group Policy if you want to be more restrictive.

Windows Defender Definitions

Windows Defender is a signature-based antimalware system, and these signatures provide the definitions that Windows Defender uses to identify malware on a Windows system. These signatures provide information about current spyware and other forms of malware. The signatures provide information about the spyware images themselves and also the types of changes the spyware makes to an infected system.

Definition updates are released on a regular basis and are typically updated once per day. However, this is not a hard and fast schedule, and if new updates are available in less than a day, Windows Defender will update itself more often (such as when there is a new piece of prevalent malware released in the wild and Microsoft wants you to get updates faster and not have to wait an entire day). In general, you should not let the database get more than 14 days old. If for some reason the database does not update itself past that time period, you should force and update. We will discuss how you can force an update later in this chapter.

Windows Defender Network Inspection System

The Network Inspection System (NIS) is a feature originally seen in the Forefront Threat Management Gateway 2010 that is used to narrow the window of opportunity for exploitation between software vulnerability disclosure and security update deployment. NIS does this by creating and deploying signatures that detect when an attempt to exploit a vulnerability is made. NIS signatures are available through the Windows Update or Windows Server Update Service.

NIS is a Network Intrusion Detection/Prevention System (IDS/IPS) for host computer. NIS is designed to detect and prevent vulnerabilities in the Windows operating system and any Microsoft applications from being exploited remotely. NIS is focused solely on protecting Microsoft services and applications and as such does not provide the range of detection that a typical enterprise-class NIDS would provide.

For detailed information on the Network Inspection System, please see http://download.microsoft.com/download/F/4/0/F40887FD-648B-40E1-B79B-AAE43CEDCA4C/NIS%20in%20TMG%20Whitepaper.docx.

Windows Defender Client-Side Configuration

There are two ways that you can configure Windows Defender:

- Local configuration
- Group Policy Configuration

Let us take a look at the local configuration interface first, then we will see what configuration options are available to you via Group Policy, which is the preferred method used in enterprise environments.

You can get to the Windows Defender interface by opening the control panel and then clicking on the **Windows Defender** icon. That will bring up the Windows Defender configuration interface as seen in Figure 8.2. On the **Home** tab you can perform manual scans, choosing from **Quick**, **Full,** and **Custom**. If you select **Custom,** you will be presented with an interface that allows you to choose which files or folders you want to scan.

On the **Update** tab, you will see an **Update** button where you can perform a manual update to the Windows Defender signatures. After clicking that button you will see a progress bar, as seen in Figure 8.3.

In Figure 8.4, you can see that the update failed because the system is pending a restart due to Windows Updates.

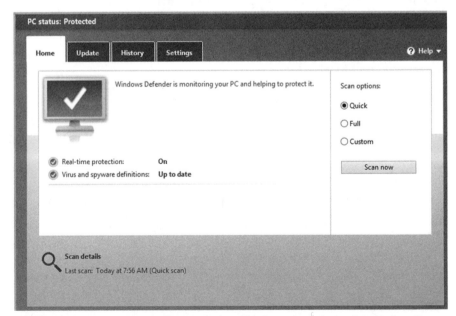

FIGURE 8.2 Windows Defender. (For color version of this figure, the reader is referred to the online version of this chapter.)

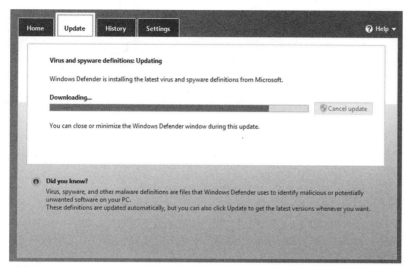

FIGURE 8.3 Updates. (For color version of this figure, the reader is referred to the online version of this chapter.)

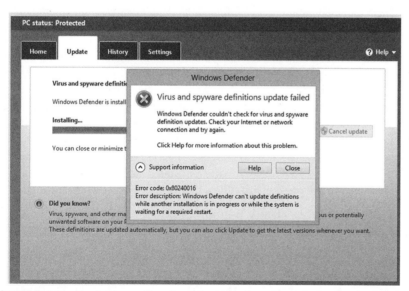

FIGURE 8.4 Checking for viruses. (For color version of this figure, the reader is referred to the online version of this chapter.)

On the **History** tab, as seen in Figure 8.5, you can use the options to see what malware has been discovered on your computer. You have three options:

- **Quarantined items**
- **Allowed items**
- **All detected items**

FIGURE 8.5 Quarantine. (For color version of this figure, the reader is referred to the online version of this chapter.)

These options are self-explanatory. We typically choose the **All detected items** since it gives you the most information. Notice a small change in the Windows Defender in Windows 8 compared to Microsoft Security Essentials. In order to view the items, you need to click the **View Details** button. These are hidden by default. While we do not know the exact reason why this would be considered a privacy issue, it could be that a good amount of malware is seen coming for pornography sites and other sites that you would not necessarily want anyone to know that you are going into—and that the malware may have a name associated with that site or perhaps has been associated in the press as infecting a particular less than wholesome site.

After you click the **View Details** button, you will see a list box like that seen in Figure 8.6.

The tab that provides you the most configuration options is the **Settings** tab. In Figure 8.7, you can see the **real-time protection** option. The **Turn on real-time protection (recommended)** option is selected by default. If you turn this off, you will no longer have real-time protection, but regularly scheduled scans will continue. This option does not turn off all Windows Defender.

The **Excluded files and locations** option allows you to exclude files and locations so that your scan will go faster—but of course, if you do this all the time, you are probably going to miss locations that malware is hiding out and you will get whacked. You can add specific files or folders or other locations by clicking the **Browse** button, as seen in Figure 8.8.

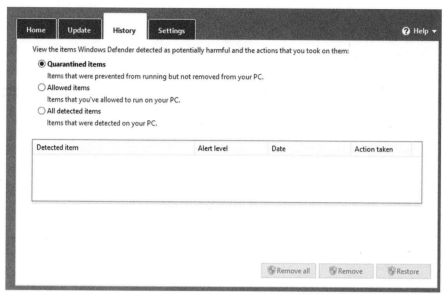

FIGURE 8.6 History. (For color version of this figure, the reader is referred to the online version of this chapter.)

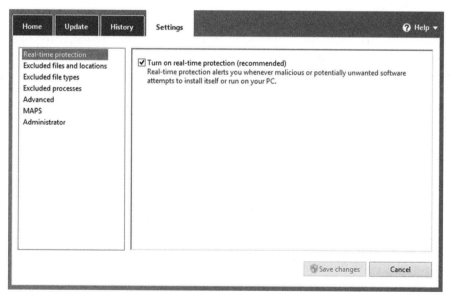

FIGURE 8.7 Settings. (For color version of this figure, the reader is referred to the online version of this chapter.)

The **Excluded file types** option is similar to the previous option, except this time you are designating file types instead of file names or locations. There are some cases where you will want to do this, such as not scanning VHD files or certain database files or logging files. Your application vendor will

FIGURE 8.8 More settings. (For color version of this figure, the reader is referred to the online version of this chapter.)

likely have information on whether certain file type associated with their application should be excluded from scans. To enter the file type, just enter the file extension in the **File extensions** text box, as seen in Figure 8.9 and then click **Add**.

The **Excluded processes** option enables you to exclude specific processes from a scan. Like excluding file types, you can get into trouble by excluding processes, and you should only do this on the recommendation of your application vendor. Note that process files, for the purpose of Windows Defender, only include files with the extensions .exe, .com, or .scr. Process image name in the **Process names** text box and click **Add** when you are down. You can use the **Browse** button if you do not want to type in the entire path as seen in Figure 8.10.

The **Advanced** option, as seen in Figure 8.11, provides you a number of choices:

- **Scan archive files**. This is enabled by default and scans archive files such as .zip and .rar files.
- **Scan removable drives**. This is not enabled by default. If you enable it, it will scan drives that are detected by the operation system as removable.
- **Create a system restore point**. If you want to make sure you can get back to where you were before the scan was run, enable this option. Note that it is not enabled by default. This is a good option to enable as it protects you from any mistakes Windows Defender might make when deleting files.

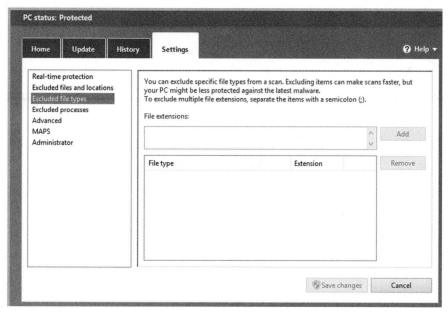

FIGURE 8.9 Exclusions. (For color version of this figure, the reader is referred to the online version of this chapter.)

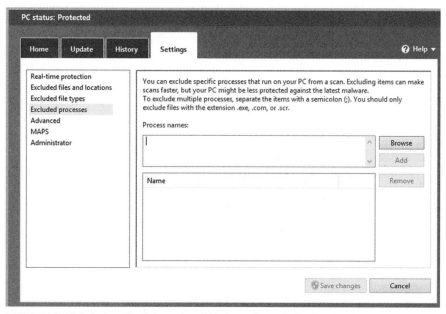

FIGURE 8.10 Exclusions. (For color version of this figure, the reader is referred to the online version of this chapter.)

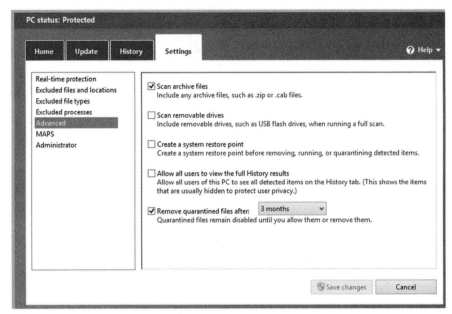

FIGURE 8.11 Quarantine. (For color version of this figure, the reader is referred to the online version of this chapter.)

- **Allow all users to view the full History results**. If you enable this, all users will be able to see the results, and as we discussed previously, you might not want that. This is disabled by default.
- **Remove quarantined files after**: This option allows you to define how long you want to keep quarantined files.

The **MAPS** option (Figure 8.12) provides you choice for various levels of participation in the Microsoft Active Protection Service (MAPS). There are three levels:

- **I don't want to join MAPS.** Participating in MAPS provides valuable feedback to Microsoft regarding the operation and performance of Windows Defender that benefits all Windows users; therefore, we recommend that you do not select this option. You want to help others, don't you?
- **Basic membership.** Only basic information is sent—such as where the malware came from, action that you apply or that were applied automatically, and if the actions actually worked.
- **Advanced membership.** Send the information that is sent when you select Basic membership, but provides more details. We recommend that you select this option as it makes the service much more effective and you end up not only helping others but also helping yourself.

For more details on MAPS and information sent to Microsoft, please see http://technet.microsoft.com/en-us/library/jj618314.aspx

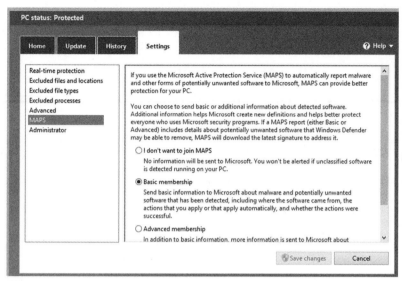

FIGURE 8.12 MAPS settings. (For color version of this figure, the reader is referred to the online version of this chapter.)

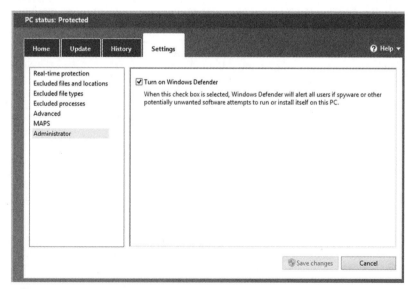

FIGURE 8.13 Turn on Windows Defender. (For color version of this figure, the reader is referred to the online version of this chapter.)

Finally, there is the **Administrator** option (Figure 8.13). This includes a single checkbox, which is the **Turn on Windows Defender**. This is enabled by default. If you uncheck this checkbox, Windows Defender becomes disabled. This might be useful if you are doing some troubleshooting work and it requires turning off the antimalware solution.

Windows Defender Group Policy Settings

In an enterprise environment, you will want to use Group Policy to control the settings. The following are the available Group Policy settings for Windows Defender in a Windows Server 2012 domain:

Table 8.2 Group Policy Settings

Check for New Signatures Before Scheduled Scans	This policy setting checks for new signatures before running scheduled scans. If you enable this policy setting, the scheduled scan checks for new signatures before it scans the computer. If you disable or do not configure this policy setting, the scheduled scan begins without downloading new signatures.
Turn off Windows Defender	This policy setting turns off Windows Defender. If you enable this policy setting, Windows Defender does not run and computers are not scanned for malware or other potentially unwanted software. If you disable or do not configure this policy setting, by default Windows Defender runs and computers are scanned for malware and other potentially unwanted software.
Configure Microsoft Active Protection Service Reporting	This policy setting allows you to configure membership in Microsoft Active Protection Service. Microsoft Active Protection Service is the online community that helps you choose how to respond to potential threats. The community also helps stop the spread of new malicious software infections. You can choose to send basic or additional information about detected software. Additional information helps Microsoft create new definitions and help it to protect your computer. This information can include things like the location of detected items on your computer if harmful software was removed. The information will be automatically collected and sent. If you enable this policy setting, you can select how Windows Defender reports potential malware threats using the following options: No Membership: No information will be sent to Microsoft. You will not be alerted if unclassified software is detected running on your computer. Basic Membership: Send basic information to Microsoft about software that Windows Defender detects, including where the software came from, the actions that you apply or that Windows Defender applies automatically, and whether the actions were successful. In some instances, personal information might unintentionally be sent to Microsoft. However, Microsoft will not use this information to identify you or to contact you. Advanced Membership: In addition to basic information, Windows Defender sends more information to Microsoft about malicious software, spyware, and potentially unwanted software, including the location of the software, file names, how the software operates, and how it has impacted your computer. In some instances, personal information might unintentionally be sent to Microsoft. However, Microsoft will not use this information to identify you or to contact you. If you disable or do not configure this policy setting, by default Microsoft Active Protection Service membership is disabled. At this setting, no information is sent to Microsoft. You are not alerted if Windows Defender detects unclassified software running on your computer. Local users can still change their Microsoft Active Protection Service membership.

Turn off Real-Time Monitoring	This policy setting turns off real-time protection prompts for known malware detection. Windows Defender alerts you when malware or potentially unwanted software attempts to install itself or to run on your computer. If you enable this policy setting, Windows Defender will not prompt users to take actions on malware detections. If you disable or do not configure this policy setting, Windows Defender will prompt users to take actions on malware detections.
Turn off Routinely Taking Action	This policy setting allows you to configure whether Windows Defender automatically takes action on all detected threats. The action to be taken on a particular threat is determined by the combination of the policy-defined action, user-defined action, and the signature-defined action. If you enable this policy setting, Windows Defender does not automatically take action on the detected threats, but prompts users to choose from the actions available for each threat. If you disable or do not configure this policy setting, Windows Defender automatically takes action on all detected threats after a nonconfigurable delay of approximately 10 min.

Windows SmartScreen

The new Windows SmartScreen application reputation service provides application reputation-based technologies that will assist in protecting users against malicious applications that they might try to download and install. This new feature uses the same technology that Internet Explorer used for years called SmartScreen (http://www.microsoft.com/security/filters/smartscreen.aspx). When you execute an application, Windows calls the ShellExecute[6] function which will verify the software acquisition and installation life cycle to verify the policies (allow, block, verify, etc.), when it needs it will verify the application reputation by retrieving information from the SmartScreen Service. If the application is not allowed, the **Windows protect your PC** modern dialog will appear as shown in Figure 8.14:

If you click **More info** hyperlink, you will have more details about the application that you are trying to run and also the option to run anyway as shown in Figure 8.15.

FIGURE 8.14 Protected. (For color version of this figure, the reader is referred to the online version of this chapter.)

---

[6] For more information about this function, read http://msdn.microsoft.com/en-us/library/bb762153(VS.85).aspx.

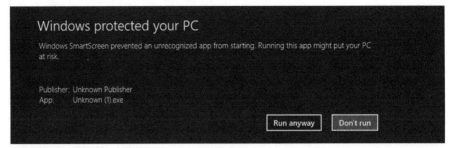

FIGURE 8.15 SmartScreen. (For color version of this figure, the reader is referred to the online version of this chapter.)

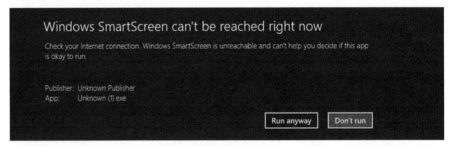

FIGURE 8.16 SmartScreen. (For color version of this figure, the reader is referred to the online version of this chapter.)

It is important to mention that this scenario assumes that the SmartScreen service was reachable and after being verified, it suggested to block the application from run. If the SmartScreen service is unreachable (for example, the Internet connection is down), then another screen will appear with the Run anyway option enabled by default as shown in Figure 8.16.

The Windows SmartScreen settings can be changed to better adequate to your needs. Follow the steps below to change these settings:

1. In the Start screen, click **Desktop**.
2. Hold the mouse in the lower-right corner of the screen until the **Charms bar** (or use Windows Key+C) appears on the right side.
3. In the **Charms bar**, click **Settings** as shown in Figure 8.17.
4. Click **Control Panel**.
5. Click **Action Center**.
6. Click **Change Windows SmartScreen settings** and the **Windows SmartScreen** dialog will appear as shown in Figure 8.18.
7. There are three modes in which you can run Windows SmartScreen. They are as follows:
   - **Get administrator approval before running an unrecognized app from the Internet (recommended)**: this option will prompt administrators and standard users for password before running unknown applications from the Internet.

FIGURE 8.17 Desktop. (For color version of this figure, the reader is referred to the online version of this chapter.)

FIGURE 8.18 Configure SmartScreen. (For color version of this figure, the reader is referred to the online version of this chapter.)

■ **Warn before running an unrecognized app, but don't require administrator approval:** this option will prompt administrators for consent and standard users for password before running unknown applications downloaded from the Internet.

■ **Don't do anything (turn off Windows SmartScreen):** this option will disable SmartScreen instead of prompting before running programs downloaded from the Internet. When this option is selected, a flag will be raised by the Action Center on the taskbar as shown in Figure 8.19.

8. Once you finish selecting the option that is most appropriate for your scenario, click **OK**.

The Windows SmartScreen is integrated with Windows User Account Control (UAC); in other words, if the ShellExecute function attempts to launch an application that requires elevation, the reputation service will be checked before prompting for UAC. If UAC is configured to Prompt for Administrator Approval, the Windows SmartScreen will show the Windows protected your computer modern dialog asking for credentials as shown in Figure 8.20.

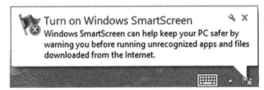

FIGURE 8.19 Warning. (For color version of this figure, the reader is referred to the online version of this chapter.)

FIGURE 8.20 Admin logon. (For color version of this figure. the reader is referred to the online version of this chapter.)

Controlling Windows SmartScreen Using GPO

There is a new policy that can be used to control how SmartScreen works via GPO, this policy is part of the *WindowsExplorer.admx* template, and it is located at Computer Configuration\Policies\Administrative Templates\ Windows Components\File Explorer. This option is called Configure Windows Smart Screen that has the settings shown in Figure 8.21.

When you click **Enabled**, the options field will allow you to select one of the following options:

■ Require approval from administrator before running downloaded unknown software
■ Give user a warning before running downloaded unknown software
■ Turn off SmartScreen

These options are available in the Windows SmartScreen UI and were previously explained.

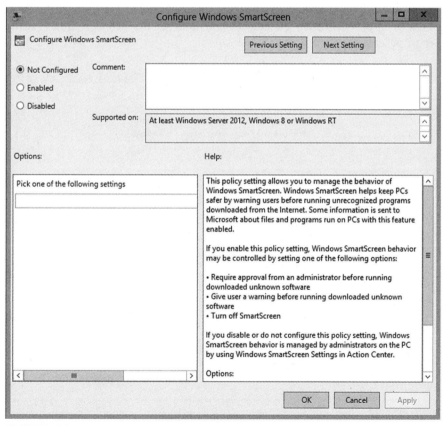

FIGURE 8.21 GP setting. (For color version of this figure, the reader is referred to the online version of this chapter.)

Action Center

The Windows Action Center will be the main portal for the end user to identify potential problems or suggestions on the Windows Security settings. Figure 8.22 has an example of how the Action Center can flag potential problems that should be fixed.

The color that appears besides the potential problem reflects the priority of the issue. Red means it is critical to be fixed, while yellow is a warning that this should be fixed as soon as possible. You can customize what will be monitored by the Action Center by selecting the option Change Action Center Settings and the window shown in Figure 8.23 will appear.

Unless guided by a Microsoft representative or automatically changed by a third-party software that hooks into the Action Center, the recommendation is to maintain these settings enabled as it is by default. The basic architecture of the Action Center is shown in Figure 8.24.

As you can see, the Action Center has the knowledge of what it is happening not only on the Windows Security components listed in the diagram but also in the third-party security-related programs that are hooked into the Windows Security Center Service.[7]

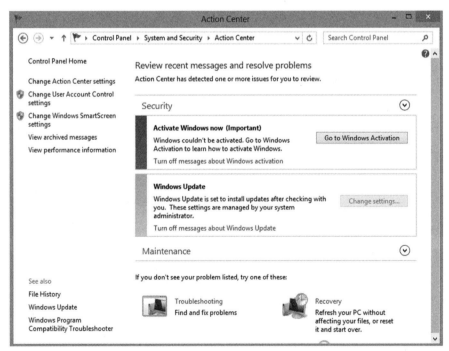

FIGURE 8.22 Action Center. (For color version of this figure, the reader is referred to the online version of this chapter.)

---

[7] For more information about Windows Security Center, see http://msdn.microsoft.com/en-us/library/gg537273(v=vs.85).aspx.

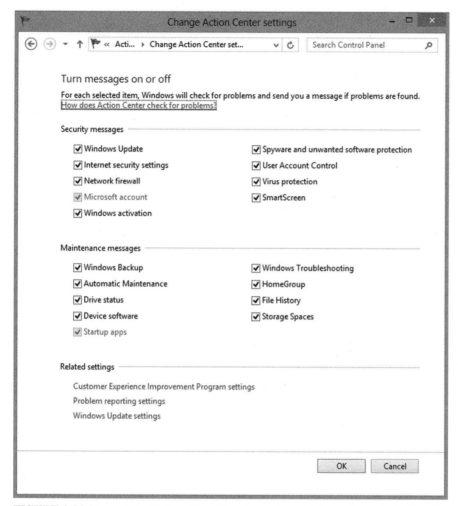

FIGURE 8.23 Change Action Center settings. (For color version of this figure, the reader is referred to the online version of this chapter.)

Encrypting File System

There are not a lot of changes in EFS on Windows 8; the architecture remains the same with the addition of elliptic curve cryptography (ECC) support. The benefit of supporting ECC is that now EFS is compliant with Suite B encryption requirements as defined by the National Security Agency (NSA). This is a requirement for protecting classified information from United States government agencies. Although Suite B does not allow the use of RSA cryptography, EFS on Windows 8 supports a new "mixed-mode" operation where ECC and RSA algorithms can coexist. This allows backward compatibility with EFS files created in previous versions.

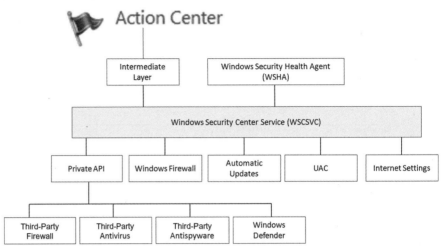

FIGURE 8.24 Architecture. (For color version of this figure, the reader is referred to the online version of this chapter.)

The important aspect to notice is that the risk area that EFS was designed to mitigate is related to data theft or compromise data due to lost or stolen mobile computers. EFS settings can be deployed equally throughout the organization by using Group Policy. The settings are available at *Computer Configuration\ Policies\Windows Settings\Security Settings\Public Key Policies\Encrypting File System*. This option allows you to create a Data Recovery Agent (DRA) and customize the EFS settings. There are other policies available in the following locations:

Table 8.3 Group Policy settings

Policy	Location	Description
EFS recovery policy processing	Computer Configuration\ Policies\Administrative Templates\System\Group Policy	Determines when encryption policies are updated.
Do not automatically encrypt files moved to encrypted folders	Computer Configuration\ Policies\Administrative Templates\System	Prevents Windows Explorer from encrypting files that are moved to an encrypted folder.
Encrypt the Offline Files cache	Computer Configuration\ Policies\Administrative Templates\Network\Offline Files	This setting determines whether offline files are encrypted.
Allow indexing of encrypted files	Computer Configuration\ Policies\Administrative Templates\Windows Components\Search	This setting allows encrypted items to be indexed by Windows Search.

ADMINISTRATOR'S PUNCH LIST

- Ensure that your company security plan addresses endpoint security as a vital part of the overall security strategy.
- If your company is encouraging the use of BYOD, endpoint security becomes even more essential since you might have to deal with more than one vendor and integration is the key.
- Be aware that the weakest point in the security chain is the end user, which means endpoint security must reduce as much as possible the possibility that the end user will perform a mistake that can compromise the system.
- The endpoint security must include all form of devices that will enable the end user to access company data. In other words, smartphone, tablets, laptops, and any other device that the end user might use to access corporate data must be included.
- Leverage built-in technology available on Windows 8 to protect the end user, such as BitLocker, RMS, and EFS.
- Ensure that your company not only has a policy in place but also enforces this policy. Leverage features such as GPO for policy enforcement.
- Evangelize the use of Security Development Life Cycle across your company. If the software that they develop is not secure in first place, the mechanisms that will be used to protect it afterward will be even harder to manage.
- Although Windows 8 comes with Windows Defender out of the box, it is important to evaluate if this solution is enough for your company. Some scenarios will require a more robust and manageable antimalware.
- Keep Windows Defender always up to date and enforce the settings by using GPO.
- Ensure that Windows SmartScreen is also enabled and enforced via GPO.

SUMMARY

In this chapter, we begin with a discussion on the threat landscape for endpoint client machines. Then, we reviewed a number of Windows Server 2012 and Windows 8 technologies that are aimed at increasing the overall level of security in a Windows client and server ecosystem. We then rounded out the chapter with more detailed discussion on Windows Defender, Windows SmartScreen, and the Encrypting File System.

CHAPTER 9

Secure Client Deployment with Trusted Boot and BitLocker

CONTENTS

CHAPTER POINTS

- Security considerations for mobile users
- Understanding the Trusted Boot process
- Understanding BitLocker full volume encryption
- Deploying Trusted Boot and BitLocker

SECURITY CONSIDERATIONS FOR MOBILE USERS

With Windows 8, Microsoft introduced one operating system that will run on desktop PCs, laptop/notebooks, and tablet devices. Many of the same security issues will apply to all three, but some risks are exacerbated by the way portable devices are used. There are a number of reasons for this:

■ Portable devices are exposed to multiple networks. Just as a person who travels extensively has a greater risk of being exposed to contagious diseases because he/she comes into contact with a greater and more diverse group of people, computers that travel from one network to another have increased risk of encountering malware or coming under attack.

■ Portable devices more often connect to wireless networks. Wi-Fi networks, because their transmissions travel over the open airwaves, are more vulnerable than wired networks to penetration by unauthorized persons who can then deliver malware to systems on those wireless networks.

■ As portable devices get smaller and lighter, they also become more likely to be inadvertently left behind. You are not as aware of their presence as with a heavy, bulky device, and thus you are also not as aware of their absence.

■ Portable devices are often transported through busy airports, left in hotel rooms while users go out, and otherwise placed into environments where it is easy to steal them.

Data Breaches: A Growing Problem

The monetary cost of replacing a lost or stolen laptop, or repairing one that has been rendered useless by a malware infestation, can be significant. However, it pales in comparison to the costs—monetary and otherwise—of a data breach. Confidential or sensitive company data stored on portable computers can include personally identifiable information about clients or employees, trade secrets and proprietary research, company financial data, and more.

There are two basic ways by which an attacker can extract confidential or sensitive data from a portable computer:

■ Physically take possession of the computer and access its drives directly, or
■ Take control remotely, which can be accomplished via the introduction of malicious software

These two methods are graphically represented in Figure 9.1.

The headlines are full of news about the loss or theft of laptops containing sensitive information. It is happening in small businesses, large corporations, nonprofits, and government agencies. NASA reported a loss or theft of 48 computers between April 2009 and 2011. One of those was a laptop that held

FIGURE 9.1 Attackers can extract data from a portable computer in two ways. (For color version of this figure, the reader is referred to the online version of this chapter.)

command and control codes for the International Space Station.[1] In August 2012, the laptop of an Apria Healthcare employee in Phoenix was stolen; it contained the protected health information of as many as 11,000 patients.[2] In September 2012, a "hacktivist" group called AntiSec (which is associated with Anonymous) claimed to have stolen over 12 million Apple users' UDIDs (Unique Device Identifiers) from an FBI database and published one million of them on the Web, although the FBI denied the claim.[3]

Even if an organization institutes a strict policy to prohibit storage of sensitive data on laptops, that does not mean a lost or stolen device does not pose a risk of data breach. If the thief is able to boot into the laptop and use the owner's credentials, he may be able to log onto the company network and get to the data that is stored on the servers there. Thus, the idea that strong security is not necessary for laptops that are "only" used to access files remotely, and not to store files locally, misses the point.

[1] NASA Breaches Leak ISS Control Code http://www.informationweek.com/government/security/nasa-breaches-leak-iss-control-code/232601867.

[2] Stolen laptop leads to health data breach at Apria Healthcare http://ehrintelligence.com/2012/08/14/stolen-laptop-leads-to-health-data-breach-at-apria-healthcare/.

[3] Anonymous is Back: 12 M Apple Device IDs Allegedly Hacked from FBI Computer http://idealab.talkingpointsmemo.com/2012/09/anonymous-is-back-12m-apple-device-ids-allegedly-hacked-from-fbi-computer.php.

Wherever the data is stored, if an employee can use the laptop to access it, so can an unauthorized person who is in control of that laptop. But that does not mean the data thief has to have physical possession of the device. The more stealthy method is to take the control of a portable (or desktop) computer remotely.

According to the Verizon 2012 *Data Breach Investigations Report*, out of 855 reported incidents, 69% of the data breaches utilized malware.

Consequences of a Data Breach

Consequences of a data breach can be severe. Although the business cost of the average data breach declined for the first time in 2011,[4] to $5.5 million from $7.2 million the year before, that is still a substantial amount of money. In addition, measurable monetary costs are not the only fallout when an organization's data is breached. Public trust and customer goodwill are also lost and can be difficult or impossible to regain. That' is particularly true for companies that hold information about customers' finances or heath status.

There may also be legal ramifications if an organization's data is breached. Many industries today, such as health care and financial services, are regulated by the government. Others are governed by industry standards. In the United States, HIPAA (the Health Insurance Portability and Accountability Act), GLB (the Gramm-Leach-Bliley Act), SOX (The Sarbanes-Oxley Act), and other federal and state laws mandate that sensitive data belonging to patients/clients be protected. The Data Protection Directive regulates processing of personal data in the European Union countries. Merchants who accept credit card payments must comply with the Payment Card Industry (PCI) data security standards. Failure to comply with regulatory mandates can result in fines, administrative penalties, loss of merchant status, and in some cases even criminal charges.[5]

The consequences can be so dire that insurance companies are now offering specific coverage for losses due to data breach. This so-called *first-party cyber insurance* reimburses companies for the costs of restoring the systems and may also compensate for revenue lost due to the data breach. It does not generally cover the cost of litigation and damages if your clients or other third parties sue you for the effects on them when your data is breached; for that, you will probably need an additional policy or rider (*third-party coverage*).[6]

---

[4] Data Breach Costs Drop http://www.informationweek.com/security/attacks/data-breach-costs-drop/232602891.

[5] HIPAA Violations and Enforcement http://www.ama-assn.org/ama/pub/physician-resources/solutions-managing-your-practice/coding-billing-insurance/hipaahealth-insurance-portability-accountability-act/hipaa-violations-enforcement.page.

[6] Big or Small Companies Need Insurance Against Data Breachers http://www.jdsupra.com/legalnews/big-or-small-cos-need-insurance-agains-24991/.

Protecting Against Data Breaches

Broadly speaking, there are two basic approaches to protect against a data breach:

- Prevent a data thief from being able to access the confidential/sensitive data
- Ensure that if a data thief does get his hands on the data, it will be in a form that cannot be read or used

Obviously, these approaches are not mutually exclusive, and a multilayered data protection plan for mobile devices will incorporate both. A physical security strategy not only involves "outer layers" of security (e.g., fences, motion detection lights, guard dogs) to keep burglars out but also includes "inner layers" (an interior alarm system, a safe for storing valuables) in case the bad guys do penetrate through the first lines of defense. Your data protection strategy should work in the same way.

Practically speaking, that means at the absolute minimum you need the following:

- Controls to keep a thief from obtaining the data
- Encryption to render the data useless if a thief does obtain it

The Windows 8 client includes built-in technologies to address both issues right out of the box. Let us take a look at how the Trusted Boot process, coupled with BitLocker full volume encryption, can serve as the foundation of organizations' mobile device data protection plans.

UNDERSTANDING THE TRUSTED BOOT PROCESS

Secure Boot is a feature in Windows 8 that has engendered more controversy than any other (with the possible exception of the missing Start menu). Code signing has been around for a long time; this refers to the process of attaching a digital signature to a driver or other software executable to verify who authored it and ensure that it has not been tampered with. Microsoft implemented this with their Authenticode technology[7] to protect users from malicious downloads. However, malware authors are always coming up with workarounds to find a way to do their dirty deeds. Rootkits are stealthy iterations of malware that can operate at different levels, including sophisticated varieties that run at the lowest level in the firmware (kernel mode). *Bootkits* are a type of rootkit that replaces the operating system's boot loader (the program that begins the OS boot process) with malicious code that runs before the OS loads. Because of the way bootkits work, they cannot be easily detected by standard antimalware tools.

---

[7] Authenticode (Microsoft TechNet Library) http://technet.microsoft.com/en-us/library/cc750035.aspx

Secure Boot protects against these malware manifestations and prevents unauthorized firmware, operating systems, and drivers from running at boot time. In the same way, software can be digitally signed; the Secure Boot feature leverages the abilities of the Unified Extensible Firmware Interface (UEFI), which replaces the old Basic Input/Output System (BIOS) in modern computers, to require Authenticode digital signatures on the firmware modules, operating system loaders (boot manager), and UEFI drivers.

How UEFI Enables Secure Boot

UEFI is an industry standard firmware interface that grew out of Intel's Extensible Firmware Interface (EFI). EFI was originally developed to provide better support for booting from disks of 2 TB or greater capacity, to provide networking capability prior to loading of the OS, and to be independent of the CPU. UEFI also supports the Secure Boot protocol, which allows the use of public key cryptography to block loading of OS loaders or drivers that are not signed with a key that matches up to the public keys (platform keys) stored in the signature database.

UEFI-aware operating systems are booted directly from a UEFI OS loader. Microsoft first supported UEFI booting with Windows Server 2008 and Vista Service Pack 1 64 bit, and it is supported by Windows 7 (64 bit) and, of course, Windows 8. The difference with Windows 8 is that secure boot will be enabled by default. This means only signed operating systems will be able to run on the device.

This led to the misperception that it would not be possible to install Linux or other alternative operating systems on Windows 8 computers. In fact, in the case of x86 PCs, it is up to hardware vendors as to whether to allow secure boot to be disabled in the firmware and/or to include digital keys for other operating systems in the signature database. The Linux Foundation has described how to make UEFI Secure Boot work with open source operating systems.[8] It is true that Microsoft has mandated that secure boot be mandatory on ARM-based Windows RT devices.

Computers are categorized according to their UEFI support as follows:

- **Class 0**: Computers with a legacy BIOS, no UEFI
- **Class 1**: Computers with UEFI CSM (Compatibility Support Module) only. Legacy BIOS interface runs on top of UEFI
- **Class 2**: Computers with both UEFI and CSM
- **Class 3**: Computers with UEFI only

---

[8] Making UEFI Secure Boot Work with Open Platforms http://www.linuxfoundation.org/publications/making-uefi-secure-boot-work-with-open-platforms.

You can learn more about UEFI specifications from the United EFI Forum's Web site at http://www.uefi.org/home/.

Windows 8 and UEFI

Windows 8, installed on firmware that meets the UEFI 2.3.1 specification, gives you the ability to use the Secure Boot feature. To install Windows 8 to boot from the UEFI on a computer that also supports the legacy BIOS compatibility mode, you might need to switch from BIOS compatibility mode to UEFI mode. To do this, you open the Boot Device menu and select the firmware mode (UEFI or BIOS), or select **Boot from file** and browse to the location of the EFI boot file. It' is also possible to use the internal shell to run the UEFI boot application from the command prompt.[9]

In order to receive Windows certification, Microsoft requires that hardware vendors ship Windows 8 computers with Secure Boot enabled by default and the firmware must not allow programs to disable the UEFI security policies in the firmware. This prevents malware from running in the boot path because only the approved signed and authenticated boot loaders can run. Here' is a simplified explanation of how it works, as shown in Figure 9.2:

1. The PC's power is turned on.
2. The firmware checks the signatures of the firmware device code (Option ROMs) for peripheral devices.
3. The firmware compares the signatures against those in the signature database that' is stored in the firmware. The databases included "Allowed" and "Disallowed" lists.
4. If a match is found, the module is allowed to run.

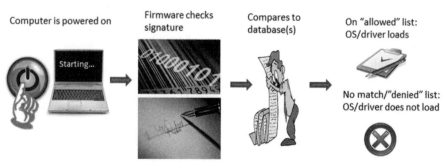

FIGURE 9.2 Secure Boot prevents malware from running in the boot path. (For color version of this figure, the reader is referred to the online version of this chapter.)

---

[9] How to Switch from BIOS compatibility Mode to UEFI Mode http://technet.microsoft.com/en-us/library/hh825112.aspx.

Certificates/keys that represent the trusted operating system loaders are stored in the "Allowed" list. Hashes of known malware are stored in the "Disallowed" list. The process is transparent to the computer user, until/unless an unverified component attempts to load.

Note that certain criteria must be met in order to use the Secure Boot feature in Windows. For example, the UEFI hard disks must use the GUID partition table (GPT) rather than the Master Boot Record (MBR).

Windows 8 Boot Hardening Features

Windows 8 and Windows Server 2012 include two separate but related features for hardening the boot process against malware:

- **Measured Boot**: Logs the boot components that start prior to the antimalware software and provides that information to the antimalware software on the local machine, which sends it to a remote server. The remote server can evaluate these components and take remedial action.
- **Early Launch Antimalware (ELAM)**: This feature ensures that antimalware loads prior to other third-party components, to protect against loading infected boot drivers and blocking malware from running.

You can use either of the boot hardening features alone or in conjunction with one another. To use the Measured Boot feature, the system must have a Trusted Platform Module (TPM), as the measurements are recorded in the TPM prior to loading of the operating system. The information recorded in the TPM is sent to the remote server after Windows loads.[10]

The ELAM driver is a registered boot driver and early launch driver. ELAM drivers must be signed by Microsoft. Their digital certificates include a special enhanced key usage (EKU) extension identifying them as ELAM driver. With ELAM, the early launch antimalware software verifies whether each driver that attempts to initialize is good, bad, or unknown and then initializes the driver or does not, depending on the policy you have defined. The malware signature data that it uses to make this determination is stored in the registry and loaded along with the antimalware driver. The malware signature data is verified by the antimalware driver when it is initialized. The ELAM driver hands off its information to the antimalware software that will run after the OS is loaded.

If Measured Boot is being used along with ELAM, the measurements of the antimalware driver are stored in the TPM. Measured Boot logs which components ran prior to the starting of the antimalware software. These measurements cannot be reset after they are recorded, without system reset, so as to

---

[10] Secured Boot and Measured Boot: Hardening Early Boot Components against Malware http://msdn. microsoft.com/en-us/windows/hardware/br259097.

keep malware from altering its own measurement. Measured Boot records information about the OS kernel components and boot drivers (third-party drivers included). The client sends the measurements to a remote computer, which evaluates them (attestation). The attestation process includes security measures to prevent replay attacks. The remote server determines whether the client is trustworthy based on a comparison of the measurements in the log with those in the TPM Platform Configuration Registers (PCRs). The PCRs are the registers where the TPM stores the measurement values. The values in each of the 24 TPM registers are shown in Table 9.1.

Measured Boot can be used with a conventional BIOS or UEFI; the process is similar, but slightly different.

To deploy Measured Boot, you must do the following:

- Enable the TPM
- Have an Attestation Identity Key (AIK) that is unique to the client, and which the server associates with the client

Table 9.1 TPM TCR Values

PCR Value	Meaning
0	Core root of trust of measurement (CRTM), BIOS, and platform extensions
1	Platform and motherboard configuration and data
2	Option ROM code
3	Option ROM configuration and data
4	Master boot record (MBR) code
5	Master boot record (MBR) partition table
6	State transition and wake events
7	Computer manufacturer specific
8	NTFS boot sector
9	NTFS boot code
10	Boot manager
11	BitLocker drive encryption access control
12	Defined for use by the static operating system
13	Defined for use by the static operating system
14	Defined for use by the static operating system
15	Defined for use by the static operating system
16	Used for debugging
17	Dynamic CRTM
18	Platform defined
19	Used by trusted operating system
20	Used by trusted operating system
21	Used by trusted operating system

- Enable boot measurements on the client
- Install antimalware as a boot driver
- Install client components to perform attestation

UNDERSTANDING BITLOCKER FULL VOLUME ENCRYPTION

Full volume encryption (FVE) refers to the encryption of a physical or virtual partition (volume) on a disk. FVE programs have been around for quite some time. For example, TrueCrypt is an open source FVE program that was released in 2004.[11] TrueCrypt is available for Windows, Linux, and Mac OS X, and there are other FVE programs for all popular operating systems. The term is sometimes used interchangeably with the term *Full Disk Encryption* (FDE) although technically the latter means that all partitions on the disk are encrypted. FDE solutions have been around since the 1990s.

Microsoft's FVE technology is called BitLocker, and it was first released in 2006 as part of Windows Vista. It has been included in all Windows client and server versions since, but not in all editions; BitLocker is available only in the high-end SKUs—Enterprise and Ultimate editions—of Windows Vista and Windows 7 and in the Pro and Enterprise editions of Windows 8.

BitLocker has been improved in Windows 8 and Windows Server 2012 to include the following new features:

BitLocker pre-provisioning: Windows 8 and Windows Server 2012 can be deployed to an encrypted state during installation prior to calling setup.

Used Disk Space Only encryption: Encrypting only the used disk space, rather than the entire volume, is now an option that can result in a much faster encryption experience.

Standard User PIN and user password change: Now a standard user can change the BitLocker PIN or password on operating system volumes and the BitLocker password on data volumes (if allowed by policy) to take the load off tech support personnel.

Network Unlock: A BitLocker system on a trusted wired network can now automatically unlock the operating system volume during the boot process, decreasing the problem due to lost PINs.

Support for hardware-encrypted hard drives: Windows 8 and Windows Server 2012 include BitLocker support for hardware-encrypted hard drives.

---

[11] TrueCrypt Free Open-source Encryption on the Fly http://www.truecrypt.org/.

Support for Cluster Shared Volumes: BitLocker now can be used with cluster-shared volumes on Windows Server 2012.

FVE vs. File/Folder Encryption

File-level encryption, as provided by Microsoft's Encrypting File System (EFS) and numerous third-party encryption programs such as CryptoForge and Folder Lock, allows you to encrypt individual files and/or folders. An advantage of file/folder encryption is that, because only specific files with sensitive data are encrypted, there is little/no reduction in general system performance, although it can slow down opening or working with the encrypted files. The user designates which files/folders to encrypt.

FVE has the advantage of requiring no action on the part of the user. That means you do not run the risk of users forgetting to encrypt a particular sensitive file. Another advantage is that FVE encrypts temporary files that might be created by applications in a folder other than the encrypted one, and it encrypts the page file/swap file which can contain copies of sensitive data that has been swapped from RAM. Finally, FVE can encrypt not only data volumes but also the operating system files. In fact, in the first version of BitLocker that was included with Windows Vista, only the operating system volume could be encrypted. Windows Vista Service Pack 1 added the ability to encrypt non-OS volumes on the internal hard drives and this ability was continued in subsequent iterations of BitLocker. Windows 7 added a new feature, BitLocker-to-Go, which allows full volume encryption of removable storage devices such as external USB hard drives and removable flash drives.

How BitLocker Works Together with Other Technologies to Protect Mobile Users

Trusted Boot protects your mobile or desktop system from malware that could—among other dirty deeds—send your confidential data to an unauthorized person across the Internet, take control of your computer, or crash the system. However, it does not protect that data and those system files from someone who gains physical access to your mobile device. If the device is stolen, you need a way to prevent the thief from accessing the data or tampering with the operating system and applications.

BitLocker can provide protection for both your OS files and the data. The two can be used in conjunction with one another. BitLocker can protect the system from a type of attack, whereby the attacker who has physical access can run another instance of an operating system on the computer and access the unencrypted files that are in your OS, even though he/she does not have your password and is not able to log into your OS instance. This is called a *parallel installation attack*.

Will not EFS keep a parallel attacker from viewing your sensitive data files? Yes—but some of the data in those files may be copied to other, temporary locations that are not encrypted by EFS. Because BitLocker encrypts all the files on the volume, including temp files, page files, and hibernation files, it protects data that may be left vulnerable when you encrypt the data files with EFS, along with protecting the operating system files. EFS can be used to encrypt files that are stored on other partitions that are not encrypted with BitLocker, and the EFS keys will be stored by default on the OS volume that is BitLocker encrypted.

How BitLocker Works

BitLocker uses the Advanced Encryption Standard (AES) to protect full volumes. Default key length is 128 bits, but you can configure it to use 256 bit keys, using Group Policy. When you encrypt the operating system files with BitLocker, it uses two partitions. The first is the encrypted volume that holds the operating system; it is called the boot drive or operating system drive and must be formatted in NTFS. The second is called the system volume and is unencrypted. Authentication and verification of system integrity take place prior to startup of the operating system, while the OS volume is encrypted; so, the Windows Pre-Execution Environment (WinPE) and boot files are on the unencrypted partition. The system volume must be formatted with NTFS on computers with a legacy BIOS, with FAT32 on computers that use UEFI, as illustrated in Figure 9.3.

BitLocker Encryption of Data Drives

In addition to encrypting the OS volume, you can use BitLocker on Windows 8 to encrypt your data volumes. This includes the following:

- Other partitions on the same drive as the operating system volume
- Partitions on other physical hard drives installed in the computer
- External USB or eSATA drives
- Removable portable USB flash drives or flash memory cards

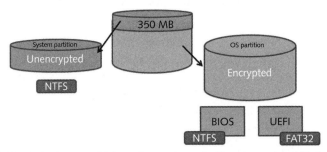

FIGURE 9.3 BitLocker imposes disk formatting requirements. (For color version of this figure, the reader is referred to the online version of this chapter.)

This means you can now encrypt practically any locally attached drive with BitLocker. When using BitLocker to encrypt a data drive (fixed or removable), it can be formatted in NTFS, FAT32, FAT16, or exFAT.

With Windows 8 BitLocker, you can access a BitLocker-protected data drive that is removed from one computer and inserted into another, using the BitLocker Control Panel.

The Encryption Process

BitLocker uses multiple encryption keys to protect your data. The full volume encryption key encrypts the data. Then the volume master key encrypts the full volume encryption key. Finally, this volume master key is itself encrypted, by RSA or AES algorithm depending on whether you are using the TPM only, a startup key only, a combination of both, or a recovery key or password.[12] Key length can be configured through Group Policy.

Starting an OS on an Encrypted Volume

When implementing a full volume/disk encryption solution, you face a dilemma: an operating system on an encrypted volume cannot boot until its boot files are decrypted; so, the key has to be available *before* the OS loads a user interface. Obviously, that key cannot be stored on the encrypted disk itself; that would be like locking your car keys inside your vehicle to keep them safe. And you do not want to store it on an unencrypted partition on the hard disk; that would make it available to unauthorized persons and negate the purpose of encryption.

The solution is to store the key externally. There are several approaches: If the computer has a TPM, the key can be stored there. Because the TPM is embedded in the motherboard, this means that if someone removes the hard drive from the computer and puts it in another one, they cannot decrypt the disk without the key. The down side of this is that if the motherboard/TPM should experience hardware failure, you might not be able to decrypt the disk—unless you have another recovery key stored elsewhere. If you move an encrypted drive to a new computer, install a new motherboard (with a new TPM), disable the TPM, or make changes to the boot configuration settings or the BIOS/EUFI; the TPM may see this as a failure of the integrity check and your drive will not be decrypted.

If the computer does not have a TPM, or even if it does, another place that you can store the decryption key for FVE is on an external removable drive such as a USB flash drive. Other alternatives that may be implemented by some FVE programs include storing the key on a smart card (which, of course, requires

---

[12] Windows BitLocker Drive Encryption Frequently Asked Questions http://technet.microsoft.com/en-us/library/cc766200(v=ws.10).aspx#BKMK_OS.

a smart card reader), a biometric authentication mechanism (which requires a fingerprint scanner or other bio reader device), or retrieving the key over the network during the Preboot Execution Environment (PXE) process.

BitLocker allows you to use a TPM and/or an external USB device. You can set a PIN on the TPM so that, in combination with the USB flash drive, you have multifactor authentication. Note that although you can use BitLocker without a TPM, you will not get the added security of verification of system integrity prior to startup. If the integrity check fails, BitLocker is placed in recovery mode, where you can use a recovery key to decrypt the volume.

Deploying BitLocker

If you want to use BitLocker in the most secure way, you need a computer that has a TPM version 1.2 or 2.0. The computer's BIOS or UEFI must be compliant with the Trusted Computing Group Static Root of Trust Measurement.[13] The BIOS or UEFI also has to support USB mass storage and be able to read the files on the USB flash drive prior to the booting of the operating system.

Prior to deploying BitLocker on a computer that has a TPM, you need to initialize the TPM. This creates a TPM owner password. When deploying BitLocker on a computer without a TPM, you must authenticate with a startup key stored on a USB flash drive. You also need to create a recovery password and recovery key, which can be used to access the encrypted data in the event of a recovery situation. The password can take the form of a numerical set of digits that you type in, or as a key stored on a USB flash drive that you simply insert during the recovery process. The recovery information can also be stored in Active Directory.

Prior to deploying BitLocker, you also need to ensure that the boot device order is set in the BIOS or UEFI to boot from the hard disk first. Note that Windows 8 adds the ability to use a hardware-encrypted drive as the boot drive. To do this, the drive must be uninitialized, and in the security inactive state, the CSM must be disabled if there is one, and the system must boot with UEFI version 2.3.1 or above.

NOTE

Hardware-encrypted drives are also called Self-Encrypting Drives (SEDs) and are available from many vendors, including Samsung, Seagate, Hitachi, Western Digital, and others. These drives use a component called a hardware encryptor and a user password is entered to unlock the disk when it powers up.[14]

---

[13] Trusted Computing Group Web site http://www.trustedcomputinggroup.org/.
[14] Self-Encrypted Drives Set to Become Standard Fare http://www.pcworld.com/article/215681/self_encrypted_hard_drives_to_become_standard_fare.html.

Although Windows 8 extends BitLocker encryption to more drive types than ever, not all drives can be encrypted with BitLocker. Local drives connected via USB, IEEE 1394/Firewire, IDE, ATA, SATA, eSATA, SAS, and SCSI are supported, and Windows 8/Windows Server 2012 add support for iSCSI and Fiber Channel.

The system partition, described above, cannot be encrypted, and by default, it is hidden when you display the contents of the Computer node in Windows Explorer. You also will not be able to encrypt a drive that is too small. You cannot use BitLocker to encrypt drive over the network or the contents of optical drives. If BitLocker is not supported for a drive, the **Turn BitLocker on** option will not appear in its right-click context menu.

BitLocker is supported for hardware-based RAID systems, but not software-based RAID disks or dynamic volumes. You also cannot use BitLocker drives formatted in any file system other than NTFS, FAT32, FAT16, or exFAT, and you cannot use BitLocker to encrypt virtual hard disks (VHDs), although you can store VHDs on a BitLocker-protected drive. You should not try to run BitLocker within a virtual machine (VM).

The BitLocker Setup Wizard

Once you have the properly formatted and sized volumes, it is very easy to deploy BitLocker on a Windows 8 computer. The encryption process itself occurs in the background, so you can still use the computer's applications while BitLocker is performing encryption. The time required to complete the encryption process depends on the size of the drive.

One of the new BitLocker features in Windows 8 and Windows Server 2012 is the ability to designate that BitLocker encrypts only the used space rather than the entire drive as it did in previous versions. This speeds up the encryption process. Then as you fill up more of the drive, BitLocker will automatically encrypt the added data at that time.

If your computer should be turned off or lose power while BitLocker is encrypting, it will automatically resume encrypting when Windows restarts.

To set up BitLocker on a data drive, you start from Control Panel. In category view, click **System and Security** and then **BitLocker Drive Encryption,** as shown in Figure 9.4.

Here, you will see a list of the drives that are BitLocker capable, and you can turn BitLocker on by clicking the down arrow at the far right and selecting **Turn on BitLocker**, as shown in Figure 9.5.

The BitLocker setup wizard begins by asking you to choose how you want to unlock the drive (password or smart card). Next, you select a method for backing up the recovery key: by saving to a USB flash drive, saving to a file or printing the key.

FIGURE 9.4 Use Control Panel to set up BitLocker on a data driver. (For color version of this figure, the reader is referred to the online version of this chapter.)

FIGURE 9.5 Turn BitLocker on via the graphical interface. (For color version of this figure, the reader is referred to the online version of this chapter.)

The next page, shown in Figure 9.6, is new to Windows 8/Windows Server 2012 BitLocker, where you choose how much of your drive you want to encrypt.

Note that if data has been previously deleted from the drive, it may still contain some or all of those deleted files (data is not erased when deleted; only the file markers are removed and it is still there and can be recovered with forensics tools until it is written over). If you choose to only encrypt the used space, that

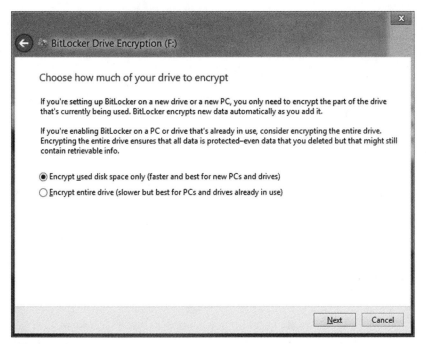

FIGURE 9.6 Choose how much of the drive to encrypt. (For color version of this figure, the reader is referred to the online version of this chapter.)

recoverable data will not be encrypted. Thus, if there is potentially sensitive deleted data on the drive, you should choose to encrypt the entire drive.

The next step is to start encrypting. This status will show in the BitLocker Control Panel until the process is finished. You will also now see BitLocker management options for the drive, as shown in Figure 9.7.

Most of these options are self-explanatory. You can back up the recovery key, change or remove the password, add a smart card, or turn off BitLocker on this drive. The only option that you might not understand is **Turn on autounlock.** This option applies only to data drives. If this option is selected, the drive will automatically unlock when you log onto Windows, so you do not have to manually unlock the drive when you want to use it. This option can only be used if the operating system drive is also encrypted with BitLocker.

Deploying BitLocker on the Operating System Drive

To protect the operating system drive, ensure that you have the two partitions described above and run the BitLocker setup wizard. On a computer with a TPM, you will be given four options for unlocking the OS drive:

- **TPM-only.** The user is not required to do anything. The TPM is validated and the user logs on normally.

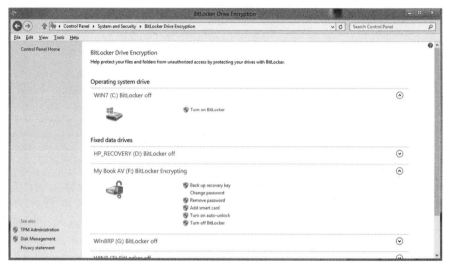

FIGURE 9.7 You can select from BitLocker management options. (For color version of this figure, the reader is referred to the online version of this chapter.)

- **TPM with startup key.** The USB flash drive that contains the encryption key must be inserted in the computer before the user can access the drive and log on.
- **TPM with PIN.** The user must enter a personal identification number (PIN) to access the drive and log on.

There is a fourth option, **TPM with startup key and PIN**, that cannot be configured through the wizard but can be set up using the Manage-bde utility (see the next section). When implemented, the USB flash drive must be inserted and the user must enter a PIN in order to access the drive and log on.

If the computer does not have a TPM, the only unlock option you have is **Startup key only.** The user must insert the USB flash drive in order to access the drive and log on.

NOTE

When a TPM is used with a startup key, only part of the encryption information is stored on the USB drive; the rest is stored in the TPM. When a startup key only is used, all of the encryption information is stored on the USB flash drive.

Configuring TPM with Startup Key and PIN

The Manage-bde utility allows you to manage BitLocker from the command line. Before you use it to configure BitLocker operating system drive protection with the highest level of security (TPM with startup key and PIN), you will need to edit Group Policy to require additional authentication. Here is how it can be done:

1. Log on with an administrative account.
2. In the Run box, type **gpedit.msc** to open the Group Policy Editor. Hold SHIFT+CTRL when you press ENTER, to run the console as an administrator.
3. Navigate to:
   Computer Configuration | Administrative Templates | Windows Components | BitLocker Drive Encryption | Operating System Drives.
4. In the right pane, double-click **Require additional authentication at startup,** as shown in Figure 9.8.
5. Click **Enabled.**
6. Make sure the box that says **Allow BitLocker without a compatible TPM** is unchecked, as shown in Figure 9.9.
7. Under the settings for computers with a TPM to:
   Set the first three settings to **Do not allow**
   Set the last setting to **Require startup key and PIN with TPM**

Next, you need to set up the TPM. Do this through the BitLocker Control Panel app. At the bottom left, click **TPM Administration.** Initialize the TPM, following the instructions in the utility. A restart may be required. After the restart, you will be prompted to back up the TPM owner key.

Next, use Manage-bde to add a recovery key:

1. Open an administrative command window.
2. Insert a USB flash drive and notice its drive letter.
3. Type the following at the command prompt:
   manage-bde -protectors -add C: -RecoveryKey <USB flash drive letter>:

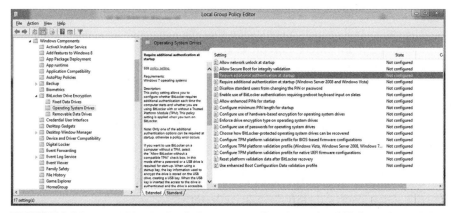

FIGURE 9.8 Require additional authentication at startup. (For color version of this figure, the reader is referred to the online version of this chapter.)

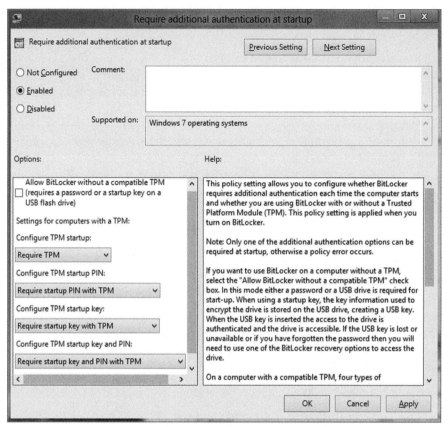

FIGURE 9.9 Uncheck the box that says **Allow BitLocker without a compatible TPM**. (For color version of this figure, the reader is referred to the online version of this chapter.)

4. The utility will return confirmation that the key protectors were added and saved to the directory represented by your USB flash drive letter, along with the external key's ID and file name.
5. Keep the USB flash drive in a safe place. This recovery key can be used to start the computer without the TPM and PIN.

Next, create the startup key (this is a second USB flash drive):

1. Insert the second USB flash drive and notice its drive letter.
2. At the administrative command prompt, type the following:
   manage-bde -protectors -add C: -TPMandPINandStartupKey -tp <your PIN> -tsk <second USB flash drive letter>:
3. The utility will return the same confirmation information as noted above.
4. Leave the second USB flash drive in the computer for now.

```
Volume C: []
[OS Volume]
ACTIONS REQUIRED:

    1. Insert a USB flash drive with an external key file into the computer.

    2. Restart the computer to run a hardware test.
    (Type "shutdown /?" for command line instructions.)

    3. Type "manage-bde -status" to check if the hardware test succeeded.

NOTE: Encryption will begin after the hardware test succeeds.
```

FIGURE 9.10 Use the Manage-bde utility to encrypt the drive.

Next, use Manage-bde to encrypt the drive by typing the following at the administrative command prompt: **manage-bde -on <drive letter of operating system drive to be encrypted>:**

The utility will return information similar to what is shown below in Figure 9.10.

After you restart and log on, and the drive passes the hardware test, the encryption will begin.[15]

Using Group Policy to Configure BitLocker Options

Windows 8/Windows Server 2012 provide additional Group Policy settings for controlling the behavior of BitLocker.

Policies you can enable for operating system drives include the following:

- **Allow network unlock at startup.** This policy allows clients configured with a BitLocker Network Unlock certificate to create and use network key protectors to unlock the computer. This is a feature new to Windows 8 and Windows Server 2012. Information to unlock the computer is exchanged with the server. You need to enable a Group Policy setting on the domain controller to distribute the certificate. This works only with client computers that have a TPM because network unlock uses two protectors: the TPM protector and the one provided by the network (or your PIN, if joined to a network without a key protector or when not connected to the network).[16]
- **Allow Secure Boot for integrity validation.** This setting determines whether BitLocker will use Secure Boot to validate platform integrity. Disabling the policy forces BitLocker to use a legacy validation method even on Secure Boot-capable computers.
- **Require additional authentication at startup.** This is used to specify what authentication options are allowed, not allowed, or required, as discussed above.

---

[15] How to configure BitLocker with TPM, PIN, and USB Startup Key https://mrhorn.com/wp/posts/bitlocker-with-tpm-pin-usb-startupkey/.

[16] BitLocker: How to enable Network Unlock http://technet.microsoft.com/en-us/library/jj574173.aspx.

- **Require additional authentication at startup (Windows Server 2008 and Windows Vista).** This policy is applicable only to computers running Windows Server 2008 or Vista and so is not relevant here.
- **Disallow standard users from changing PIN or password.** When Enabled, this policy prevents standard users from changing the BitLocker volume PINs if they first provide the existing PIN.
- **Enable use of BitLocker authentication requiring preboot keyboard input on slates.** This policy allows users to use authentication options requiring input before booting, on devices such as slates that do not have a hardware keyboard. This should only be enabled on devices that allow alternatives to the on-screen keyboard, such as attaching a USB keyboard.
- **Allow enhanced PINs for startup.** By default, all new startup PINs will be "enhanced"—that is, PINs permit use of upper/lowercase characters, symbols, numbers, and spaces. If you disable the policy, enhanced PINs will not be used. PINs will be numeric characters. Some devices do not support enhanced PINs in a preboot environment.
- **Configure minimum PIN length for startup.** This policy lets you set a minimum PIN length for the TPM startup PIN. The default is four characters. You can set it to four or more characters, up to 20.
- **Configure use of hardware-based encryption for operating system drives.** This policy lets you define whether to use BitLocker software-based encryption when hardware-based encryption is not available. You can also restrict the encryption algorithms and cipher suites for hardware-based encryption to the ones you specify. If you disable the policy, software-based encryption will be used by default.
- **Enforce drive encryption type on operating system drives.** This policy lets you select the encryption type to be used by BitLocker. You can allow the user to choose, specify full encryption only, or specify used space encryption only.
- **Configure use of passwords for operating system drives.** This policy lets you specify password complexity requirements for operating system drives. You can allow, disallow, or require complex passwords, and you can set a minimum password length (default is eight characters).
- **Choose how BitLocker-protected operating system drives can be recovered.** This policy lets you select whether to allow a data recovery agent and configure user storage of BitLocker recovery information. You can omit the recovery options from the BitLocker setup wizard and select to save BitLocker recovery information to Active Directory Services for operating system drives. You can also configure storage of recovery information to AD DS (store recovery passwords and key packages, or store passwords only).
- **Configure TPM platform validation profile for BIOS-based firmware configurations.** With this policy, you can configure how the TPM secures

the BitLocker encryption key when the computer has a legacy BIOS or UEFI with CSM enabled.

- **Configure TPM platform validation profile (Windows Vista, Windows Server 2008, Windows 7, Windows Server 2008 R2).** This policy is used to configure how the TPM secures the encryption key on the operating system platforms named.
- **Configure TPM platform validation profile for native UEFI firmware configurations.** This policy is used to configure how the TPM secures the encryption key on computers with a native UEFI firmware without CSM enabled.
- **Reset platform validation data after BitLocker recovery.** This policy lets you control whether to refresh the platform validation information when Windows starts following BitLocker recovery.
- **Use enhanced Boot Configuration Data validation profile.** With this policy, you can select to verify specified BCD settings during platform validation.

Policies you can enable for fixed data drives, which are mostly self-explanatory, include the following:

- Configure use of smart cards on fixed data drives.
- Deny write access to fixed drives not protected by BitLocker.
- Configure use of hardware-based encryption for fixed data drives.
- Enforce drive encryption type for fixed data drives.
- Allow access to BitLocker-protected fixed data drives from earlier versions of Windows.
- Configure use of passwords for fixed data drives.
- Choose how BitLocker-protected fixed data drives can be recovered.

Policies you can enable for removable data drives include the following:

- Control use of BitLocker on removable drives (allow or disallow users to use BitLocker on removable drives or to suspend and decrypt BitLocker-encrypted drives).
- Configure use of smart cards on removable data drives.
- Deny write access to removable drives not protected by BitLocker.
- Configure use of hardware-based encryption for removable data drives.
- Enforce drive encryption type on removable data drives.
- Allow access to BitLocker-protected removable data drives from earlier versions of Windows.
- Configure use of passwords for removable data drives.

Automating BitLocker Deployment in the Enterprise

In the enterprise, you can automate BitLocker deployment using scripts. You can use WMI or Windows PowerShell, and you can script BitLocker operations with Manage-bde. The Manage-bde utility can be used with both operating system and data volumes. Note that the on command encrypts the operating system volume with a TPM-only protector and no recovery key. On a computer that does not have a TPM, you cannot encrypt the drive without protectors. You can add protectors using this command: **manage-bde -protectors -add C: pw-sid <user or group >**. You will be required to enter and confirm the password protector.

The following parameters are available in Manage-bde:

Table 9.2 Manage-bde Parameters

■	**status**	Provides information about BitLocker-capable volumes
■	**-on**	Encrypts the volume and turns BitLocker protection on
■	**-off**	Decrypts the volume and turns BitLocker protection off
■	**-pause**	Pauses encryption, decryption, or free space wipe
■	**-resume**	Resumes encryption, decryption, or free space wipe
■	**-lock**	Prevents access to BitLocker-encrypted data
■	**-unlock**	Allows access to BitLocker-encrypted data
■	**-autounlock**	Manages automatic unlocking of data volumes
■	**-protectors**	Manages protection methods for the encryption key
■	**-SetIdentifier or -si**	Configures the identification field for a volume
■	**-ForceRecovery or -fr**	Forces a BitLocker-protected OS to recover on restarts
■	**-changepassword**	Modifies password for a data volume
■	**-changepin**	Modifies PIN for a volume
■	**-changekey**	Modifies startup key for a volume
■	**-KeyPackage or -kp**	Generates a key package for a volume
■	**-upgrade**	Upgrades the BitLocker version
■	**-WipeFreeSpace or -w**	Wipes the free space on the volume
■	**-ComputerName or -cn**	Runs on another computer. Examples: "ComputerX", "127.0.0.1"
■	**-? or /?**	Displays brief help. Example: "-ParameterSet -?"
■	**-Help or -h**	Displays complete help. Example: "-ParameterSet -h"

PowerShell cmdlets can be used in a similar manner to Manage-bde, to add configuration options beyond what is available in the Control Panel GUI. The PowerShell cmdlets available for BitLocker are shown in Table 9.3.[17]

Provisioning BitLocker Prior to Operating System Installation
Another new feature in Windows 8 and Windows Server 2012 is the ability to provision BitLocker prior to the installation of the operating system. You can enable BitLocker from the Windows Pre-installation Environment (WinPE). You will need WinPE version 4 installed.

[17] BitLocker: Use BitLocker Drive Encryption Tools to Manage BitLocker http://technet.microsoft.com/en-us/library/jj647767.aspx. http://technet.microsoft.com/library/cc732148(WS.10).aspx.

Table 9.3 BitLocker-Related PowerShell Cmdlets

Name	Parameters
Add-BitLockerKeyProtector	- ADAccountOrGroup - ADAccountOrGroupProtector - Confirm - MountPoint - Password - PasswordProtector - Pin - RecoveryKeyPath - RecoveryKeyProtector - RecoveryPassword - RecoveryPasswordProtector - Service - StartupKeyPath - StartupKeyProtector - TpmAndPinAndStartupKeyProtector - TpmAndPinProtector - TpmAndStartupKeyProtector - TpmProtector - WhatIf
Backup-BitLockerKeyProtector	- Confirm - KeyProtectorId - MountPoint - WhatIf
Disable-BitLocker	- Confirm - MountPoint - WhatIf
Disable-BitLockerAutoUnlock	- Confirm - MountPoint - WhatIf
Enable-BitLocker	- AdAccountOrGroup - AdAccountOrGroupProtector - Confirm - EncryptionMethod - HardwareEncryption - Password - PasswordProtector - Pin - RecoveryKeyPath - RecoveryKeyProtector - RecoveryPassword - RecoveryPasswordProtector - Service - SkipHardwareTest - StartupKeyPath - StartupKeyProtector - TpmAndPinAndStartupKeyProtector - TpmAndPinProtector - TpmAndStartupKeyProtector - TpmProtector - UsedSpaceOnly - WhatIf

Continued

Table 9.3 BitLocker-Related PowerShell Cmdlets—Continued

Name	Parameters
Enable-BitLockerAutoUnlock	- Confirm - MountPoint - WhatIf
Get-BitLockerVolume	- MountPoint
Lock-BitLocker	- Confirm - ForceDismount - MountPoint - WhatIf
Remove-BitLockerKeyProtector	- Confirm - KeyProtectorId - MountPoint - WhatIf
Resume-BitLocker	- Confirm - MountPoint - WhatIf
Suspend-BitLocker	- Confirm - MountPoint - RebootCount - WhatIf
Unlock-BitLocker	- AdAccountOrGroup - Confirm - MountPoint - Password - RecoveryKeyPath - RecoveryPassword - RecoveryPassword - WhatIf

To install BitLocker using PowerShell, use the servermanager module and the Install-WindowsFeature cmdlet. To install BitLocker with available management tools and subfeatures, use the following command: **Install-WindowsFeature BitLocker -IncludeAllSubFeature -IncludeManagementTools**.

This installs the administration tools for BitLocker and the AD DS Tools.

You can use System Configuration Manager 2012 with Service Pack 1 installed to automate the process of pre-provisioning BitLocker. You will create a new deploy task sequence on the Configuration Manager server where you select a Windows 8 boot image and select **Configure task sequence for use with BitLocker.** You will need to edit the task sequence to enable the TPM in WinPE and set it up to store the recovery key in Active Directory Domain Services.[18]

---

[18] How Can I Pre-Provision BitLocker in WinPE for Windows 8 Deployments using Configuration Manager 2012 SP1 http://www.windows-noob.com/forums/index.php?/topic/6451-how-can-i-pre-provision-bitlocker-in-winpe-for-windows-8-deployments-using-configuration-manager-2012-sp1/?

Troubleshooting, Recovery, and Repair

BitLocker will go into recovery mode if the computer attempts to start the operating system and cannot access the BitLocker-protected drive. This can happen when you change the boot order, make changes to the NTFS partition, enter the PIN incorrectly, add or remove some hardware components, make changes to the boot manager or MBR, or if the TPM is damaged, turned off, fails, or is hidden from the operating system. You will also see recovery mode at startup under other circumstances. In this case, you will need the recovery key or recovery password to unlock the encrypted drive.

The BitLocker Repair tool, repair-bde, is useful when part of a BitLocker-encrypted disk becomes corrupted (for example, by an ungraceful shutdown of Windows or a disk hardware failure). You can use this command line utility to access encrypted data on the damaged drive and reconstruct parts of the drive. You will need a valid recovery key or recovery password (the key package may be backed up in AD DS if you used the default setting). Repair-bde can be used when you are unable to start the BitLocker recovery console.

SUMMARY

Mobile computer users are at special risk due to the portability of their devices. The Windows 8 client operating system, in conjunction with Windows Server 2012, provides new security features and functionality to help counter those risks so users can enjoy the benefits of connected-anywhere mobile devices for getting work done on the go, without exposing the devices and the corporate network to security breaches.

Secure Boot is enabled by default on Windows 8 systems and helps to protect those systems from malicious code that can emulate the boot loader and hide from traditional malware detection software. BitLocker drive encryption can protect lost or stolen portable computers from parallel installation attacks and keep both the operating system files and the data secure and inaccessible to an unauthorized person who gains physical access to the system in a pre-boot state. Together, these technologies help to make mobile devices running Windows 8 among the most secure portable systems available for business use.

CHAPTER 10

Mitigating Application's Vulnerabilities

CONTENTS

CHAPTER POINTS

- Living in the world of Apps
- Browser Protection
- The old friends are still here: UAC and AppLocker
- Extra Tools

LIVING IN THE WORLD OF APPS

The natural trend of apps all around tablets, smartphones, game consoles, and social networks is now a reality on PCs and that is thanks to Windows 8. The growing number of apps available in different stores and marketplaces also brings challenges around security. There are many cybercriminals taking advantage of this way of commercializing applications to spread malware to consumers. What starts on the consumer's device can easily proliferate to an enterprise environment with this new paradigm of BYOD (Bring your Own Device) and the embracement of this paradigm by big corporations. For this reason, it is important to be diligent when dealing with application development and management in the enterprise. Developers must be using the Microsoft Security Development Lifecycle[1] principles to enhance the overall protection of the application by thinking about security from the conception of the project and through its maintenance.

Despite all the efforts to make Windows 8 the most secure OS that Microsoft ever released, there are still concerns regarding the App platform. Some specialists are comparing the Windows App Security to Android Apps security.[2] As a Security Professional, your role is to evangelize to the developers on how to make their apps more secure and evangelize to the users on how to securely interact with third party apps that were downloaded from the marketplace. Windows 8 comes with built-in features that will assist the end user in identifying a rogue application as we explained in Chapter 8 when discussing the Windows SmartProtection.

For a developer or an IT PRO, it is very important to understand the most common attack surfaces in Windows system. This is the only way you can understand the communication channels that you need to protect. The main ones are

- RPC endpoints
- Network endpoints
- ActiveX parsers
- DCOM objects
- LPC endpoints
- Protocol Handlers
- Registry Keys
- Kernel Entry Points

Understanding the attack surface is the first step to enhance your operating system and application security.

Windows App Store Security

Developers that focus on building Windows Store apps should also understand the platform security capabilities in order to better leverage its resources while developing their application. For example, Windows Store apps[3] cannot

---

[1] More information about SDL visit www.microsoft.com/sdl.

[2] Read more about this here http://blogs.mcafee.com/mcafee-labs/stronger-windows-8-still-vulnerable-through-apps-users.

[3] For more information on how to developer Windows Store Apps, read http://msdn.microsoft.com/en-us/library/windows/apps/br211386.aspx.

use interprocess communication (IPC) calls to communicate with any process outside the AppContainer (we will talk about AppContainer in more detail later in this chapter). IPC is only allowed between processes that are part of the same AppContainer.

The same isolation is also true for Windows Store app data storage, which is something very important to prevent data leakage. The access to the data storage is restricted by default and it is only allowed if the user explicitly grants access to it. By default, the Windows Store apps have access only to local settings and storage in the following locations (under *Windows::Storage::Appl icationData::Current*):

- LocalSettings
- LocalFolder
- TemporaryFolder
- RoamingSettings
- RoamingFolder

Isolation is also present from a network standpoint by not allowing access to the network unless it is explicitly granted. The access levels are shown in Table 10.1:

Table 10.1 Security Levels

Level	Description	Applicability
Internet (Client)	Allows outbound access to Internet and public networks through firewalls	Usually the preferred method for most or all apps
Internet (Client & Server)	Allows outbound and inbound access to Internet and public networks through firewalls	Usually used by peer-to-peer (P2P) apps
Private Networks (Client & Server)	Allows outbound and inbound access to home and work networks through firewalls	Usually used by games that need communication within the LAN

Last but not least, it is also important to protect other peripherals that might be attached to the system, such as webcams, GPSs, and other devices. Windows App device isolation happens by blocking all devices, passive sensors, and 3 G/4 G/Dial connections by default. The user must be prompted in case an app requires access to those devices.

TIP

For more information about Windows 8 app development, watch this session from BUILD conference http://channel9.msdn.com/Events/BUILD/BUILD2011/TOOL-930C

BROWSER PROTECTION

The other important element to consider is the fact that most apps are going to use either the browser itself or components from the Browser to operate. Which means that by having security controls embedded into the Browser can assist the overall protection of the system. Microsoft Internet Explorer has achieved an excellent reputation in the market; while we were writing this chapter, Internet Explorer 9 received recognition from NSS Labs[4] to be the most effective browser in the market to combat fraud and malicious downloads. There are a series of security enhancements that were added to Internet Explorer 10 as well as new security features that will continue to drive this trend moving forward. While IE10 (we will be calling it this from now on) inherits all functionalities from IE9, it adds the following:

- AppContainer: architecture change in Windows 8 that allows applications to run at low integrity level, which basically means that it prevents read/write access to System.
- Enhanced Protected Mode (EPM): extends the traditional Protected Mode by adding restriction capabilities to prevent some Internet Explorer functions to be exploited.
- Extensibility: IE 10 has a feature called *immersive site experiences* which enhances the overall user experience when using chromeless UI and maximized screen real estate. When it is running on this mode it will disable all third party applications (ActiveX control is an example).
- HTML5 Sandbox: it allows app developers to create applications with reduced privileges. It enables security restrictions for inline frame (iframe) elements that might contain untrusted content.
- Address Space Layout Randomization (ASLR) Improvements: by using the new ForceASLR loader option for developers. This option instructs the Windows operating system to randomize the location of all modules that are currently loaded by the browser.[5]
- SmartScreen Enhancements: enhancement of the data collection capability.

A Sandbox Called AppContainer

This new sandbox allows developers to have more security control and granularity to protect their applications. All Modern UI applications will be running by default in an AppContainer,[6] which means that goes beyond IE10 and

---

[4] See an article about this here http://www.eweek.com/security/internet-explorer-shines-in-nss-labs-browser-security-test/.

[5] For more information about memory protection in IE10, see http://blogs.msdn.com/b/ie/archive/2012/03/12/enhanced-memory-protections-in-ie10.aspx.

[6] For more information about AppContainer in Windows Apps, visit http://msdn.microsoft.com/en-us/library/windows/apps/hh464936.aspx.

extends to the desktop. What IE10 does is to use this capability by leveraging it in some scenarios to provide a better protection to the end user.

When a user opens a new tab in IE10 and this tab is configured to run in Enhanced Protected Mode (Internet and Restricted Zone are by default), it will automatically run inside an AppContainer sandbox (64 bit only). The IE10 tabs on Windows 8 desktop will not behave like that by default, but it will also be protected by running in low integrity protected mode (32 bit). You can change this behavior by enabling the Enhanced Protected Mode (EPM) using the option shown in Figure 10.1 (available in Internet Options).

When this option is enabled, the Windows 8 desktop's Internet Explorer tabs will run in an AppContainer 64-bit mode (if the system is running on a 64 bit processor).

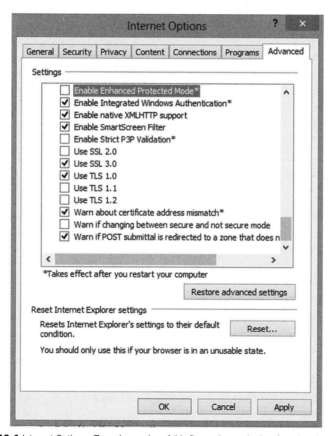

FIGURE 10.1 Internet Options. (For color version of this figure, the reader is referred to the online version of this chapter.)

IMPORTANT

During the Beta timeframe, a blog called "Delivering reliable and trustworthy Metro style apps" explained the security elements around application confidence. We recommend you to read this chapter to understand the details about the overall solution. Read more at http://blogs.msdn.com/b/b8/archive/2012/05/17/delivering-reliable-and-trustworthy-metro-style-apps.aspx.

Some network restrictions are introduced by AppContainer when used in conjunction with Enhanced Protection Mode. The restrictions are

- An EPM process does not accept inbound connection attempts from the network. Although this is already blocked by the web platform, there are some third party add-ons that offer this capability. When EPM is enabled, those add-ons will not be able to make remote access connections.
- Applications that are running inside of an AppContainer cannot make connections to local running processes that are outside their own package. There is a tool that allows you to create exemptions for this behavior.[7]
- "This page cannot be displayed" problem when accessing Internet pages that refer to objects coming from Intranet pages. This happens because intranet resources are protected from cross-zone attacks, also known as Cross-Site-Request-Forgery (CSRF) and Intranet Port Scanning. The workaround for that is to add the intranet site into the security trusted list as shown in Figure 10.2.

AppContainers also provide isolation of cookies and cache information, which means that apps running within this container will not have read/write access outside of it as shown in Figure 10.3.

By using this, isolation applications will be more secure and provide a better privacy for the end user. This is very important when dealing with applications that need this level of security, such as online banking, health information, and other apps that deal with private data.[8]

SmartScreen

SmartScreen feature will assist the end user to have a more secure browsing experience by detecting phishing websites and blocking access to it.[9] When trying to access a piece of content that was categorized by SmartScreen as malicious, the warning showed in Figure 10.4 appears:

---

[7] You can download the EnableLoopback Utility Tool to create exemptions for that. More info on this at http://blogs.msdn.com/b/fiddler/archive/2011/12/10/fiddler-windows-8-apps-enable-loopback-network-isolation-exemption.aspx.

[8] Previous versions of Internet Explorer could in some instances allow applications to access information from others as exemplified in the this post http://blogs.msdn.com/b/ieinternals/archive/2011/03/10/internet-explorer-beware-cookie-sharing-in-cross-zone-scenarios.aspx.

[9] For more information on how SmartScreen works, see http://windows.microsoft.com/en-US/windows-vista/SmartScreen-Filter-Information-for-administrators-and-website-owners.

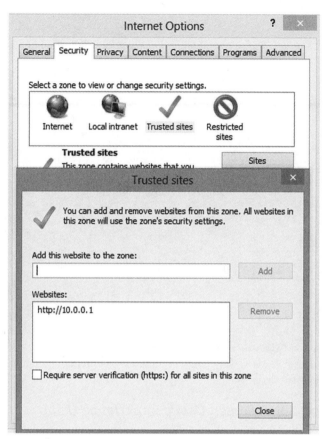

FIGURE 10.2 Trusted Sites. (For color version of this figure, the reader is referred to the online version of this chapter.)

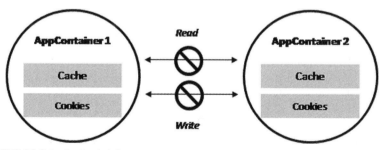

FIGURE 10.3 Application isolation.

TIP

To test the functionality of SmartScreen Application Reputation use this site http://ie.microsoft.com/testdrive/Browser/DownloadReputation/Default.html?o=1.

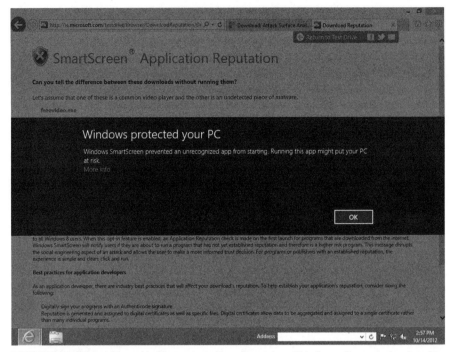

FIGURE 10.4 SmartScreen blocking content. (For color version of this figure, the reader is referred to the online version of this chapter.)

Controlling SmartScreen User's Experience Using Group Policy

In a corporate environment, administrators might want to enforce company's policy by ensuring that users are not able to make changes to Smartscreen configuration. For that they can leverage some group policies that are available for this feature. In order to exemplify this situation, let us use the scenario below.

SCENARIO

Deb is the Security Analyst of EndtoEdge.com, and she is reviewing the new corporate security policy strategy for 2013. There are plans to upgrade all workstations to Windows 8 and ensure that the following requirements are met:

- Users cannot manage how the filtering platform operates.
- Users cannot bypass the filtering platform in any scenario.
- All settings must be applied regardless of the user; they should be tight with all computers from the Financial department.

In order to implement those requirements, follow the steps below on your Domain Controller:

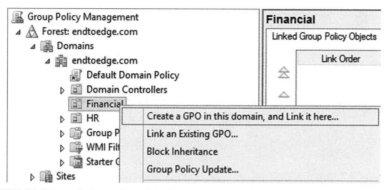

FIGURE 10.5 Group Policy configuration. (For color version of this figure, the reader is referred to the online version of this chapter.)

1. In the Server Manager, click **Tools** and then click **Group Policy Management**.
2. Expand Domains, expand your domain (in this case endtoedge.com) and right click in the Financial OU.
3. Click **Create** a GPO in this domain, and Link it here as shown in Figure 10.5.
4. In the New GPO dialog box, type SmartScreen Policy Financial Department and click **OK**.
5. On the left pane, under Financial OU, click **SmartScreen Policy Financial Department**, click **OK** on the dialog box, right click on this policy, and choose Edit.
6. Expand the following path: Computer Configuration/Policies/ Administrative Templates/Windows Components/Internet Explorer.
7. To comply with the first requirement, double click Prevent managing SmartScreen Filter policy on the right pane and the Prevent managing SmartScreen Filter window appears. Configure this setting as shown in Figure 10.6.
8. Once you finish configuring this option, click **OK**.
9. To comply with the second requirement, two policies must be configured. To configure the first one, double click Prevent bypassing SmartScreen Filter warning and Enabled it as shown in Figure 10.7.
10. Once you finish click **OK**, double click Prevent bypassing SmartScreen Filter warnings about files that are not commonly downloaded from the Internet policy and then Enabled it as shown in Figure 10.8.
11. Once you finish, click **OK**.
12. Close Group Policy Management Editor and close Group Policy Management.

From the user perspective, there is one more policy that can be applied to control whether SmartScreen Filter scans pages in the zones below for malicious content:

- Internet
- Trusted Sites

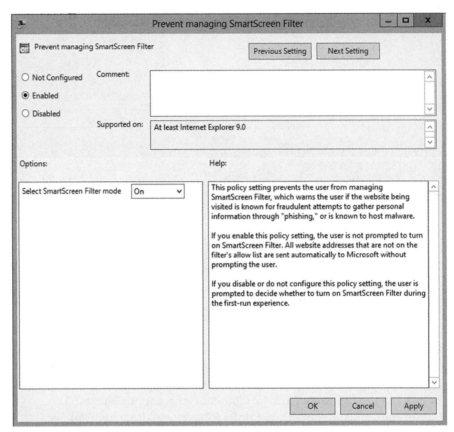

FIGURE 10.6 Group Policy settings. (For color version of this figure, the reader is referred to the online version of this chapter.)

- Locked-Down Internet
- Local Machine
- Restricted sites

The policy is called **Turn on SmartScreen Filter** scan, and it is located at **User Configuration\Policies\Administrative Templates\Windows Components\ Internet Explorer\Internet Control Panel\Security Page**.

THE OLD FRIENDS ARE STILL HERE: UAC AND APPLOCKER

When you provide your users too many rights on their computers, you are automatically increasing your risk[10]; this is a well-known side effect of just allowing users do what they want to do on their workstations. Although User Access

---

[10] Read this article for more facts around this http://blogs.technet.com/b/yuridiogenes/ archive/2011/04/14/too-much-rights-means-more-risk-using-standard-users.aspx.

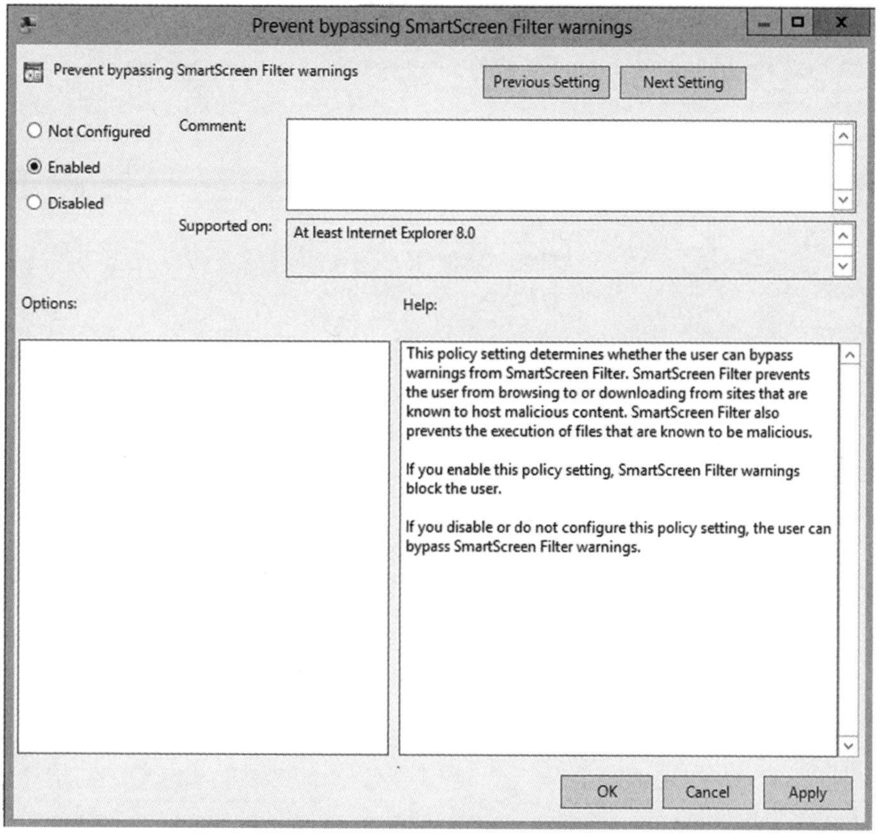

FIGURE 10.7 Enable SmartScreen. (For color version of this figure, the reader is referred to the online version of this chapter.)

Control (UAC) feature introduced in Windows Vista had caused many to hate this approach, with time it was noticeable that such approach reduces the likelihood that the user will perform an operation that might compromise his system. Although Microsoft recommends keeping UAC enabled on the workstation (in this case Windows 8), it has guidelines around disabling UAC on Servers.[11]

In Windows Server 2012 and Windows 8, there are not a lot of changes in UAC; from the control perspective, the major change is in the behavior of the UAC slider shown in Figure 10.9.

The change is specifically to the bottom position's meaning as appears in Figure 10.10. In Windows 7, the bottom position turns UAC all the way off, disabling User Interface Privilege Isolation (UIPI) and Protected Mode Internet Explorer (PMIE) all together (this happens after the restart of the system). In

---

[11] Read this KB (that also applies to Windows Server 2012) for more recommendations on that http://support.microsoft.com/kb/2526083.

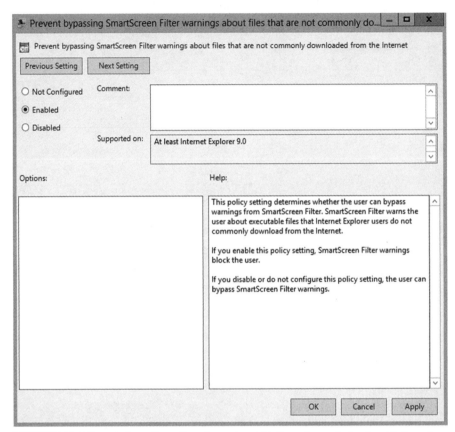

FIGURE 10.8 Group Policy settings. (For color version of this figure, the reader is referred to the online version of this chapter.)

Windows 8, the bottom position completely suppresses UAC prompting by auto-answering the prompts, which means it has an (auto-yes for protected administrators and an auto-no for standard users. This will enable UIPI to continue to run bringing core security to the end user.

Hardening Application Environment

Many IT administrators who are not used to dealing with security incidents might think that the solution to block users from running unauthorized programs that they download from the Internet is to block everything on the edge[12]; unfortunately, it is not that simple. In today's mobile environment, the nature and location of the edge changes from day to day or even hour to hour. Ideally you should always leverage the concept of defense in depth when protecting

---

[12] Read this article for more information about this http://blogs.technet.com/b/yuridiogenes/archive/2011/09/09/blocking-traffic-via-the-edge-device-is-not-the-answer-for-everything-that-you-need-to-block.aspx.

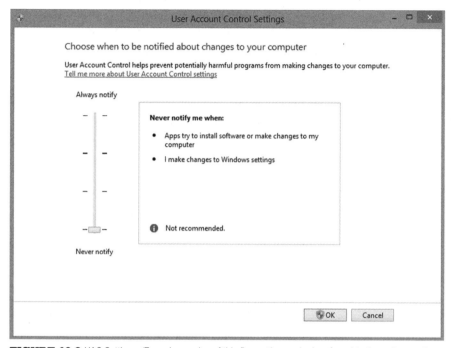

FIGURE 10.9 UAC Settings. (For color version of this figure, the reader is referred to the online version of this chapter.)

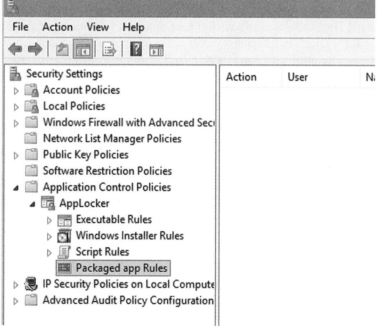

FIGURE 10.10 Packaged app Rules. (For color version of this figure, the reader is referred to the online version of this chapter.)

assets on your environment. From the application perspective is necessary that the operating system have total control on the application's boundaries. With AppLocker, it is possible to enhance the overall operating system protection against rogue applications that are not supposed to be running on the system.

One of the challenges of using AppLocker is the creation and maintenance of an application inventory. This happens because AppLocker works by querying an allow list of applications, which means that administrators will have to create a list of all applications that they want to allow. This is called an inventory. The advantage with Windows 8 is that Modern apps will run within an AppContainer, which already mitigates part of the problem by restricting what they are allowed to do. With this new model, it is expected that administrators only leverage the AppLocker feature for applications that require more customization.

There are not a lot of changes in AppLocker on Windows 8[13]; the core changes are the capability of creating rules for packaged apps and package apps installers as well as the addition of new file formats (mst and appx) with the option shown in Figure 10.10.

On Windows 8 workstations,[14] AppLocker can control installation and execution of all Modern apps. AppLocker has three different kinds of rules to control that

- Path rules: based on the Fully Qualified Path Name (FQPN) of the binary being executed.
- Hash rules: based on the SHA256 hash of the binary.
- Publisher rules: based on the Fully Qualified Binary Name (FQBN) of the binary. The FQBN is composed of four pieces of information (also known as 4-tuple), which are *Publisher Name*, *Product Name*, *File Name*, and *Version*. The publisher name is extracted from the signing certificate of the binary, and the rest of the fields are extracted from the binary itself.

In Windows Server 2012 and Windows 8, AppLocker behaves differently for packaged apps versus traditional desktop applications. For packaged apps, AppLocker rules will be enforced at both runtime and install time. The difference between both is that at run time the rules will be enforced by the kernel and at install time will be enforced by AppX (Modern Apps) installer.

Creating an AppLocker Packaged App Rule
In order to exemplify a typical scenario where AppLocker can be used to control Modern applications, let us use the scenario below:

---

[13] If you are not familiar with AppLocker, we recommend you to watch this demo http://technet.microsoft.com/en-us/windows/dd320283.aspx since this feature has not change too much the steps can be followed using Windows 8.
[14] For more information regarding the Windows 8 and Windows Server 2012 editions that support AppLocker, see this chapter http://technet.microsoft.com/en-us/library/ee424382(WS.10).aspx.

SCENARIO

Deb is the Security Analyst of EndtoEdge.com, and she is reviewing the new corporate security policy for Modern Apps. As EndtoEdge.com is planning to migrate all workstations to Windows 8, they also want to mitigate how Modern Apps operate. These are the requirements that Deb found relevant in this new policy:

- Deny access to all users to use the following Modern Apps that comes out of the box with Windows 8:
  - Windows Store
  - News
  - Sports
  - Weather
  - Games
  - Music
- Even if those applications are updated by the vender, the AppLocker must still block access to it, which means that this rule should be version agnostic.

Follow the steps below to create a new Packaged App Rule to control your Modern Apps using AppLocker:

1. In the Start screen, click **Desktop**.
2. Hold the mouse in the lower-right corner of the screen until the **Charms bar** appears on the right side.
3. In the **Charms bar**, click **Search**.
4. Type **secpol.msc** and click the apps's name in the right as shown in Figure 10.11.
5. On the **Local Security Policy** console, expand **Application Control Policies**, expand **AppLocker**, and click **Packaged app Rules**.
6. Right click **Packaged app Rules** and click **Create New Rule**.
7. In the **Before you Begin** page of the **Create Packaged app Rules** Wizard, click **Next**.
8. In the **Permissions** page, change it to **Deny** and click **Next**.
9. In the **Publisher** page, select **Use an installed packaged app as reference** and click **Select** button.
10. In the **Select applications** dialog, select the application Windows Store as it shows in Figure 10.12 and click **OK**.
11. In the **Create Packaged app Rules** dialog, position the slide one level up (Package name) as it shows in Figure 10.13 and then click **Next**.

IMPORTANT

Notice that the package version shows as *, which means that it will apply to any version of the package name WinStore.

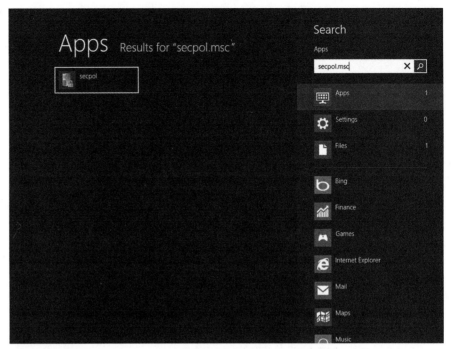

FIGURE 10.11 Searching for apps. (For color version of this figure, the reader is referred to the online version of this chapter.)

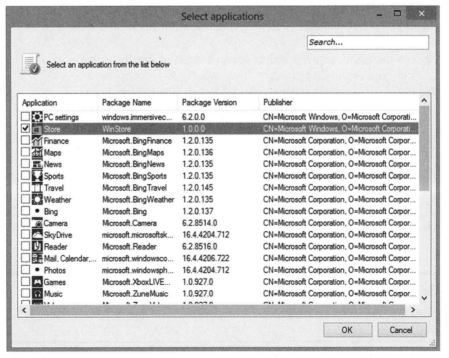

FIGURE 10.12 Selecting Winstore. (For color version of this figure, the reader is referred to the online version of this chapter.)

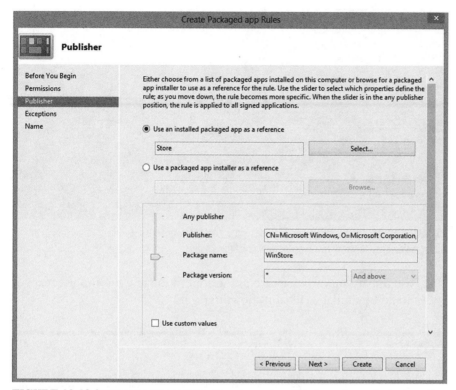

FIGURE 10.13 Create packaged app Rules. (For color version of this figure, the reader is referred to the online version of this chapter.)

FIGURE 10.14 Configuring Deny. (For color version of this figure, the reader is referred to the online version of this chapter.)

12. In the **Exceptions** page, leave the default selections and click **Next**.

13. In the **Name** page, you can add a custom name to this rule or leave it as default. Once you finish it, click **Create** button. Your policy should look like the one shown in Figure 10.14.

NOTE

In order to comply with the scenario's request you must repeat all the steps for each application. Now try out, that's your home works!

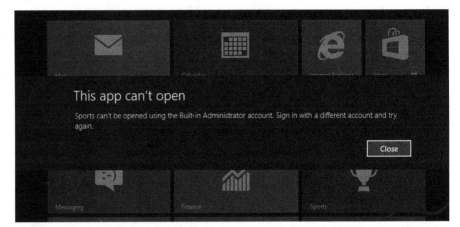

FIGURE 10.15 Application getting blocked by the rules that were created. (For color version of this figure, the reader is referred to the online version of this chapter.)

Once you finish, you can try to access the application and the end user experience should be similar to what it shows in Figure 10.15.

NOTE

You might have to run gpupdate/force to commit the changes.

Ideally you will have a reference computer to perform all the AppLocker hardening and then use this reference[15] to deploy the GPO with the list of applications that AppLocker will monitor.

Software Restriction Policy

In Windows Server 2012, the Software Restriction Policies (SRP) Group Policy-based feature has not changed when compared to its previous version. The ultimate goal of SRP is to identify programs running on workstations that belong to the domain and restrict those programs to run, which increases the reliability, integrity, and manageability of the company's workstations.

NOTE

For more information on how to implement software restriction policy see http://technet.microsoft.com/en-us/library/hh994606.aspx.

---

[15] Use the steps from http://technet.microsoft.com/en-us/library/dd723675(WS.10).aspx in order to create a reference computer.

EXTRA TOOLS

Microsoft offers many tools that can help you to build more secure applications during the development phase and also tools that assist mitigating vulnerabilities for programs that are already installed. As stated earlier in this chapter, the best way to develop applications that can provide the functionality that your customer wants aligned with the security that it is necessary to use the Security Development Lifecycle.

SDL Threat Modeling Tool

The SDL Threat Modeling Tool can help you to identify the attack surface of your application during the development phase. The goal is to use this tool during the design phase of your application and reduce the likelihood of exploitation once the application is ready to ship. Figure 10.16 shows the initial screen of this tool.

TIP

You can download the SDL Threat Modeling Tool from http://www.microsoft.com/en-us/download/details.aspx?id=2955.

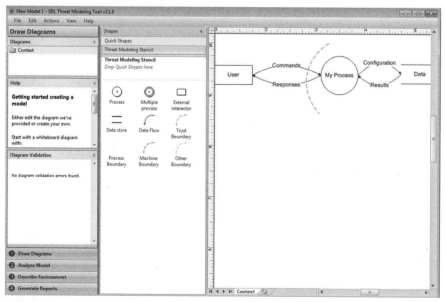

FIGURE 10.16 SDL Threat Modeling Tool. (For color version of this figure, the reader is referred to the online version of this chapter.)

When using this tool, it is very important that you understand the following core elements:

- Data Flow: first step is to know the feature design and understand how data flow across the Operating System.
- Identify Threats: what are the potential threats that you found by reviewing the data flow?
- Mitigate: once you identify the threats, you should mitigate them or accept the risk.
- Validate: after finishing all steps, you must run through an exercise of validation to see if those threats were really mitigated.

On the SDL Treat Modeling Tool, you can identify the attack surface according to the element and define the impact of the threat. Figure 10.17 shows an example of what are the threats (based on the STRIDE[16] concept) for the data flow from the "User" to the "Process" that you are building. The threats are categorized accordingly; for this particular command (from "User" to "Process") is possible to identify three categories: Tampering, Information Disclosure, and Denial of Service.

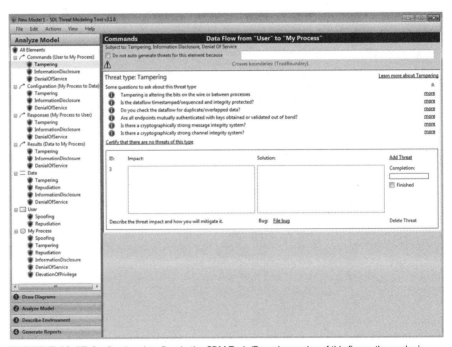

FIGURE 10.17 Configuring data flow in the SDM Tool. (For color version of this figure, the reader is referred to the online version of this chapter.)

---

[16] STRIDE is an acronym for the following classes of threats: Spoofing, Tampering, Repudiation, Information Disclosure, Denial of Service, Elevation of Privilege.

Attack Surface Analyzer

With the Microsoft Attack Surface Analyzer, you can create a report before installing the application and run the report again after installing the application to identify if there was any change on the system that can potentially expose one or more vulnerabilities. It can assist you understanding if the installed app opened any hole in the Windows operating system, for example, the Attack Surface Analyzer (Figure 10.18).

TIP

You can download this tool from http://www.microsoft.com/en-us/download/details.aspx?id=24487.

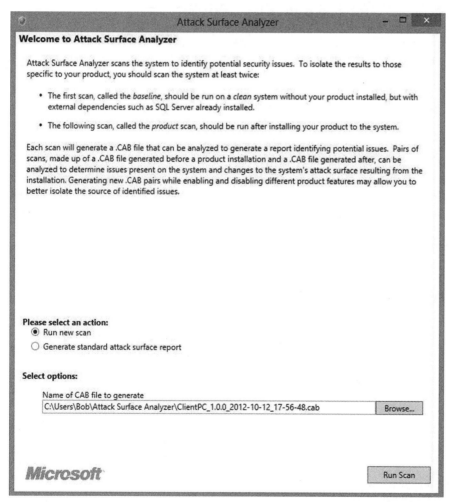

FIGURE 10.18 Running a scan via Attack Surface Analyzer. (For color version of this figure, the reader is referred to the online version of this chapter.)

Enhanced Mitigation Experience Toolkit

When you read an out of band tool making the news,[17] it is because there is something really good on this tool. EMET is a powerful tool that can even mitigate zero day vulnerabilities as well as vulnerabilities that were not yet patched. This tool can be installed standalone in the Windows system or can be deployed via GPO or SCCM.[18]

TIP

You can download this tool from http://www.microsoft.com/en-us/download/details.aspx?id=29851.

Security Tools Community Edition

One initiative that can help you and the community is the addition of new tools in a TechNet Wiki page that was specifically created for that. If you have any Windows security tool that you documented or just that you worked with and wants to share your knowledge with the community, go to http://social. technet.microsoft.com/wiki/contents/articles/3807.aspx and add this tool there. This page can be changed at any time.

SUMMARY

In this chapter, we looked at a number of new features and capabilities in Windows Server 2012 and Windows 8. In addition, we called out some useful tools that you can use to assess the security of your applications and of your Windows 8 workstations and Pad PCs, as well as your Windows Server 2012 environment. Improvements in Internet Explorer security were detailed, and a discussion of our old friends UAC and AppLocker was included. Finally, we took a look at some useful tools, such as the SDL Threat Modeling Tool and the Enhanced Mitigation Experience Toolkit.

---

[17] This tool was mentioned by Ed Bott on his blog right after Microsoft released the Security Advisory 2488013. More info at http://www.zdnet.com/blog/bott/the-one-security-tool-every-windows-user-should-know-about/2848.

[18] More details on how to deploy using SCCM can be found it here http://blogs.technet.com/b/configmgrteam/archive/2012/05/15/deploying-and-configuring-the-enhanced-mitigation-experience-toolkit.aspx.

Mitigating Network Vulnerabilities

> **CHAPTER POINTS**
>
> - Using Windows Firewall for host-based protection
> - Securing the endpoint with IPsec rules
> - Common Windows Firewall/IPsec Deployment Scenarios
> - Using SMB encryption to protect data traversing the network

UNDERSTANDING WINDOWS FIREWALL WITH ADVANCED SECURITY

Much has been made of the "death of the firewall," and some have postulated that firewalls are no longer necessary.[1] Microsoft announced in September 2012 the discontinuation of their premier network firewall, Forefront Threat Management Gateway (TMG), over a year after one of the authors of this book wrote about the impending demise of the product.[2] And indeed, the network firewall is fast becoming thought of as an obsolete technology. At the RSA 2012 conference, RSA called on the IT industry to move away from perimeter-based security and embrace a more "intelligence-driven" model.

The premise behind this evolution is that the "moat around the castle" approach to security is outmoded and inefficient. It makes sense to move the protection closer to the data; after all, that is really what you need to protect. Operating systems and applications can be reinstalled, but data may contain information that cannot be replaced and/or that can create irreparable problems if it is divulged to unauthorized persons. Think of the physical security analogy: Why spend the money to hire 50 guards to patrol the perimeter of a large estate consisting mostly of woodlands, when the real valuables are housed in a building in the center of the acreage? Instead, you can place one guard on each side of the building and have better protection at a much lower cost.

This new security model does not mean firewalls are useless; but it does mean network firewalls may be falling out of fashion in favor of host-based firewalls and other security measures that "live" further inward, where the data is created, viewed, and manipulated. The Windows Firewall with Advanced Security

---

[1]*Why you do not need a Firewall*, by Roger Grimes; InfoWorld Security Central, 15 May 2012. http://www.infoworld.com/d/security/why-you-dont-need-firewall-193153?page=0,0.
[2]*The Demise of Threat Management Gateway: Is Microsoft backing away from the Edge?* By Debra Littlejohn Shinder; TechRepublic, 31 May 2011. http://www.techrepublic.com/blog/window-on-windows/the-demise-of-threat-management-gateway-is-microsoft-backing-away-from-the-edge/4387.

is a host-based firewall that has matured into a surprisingly capable security tool in its latest iteration.

Evolution of the Windows Firewall

Prior to Windows XP, Windows users who wanted a host-based firewall to protect their systems had to rely on third-party products. The initial release of XP in 2001 included the Internet Connection Firewall, but it was disabled by default; users had to explicitly hunt it down and turn it on. Many users did not even know it was there and most did not use it. However, when Microsoft released Service Pack 2 for XP in 2004, the firewall was enabled by default. It was improved and its name was changed to Windows Firewall. However, the firewall was still fairly rudimentary and true to its original name, and it filtered only inbound connections.

Vista Adds Advanced Security

With Vista, Microsoft made the Windows Firewall far more robust. They added the capability of filtering outbound connections, although many casual users did not discover this because the firewall had two interfaces: the simple interface accessible through the Control Panel applet and a management console interface where its more advanced features (including outbound filtering) could be configured. While somewhat confusing at first glance, this two-tiered approach to configuration options served a purpose. Less technical users were less likely to stumble into the advanced firewall settings and "experiment," and possibly block or open the wrong ports and thus either shut down their connectivity or make themselves vulnerable to threats. To get to the advanced settings, you had to create an empty MMC and add the snap-in.

You could set up profiles for both public and private networks, but only one profile could be active at a given time, so that if your computer was connected to both, the most restrictive settings were applied.

Windows 7 Adds More Options

Windows 7 added the ability to reach the Advanced Security configuration console by clicking the **Advanced Settings** option in the left pane of the Control Panel applet (which might or might not be a good thing). Windows 7 also added a third-network type; instead of choosing between a public and private network, you could choose public, home, or work network. The latter two are treated as private networks, but Microsoft recognized that there are differences between the two. Network discovery was automatically turned on when you picked the "home network" selection and you could set up a homegroup to share media, documents, and devices with other members. If you chose "work network," you could not create or join a homegroup.

The firewall settings for each network type could be modified separately, and we were given the ability to have multiple profiles active on different network adapters. Thus, different rules could be applied to the traffic on the public or private networks.

Windows Firewall with Advanced Security in Windows 8

Windows 8 continues with the dual-administration approach. If you open Windows Firewall through the Control Panel (in the **System and Security** category when in Category View), you will see the simplified interface shown in Figure 11.1.

As you can see, three different network types are supported:

- **Domain networks:** networks that are joined to a Windows Server domain
- **Private networks:** networks such as home networks or business networks that are not joined to a Windows domain
- **Guest or public networks:** networks such as hotspots or Ethernet networks at hotels, airports, coffee shops, and so forth that are shared with unknown/untrusted users and computers

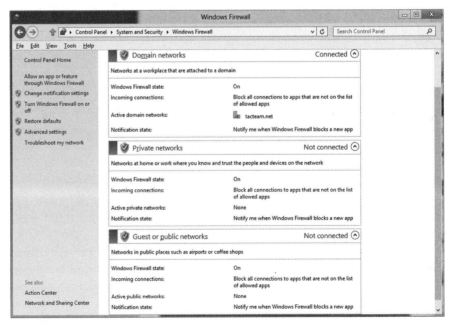

FIGURE 11.1 Windows Firewall as accessed through Control Panel. (For color version of this figure, the reader is referred to the online version of this chapter.)

This interface can be used to allow an application or feature to function through the firewall, to change the notification settings, to turn the firewall on or off, or to restore the firewall to the default settings. As with Windows 7's firewall, clicking the **Advanced Settings** option will take you to the MMC.

The Advanced Security settings are managed through a standard Microsoft Management Console (MMC), which is shown in Figure 11.2.

Interestingly, if you take a look at the Help file, you will see a message labeled "Important," informing you that "Windows Firewall with Advanced Security is designed for use by IT administrators who need to manage network security in an enterprise environment. It is not intended for use in home networks. Home users should consider using the Windows Firewall program available in Control Panel instead."

However, if you do not want to leave it up to users to heed this advice, you can set a Group Policy to prohibit the use of the Windows Firewall with Advanced Security MMC snap-in, which will restrict users from adding it to an MMC or

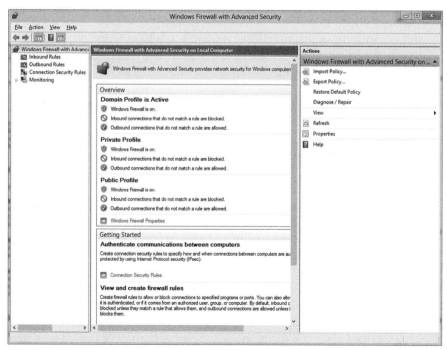

FIGURE 11.2 Windows Firewall Advanced Security configuration MMC. (For color version of this figure, the reader is referred to the online version of this chapter.)

running it as a standalone console. We will discuss how to do that in the section "Controlling the Windows Firewall Through Group Policy."

DEPLOYING AND MANAGING THE WINDOWS FIREWALL WITH ADVANCED SECURITY

The Windows Firewall with Advanced Security in Windows 8 builds on its Windows 7 predecessor, supporting detailed rules that will allow you to filter traffic based on such criteria as:

- Active Directory users and groups
- Source and destination IP addresses
- IP port numbers
- ICMP settings
- Types of interfaces and services
- IPsec settings

What Is New in Windows 8 and Windows Server 2012

There are three new key features that have been added to the Windows Firewall with Advanced Security in Window 8 and Windows Server 2012:

- **Internet Key Exchange version 2 (IKEv2) for IPsec transport mode:** This has been added to support scenarios securing IPsec end-to-end transport mode connections, making IKEv2 available as a VPN tunneling protocol that supports automatic VPN reconnection. IKEv2 will be discussed in more detail in Chapter 13.
- **Windows Store app network isolation:** This allows administrators to set and enforce boundaries to help protect the network from Windows 8 Store apps that are compromised. This limits the impact that such compromise can have on the network, system, and other apps. We will discuss it in further detail below, in the immediately following section "Controlling Network Access of Windows Store Apps."
- **Windows PowerShell cmdlets for Windows Firewall:** New PowerShell cmdlets have been added so that administrators can now fully configure and manage WFAS and IPsec from the command line, replacing Netsh administration. We will discuss this further in the section "Managing the Windows Firewall with PowerShell and Netsh."

Controlling Network Access of Windows Store Apps

Network isolation controls access to the network for apps that are downloaded and installed through the Windows Store. Network isolation is part of Windows 8's application security model. Developers of apps can select different levels of network access when they build the apps, depending on the app's needs for network access.

Windows 8 divides remote computers into two groups:

- **Home/work network:** These are on local subnets and also include local proxies on that network. This includes computers that are on a network the user has marked as trusted, computers on the network that are authenticated to a domain controller, and computers configured for DirectAccess when the network endpoint is part of the Intranet address space.
- **Internet:** This refers to any network access that is not part of the home/work network, including Internet proxies.

Windows 8 uses security identifiers (SIDs) and globally unique identifiers (GUIDs) to enforce the boundaries. Windows 8 discovers addresses on the local computer's NICs to find gateways and other IP addresses that provide access to the Internet. This includes both IPv4 and IPv6 addresses. Windows also identifies a network as trusted or nontrusted, based on whether the user enables sharing on the network. You use Group Policy to configure the Intranet address space for Windows network isolation.

The system checks each app's capabilities (SIDs and GUIDs) when it tries to make an outbound request such as an HTTP request. The system blocks or allows the request based on the configuration.

If you develop Windows Store apps, you can find more information on Microsoft's MSDN Web site about configuring network isolation for your apps.[3] Firewall rules are created automatically based on how the developer configured the app.

If you are a network administrator, you can further customize the WFAS configuration so that Windows Store apps are subject to isolation of network access. You can restrict the app's access to resources within the boundaries set by the developer. You do this using Group Policy, and we will discuss the details in the section "Controlling the Windows Firewall Through Group Policy."

Configuring the Windows Firewall with Advanced Security

As mentioned above, there are two ways to configure the Windows Firewall with Advanced Security in Windows 8 and Server 2012, and we will take a look at how to do each.

Using the Control Panel Interface

Basic firewall settings can be configured through the Control Panel interface. In the Control Panel, select the **System and Security** category and then **Windows**

---

[3]*How to configure network isolation capabilities*, MSDN Windows Dev Center. http://msdn.microsoft.com/en-us/library/windows/apps/hh770532.aspx.

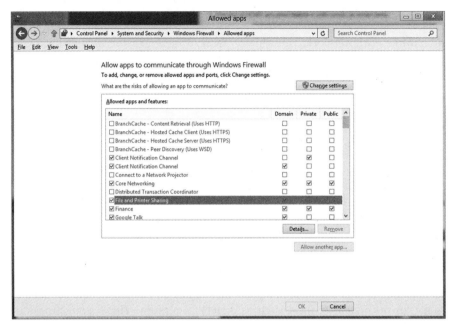

FIGURE 11.3 Configuring allowed apps and features through the Control Panel interface. (For color version of this figure, the reader is referred to the online version of this chapter.)

Firewall, as discussed above. To allow a specific program or service to communicate through the firewall, select the option (in the left pane) to **Allow apps to communicate through the Windows Firewall.**

As you can see in Figure 11.3, you can check boxes in a list of apps and features and then you can choose the network type(s) on which these apps and features will be allowed to communicate through the firewall. Before you can add, change, or remove allowed apps and ports, you must click **Change settings.**

If the program that you want to allow does not appear in the list, you can add it. Click the button that says **Allow another app…** (if this choice is grayed out, it is probably because you did not click the **Change settings** button). This selection brings up an **Add an app** window that displays apps installed on your computer, as shown in Figure 11.4.

If you do not find the desired application in this list, either you can type in the path to the program file, or you can click the **Browse** button and find it through the Windows Explorer interface. Note that you choose which network type(s) the app will be able to communicate on by selecting the **Network types…** button.

FIGURE 11.4 Adding an app to the "allowed" list when it does not appear in the list. (For color version of this figure, the reader is referred to the online version of this chapter.)

This is all very straightforward and works fine for most home users, but in a business environment, you may want to make much more specific filtering rules. That brings us to the Windows Firewall management console (WFAS MMC).

Using the Windows Firewall with Advanced Security MMC

The management console in Windows 8/Server 2012 is version 3.0, and it follows the standard MMC layout, with the console tree in the left pane and the Action pane on the right. You can access the snap-in from the Control Panel Home in the Windows Firewall Control Panel applet or by typing **Windows Firewall** on the Windows Start Screen.

The "Getting Started" section in the bottom middle pane provides links for creating IPsec connection security rules (which we will address in the section "Protecting the Windows Endpoint with IPsec"), viewing and creating firewall rules, and viewing current firewall and IPsec policy and activity.

The advantage here, over the Control Panel interface, is that you can create both inbound and outbound rules. There is also much more information available about the rules that you create, as shown in Figure 11.5.

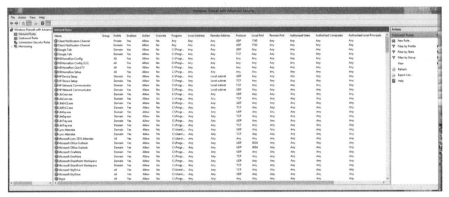

FIGURE 11.5 Configuring and viewing inbound and outbound firewall rules. (For color version of this figure, the reader is referred to the online version of this chapter.)

Of course, you can add or remove columns to customize the view, and you can choose whether to hide or display specific elements such as the console tree, standard menus, standard toolbar, status bar, description bar, taskpad navigation tabs, and/or Action pane.

General Settings

When you are in the top level of the console tree in the left pane (**Windows Firewall with Advanced Security**), you can configure the firewall's general settings by clicking **Properties** in the right Action pane, in the Action menu, or by right-clicking **Windows Firewall with Advanced Security** in the left console tree and selecting it from the context menu. Here, you can configure settings separately for each of the profile types (domain, private, and public) as well as IPsec settings, which we will address in the section "Protecting the Windows Endpoint with IPsec."

For each profile, you can choose whether to use the firewall at all (firewall state on/off setting) and whether to block or allow each connection type (inbound and outbound) by default, as shown in Figure 11.6.

You can specify which network connection(s) you want to protect with Windows Firewall (local area, wi-fi, etc.) by clicking the **Customize** button for **Protected network connections.**

Under the **Settings** section of each profile tab, you can specify settings that control the firewall's behavior when using that profile, as shown in Figure 11.7.

Here, you can choose whether to display notifications to users when a problem is blocked and whether to allow unicast responses to multicast or broadcast network traffic. You will also notice a section titled **Rule merging**, but the options are grayed out. The setting can only be changed by application of Group Policy; this interface merely shows you what the current setting is.

FIGURE 11.6 You can configure general settings separately for each profile type. (For color version of this figure, the reader is referred to the online version of this chapter.)

FIGURE 11.7 You can customize settings to control WFAS behavior for each profile. (For color version of this figure, the reader is referred to the online version of this chapter.)

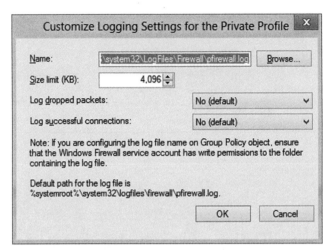

FIGURE 11.8 You can create custom logging settings for each profile. (For color version of this figure, the reader is referred to the online version of this chapter.)

Finally, you can customize the logging settings for each of the profiles, as shown in Figure 11.8.

Here, you set the location path and name of the log file and a size limit in kilobytes. You can choose whether or not to log dropped packets and successful connections (for both, the default is not to log, in order to save log space). You will find a summary of the current logging settings in the **Monitoring** node, as shown in Figure 11.9.

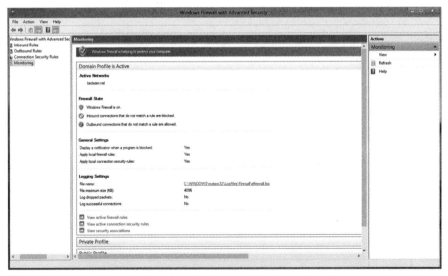

FIGURE 11.9 The **Monitoring** node displays current logging settings. (For color version of this figure, the reader is referred to the online version of this chapter.)

Logging creates a text file that shows you which network connections the firewall allowed or dropped. Windows Firewall with Advanced Security also records important events in the **Applications and Services** node in Event Viewer. We will talk more about using these resources in the section "Troubleshooting the Windows Firewall with Advanced Security."

Creating New Rules

Click **New Rule…** in the Action Pane or Action menu invokes the new rules wizard. If you happen to have hidden both the Action pane and toolbar, you can get to this option by right-clicking either **Inbound Rule** or **Outbound Rule** in the left console tree and selecting **New Rule…** there. The wizard makes it easy to create a new rule to control connections for a specified program or for a particular TCP or UDP port. You can also select a predefined rule or make a custom rule. You start off by selecting one of these four rule types, as shown in Figure 11.10.

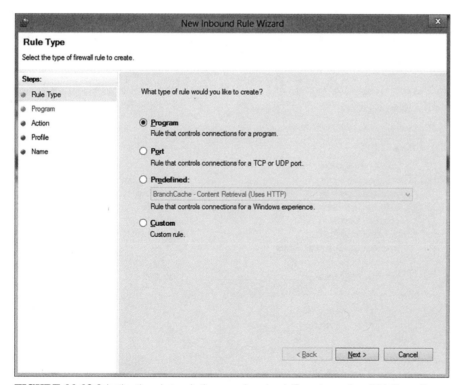

FIGURE 11.10 Selecting the rule type in the new rules wizard. (For color version of this figure, the reader is referred to the online version of this chapter.)

You might be wondering about the option to create a "custom rule." Are not all the rules you create (that are not predefined) custom rules? In this instance, the term is being used to refer to a rule that is based on more than one of the options. In other words, instead of choosing to base the rule on the program *or* the port, you can configure a custom rule to apply to a specific program *and* a specific port.

In addition to applying to programs, custom rules can also be applied to all services or only to specific services, as shown in Figure 11.11.

Custom rules also allow you to apply rules to many different types of protocols other than just TCP and UDP, as shown in Figure 11.12.

If you select to apply a rule to the Internet Control Message Protocol (ICMP), you can further customize the settings to apply it to all ICMP types or to only specific ICMP types (e.g., echo request or router advertisement), as shown in Figure 11.13.

Custom rules can even be applied to specific IP addresses; you can select both local and remote addresses to which the rule will apply, as shown in Figure 11.14.

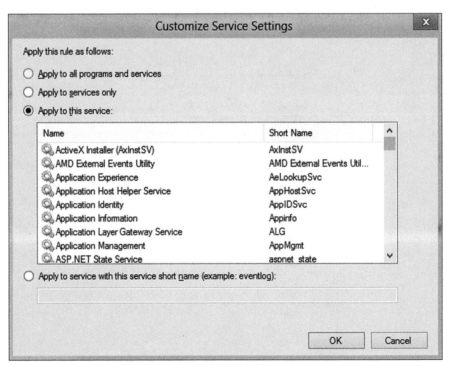

FIGURE 11.11 Custom rules can be applied to all or specific services, as well as programs. (For color version of this figure, the reader is referred to the online version of this chapter.)

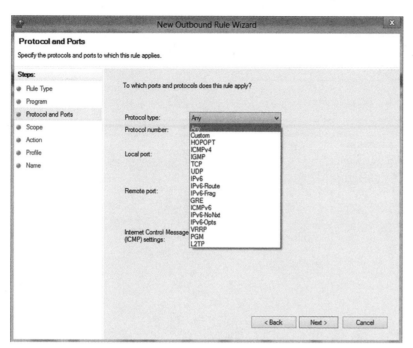

FIGURE 11.12 Custom rules can be applied to many different types of protocols. (For color version of this figure, the reader is referred to the online version of this chapter.)

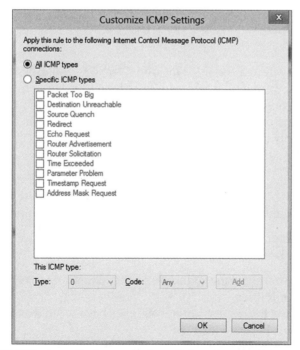

FIGURE 11.13 ICMP rules can be fine-tuned to be applied to only specific ICMP types. (For color version of this figure, the reader is referred to the online version of this chapter.)

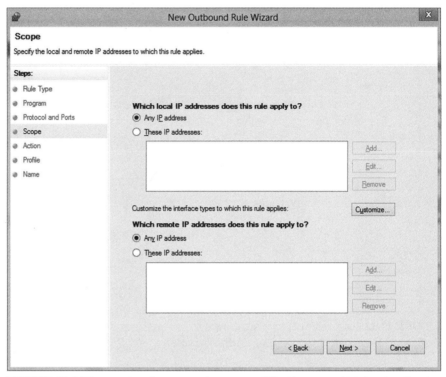

FIGURE 11.14 Custom rules allow you to select a scope of IP addresses to which the rule will apply. (For color version of this figure, the reader is referred to the online version of this chapter.)

After you have selected the rule type, the selections will differ slightly based on which type you have chosen. If you choose to create a rule that applies to programs, you can designate whether your new rule is to apply to all of the connections on the computer that match the rule's other properties or whether to apply it only to a specific program, as shown in Figure 11.15. You can type in the path or browse to find it.

If you are creating a rule that applies to a port, you will need to specify the protocol (TCP or UDP) and either "all ports" or specific remote port numbers, as shown in Figure 11.16. You can designate a single port or a range of ports.

For inbound rules, you have three choices as to how you want these types of connections to be handled, as shown in Figure 11.17.

- You can always allow the connection, whether or not it has been protected with IPsec;
- You can allow the connection only if it has been secured and authenticated by using IPsec; or
- You can block all connections from this program.

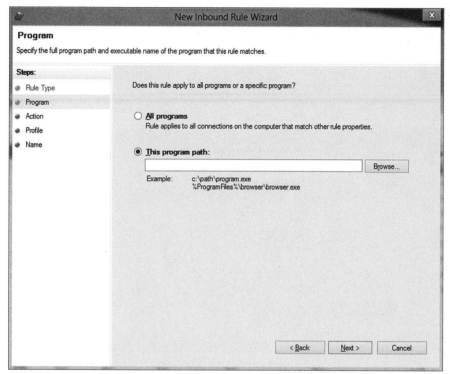

FIGURE 11.15 Selecting the programs to which your new rule will apply. (For color version of this figure, the reader is referred to the online version of this chapter.)

When you choose to allow a connection only if it is secured with IPsec, you will then be given the option to customize the settings for how those connections are handled, as shown in Figure 11.18.

As you can see, the default is to allow the connection if it is both authenticated and integrity protected. However, this is not the most secure settings. The second option, to require connections to be encrypted, will provide privacy for the data traveling across the connections, in addition to integrity and authentication.

Allowing the connection to use null encapsulation is less secure than the other two, and it requires the connection to be authenticated but neither provides privacy nor guarantees integrity of the packets governed by this rule. There is no AH or ESP header used to encapsulate the data, so this option would generally only be used with software or network equipment that is not compatible with AH or ESP. We will talk about this more in the section "Protecting the Windows Endpoint with IPsec."

Finally, you can set the option to override any block rules, if you need to ensure that the program will always be available.

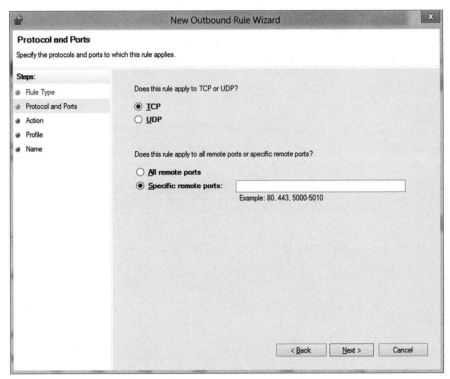

FIGURE 11.16 Protocol/port-specific rules require that you identify the transport protocol and the applicable port(s). (For color version of this figure, the reader is referred to the online version of this chapter.)

You can also select which of the network types this rule will apply to; the rule can be invoked when connected to the Windows domain, when connected to a private home or (nondomain) work network, and/or when connected to public networks, as shown in Figure 11.19.

After you give the rule a name and description and click **Finish**, the wizard is completed and the new rule will show up in your list of rules in the WFAS MMC. The wizard for creating an outbound rule involves identical steps.

Filtering Rules

As you can see in Figure 11.20, you are likely to have a large number of firewall rules even if you have not explicitly added them.

You might be wondering how you are ever going to find the one(s) that you want to view or modify. Microsoft helps you to narrow down the list by allowing you to filter by various criteria:

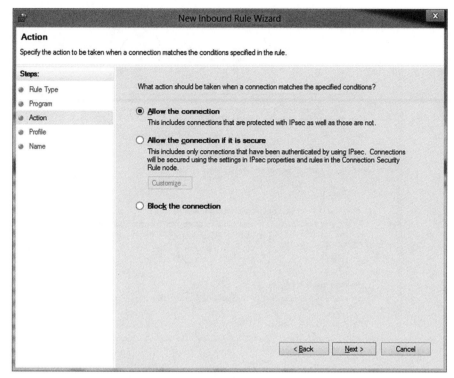

FIGURE 11.17 You can allow or block the specified connection, or allow it only if it is secured with IPsec. (For color version of this figure, the reader is referred to the online version of this chapter.)

- Profile (domain, private, or public)
- State (enabled or disabled)
- Group (for example, all rules pertaining to core networking or to file and printer sharing)

Disabling and Modifying Rules

Disabling a rule is as easy as right-clicking its name in the list and selecting **Disable** from the context menu. Of course, if you are sure that you will never use the rule again, you can select **Delete** to remove it entirely.

Sometimes you might need to modify a rule after it was created. In that case, just right-click it and select **Properties.** This will display the multitabbed Properties sheet as shown in Figure 11.21.

You will note that if a rule is "predefined" (which means it was a default rule that was created automatically by the system), you may not be able to modify some of its properties. You can, however, change the action field (allow, allow if secure, or block). Settings that cannot be changed will be grayed out, as shown on the **Protocols and Ports** tab in Figure 11.22.

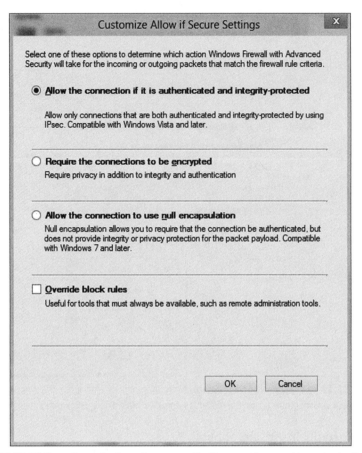

FIGURE 11.18 If you choose to allow when secured by IPsec, you then need to customize those settings. (For color version of this figure, the reader is referred to the online version of this chapter.)

Through the Properties sheet's **Local Principals** tab, you can specify to only allow connections under the rule for specific users and you can also create exceptions to the rule for specified users, as shown in Figure 11.23.

Another useful configuration option in the Properties sheet is the ability to only allow connections to specific remote computers or to create exceptions to the rule for specific remote computers. The **Remote Computers** tab's configuration sheet is very similar to the one used to designate authorized or excepted users.

The **Advanced** tab gives you the option to further narrow down the connections to which the rule will be applied. Here, you can select one or more interface types as shown in Figure 11.24. The rule will be applied only to connections using the checked interface types (local area network, remote access, and/or wireless network).

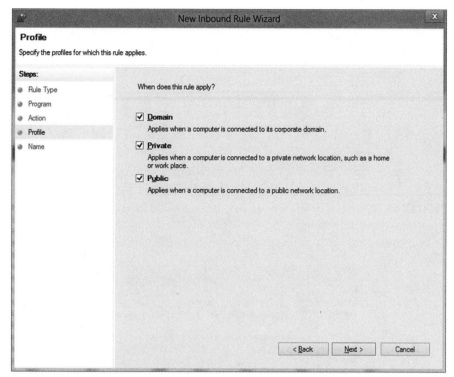

FIGURE 11.19 You can select one or more network types to which the rule will apply. (For color version of this figure, the reader is referred to the online version of this chapter.)

Exporting and Importing Policies

In addition to creating new firewall rules and modifying existing ones, you can also use the **Export Policy…** function in the right Action pane (when you are at the top level of the console tree in the left pane) to back up the firewall's configuration to a tab- or comma-delimited text file or to Unicode file. The **Import Policy…** option is used to import a saved backup file.

NOTE

If you import a policy, it will overwrite all the current policy, so you should export the current policy first if you want to save a copy of it.

Controlling the Windows Firewall Through Group Policy

Note that the user, even a local administrator, may not be able to change the configuration settings for Windows Firewall with Advanced Security. If you find that these settings are grayed out, this indicates that the computer has

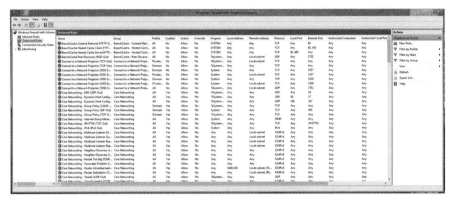

FIGURE 11.20 You are likely to have a large number of inbound and outbound rules in Windows Firewall. (For color version of this figure, the reader is referred to the online version of this chapter.)

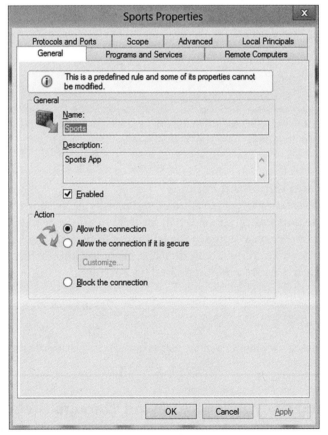

FIGURE 11.21 Use the Properties sheet to modify existing rules. (For color version of this figure, the reader is referred to the online version of this chapter.)

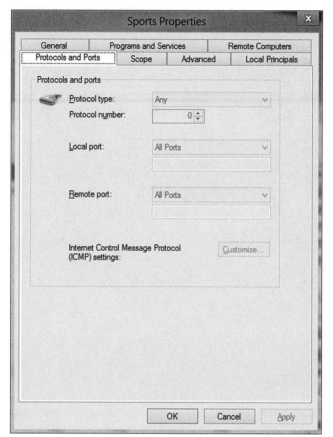

FIGURE 11.22 Predefined rules do not allow changes to some of the settings; those settings are grayed out. (For color version of this figure, the reader is referred to the online version of this chapter.)

Group Policy settings configured (either locally or through the application of domain policies) that control the WFAS settings.

Prohibiting Running the Windows Firewall with Advanced Settings MMC

As an administrator, you can use Group Policy to prevent users from running the Windows Firewall with Advanced Settings management console, but you will find that setting in a location in the Group Policy Editor that is completely different from other firewall settings. To do this, navigate to the following location in the GPE MMC:

> **User Configuration | Administrative Templates | Microsoft Management Console | Restricted/Permitted Snap-ins**

In the right pane, scroll down and double-click **Windows Firewall with Advanced Security**, as shown in Figure 11.25.

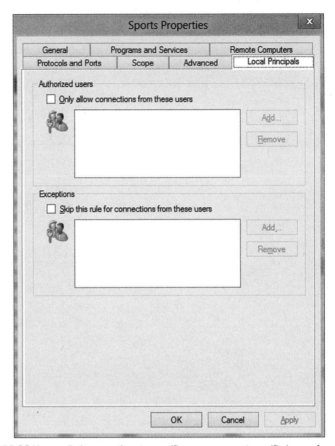

FIGURE 11.23 You can limit connections to specific users or except specified users from the rule. (For color version of this figure, the reader is referred to the online version of this chapter.)

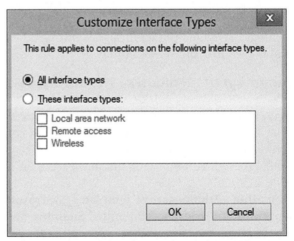

FIGURE 11.24 You can specify that the rule applies only to selected interface types. (For color version of this figure, the reader is referred to the online version of this chapter.)

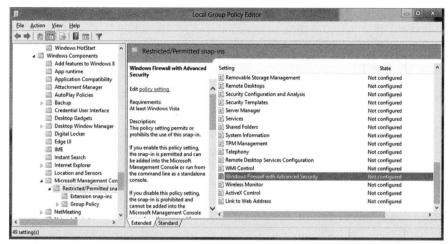

FIGURE 11.25 Restricting the use of the Windows Firewall with Advanced Security snap-in. (For color version of this figure, the reader is referred to the online version of this chapter.)

Select **Disabled.** This prevents the snap-in from being added to an MMC, and it will not appear in the **Add/Remove Snap-ins** list in the MMC. It also prevents running this console from the command line as a standalone console. A user who tries to do so will receive an error message, stating that policy prohibits the use of this snap-in.

Note that you can also enable the policy **Restrict users to the explicitly permitted list of snap-ins.** If that policy is enabled, the Windows Firewall with Advanced Security snap-in will be prohibited when the **Windows Firewall with Advanced Security** policy is not configured. Otherwise, it will be allowed when this policy setting is not configured.

Deploying Firewall Rules or Settings Through Group Policy

In an enterprise environment, Microsoft recommends that Windows Firewall with Advanced Security settings and rules be deployed using Group Policy in Active Directory Domain Services.[4] This involves the following steps:

- Create a group in AD DS where you will place computers to which the Group Policy will be applied.
- Create a Group Policy Object (GPO) for each version of Windows.
- Create security group filters to fine-tune the group members.

---

[4]*Checklist: Creating Group Policy Objects, Windows Firewall with Advanced Security*, TechNet Windows Server 2012 Web site. http://technet.microsoft.com/en-us/library/jj717258.aspx.

- Create Windows Management Instrumentation (WMI) filters for setting criteria that computers must match to receive the GPO.
- Link the GPO to the domain level of the AD hierarchy.
- Add computers to the group.
- Configure the GPO with default firewall settings.
- Create inbound and outbound firewall rules.

Controlling Network Access of Windows Store Apps

As discussed earlier in this chapter, network isolation for Windows Store apps is one of the new features in WFAS for Windows 8 and Server 2012. To fine-tune access to resources for Windows Store apps using Group Policy, you need to be a domain administrator and perform the following tasks, which we will break down into steps:

Define the Address Space of Your Intranet Network

1. In the Group Policy Management snap-in (gpmc.msc), open the **Default Domain Policy.**
2. From the Group Policy Management Editor, expand **Computer Configuration, Policies, Administrative Templates, Network** and then click **Network Isolation**.
3. In the right pane, double-click **Private network ranges for apps**.
4. In the Private network ranges for apps dialog box, click **Enabled**. In the Private subnets text box, type the private subnets for your intranet (separated by commas).
5. Double-click **Subnet definitions are authoritative**. Click **Enabled** if you want the subnet definitions that you previously created to be the single source for your subnet definition.

Configure Proxy Addresses

1. Double-click **Internet proxy servers for apps.**
2. Click **Enabled.**
3. In the Domain Proxies text box, type the IP addresses of your Internet proxy servers, separated by semicolons.
4. Double-click **Intranet proxy servers for apps.**
5. Click **Enabled.**
6. In the IP address text box, type the IP addresses of your intranet proxy servers, separated by semicolons.
7. Double-click **Proxy definitions are authoritative**. If you want the proxy definitions that you previously created to be the single source for your proxy definition, click **Enabled**. If you want to add additional proxies by using local settings or network isolation heuristics later, leave the **Not Configured** default setting in place.

Create Custom Firewall Rules

Create firewall rules based on Windows Store app capabilities. You can set firewall policies to block Internet access for any apps on the network that have a particular capability. The Windows Store capabilities include the following:

- Internet (Client)
- Internet (Client and Server)
- Home/Work Networking
- Document Library access
- Picture Library access
- Video Library access
- Music Library access
- Default Windows credentials
- Removable Storage
- Shared-User Certificates
- Location
- Microphone
- Near-field proximity
- Text messaging
- Webcam
- Other devices (based on GUID)

Here is an example of how to create a custom firewall rule that blocks access to the intranet for a media sharing app:

1. Open the Group Policy Management snap-in (gpmc.msc) and in the left pane, right-click your domain name, and then click **Create a GPO in this domain, and link it here.**
2. Type a name for your GPO in the **Name text box** and then click **OK**.
3. Right-click your new GPO and then click **Edit**.
4. From the Group Policy Management Editor, expand Computer Configuration, Policies, Windows Settings, Security Settings, Windows Firewall with Advanced Security and then click **Windows Firewall with Advanced Security—LDAP://…**
5. Right-click **Outbound Rules** and then click **New Rule.**
6. Click **Custom** and then click **Next**.
7. Click **Next** on the **Program** page, the **Protocols and Ports** page, and the **Scope** page.
8. On the **Action** page, check the box for **Block the Connection** and then click **Next**.
9. Click **Next** on the **Profile** page.
10. On the **Name** page, type a name for your rule and then click **Finish**.
11. In the right pane, right-click your new rule and then click **Properties**.
12. Click the **Local Principals** tab.

13. Select the **Only allow connections from these users** box and then click **Add**.
14. Click **Application Package Properties** and then click **OK**.
15. In the Choose Capabilities dialog box, click **APPLICATION PACKAGE AUTHORITY\A home or work network** and then click **OK**.
16. Click the **Programs and Services** tab under Application Packages and then click **Settings**.
17. Click **Apply to this application package**.
18. Select the app in the text box and click **OK**.
19. Click **OK** to close the Properties dialog box.
20. Close the Group Policy Management Editor.
21. In Group Policy Management, select your new GPO.
22. In the right pane under Security Filtering, select **Authenticated Users**.
23. Click **Remove** and then click **OK**.
24. Under Security Filtering, click **Add**.
25. Type **domain computers** in the text box and click **OK**.
26. Close Group Policy Management.

For more information, see *Isolating Windows Store Apps on your Network* in the TechNet Library.[5]

Group Policy Settings That Control Windows Firewall Behavior

There are a number of Group Policy settings available through the local Group Policy Editor or the Group Policy Management Console (GPMC), which pertain to the Windows Firewall with Advanced Security, as shown in Figure 11.26.

These policies include the following:

- **Allow authenticated IPsec bypass:** Allows unsolicited incoming messages from specified systems that authenticate using the IPsec transport.
- **Allow ICMP exceptions:** Defines the set of Internet Control Message Protocol (ICMP) message types that Windows Firewall allows. Note that if you do not enable the "Allow inbound echo request" message type, Windows Firewall blocks echo request messages sent by Ping running on other computers, but it does not block outbound echo request messages sent by Ping running on this computer.
- **Allow inbound file and printer sharing exception:** Windows Firewall opens UDP ports 137 and 138, and TCP ports 139 and 445 to allow inbound file and printer sharing.

---

[5]*Isolating Windows Store Apps on your Network,* TechNet Library Windows Server Web site http://technet.microsoft.com/en-us/library/hh831418.aspx.

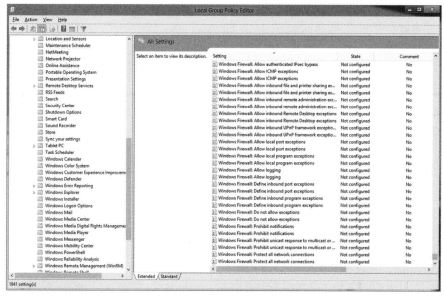

FIGURE 11.26 Group Policy settings that control WFAS. (For color version of this figure, the reader is referred to the online version of this chapter.)

- **Allow inbound remote administration exception:** Allows remote administration of the computer using administrative tools such as the Microsoft Management Console (MMC) and Windows Management Instrumentation (WMI) by opening TCP ports 135 and 445.
- **Allow inbound Remote Desktop exceptions:** Allows the computer to receive inbound Remote Desktop requests by opening TCP port 3389.
- **Allow inbound UDP framework exceptions:** Allows this computer to receive unsolicited inbound Plug and Play messages sent by network devices, such as routers with built-in firewalls, by opening TCP port 2869 and UDP port 1900.
- **Allow local port exceptions:** Allows administrators to use the Windows Firewall component in Control Panel to define a local port exceptions list.
- **Allow local program exceptions:** Allows administrators to use the Windows Firewall component in Control Panel to define a local program exceptions list.
- **Allow logging:** Allows Windows Firewall to record information about the unsolicited incoming messages that it receives.
- **Define inbound port exceptions:** Allows users to view and change the inbound port exceptions list defined by Group Policy.
- **Define inbound program exceptions:** Allows users to view and change the program exceptions list defined by Group Policy.

- **Do not allow exceptions:** Blocks all unsolicited incoming messages and overrides all other Windows Firewall policy settings that allow such messages.
- **Prohibit notifications:** Prevents Windows Firewall from displaying notifications to the user when a program requests that Windows Firewall add the program to the program exceptions list.
- **Prohibit unicast response to multicast or broadcast requests:** Prevents the computer from receiving unicast responses to its outgoing multicast or broadcast messages, other than DHCP unicast responses.
- **Protect all network connections:** Turns on Windows Firewall; disabling this policy prevents WFAS from running and prevents locally logged-on administrators from starting it.

Managing the Windows Firewall with PowerShell and Netsh

For those who prefer to use the command-line interface for administrative tasks, there are a number of Netsh commands and PowerShell cmdlets available to configure and manage the Windows Firewall with Advanced Security in Windows 8 and Windows Server 2012.

Netsh Commands for WFAS

Note that the Netsh commands for Windows Firewall with Advanced Security are the same in Windows 8/Server 2012 as in Windows 7/Server 2008 R2. These include the following contexts:

- Netsh AdvFirewall context
- Netsh AdvFirewall Consec Commands
- Netsh AdvFirewall Firewall Commands
- Netsh AdvFirewall MainMode Commands
- Netsh AdvFirewall Monitor Commands

For more information about the available Netsh commands, see *Netsh Commands for Windows Firewall with Advanced Security* in the TechNet library.[6]

PowerShell Administration

Microsoft recommends that administrators transition from the use of Netsh to Windows PowerShell for configuration and management of the Windows Firewall with Advanced Security, as the Netsh functionality may be removed in future versions of Windows.

---

[6]*Netsh Commands for Windows Firewall with Advanced Security*, TechNet, Windows Server Web site. http://technet.microsoft.com/en-us/library/cc771920(v=ws.10).aspx.

The following are examples of cmdlets that can be used to accomplish common tasks involving WFAS:

- **Enable Windows Firewall:** `Set-NetFirewallProfile -Profile Domain,Public,Private -Enabled True`

- **Set default inbound/outbound actions, specify protected network connections, allow notifications to be displayed to the user when a program is blocked, allow unicast response and specify logging settings:** `Set-NetFirewallProfile -DefaultInboundAction Block -DefaultOutboundAction Allow –NotifyOnListen True -AllowUnicastResponseToMulticast True -LogFileName %SystemRoot%\ System32\LogFiles\Firewall\pfirewall.log`

- **Create a firewall rule to allow Telnet to listen on the network, scoped to the local subnet:** `New-NetFirewallRule -DisplayName "Allow Inbound Telnet" -Direction Inbound -Program %SystemRoot%\System32\tlntsvr. exe -RemoteAddress LocalSubnet -Action Allow`

- **Create a firewall rule to block outbound traffic from a specific location and local port to a GPO in Active Directory:** `New-NetFirewallRule -DisplayName "Block Outbound Telnet" -Direction Outbound -Program %SystemRoot%\System32\tlntsvr.exe –Protocol TCP –LocalPort 23 -Action Block -PolicyStore domain.contoso.com\gpo_name`

- **Add inbound and outbound rules to a group:** `New-NetFirewallRule -DisplayName "Allow Inbound Telnet" -Direction Inbound -Program %SystemRoot%\System32\tlntsvr.exe -RemoteAddress LocalSubnet -Action Allow –Group "Telnet Management"`

  `New-NetFirewallRule -DisplayName "Block Outbound Telnet" -Direction Inbound -Program %SystemRoot%\System32\tlntsvr.exe -RemoteAddress LocalSubnet -Action Allow –Group "Telnet Management"`

- **Delete a firewall rule:** `Remove-NetFirewallRule -DisplayName "Allow Web 80"`

- **Return all firewall rules on a remote computer:** `Get-NetFirewallRule -CimSession RemoteComputer`

- **Create a firewall rule that requires traffic to be authenticated:** `New-NetFirewallRule -DisplayName "Allow Authenticated Telnet" -Direction Inbound -Program %SystemRoot%\System32\tlntsvr.exe -Authentication Required -Action Allow`

For more information about using PowerShell to configure and manage the Windows Firewall with Advanced Security on Windows 8/Server 2012, as well as links to PowerShell guides and Help, see the TechNet library.[7]

---

[7]*Windows Firewall with Advanced Security Administration with Windows PowerShell*, TechNet, Windows Server Web site. http://technet.microsoft.com/en-us/library/hh831755.aspx.

Troubleshooting the Windows Firewall with Advanced Security

Troubleshooting firewall issues begin with checking simple settings and continue with collecting information about the firewall's behavior and what network connections it has allowed or blocked.

Checking Status of Services

The first step is to make sure that the necessary services are started; otherwise, WFAS will not be able to work properly. In the **Services** MMC snap-in (**Control Panel | System and Security | Administrative Tools | Services**), check the following services and ensure that they are running:

- Windows Firewall Service
- Base Filtering Engine
- Group Policy
- Client IKE and AuthIP IPsec Keying Modules
- IP Helper IPsec Policy Agent
- Network Location Awareness
- Network List Service

If all are started and running, it is time to move on to collecting more information by examining the relevant logs.

Using Event Logs

You can find information about the firewall's operational events in the Event Viewer log, in **Applications and Services | Microsoft | Windows | Windows Firewall with Advanced Security**, as shown in Figure 11.27.

The Event log records five different types of firewall events:

- **ConnectionSecurity**: This log records events that pertain to the configuration of IPsec rules and settings, such as when a connection security rule is added or removed or the settings of IPsec are changed.
- **ConnectionSecurityVerbose**: This log records events that are relevant to the operational state of the IPsec engine, such as when a connection security rule is activated.
- **Firewall**: This log records events concerning the configuration of Windows Firewall itself, such as when a rule is added, removed, or changed.
- **FirewallVerbose**: This log records events regarding the operational state of the firewall, such as when a firewall rule is activated or the settings of a profile change.
- **Network isolation operational log**: This log records events pertaining to network isolation.

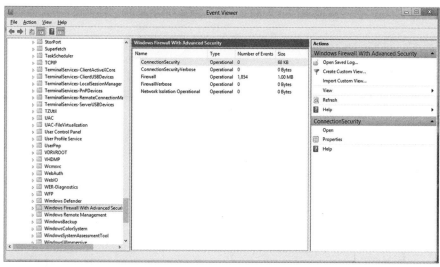

FIGURE 11.27 WFAS logs important events in the Applications and Services Event Log. (For color version of this figure, the reader is referred to the online version of this chapter.)

Note that the ConnectionSecurityVerbose and the FirewallVerbose logs are disabled by default. To enable either of these logs, select it and click the **Action** menu and then choose **Properties.** On the **General** tab of the Log Properties dialog box, click **Enable Logging**.

In this dialog box, shown in Figure 11.28, you can also set the log file path, set a maximum log size and specify what is to happen when the maximum log size is reached. You can also manually clear the log.

Each event recorded provides detailed information regarding date and time, source, an event ID, the user and computer, and more, as shown in Figure 11.29. The **Details** tab contains the raw data generated by the event. This information can be useful in tracking down the causes of problems with the firewall.

Using Firewall Log Text Files

Earlier in this chapter, we discussed how to configure Windows Firewall with Advanced Security to create a text log file. To view the log file, navigate in Windows Explorer to the location you selected for storing the log file and open it with Notepad or another text editor. Note that you must be a member of the local administrators group in order to view the firewall log.

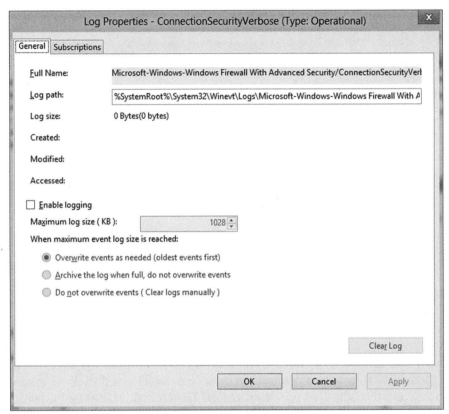

FIGURE 11.28 You can configure the properties for the WFAS event logs. (For color version of this figure, the reader is referred to the online version of this chapter.)

The log file contains information including the following:

- Date and time of the recorded transactions
- Action taken by the firewall
- Protocol used for the communication
- IP address of the sending computer
- IP address of the destination computer
- Source port number of the sending computer
- Port number of the destination computer
- Size of the packet (in bytes)
- TCP control flags
- TCP sequence number
- TCP acknowledgment number
- TCP window size of the packet (in bytes)

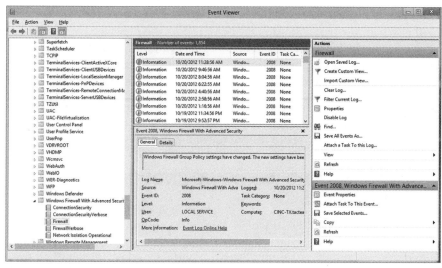

FIGURE 11.29 You can gather information about firewall events from the applicable event log. (For color version of this figure, the reader is referred to the online version of this chapter.)

- ICMP type
- ICMP code
- Info (depending on the action that occurred)

Creating Custom Log Files

You can also create two types of custom log files that can be helpful in troubleshooting WFAS:

- **Network Statistics file**: displays network statistics, listing all listening ports.
- **Task List file**: lets you view the task lists of programs and services and provides the event PID (which you can then find in the Network Statistics file).

Here is how you create these two custom files:

1. At the command prompt, type **netstat -ano > netstat.txt**, and then press ENTER.
2. At the command prompt, type **tasklist > tasklist.txt** and then press ENTER or (to create a task list for services, type **tasklist /svc > tasklist.txt**).
3. Open the tasklist.txt and the netstat.txt files in a text editor such as Notepad.
4. In the tasklist.txt file, record the Process Identifier (PID) for the process you are troubleshooting and then compare the PID with the one in the Netstat.txt file. Also record the protocol that is used. This information can be useful when you review the information in the firewall log file.

Restoring Default Settings

If all else fails, the best solution may be to restore the firewall to its default settings and start over. Before you do this, you might want to save the current configuration, using the **Export Policy...** option in the WFAS MMC's right Action pane. Then reset the firewall to the default configuration by following these steps:

1. In the Windows Firewall with Advanced Security snap-in, click **Restore Default Policy** in the right Actions pane.
2. At the prompt, click **Yes** to restore firewall defaults.

PROTECTING THE WINDOWS ENDPOINT WITH IPSEC RULES

Internet Protocol Security (IPsec) is a popular choice for securing network communications because it can protect data in transit over the network by authenticating and/or encrypting each individual packet. IPsec differs from other in-transit encryption technologies such as Secure Sockets Layer (SSL) and Transport Security Layer (TLS) in that it operates at the network layer of the OSI model, whereas the others operate in the upper layers. The advantage is that applications do not have to be specifically designed to use IPsec.

IPsec uses the Authentication Header (AH) and Encapsulating Security Payload (ESP) protocols to provide authentication, integrity, and confidentiality for data packets sent between two hosts, two gateways, or a gateway and host. IPsec uses security associations (algorithms and keys) to perform encryption and authentication of one-way traffic between two points. Thus, a two-way communication between two computers uses two security associations, one for traffic going in one direction and another for the traffic flowing in the opposite way. IPsec can be implemented in either transport mode for host-to-host communications or tunnel mode for creating virtual private networks.

The Windows Firewall with Advanced Security console is used to create and manage IPsec rules (which are called "connection security rules" in the firewall interface) in addition to firewall rules. Connection security rules authenticate the computers involved in communications going through the firewall and encrypt that traffic.

To understand the difference between firewall rules and connection security rules, it is important to note that firewall rules are generally applied to programs, services, and protocols. Connection security rules are applied to computers—the endpoint computers between which the communication is being exchanged. Windows Firewall is now more fully integrated with IPsec settings and can allow or block traffic based on some IPsec negotiation outcomes.

Configuring IPsec Rules on Windows Firewall with Advanced Security

In order to use connection security rules, both of the computers involved in the communications must have IPsec policies configured. Authentication for connection security rules can be based on Kerberos in an Active Directory domain, or on certificates or preshared keys. There are five different types of connection security rules that you can create:

- **Isolation**—allows you to restrict communication to only those hosts that can authenticate using specific credentials. For example, you can allow communications only to computers that are joined to an Active Directory domain.
- **Authentication exemption**—allows you to configure exemptions to the isolation rules, such as an exemption to our previous example that would allow connections to a DNS server without the requirement to authenticate.
- **Server-to server**—allows you to secure the connections between two specific computers, such as a connection between a database and an application server.
- **Tunnel**—allows you to create rules that work in the same way as server-to-server rules but are implemented through tunnels (site-to-site connections).
- **Custom**—allows you to create rules with special settings based on your specific needs.

The first step in securing communications with IPsec is to create a rule. In the WFAS console, right-click **Connection Security Rules** in the left pane and select **New Rule…** or select it in the **Action** menu or the right Action pane. The New Connection Security Rule Wizard opens by asking you to select the rule type from the list discussed above, as shown in Figure 11.30.

When you create an isolation rule, the next step is to select when you want authentication to take place. You have three choices here, as shown in Figure 11.31:

- You select **Request authentication for inbound and outbound connections** to have the communications authenticated whenever possible, but authentication is not required so communication can still be established if the computer on the other end does not support it.
- You can select **Require authentication for inbound connections and request authentication for outbound connections** if you want to ensure that only authenticated incoming communications will be allowed. If the computer sending the request is unable to authenticate, the connection will be rejected. Outbound communications will be treated in the same way as above—authenticated when possible but allowed without authentication.

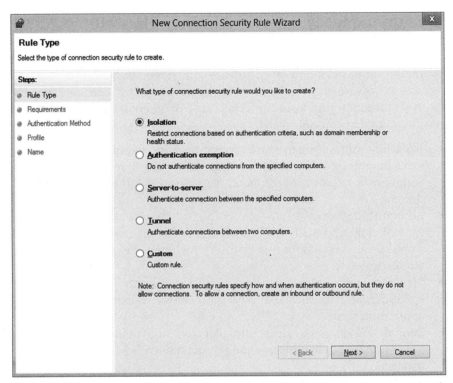

FIGURE 11.30 You can create one of the five types of connection security rules. (For color version of this figure, the reader is referred to the online version of this chapter.)

- For the highest level of security, you can select **Require authentication for inbound and outbound connections.** With this choice, only authenticated connections are allowed.

On the next page of the wizard, shown in Figure 11.32, you specify what authentication method you want to use for this rule.

You have four choices here:

- You can choose **Default** and use the authentication methods that are defined in the IPsec settings.
- You can choose **Computer and User** to use Kerberos v5 and restrict communications to connections from domain-joined users and computers only.
- You can choose **Computer** to use Kerberos v5 and restrict communications to connections from domain-joined computers only.
- You can choose the **Advanced** option and specify custom settings for first and second authentication methods.

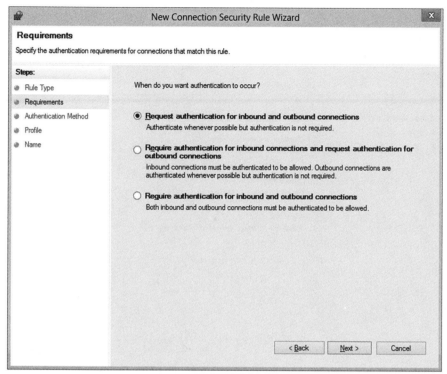

FIGURE 11.31 You must select when you want authentication to occur. (For color version of this figure, the reader is referred to the online version of this chapter.)

When you choose to customize the authentication methods, you can list multiple methods to be tried, and they will be tried in the order in which you place them in the list. You do this for both first and second authentication, and you can also choose whether to make first or second authentication optional. You will not be able to specify a second authentication if a preshared key is listed in the first authentication methods list.

The next step is to select the network type(s) to which the rule applies, just as you do with firewall rules (domain, private, or public).

Then you give the rule a name (and description if you want) and it will appear in your list of Connection Security Rules in the middle pane of the WFAS console, as shown in Figure 11.33.

To disable or delete it, right-click it and choose the appropriate option. To modify it, choose **Properties.** This opens its Properties sheet with tabs for General info, Remote Computers, Protocols and Ports, Authentication, and Advanced, as shown in Figure 11.34. Here, you can make changes to the selections you made in the wizard and also configure some settings that did not appear in the wizard.

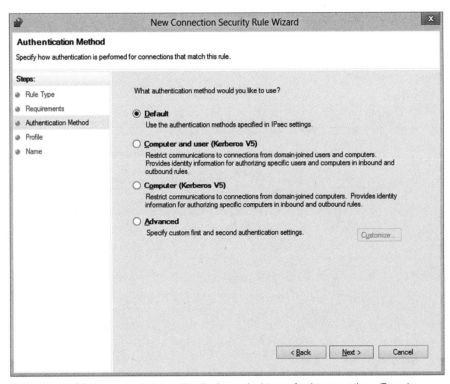

FIGURE 11.32 You must select an authentication method to use for the connections. (For color version of this figure, the reader is referred to the online version of this chapter.)

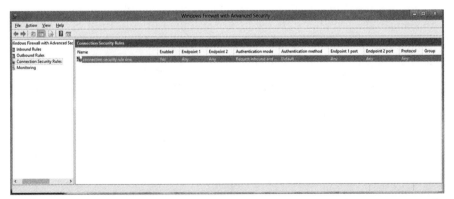

FIGURE 11.33 Your new rule appears in the middle pane of the WFAS console. (For color version of this figure, the reader is referred to the online version of this chapter.)

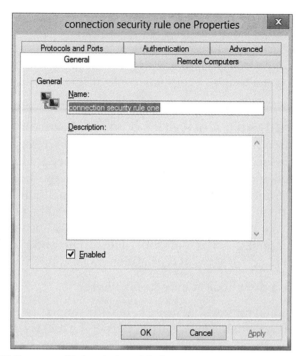

FIGURE 11.34 You can modify the rule through its Properties sheet. (For color version of this figure, the reader is referred to the online version of this chapter.)

On the **Remote Computers** tab, you can specify the IP addresses of the endpoints to which you want the rule to apply. On the **Protocols and Ports** tab, you can apply the rule only to specific protocol types (for example, IPv6 or L2TP) or specific ports on each of the endpoints. On the **Authentication** tab, you can change the authentication mode (Request/ require on inbound/outbound) and/or the authentication method that you set in the wizard. On the **Advanced** tab, you can not only change the network type(s) to which the rule applies but also specify that it applies only to certain interface types (local area network, remote access, and/or wi-fi), and you can specify whether IPsec tunneling should be used. When tunneling is used, you need to set the authentication mode to "Require inbound and outbound."

You can also create IPsec policies through the IP Security Policies snap-in in the Microsoft Management Console, via the command-line netsh tool or PowerShell, but that is beyond the scope of this chapter.

COMMON DEPLOYMENT SCENARIOS

Now that you have a good understanding of how the Windows Firewall with Advanced Security works and how to use it to create firewall rules and IPsec rules, let us look at a couple of common deployment scenarios where you can put those skills to work.

Host Firewall with Network Location Awareness

Network Location Awareness (NLA) is an important concept by which the operating system and applications can detect when they are moved from one network to another (for example, from the Ethernet network at the office to a wi-fi network at home or a public hot spot). When applications are aware of location, they can be configured to act differently depending on the network on which they are currently running. This is the basis for the different firewall profiles for public, home, and work (domain) networks in the Windows Firewall, as the Windows Firewall is a location-aware application.

Now let us take a closer look at the network types:

- **Guest or Public networks:** When you initially connect to a network, by default it is set to the public network type. The user is asked to select whether the network is public or private. The user must be a local administrator to set the network as private. The rules that are associated with public networks are most restrictive because the public network is presumed to be untrustworthy because it is shared with users and computers that are not known, managed, or under your control.
- **Private networks:** Private networks are not open to the public and are generally restricted to known users and computers; thus they are more trustworthy than public networks. Private networks generally have an edge firewall or Network Address Translation (NAT) device separating them from the Internet and other publicly accessible networks. Private networks can be wired or wireless. Wireless private networks should be encrypted with a strong encryption protocol (WPA; WPA2). Networks are designated as private by administrators, either during the setup process or through manually changing the network type later. When you set a network as private, Windows remembers that designation the next time you connect to it. Because private networks are more trustworthy, rules are generally less restrictive than for the public networks.
- **Domain networks:** If the computer is a member of an Active Directory domain and authenticates to the domain controller, Windows detects this and designates the network as a domain network. You cannot manually set the network type to domain network. Domain networks comprise computers that are managed and controlled by administrators through Group Policy and thus are highly trustworthy, so rules governing domain networks are generally less restrictive.

When deploying the Windows Firewall with Advanced Security as a network location-aware host firewall, you create a different profile for each of the types of networks. The profiles can contain different types of firewall policies.

When you create firewall rules as described earlier in this chapter, you can enforce specific rules on public, private, domain, or all network profiles. Thus, you can allow traffic for a specific service or application when connected to one network type, but not when connected to another.

Server and Domain Isolation with Windows Firewall and IPsec

Windows Firewall with Advanced Security supports the creation of rules for server and domain isolation. This allows you to isolate the server and domain resources so that only authenticated, authorized computers will be able to access those resources. To do this, you create a logical network within the physical network and the computers in the logical network are required to provide authentication credentials before they can connect to other computers in the isolated network. Computers outside the isolated network cannot gain access.

Server isolation allows you to configure servers that need special protection so that the IPsec policy will accept only authenticated communications from other computers. You have already seen how you can create IPsec rules through WFAS to do this.

Domain isolation involves restricting domain member computers to accepting only requests from other domain-joined computers. All computers in the isolated network are part of the domain. IPsec policy secures the communications sent between all clients and servers within the domain.

Server and domain isolation is a complex topic, and you can find more resources detailing server and domain isolation deployments on the Microsoft TechNet Web site.[8]

USING SMB ENCRYPTION TO PROTECT DATA TRAVERSING THE NETWORK

You know that, as a security professional, you should trust no network—even the internal network, where the authenticated and authorized users are located. IPsec protects data in transit over the network, but it can be complicated to deploy. On a Windows network, the Server Message Block protocol runs on top of TCP/IP and is used by applications to read and write to

---

[8]*Server and Domain Isolation*, TechNet Networking and Access Technologies Web site. http://technet. microsoft.com/en-US/network/bb545651.aspx.

files and request services from servers. These SMB communications can be encrypted to protect the data without the need to deploy IPsec and without specialized hardware. The feature in Windows Server 2012 that can help you to mitigate eavesdropping/snooping attacks while data is in transit in the network is called SMB encryption. One of the greatest advantage of this feature is that it has zero (yes zero) deployment cost, because it does not require other components (no PKI, no certificate deployments, trust, special hardware, and so forth).

Although this sounds great, you have to remember that the name of this feature is SMB encryption, which means only data that is transmitted using the SMB 3.0 Protocol will be encrypted. A client that supports encryption will leverage the new SMB2_GLOBAL_CAP_ENCRYPTION capability during the SMB negotiation request packet (within the Capabilities field). The server (or the workstation acting as a server) will reply with SMB2_GLOBAL_CAP_ENCRYPTION. This is like an initial handshake, so that once the negotiation is completed, both parties will know the other side's encryption capability. Note that encryption can be enabled per share or for the entire server. The main difference is that if you want to enable encryption on the entire server, you will need to use PowerShell.

The algorithm that is used by SMB encryption is the Advanced Encryption Standard (AES) 128 bit, and it does not offer a negotiation capability.[9] The good news is that there is almost no impact on performance because most new processors use AES acceleration.[10] There is one caveat that goes along with this: it only works with Windows 8/Windows Server 2012 because it requires SMB 3.0. In other words, if you try to use a Windows 7 workstation (or any other previous version of Windows) to access a share that has SMB encryption enabled, you will receive an "Access Denied" error message.

As long as all the computers involved are running Windows 8 or Windows Server 2012, you are good to go, so in the next section, we will discuss the "how to" of enabling SMB encryption.

Enabling SMB Encryption
The SMB encryption feature can be enabled in one of the two ways:

- Using the Server Manager
- Using PowerShell

---

[9] TechNet Video, *From End to Edge and Beyond* with Jose Barreto, Microsoft Product Manager http://technet.microsoft.com/en-us/video/from-end-to-edge-and-beyond-episode-20.
[10] Wikipedia, *AES Instruction Set* http://en.wikipedia.org/wiki/AES_instruction_set.

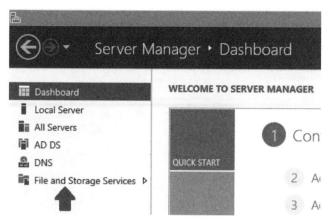

FIGURE 11.35 Click **File and Storage Service** in Server Manager. (For color version of this figure, the reader is referred to the online version of this chapter.)

Since you are already familiar with the Server Manager interface, we will start by using the graphic interface to enable SMB encryption for a new share in an existing folder. Here are the steps:

1. On the **Server Manager**, click **File and Storage Service** in the left pane, as shown in Figure 11.35.
2. Click **Shares** and under **Tasks**, click **New Share** as shown in Figure 11.36.
3. On the **New Share Wizard**, in the **Select the profile for this share** page, shown in Figure 11.37, leave the default selection (**SMB Share—Quick**) as is and click **Next**.
4. On the **Select the server and path for this share** page, shown in Figure 11.38, click **Type a custom path**, select the location for your share (in this case C:\FEEAB), and then click **Next**.
5. On the **Specify share name** page, accept the default selection and click **Next**.

FIGURE 11.36 Select **New Share** under **Shares | Tasks**. (For color version of this figure, the reader is referred to the online version of this chapter.)

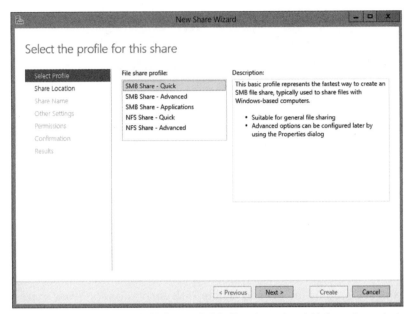

FIGURE 11.37 Leave the default **SMB Share - Quick**. (For color version of this figure, the reader is referred to the online version of this chapter.)

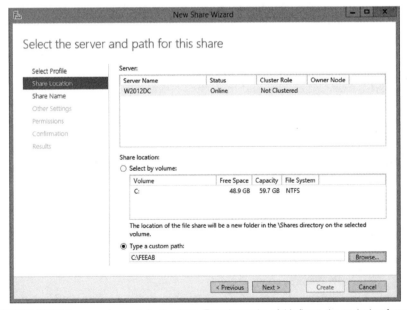

FIGURE 11.38 Type a custom path for the share. (For color version of this figure, the reader is referred to the online version of this chapter.)

FIGURE 11.39 Check the option to **Encrypt data access**. (For color version of this figure, the reader is referred to the online version of this chapter.)

6. On the **Configure share settings** page, check the **Encrypt data access** option as shown in Figure 11.39 and click **Next**.
7. On the **Specify permission to control access** page, you can change the permission level. For this example, we will leave the default selection in place and click **Next**.
8. On the **Confirm selections** page, click **Create**.
9. On the **View results** page, confirm that the share was successfully created as shown in Figure 11.40 and click **Close**.

This provides quick and effective encryption for SMB shares in just nine steps. However, if you prefer the command line and want to speed up the process a bit, you can reduce that to a one-line PowerShell command.

To perform the same operation using PowerShell, type the following command:

```
Set-SmbShare -Name FEEAB -EncryptData $True
```

NOTE

Use $False to disable encryption.

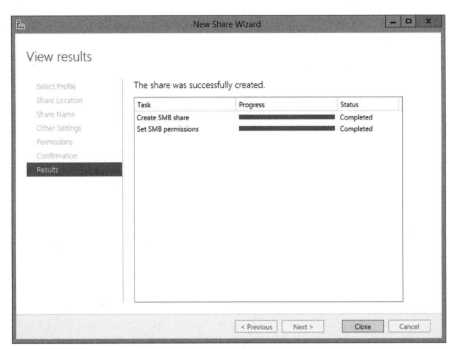

FIGURE 11.40 Confirm that the share was successfully created. (For color version of this figure, the reader is referred to the online version of this chapter.)

FIGURE 11.41 You can also use PowerShell to encrypt the data. (For color version of this figure, the reader is referred to the online version of this chapter.)

The result of this command is shown in Figure 11.41.

If you want to verify that this folder was really encrypted, you can use the following command:

```
Get-SmbShare -Name FEEAB | Format-List -Property *
```

The result of this command is shown in Figure 11.42.

Notice that the *EncryptData* property is set to True, which means that the share is encrypted. You can also use Server Manager to access the properties of the share and validate the configuration. In that case, you only need to right-click on the share, choose **Properties** and in the share's properties, and click **Settings** as shown in Figure 11.43.

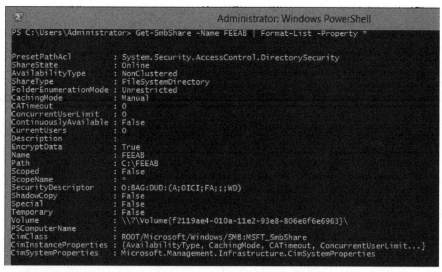

FIGURE 11.42 Verify that the data was really encrypted, using PowerShell. (For color version of this figure, the reader is referred to the online version of this chapter.)

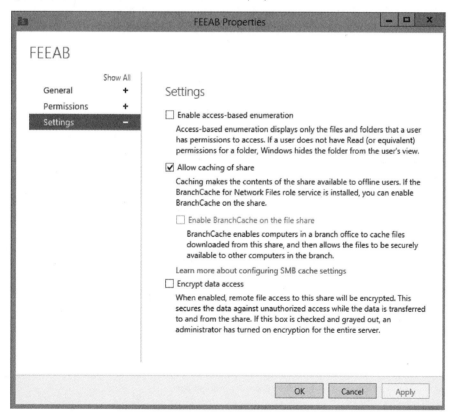

FIGURE 11.43 You can validate the configuration through Server Manager, as well. (For color version of this figure, the reader is referred to the online version of this chapter.)

If you want to encrypt all the shares on this particular server, you can use the PowerShell command below:

```
Set-SmbServerConfiguration -EncryptData $true
```

IMPORTANT

Be very careful when doing this, because the result of this command is that *all* shares that are going to be created on this server will be encrypted. This means that all clients that are accessing shares located on this server must be using either Windows 8 or Windows Server 2012 (remember that legacy clients will get the "Access Denied" error message).

Under the Hood

Now that you know what SMB encryption is all about and how to enable it, let us take a look at the before and after of enabling SMB encryption from another perspective: from that of the network itself. Using Network Monitor 3.2 with the latest parses, you can compare the traffic patterns across the same folder and the same file when encryption is enabled and when it is not enabled. However, note that even after installing the latest parser, you will not see the SMB 3 Protocol in the Network Monitor filter. Do not worry; this is an expected behavior.[11]

Figure 11.44 shows the client (10.0.0.160) accessing the share (FEEAB) on the server (10.0.0.160) without SMB encryption enabled. You can clearly see all

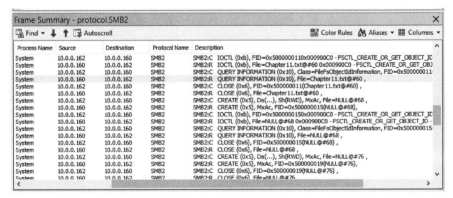

FIGURE 11.44 This client is accessing a share without SMB encryption enabled. (For color version of this figure, the reader is referred to the online version of this chapter.)

---

[11]Yuri Diogenes' Blog, *Where is my SMB3 in Network Monitor?* http://blogs.technet.com/b/yuridiogenes/archive/2012/10/15/where-is-my-smb3-in-network-monitor.aspx.

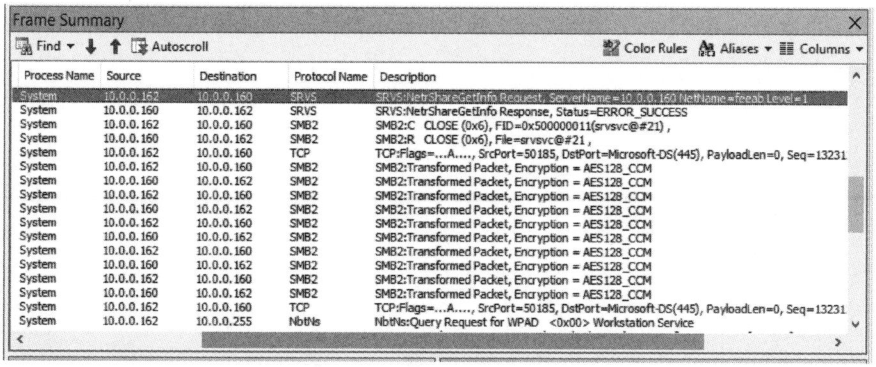

FIGURE 11.45 Here is the same traffic with SMB encryption enabled. (For color version of this figure, the reader is referred to the online version of this chapter.)

SMB commands, which file is being accessed (Chapter11.txt), and if you look at the hex code in Network Monitor, you can even see the file's content.

Next, we will look at the same traffic from the same client and server when SMB encryption is enabled. Take a look at Figure 11.45 and notice that, immediately after the initial SMB connection (C and R), all the rest of the SMB traffic is encrypted.

SUMMARY

In this chapter, we have delved deeply in the new Windows Firewall with Advanced Security that comes built into Windows 8 and Windows Server 2012. We discussed the evolution of the Windows Firewall over the years, improvements to this latest version of Windows Firewall, and its features and capabilities. We demonstrated detailed step-by-step instructions for using the WFAS console, netsh, PowerShell and Group Policy to create, manage and control firewall, and IPsec rules and settings. The Windows Firewall continues to develop into a sophisticated host-based firewall that is capable of protecting Windows servers and clients in a wide variety of scenarios, supplementing network-based security controls to keep Windows machines safe from attacks originating from both Internet and local network sources.

CHAPTER 12

Unified Remote Access and BranchCache

CONTENTS

CHAPTER POINTS

- The Evolving Remote Access Landscape
- New Capabilities in DirectAccess
- DirectAccess Requirements
- New Capabilities in BranchCache
- Overview of a BranchCache Deployment

THE EVOLVING REMOTE ACCESS LANDSCAPE

Remote access to corporate resources has gone through several major changes over the years. If you have been in the business long enough, you might remember your first "remote access" experience with a phone coupler-based modem. The ability to connect to another network (or actually, even another computer) was exhilarating! When the 2400 baud modem became mainstream, it also became a mainstream practice for large companies to allow their users access to information on the corporate network from remote locations.

If you were not around during the modem age, the end-user experience was that you connected the modem to a phone line using a regular POTS (plain old telephone service) connection. Just like the landlines in homes today (do you still have a land line? We have not had one for years). You would use the modem dial-up software to dial the number of the modem that you wanted to call—which was typically a "modem bank" managed by your IT department on the corporate campus. You could hear the sound of the modems negotiating the connection and it sort of sounded like a jaw harp. If you were not around in those days, you can hear the sound of a modem at http://www.youtube.com/watch?v=oDyqctIw0SE.

Modem speeds gradually increased in the 1990s. In the early 1990s, the 1200 baud modem gave the way to the 2400 baud modem. After that the 9.2K and the 14.4K modems began to be popular. The switch between 2400 baud and 14.4K was definitely noticeable—you could actually start seeing pictures on Web pages and you could download software far faster than ever before! But that was nothing. Soon afterward it was the 28.8K modem. Wow! That was twice as fast. The end of the modem age found the 56K modem to be the final popular standard.

Classic POTS modem technology had a number of limits that made it difficult to get much higher than 56K. While there were attempts to go over that number, none of them really stuck. And interest in modems was declining anyhow, because this new thing called "broadband" Internet began to take hold. And the beginning of that broadband Internet was DSL.

Most of you probably have had some experience with DSL and maybe are even using it now. DSL (which stands for "Digital Subscriber Line") was a new technology that made it possible to send digital signals over a POTS line. Unlike traditional modems, which used analog technology (similar to the technology used in POTS voice calls), DSL would enable much faster data transfer rates because of it used broadband instead of baseband technology. Of course, you needed some added equipment, known as a "line conditioner" to make this work.

"Broadband" then became synonymous with "fast Internet access" even if broadband signaling was not used. Sort of like anything connected to the Internet or virtualization is now called "cloud." The definition of fast started out fairly modest. I recall my first DSL connection. I got it as a replacement for the 128K ISDN line I had. It was a blazing 512K! At the time the definition of "broadband" access was anything over 128K, so as to differentiate it from ISDN speeds. Of course, it was also differentiated by the fact that it was many times less expensive than ISDN and did not require specialized ISDN equipment or lines to be installed at your house.

The remote access experience changes significantly with the advent of broadband connectivity as well. In the modem days, you did not connect to the Internet to get access to the corporate network. Instead, you dialed into the companies modem bank. You had a direct point-to-point connection with the corporate network—in the same way that you had a direct point-to-point connection with a person that you establish a normal landline phone call with. There was an implicit trust in the privacy of the POTS network because there was a large body of laws that forbade wiretapping and also because it took special skills and equipment to "tap" a phone line and decipher the modem signals. Not that it could be done and not that it was not done—but people were a lot more naïve about computer security in those days.

With the advent of widespread broadband access, new methods were developed that allowed people to access the corporate network. Instead of dialing directly into a modem bank, users would first connect to the Internet. Unlike today where broadband connections are "always on," in the early days of broadband you often had to start the Internet connection. After you connected to the Internet, you could then go through the process of connecting to the corporate network.

How did you connect to the corporate network in the new age of the broadband Internet? Well, the method was actually developed before broadband networking was available. Before broadband, but after the days of the modem banks, companies found that they could achieve more cost-effective remote access connectivity by leveraging the Internet. The company could install a T1, T3, or multiple T-lines and get rid of all the hardware they had to purchase and maintain. Remember, modem banks required that each user that wanted to dial in had to have a dedicated modem port to connect to. If you want to allow hundreds or thousands of simultaneous modem connections, the cost of the service could run up very quickly. With high-speed Internet connections at the main office, the company only needs to manage a handful of Internet links, not hundreds or thousands of modem. The modem companies saw the writing on the wall and the decline of the modem, and almost all of them have faded into the dustbin of history.

Since the Internet connection is a shared connection, you cannot have actual point-to-point connections between the remote access clients and the remote access endpoint at the corporate network. The solution was to create a "virtual" point-to-point connection. In that way, you could take advantage of the existing point-to-point protocol (PPP) that was used to negotiate a connection on an analog modem to modem connection, but wrap that PPP connection inside and Internet head. The solution ended up being what we know today as a "virtual private network."

And you thought that virtualization did not exist before VMware! The reason why it is called a "virtual" private network is that the VPN protocol enables the connection to create a PPP connection over the shared Internet. The VPN connection enabled the user to take advantage of the cost efficiencies of the Internet connection to create a virtual "cable" or link to the VPN server. The VPN server replaced the modem bank. The big advantage of using a VPN server over a modem bank was that a single VPN server could accept hundreds or even thousands of remote access VPN connections.

Another big difference between the point-to-point modem connections and a VPN connection over a shared Internet was that the illusion of security that you had with the point-to-point modem connections was not there for the VPN connections. Network security specialist knew that the "protections" of the telco connection just were not there for the Internet. Anyone could hook into an Internet connection, and with the right network analysis tools, read the entire contents of a virtual point-to-point connection over the Internet. Therefore, something had to be done about securing that connection.

For Microsoft, its first major foray into VPN networking was the Point-to-Point Tunneling Protocol or PPTP. As the name implies, the point-to-point connection was tunnel inside another protocol. In this case, it was GRE, the Generic Routing Encapsulation Protocol. PPTP quickly became very popular. It was easy to set up, both on the client and on the server side, and had an acceptable level of encryption for the time that it was released. Unfortunately, the core encryption methods used by PPTP and the way that it handles authentication outside the encrypted session makes PPTP a less viable alternative for VPN networking.

Microsoft's second attempt at a secure VPN protocol was the Layer 2 Tunneling Protocol over IPsec (L2TP/IPsec). Microsoft worked together with Cisco in developing this protocol. Sadly, Cisco decided later to abandon the L2TP/IPsec protocol and decided to go in another direction by promoting the IPsec transport remote access VPN client/server protocol.

In spite of Microsoft and Cisco going their separate ways, L2TP/IPsec became very popular. In contrast to PPTP, where credential exchange took place outside the encrypted session, the L2TP/IPsec protocol first established a secure IPsec tunnel before the credential exchange took place. Initially, a Public Key Infrastructure was required. A server certificate was required on the VPN server and the L2TP/IPsec VPN client needed to trust the issuing authority for the VPN server certificate. There was also the option to require mutual certificate authentication. In this case, the server would have to present a trusted certificate to the client and the client would have to present a trusted certificate to the server. The use of the Extended Authentication Protocol (EAP) expanded the number of authentication options to make this VPN protocol even more secure.

PPTP and L2TP/IPsec worked great when they were released because firewalls were not in widespread use on most of the client-side outbound connections. However, as the number of Internet-based attacks began to get a good amount of media attention, more and more end users found themselves behind restrictive firewalls. The problem with PPTP at this point is that there needed to be a PPTP NAT Editor on the firewall in order for PPTP to work correctly. L2TP/IPsec did not have this problem, but there were issues with having the correct ports available on the outbound connection—ports that were not typically enabled for outbound access on the client side of the connection. Also, some firewalls limited packet fragmentation in order to prevent attacks. This created problem for L2TP/IPsec as well.

Microsoft realized that firewalls were not going away (this was before the cloud and IPv6, where there are serious discussions about the firewall going away—and the authors as well as the technical reviewer of this book strongly disagree that they are going away), so they had to come up with a solution that was "firewall friendly." I have always thought that this was a bit of a misnomer, since so-called firewall friendly protocols are actually firewall "unfriendly" since they typically seek to subvert the intent of the firewall—which is to allow only the protocols that are explicitly enabled inbound or outbound through the firewall.

The solution was to enable a VPN protocol that could be tunneled through a protocol that almost all firewalls allow outbound. It is well known that the HTTP and HTTPS (SSL) are the "universal firewall protocols" because virtually every firewall in the world allows these protocols outbound. Unfortunately, this has led to a lot of abuse by both legitimate and illegitimate users.

Legitimate use of tunneling protocols can be seen with the Outlook Anywhere protocol, which encapsulates RPC traffic in an SSL header so that it can easily traverse firewalls. The problem is that writers of malicious software also know that firewall admins make the mistake of allowing SSL access to all sites. The malware can be configured to gather whatever information it needs to get and then call back home over an SSL connection and the firewall will allow it. It had never ceased to amaze me that even "firewall experts" continue to allow unrestricted access to SSL to all locations or that they have not implemented outbound SSL to SSL bridging.

But things are what they are, and therefore, tunneling protocols in an SSL header are a fact of life and we can take advantage of that for VPN connectivity. This is where the Secure Sockets Tunneling Protocol (SSTP) comes in. SSTP tunnels the point-to-point connection in a TLS secured HTTP header. The authentication process is secure because credentials are not passed until after the SSL session is established. SSTP is available for Windows Server 2008 and above and Windows Vista SP1 and above. Sadly, there had been no backporting of this wonderful VPN protocol to download clients like Windows XP.

Until this point I have been talking about network-level VPNs. Sometime in the first half of the first decade of the twenty-first century, there was a short-term "craze" for something that was called an "SSL VPN." Like cloud computing today, the term *SSL VPN* could mean just about anything the vendor wanted it to mean. It could mean a very proxy, it could mean tunneling application protocols in an SSL header, it could mean port forwarding, it could mean socket forwarding, or it could even mean using customer methods to tunneling point-to-point connections within an SSL header, which would be a real SSL VPN. Regardless of the confusion that the SSL VPN vendors introduced into the market, the solutions never really took off, because they could not deliver on most of their promises.

Sometime after the dust settled on the SSL VPN bubble, some smart guys figured out that maybe terminal services was useful not only for intranet use, but it could also be used to provide remote access. After all, what you really need is a desktop, some applications, and access to the data on the corporate network. There is no requirement that the computing device needs to be the one that the user is actually sitting right in front of.

The problem was that the remote desktop protocol was not really optimized for WAN use. Sure, it worked great when the users were connected to a 100 Mbps or 1 Gbps network, but what about when all you got it about 128K? Microsoft understood that if this was going to work, they would have to make some significant improvements in the remote desktop protocol.

And improvements they did make! They also solved another problem, which was the old firewall outbound ports problem. The default RDP port is TCP

3389. Back then you might get lucky and the firewall would already have that port open outbound, but in most cases it was not. Even worse, if you were behind a Web proxy, then you could not get out at all.

Just like with the SSL VPN story, where they took advantage of wrapping the RPC protocol in a TLS encrypted SSL header, Microsoft did the same thing with the RDP protocol. In fact, Microsoft took advantage of the work they already did with RPC/HTTP and then just encapsulated the RDP protocol inside the HTTP and RPC headers and used a similar RDP gateway to remove the headers and forward the connections to the appropriate terminal servers.

So, there is the history of remote access, at least from a mostly Microsoft perspective. But, is it a VPN that we always wanted? What is the point of VPN anyhow? We use VPN connections so that our uses can get to the information they need when they need it. We really do not care how this is done, but we do care what the end-user experience is like. Why? Because if the end-user experience sucks, the users would not use the access technologies we give them, and that will lead to the users being less productive than they should be.

What would the ideal solution be? I think that the ideal solution for enabling always on access for end users would have the following characteristics:

- The user can access any information on the corporate network that the user is authorized to use at all times.
- The user does not have to "do anything" before accessing that information.
- The user experience is the same regardless of location—there is no difference in the experience the user has to get information when connected to corpnet and when the user is connected to a hotel wireless connection a continent away.
- The connection takes place automatically, even if the user is not logged in.
- The connection is always on.
- IT is able to always use this connection to service and manage all mobile clients.

These are the things that we want. The question then becomes "is there any way we can get these things using a VPN or some other technology?" The answer is a resounding "yes!" That is because we now have DirectAccess. DirectAccess is an always on, always connected remote access technology that enables users to always be connected to corporate network and also allows IT to always be connected to the users and their computers.

The DirectAccess connection starts automatically and does not require user action in order to establish the connection. The connection starts before the user even logs on, so that IT can always connect to the device even if the user is logged off. This means that the DirectAccess link to the corpnet is a bidirectional connection.

In addition, DirectAccess can use a number of protocols so that it can traverse firewalls and other network devices. Even if the user is located behind a restrictive firewall or a Web proxy, the connection to the corpnet will be made.

One could say that DirectAccess is the answer to every network admin's dream of providing remote connectivity to his end users. However, like all dreams, they end when the person wakes up. DirectAccess is the answer to many admin prayers, but there is a catch: only Windows 7 (Enterprise or Ultimate) and Windows 8 (Enterprise) devices can be DirectAccess clients. That means that if you still have a fleet of Vista or Windows XP machines (and who does not?), then they would not be able to use DirectAccess and they will have to fall back on traditional methods of remote access.

Figure 12.1 shows how you might plan for remote access to support the heterogeneous collection of devices that need to access the corporate network. To summarize the following:

- Pre-Windows 7 and non-Windows devices. These devices can use traditional VPN technology. In most cases, they will be limited to PPTP or L2TP/IPsec. Given that PPTP is a deprecated VPN protocol because of security concerns, L2TP/IPsec is on the only practical solution.
- Windows 7 and Windows 7 devices. These can use either VPN or

FIGURE 12.1 Varieties of remote access. (For color version of this figure, the reader is referred to the online version of this chapter.)

DirectAccess. DirectAccess does require that the device be a domain member, so for those Windows 7 and Windows 8 devices that are not domain members, then they will need to use traditional VPN.

- All RDP client-enabled devices. They devices can use RDP-based solutions. This can be in the form of a terminal server connection, a Remote App connection, or some form of Virtual Desktop Infrastructure (VDI) solution.
- Smart Phones. Most smart phones have a VPN client built in that can take advantage of the L2TP/IPsec protocol.

In Windows Server 2012, DirectAccess and the remote access VPN configuration can be done in a single console and you can configure and manage all of the remote access solutions from this console. The console also provides a single place where you can monitor all of your remote access connections.

Let us now take a look at what some of the new capabilities are in Windows Server 2012 DirectAccess. I bet you are going to like them.

NEW CAPABILITIES IN DIRECTACCESS

The following represent new or improved capabilities in Windows Server 2012 DirectAccess:

- DirectAccess and RRAS coexistence
- Simplified DirectAccess management for small and medium organization administrators
- Removal of PKI deployment as a DirectAccess prerequisite
- Built-in NAT64 and DNS64 support for accessing IPv4-only resources
- Support for DirectAccess server behind a NAT device
- Simplified network security policy
- Load-balancing support
- Support for multiple domains
- NAP integration
- Support for OTP (token-based authentication)
- Automated support for force tunneling
- IP-HTTPS interoperability and performance improvements
- Manage-out support
- Multisite support
- Support for Server Core
- Windows PowerShell support

Let us take a look at each of these.

DirectAccess and RRAS Better Together

If you recall how the Windows DirectAccess worked in the past, you will remember that there was a dedicated DirectAccess console. It looked a little bit like the UAG DirectAccess console but was limited compared to UAG. In Windows Server 2012 you get a single console, the Unified Remote Access Console, where you configure DirectAccess, remote access client VPNs, and site to site VPNs. This provides a single place of configuration, management, and monitoring of all remote access connections, regardless of how the connection was established.

But there is another reason why Unified Remote Access in Windows Server 2012 is a big advancement. If you had not set up DirectAccess using the Windows DirectAccess in the past, you might not know that the DirectAccess could not be configured as a remote access VPN server. There were a number of reasons for this, most of them related to the packet filters RRAS configured to support the remote access VPN client connections and also the DirectAccess Denial of Service Protection (DoSP), which prevented all IPv4 packets and all non-IPv6-protected packets from being forwarded by RRAS.

With the new Unified Remote Access console, Windows Server 2012 prevents these services from stepping on each other. Now you can have your

DirectAccess, remote access VPN server, and site-to-site VPN gateway all on the same machine.

Simplified DirectAccess Management

DirectAccess in the past was not an easy thing to get up and running. You have to make sure your DNS infrastructure was in place to support DirectAccess, you had to have some kind of PKI to support IPsec and SSL, and you needed the Network Location Servers to be up and running, and there were several other requirements that took various levels of sophistication just to get the thing up and running.

Given the level of complexity, a lot of small- and mid-sized businesses did not deploy DirectAccess. But it is just these kind of businesses that would really benefit from the DirectAccess solution. The new Getting Started Wizard can be used by anyone to get a simple DirectAccess deployment working, without the need of setting up a PKI or Network Location Servers.

Deploy DirectAccess Without a PKI

Previously in Windows DirectAccess, certificates were used in multiple places. You had to have certificates to support the two DirectAccess tunnels that were created. The first tunnel, called the infrastructure tunnel, represented an IPsec transport mode connection that enabled the DirectAccess client to access DNS servers and domain controllers so that the user could log on. The infrastructure tunnel required both computer certificate and machine account NTLM authentication. After that connection was established, the client had access to a domain controller so that the second tunnel, the intranet tunnel could be established using computer certificate authentication and user account Kerberos authentication.

In addition to the computer certificates that were required on the client, a server certificate was required on the DirectAccess server so that the mutual authentication of the IPsec tunnels could be established. A Web site certificate was also required on the DirectAccess server so that the DirectAccess clients could establish IP-HTTPS connections to the DirectAccess server.

Finally, another certificate was required so that the client could establish connections to the Network Location Server while they were on the corpnet. As you can see, there were a lot of certificates going around and it was easy to mess things up by not using the right type of certificates, or by failing to renew certificates before they expired.

While you do have the option of creating similar DirectAccess deployments in Windows Server 2012 (and in some cases, you will need to), you now have the option of creating a much simpler DirectAccess deployment that does not require the same level of depth in terms of infrastructure requirements. This is made possible by a new feature in Windows Server 2012 known as the Kerberos Proxy.

Instead of creating two IPsec tunnels, the DirectAccess client can create a single IP-HTTPS connection with null encryption which tunnels the IPsec transport mode connection. When the authentication request is made, they are sent to the Kerberos Proxy service and the service then forwards the Kerberos requests behalf of the DirectAccess client.

For this to work, the DirectAccess server needs to have a server certificate installed so that the IP-HTTPS connection can be established. The DirectAccess clients must trust this certificate. You can use private certificates (those created by your own PKI), you can use commercial certificates (those you purchase from a public certificate authority), or you can allow the DirectAccess setup wizard to create a self-signed certificate. The latter option is most applicable to small businesses that do not have the in-house expertise for acquiring and maintaining even a small PKI. Note that the Kerberos Proxy service will also need a certificate.

NOTE

This simplified deployment does have some limitations and thus is aimed primarily at small and mid-sized businesses. For example, options such as force tunneling and Network Access Protection (NAP) and two-factor authentication methods such as one-time password (OTP) are not available when you set up DirectAccess using the simplified approach.

Say Goodbye to IPv6 and Hello to IPv4

One of the primary reasons why DirectAccess had not been more popular and more frequently implemented is because there was the impression that IPv6 was required. Unfortunately, for the Windows DirectAccess solution previously available, that was true. You needed to have an intranet that was native IPv6 (which means all the resources you wanted your users to have access to would need to have IPv6 addresses) or you would need to deploy ISATAP (Intra-Site Automatic Tunnel Addressing Protocol). The problem is that almost no one had a native IPv6 network and ISATAP really was not a long-term solution—on top of the fact that it was difficult to set up and configure.

The reason why IPv6 was important and required with the Windows DirectAccess is that the DirectAccess client only "speaks" IPv6 to the DirectAccess server. When the DirectAccess client connects to the DirectAccess server, the DirectAccess client is assigned a valid IPv6 address that enables it to connect to resources on the corporate network. All client-side application must be IPv6 capable, and protocols used by these applications must not imbed IPv4 addresses in them. If either of these situations is not true, then connections over the DirectAccess tunnels will fail.

It is unfortunate that the Windows DirectAccess came out before the UAG DirectAccess solution. The reason for that is DirectAccess got a bad reputation among network admins for the IPv6 requirement. UAG solved the problem of IPv6 by including an IPv6 to IPv4 protocol translator called "NAT64" and an IPv6 to IPv4 name resolution mapping service called DNS64. With UAG and its NAT64/DNS64 feature set, you no longer needed any IPv6 capable hosts on the corporate network. The NAT64/DNS64 tandem would translate the IPv6 connection and name resolution requests made by the DirectAccess client and forward the connections to the IPv4-only resources on the intranet. That meant that *no* IPv6 infrastructure was required anywhere on the network.

Windows Server 2012 DirectAccess now had its own NAT64/DNS64 solution. And the good news is that you do not have to do anything to make it work. All you need to do is run the DirectAccess server setup Wizard, and NAT64/DNS64 are good to go!

So, how does this magic work? The NAT64/DNS64 sequence works something like this:

1. The DirectAccess client sends an AAAA DNS query to the DNS64 service that is running on the DirectAccess server. Remember, the DirectAccess client only "understands" IPv6; that is why it sends a "quad A" query. The DNS server assignment for the DirectAccess client is something assigned to the DirectAccess client through Group Policy.
2. The DirectAccess server is configured with one or more internal DNS server addresses in the configuration of the DirectAccess server's internal interface (if the DirectAccess server has more than one interface, we will see later that you can now configure a DirectAccess server with a single interface). The DNS64 service sends both an A and an AAAA query to its configured DNS servers. The AAAA query is sent first and then the A query a very short time after that (this is a configurable option.)
3. The internal DNS server then responds to the AAAA or to the A queries (or both). If the DNS server responds with an AAAA record, then it forwards that response to the DirectAccess client and then the DirectAccess client connects directly to the IPv6 address included in the query response.
4. If the DNS server returns only an A response, then we have to do something with that IPv4 address, since we cannot return an IPv4 address to the DirectAccess client because the DirectAccess client does not understand IPv4. The IPv4 address is mapped to a "phony" IPv6 address by the DNS64 service. The "phony" IPv6 address is returned to the DirectAccess client as part of the DNS query response sent to the client.
5. The client, having received this "phony" IPv6 address, gladly makes a connection attempt to that address. Now, since this is a "phony" address, we have to do something with it. Fortunately, our friend, the DNS64 service, let its buddy, the NAT64 service, know about this phony address.

The NAT64 service sees the request sent to this "phony" IPv6 address and changes the IPv6 header into an IPv4 header with the actual IPv4 address of the destination server. After the header change is made, the NAT64 service forwards the packet to the destination IPv4 server.

6. The NAT64 service is not done yet! When the IPv4-only server responds to the DirectAccess client, the NAT64 service steps in again and converts the IPv4 header into an IPv6 header so that the response can then be returned to the DirectAccess client.

There are a few things to keep in mind regarding the use of NAT64/DNS64:

- The NAT64/DNS64 service does not perform any kind of "reverse NAT." What this means is that you cannot initiate connections from inside the intranet to a DirectAccess client. Only an IPv6 capable host on the intranet can initiate connections to DirectAccess client (this is sometimes referred to as "manage out").
- The DNS64 service will only forward A, AAAA, and PTR requires and will only return these types of records to the DirectAccess client. Requests for any other record types will be passed directly to the DNS server, which means if the response does not include IPv6 information, the DirectAccess client will not be able to use it.
- There is a small performance and memory hit when you use NAT64/DNS64. In most instances, this would not present any problems, but a heavily loaded DirectAccess server may be challenged. Make sure that you perform frequent performance monitoring to make sure you know what your limits will be.

Put the DirectAccess Server Behind Your Firewall

In the previous version of Windows DirectAccess, the DirectAccess server required two consecutive public IP addresses. The reason for this is that in order for the IPv6 transition protocol Teredo to work, you needed these addresses so that the DirectAccess client could figure out what type of NAT device it was behind and configure itself accordingly.

While that is all well and good, the problem is that the IPv4 address space is exhausted, and getting more IPv4 addresses is not a trivial affair any more. Perhaps even more problematic is the fact that almost no one wanted to put the DirectAccess on the edge of the network. They wanted to put the DirectAccess server behind an existing firewall, and just about all firewalls use NAT. In fact, there were a lot of discussions around this issue, as many of the firewall admins I talked to literally equated firewalls with NAT and they never thought about the fact that most firewalls can be configured without using NAT.

Needless to say, trying to get the DirectAccess on the edge of the network was a losing battle. The good news is that the Windows Server 2012

DirectAccess does not require two consecutive public IP addresses on the external interface (if you choose to go with a multi-interface DirectAccess server). Instead, you can use a single IP address on the interface the DirectAccess clients will connect to, and that address can be a private IP address. That means that you can now put the DirectAccess server behind a NAT device. Yay!

There is a limitation though. In this configuration, the DirectAccess clients will only be using IP-HTTPS to connect to the DirectAccess server. The reason for this is that since IP-HTTPS is wrapped in an HTTP header, it is entirely amenable for NAT. In the previous version of Windows DirectAccess, the IP-HTTPS protocol was considered the "protocol of last resort" because of all the processing overhead and "double encryption" for both DirectAccess tunnels, which incurred a large amount of processing overhead. In Windows Server 2012, we do not have that situation anymore because the IP-HTTPS protocol has been improved so that the HTTPS connection is made using null encryption. Now we have a single DirectAccess tunnel that is only encrypted once using IPsec.

Real High Availability

The high availability story for the previous version of the Windows DirectAccess solution was not a good one. There was no support for clusters, and the only way you could have some level of high availability was to run the DirectAccess server as a virtual machine in a Failover Cluster. While this did achieve a certain level of HA, it was still limited to a single machine. The problem is that a single machine is pretty limiting from a scalability perspective.

DirectAccess in Windows Server 2012 benefits from the high availability features that were given to DirectAccess as part of the UAG DirectAccess solution. Like the UAG DirectAccess offering, it uses NLB and supports up to eight servers in an NLB cluster. And because it uses NLB, if a connection is broken, it is not automatically assigned to another server in the cluster. The DirectAccess client will need to establish a new link with another member of the NLB cluster.

Multiple Domains Made Easy

The initial version of the Windows DirectAccess solution did not contain integrated support for multiple domains. While there were some workarounds that you could do to make it work, you had to do a lot of manual steps to make it work. And if you changed the configuration, you had to repeat those steps because any domain outside the domain that the DirectAccess server belonged to would not receive the changes. Yes, we will able to make it work, but it was not easy or fun.

In Windows Server 2012, multi-domain support changes and is now fully integrated into the product. You can configure the DirectAccess policies as you run the DirectAccess wizard and those policies will be deployed to each of the domains that you want the users to have access to.

NAP Integration

In the initial version of the Windows DirectAccess solution, you had to do a lot of manual configuration of Group Policy Objects so that NAP would be required for DirectAccess clients. This situation was fixed to a greater or lesser extent with the UAG DirectAccess solution, where the configuration for NAP was integrated into the DirectAccess setup wizard. Windows Server 2012 carries on the great tradition of UAG DirectAccess, and now the NAP setup is integrated into the Windows Server 2012 DirectAccess wizard.

That said, you still need to set up the NAP infrastructure before you configure the Windows Server 2012 DirectAccess wizard to require NAP enforcement for your DirectAccess clients. That means that you will need to set up the Network Policy Server (NPS) yourself, as well as the PKI required by NAP.

One-Time Password Support

As discussed earlier, there are two tunnels that are used for the DirectAccess connection (unless you are using the IP-HTTPS only solution)—the infrastructure tunnel and the intranet tunnel. The infrastructure tunnel uses computer certificate and machine account NTLMv2 authentication. The intranet tunnel uses computer certificate and user account Kerberos authentication. While this is a reasonable level of security, many organizations are moving toward two-factor authentication solutions to increase the level of authentication and authorization security for remote access.

The previous version of Windows DirectAccess did have support for smart card-based two-factor authentication. However, smart cards are not as popular as other types of two-factor authentication solutions, such as the RSA SecurID. In addition, a great number of newer OTP-based two-factor authentication solutions have been released in recent years, and DirectAccess should be able to support most of these.

That is why in Windows Server 2012 we now have support for OAuth-based OTP solutions. You can still use smart cards, but if you want to use other one-time password solutions, you can now do that. And if you do not want to use a smart card or some other OTP solution, and if you have Windows 8 clients, you can take advantage of the new "virtual smart card" solution where TPM-enabled devices can be configured to present the virtual smart card to the DirectAccess server.

Split Tunnel or Forced Tunneling? It Is Your Choice

Split tunneling is when a client system can not only remote access the corporate network but also access the Internet directly. This was seen as an issue for VPN clients in the past because you could configure the VPN connection on a Windows host to "share" the VPN connection. This would allow users to share the corporate network VPN connection with other users on the same network as the client system. This is clearly a security issue, and therefore, split tunneling has earned itself a "bad name." For Windows clients, this can be controlled through Group Policy.

The situation with DirectAccess is a bit different because users cannot "share" the DirectAccess tunnel with any other computer. The reason for this is that IPsec rules force authentication for all machines that connect to the corporate network through the DirectAccess server. Thus, the issue of having unauthenticated and unauthorized machines connecting to the corporate network through the DirectAccess client connections is not possible.

Of course, there are other issues with split tunneling that some network security experts have brought up. For example, suppose some malware infects the DirectAccess client. That malware can now obtain information from the corporate network and immediately share that information with a "control server" somewhere on the Internet in real time. There have even been concerns about real-time remote control of the infected DirectAccess client and what the effect of that kind of compromise might be.

The nature modern malware is such that real-time connectivity to the network is not required for it to do its damage. Malware can detect when the client is on the corporate network, and then when disconnected, it can send information back to its controllers. Of course, with the DirectAccess situation, the client is always connected to the network.

I do not consider split tunnel to be a major security issue for DirectAccess. But if your team has decided that split tunneling is not a viable option for your company, you can configure the DirectAccess clients to use something called force tunneling. When you configure the DirectAccess to use force tunneling, you force all network traffic over the DirectAccess connection. If the client wants to connect to corporate resources, then that connection goes through the DirectAccess tunnel. If the client wants to connect to the Internet, those connections also go over the DirectAccess tunnel.

You will need to provide a proxy address for the DirectAccess clients to use when connecting to the Internet. The Windows Server 2012 DirectAccess setup wizard will help you with that. This is a major advance over the previous Windows DirectAccess offering, where you had to do some customer GPO changes to get force tunneling enabled.

NOTE

If you decide to use force tunneling, be aware that your DirectAccess clients will be limited to use the IP-HTTPS protocol only. This is a major planning decision in the past, because the IP-HTTPS protocol could create a performance issue. However, with the improvements in the new IP-HTTPS protocol, this should not be so much of a problem. In addition, it will use the NAT64/DNS64 features for name resolution so that the DirectAccess clients can connect to your IPv4 proxy server.

Improved IP-HTTPS Performance and Authentication Support

As mentioned earlier, IP-HTTPS was considered the IPv6 transition technology of last resort. This is due to the fact that there is a large amount of protocol overhead and double encryption due to using both IPsec and TLS (SSL). That is why 6to4 is tried first and used when the client has a public IP address and why Teredo is tried first when the client has a private IP address. Only after these two methods failed did the DirectAccess client use IP-HTTPS.

This was clearly a subpar situation. IP-HTTPS is a very useful protocol, and there had to be a way to make it more performant. And that is what you get in the Windows Server 2012 IP-HTTPS protocol. Several improvements were made that focus on performance, with the most significant one being the fact that you can configure IP-HTTPS to use NULL encryption. So you get the benefits of server authentication, and the benefits of single encryption. It is estimated that IP-HTTPS performance is almost on par with the alternative IPv6 transition protocols.

Another problem that the previous IP-HTTPS protocol had was due to the fact that it was designed to work with proxies. However, its design was more useful for *open* Web proxies. Problems appeared when the proxy required authentication or proxy assignment was not made using Web Proxy Automatic Discovery (WPAD). Since the IP-HTTPS service works within a system context and not a user context, it was not easy to configure the Web proxy settings that the IP-HTTPS protocol should use. Windows Server 2012 solves this problem by making these setting users configurable so that proxy addressing and authentication information can be provided by the client who needs to make these settings manually.

Finally, you no longer need to install client certificate for mutual client/server authentication to support the IP-HTTPS connection.

Force Manage Out Only

Even though most of the press goes to how great DirectAccess is as a remote access solution, there is another perspective—and that comes from the view of the IT department. There are many scenarios where enabling always on remote access is not what you want. Instead, what you want is the ability to always be able to "touch" all the machines in your mobile fleet—to check on your inventory, to make sure security and other updates are applied, and to be able to provide remote support in case something goes haywire.

This is where "manage out" support comes in. When you "manage out" a DirectAccess client, you are able to initiate connections from the intranet to the DirectAccess clients, no matter where those DirectAccess clients are located. In the previous version of Windows DirectAccess, you could configure for manage out, but again, it took a lot of manual configuration. With the Windows Server 2012 DirectAccess, you can configure DirectAccess so that only manage out is available.

Keep in mind that when you configure DirectAccess client for manage out only—there is no intranet tunnel established. The users do not log on to the network and they are not able to access intranet resources. That means that support for two-factor authentication, NAP, and force tunneling is irrelevant.

DirectAccess at Multiple Sites

One of the most difficult challenges with DirectAccess in the previous Windows and UAG versions was to get a multiple site DirectAccess server configuration setup. There were multiple issues, and while I was able to come up with a workaround, it was a very stable or compelling one and required a high level of experience in IPv6 and Active Directory Group Policy. The solution was complex and fragile, and ultimately, we took down the article that showed how to do it.

That did not mean that the DirectAccess was going to give up on the situation. In Windows Server 2012, we now have full multisite support for DirectAccess. The reason for this is that in a multinational company, it is likely that employees are going to travel all over the world. If the employee flies from New York to Tokyo, you do not want that employee to connect to the NYC office's DirectAccess server, but you want that employee to connect to the Tokyo office's DirectAccess server.

The new DirectAccess client is able to be configured with multiple DirectAccess server names or IP addresses. The client will ping all the servers on the list and determine which will be the best response time. Then it will connect to that DirectAccess server. Also, if some of the servers are not available, the DirectAccess client will connect to any available server, which will be the one with the best response time. There is also an option for the users to configure their own DirectAccess addresses. This is most useful in a support case situation, where the Help Desk instructs the user to use a specific address.

Support for Server Core

Given that the DirectAccess server is a security server at its core, it is important that we are able to lock down the server as much as possible. Windows Server 2012 makes this possible by allowing you to install and configure your DirectAccess server on a Core installation of Windows Server 2012.

DirectAccess Remote Domain Offline Join

One of the primary requirements for a DirectAccess client is that it is a member of a domain that is hosting the Group Policy Object entries that are used to configure the DirectAccess client. This creates a bit of a dilemma for IT organizations that need to deal with an increasing number of employees that never physically (or through wireless) connect to the corpnet. One way this has been dealt with in the past is to have an IT image in the user's machine and join it to the domain during the imaging process. Then IT ships the device to the user.

While that does work, there is a lot of overhead involved. Someone has to image the machine, join it to the domain, box it, and then get it mailed out to the end user. Multiple this activity by thousands of machines and you can see that it takes a good amount of time and money.

Perhaps even more problematic is the growing trend of Bring You Own Device (or maybe Buy Your Own Device). More organizations are willing to allow users to purchase their own devices and then let them use those devices to connect to the corporate network. There are still security concerns, so IT wants to be able to control those devices. And if those devices are going to be configured as DirectAccess clients, they must be domain joined.

Windows Server 2012 introduces a solution to this problem—DirectAccess Offline Domain Join. It works as follows:

1. First, you create computer accounts for the machines that you want to join to the domain.
2. Then you create a provisioning package from a domain-joined computer that is already on the corporate network.
3. Now you add the computers to the DirectAccess security group—this is a security group that you need to create so that you can apply the DirectAccess Group Policy settings to it by using Group Policy Security Group filtering.
4. Next, make the package available to the users. The package is fairly small, so you can e-mail it to them, or make it downloadable from a published Web site, or send it in a password-protected USB key, depending on your security concerns.
5. The user then runs the package, which joins the computer to the domain and applies the initial Group Policy settings required for the machine to become a DirectAccess client.

6. Reboot the computer. When the computer reboots, it will automatically establish the DirectAccess connection. The user does not need to launch any applications for this to happen, as the DirectAccess connection is established automatically.

For more information and the details on how to configure DirectAccess Offline Domain Join, please see http://technet.microsoft.com/en-us/library/jj574150.aspx.

DirectAccess and Windows To Go

Another option that solves the domain join and BYOD problems is to take advantage of the new Windows To Go feature. Windows To Go is a cool new way to deploy enterprise desktop environments to your users and still let your users use their own devices. The way it works is that you create a full operating system on a USB key. That operating system contains your corporate image and included in the image is the full DirectAccess configuration. You mail the user the USB key and they boot that key. It is as easy as that!

Things you should know about Windows To Go are as follows:

■ When you boot the Windows To Go system, the hard disk on the computer that you are running Windows To Go on will be inaccessible. This is a core security requirement, because you do not want the host system to compromise your Windows To Go system and vice versa. If you stick the Windows To Go USB key into a running Windows 8 system, that key and its contents will not be visible in the Windows Explorer.

■ Windows To Go does not use a TPM, since a TPM is associated with a single physical system and the Windows To Go system can be connected and run from any system that can boot a USB key. Instead, a boot password can be required if you want to take advantage of BitLocker.

■ You can recover a Windows To Go system using the Windows Recovery Environment like you can with a physical computer. You can reimage the key or use a backup of the original Windows To Go system. While user state virtualization is always something you should strive to achieve, it is even more important if you decide to go ahead with widespread deployment of Windows To Go system.

■ You can use the Push Button Reset feature in Windows 8 to get back to the manufacture's original configuration, since there is not an actual OEM configuration to go back to. Just use a new copy of the Windows To Go image.

■ You cannot use "just any" USB key for Windows To Go. They need to be high-performance devices and need to be drives that are certified for use with Windows To Go. Noncertified drives are not supported.

Finally, I want to point out that while I have used the term "USB key" as the medium on which you store the Windows To Go imagine, you can also use a USB laptop drive. As long as it is certified for Windows To Go, you are good.

For more information on Windows To Go, please see http://technet.microsoft. com/en-us/library/hh831833.aspx.

For information on how to set up Windows To Go, please see http://social. technet.microsoft.com/wiki/contents/articles/6991.windows-to-go-step-by-step-en-us.aspx?PageIndex=3.

DIRECTACCESS REQUIREMENTS AND PLANNING

While I have spent a lot of time so far trying to convince you that the Windows Server 2012 DirectAccess setup and configuration experience is easier than it has ever been before, the fact is that DirectAccess still requires some work on the back end before you get it going. However, depending on your deployment, that amount of work you need to do can be significantly less than what it used to be with the previous Windows DirectAccess or even with the UAG DirectAccess solutions.

Basic DirectAccess requirements need to be met before you start thinking about setting up the infrastructure. The core requirements are as follows:

- Windows Server 2012 with the Unified Remote Access role enabled.
- Windows 7 clients for basic DirectAccess functionality.
- Windows 8 client for rich DirectAccess functionality (multisite support, remote domain join, and other new Windows 8 features).
- DirectAccess clients and servers must belong to a domain that contains the DirectAccess GPO objects that configure the DirectAccess clients and servers.
- A basic PKI to support certificate requirements for the DirectAccess server, DirectAccess clients, and Network Location Server.

The basic DirectAccess solution can be as simple as a single DirectAccess server with a single network interface which is configured with a private IP address and is located behind a NAT device. This basic setup will support only the IP-HTTPS protocol and does not support more advanced features such as multifactor authentication, multisite deployment, or high availability scenarios. This is design for very small organizations that do not require enterprise levels of support and availability.

For details on planning a simple deployment, please see http://technet. microsoft.com/en-us/library/hh831520.aspx.

The more complex scenarios that require two-factor authentication, multisite access, and load-balanced arrays are going to require the same level of back-end planning and deployment that was required by the previous UAG version of DirectAccess. The means that you will need a fairly robust DNS and PKI infrastructure to support your DirectAccess solution. While planning and deployment will be much easier than it was with the previous Windows version of DirectAccess and even the UAG version (if you take into account how difficult it was to deploy multisite and multiple domains in the past), there is still a good deal of footwork required to get the infrastructure setup and stabilized before you even think about enabling the DirectAccess server and clients.

There is a good review of the planning requirements for the enterprise setup of DirectAccess at http://technet.microsoft.com/en-us/library/jj134262.aspx.

In addition, many of the same requirements existed for the UAG DirectAccess solution. There is a nice "Complete Guide to UAG DirectAccess" that can give you some additional insights into planning your infrastructure at http://www.windowsnetworking.com/articles_tutorials/Complete-Guide-UAG-DirectAccess-Part1.html.

WHAT IS BRANCHCACHE?

BranchCache is a WAN bandwidth optimization technology that you can use to reduce the overall bandwidth usage on your WAN links that connect branch offices to the main office. The assumption is that most of the information that branch office users need is located at the main office. What BranchCache does is allow cached copies of content to be stored in branch offices so that when subsequent requests are made for the same content, the content request is answered by a host at the branch office. A small amount of information that is associated with the file is actually served by the actual server that is hosting the information.

In addition to reducing bandwidth requirements on WAN links that connect branch offices to cloud services, such as hosted private cloud. Information that you want to be located in the hosted private cloud can take advantage of BranchCache too, so that information requested by servers in your hosted private cloud only needs to be called for once to the main office server.

You can choose to deploy BranchCache in one of two modes:

- **Distributed mode**. In this mode, Window 7 and Windows 8 computers host the cached content. There is no central server. Instead, when a host on the branch network asks for content on the main office server, that content is cached on the client itself. When subsequent clients ask for the same content, the client that first requested the content from the server will fulfill the request. This mode works for a single subnet only, but does have the advantage of not requiring any additional hardware.
- **Hosted mode**. In this mode, you configure one of more Windows Server 2008 R2 or Windows Server 2012 servers to host the cached content.

When a client system at the main office requests a file from a main office server, it obtains the content and then shares the content with the BranchCache server at the branch office. When a subsequent client requests the same content, that content is returned from the BranchCache server at the branch office.

You can deploy both kinds of BranchCache servers in your organization. However, each branch office can host only one of the caching modes—either distributed or hosted, but not both.

BranchCache does not work for all protocols. In fact, it is limited to a small set of protocols. These include the following:

- HTTP/HTTPS Web servers
- SMB-based file servers
- Application servers that use the BITS protocol

Each of these server types must be configured to support BranchCache through Group Policy settings. We go through that procedure in the BranchCache configuration section of this chapter.

BranchCache was initially introduced in Windows Server 2008 R2. The "content information" that reflects attributes of the content hosted on the server for this version of Windows Server is called "version 1." The content information used by Windows Server 2012 content servers is called "version 2." You can deploy version 1 only, version 2 only, or version 1 and 2. Note that only Windows 8 clients can take advantage of the higher performance version 2.

Security is a key consideration when you work with BranchCache. The cached information is going to be stored in inherently less secure branch offices. Therefore, you need to be aware of how this information is secured and what access controls are used to gain access to the cached information.

Some key security-related issues with BranchCache include the following:

- Access to the cached data is consistent with the ACLs set on that data on the source server. The same access controls put on the data on the server are put on the data in the cached location.
- Metadata is calculated for all content on the content server in the form of hashes—this is the "content information" discussed earlier. After the content is downloaded to the branch office, only this metadata is exchanged between the branch office and content server.
- Content information is obtained using the protocol that would be used to access the actual file. If the file is delivered to the client over HTTP, then the content information will be returned using HTTP. If over HTTPS, then the content information will be delivered over HTTPS.
- All content-related activity between clients (in distributed mode) or clients and servers (in hosted mode) is encrypted over the wire using AES128.

- Potential Denial of Service attacks secondary to a client being overwhelmed by request for data are mitigated BranchCache protocols queue manager counters and timers, which prevent clients from becoming overloaded.
- In distributed mode, the cached content is not encrypted on disk. The reason for this is that it is likely not encrypted on any of the client's disks. However, if you are concerned about information leakage, it is a good idea to apply BitLocker to all the clients at the branch office.
- In hosted mode, cached content is encrypted by default. Although there is this encryption, general concerns over information leakage are still valid from the volume perspective, as all the content requested from all the clients in the branch office is stored on the server, which makes it easier for an attacker to get a large amount of information more easily. Like with distributed mode, ACLs protect the content using the same access controls that applied to the content when it was on the content server. However, it becomes even more important to use BitLocker in the hosted mode scenario.

Key deployment requirements for BranchCache include the following:

- Windows Server 2008 R2 and/or Windows Server 2012 content servers (Web servers, file servers, or BITS servers).
- Windows 7 or Windows 8 clients. Windows 8 clients are required to take advantage of the higher performance BranchCache protocols and new content information model.
- In hosted cache mode, you can support Windows 7 clients when the BranchCache server is running Windows Server 2012, but you will need to assign a computer certificate to it so that HTTPS can be used when communicating with the Windows 7 clients.
- While not an absolute requirement, it is a good idea to have an Active Directory domain so that you can configure the clients and servers to use BranchCache correctly. Otherwise, you will have to manually configure the clients and/or servers using local policy settings—something that can take a lot of time even if you have only a few branch offices.
- Active Directory sites make it easier and more efficient for hosted cache servers to be automatically discovered by clients at the branch office. In order to be automatically discovered, the BranchCache server at the branch office must be configured to be on the same Active Directory site as the clients it serves.

OVERVIEW OF BRANCHCACHE DEPLOYMENT

There are number of ways you can configure BranchCache, with the major differences being which mode you want to use and whether your clients and servers are going to be domain members or not. We assume that for security purposes and for ease of management, almost all BranchCache deployments are going to be on Windows Active Directory domain networks. Note that your domain controllers do not need to be Windows Server 2012. You can load the Windows Server 2012 administrative templates onto your 2008 or 2008 R2 servers.

The main steps that you will need to carry out include the following:

- **Configuring the content servers.** Recall that there are three types of content servers you can configure to support BranchCache: file servers, Web servers, and BIT-enabled application servers, such as Windows Server Update Services (WSUS). Configuration for each type of server will be different somewhat.
- **Configuring the hosted cache servers.** If you choose to go down the hosted cache route, you will need to deploy hosted cache servers. If you choose to use distributed caching instead, you do not have to go through this step.
- **Configuring the clients.** Client configuration is required in two main areas: first, if you choose to use the distributed cache option, you need to configure the clients to be able to host the cached files for the other clients; second, you need to configure the clients so that they can figure out what type of BranchCache mode they should be using and then determine if they need to let all the clients on the network know they need a file or request the file from a hosted mode cache server.

Let us now take a closer look at the steps involved.

Content Server Configuration

The first step is to configure the content servers. These include Web/BITS application servers and file servers.

Web (Including WSUS) and BITS Application Servers

For both new and existing Web and BITS application servers, all you need to do is install the BranchCache feature. In general, we recommend that you install the services first before you enable BranchCache on the servers. You can use PowerShell or Server Manager to do this.

The PowerShell lines to install and enable BranchCache are as follows:

```
Install-WindowsFeature BranchCache

Restart-Computer
```

If you use the Server Manager, perform the following steps:

1. In **Server Manager**, click **Manage**, and then click **Add Roles and Features**. The **Add Roles and Features wizard** opens. Click **Next**.

2. On the **Select Installation Type** page, select **Role-based or feature-based installation** and then click **Next**.
3. On the **Select destination server** page, make sure that the correct server is selected and then click **Next**.
4. On the **Select server roles** page, click **Next**.
5. On the **Select features** page, click **BranchCache** and then click **Next** (Figure 12.2).
6. On the **Confirm installation selections** page, click **Install**. On the **Installation progress** page, you can see the BranchCache feature installation progress. Click **Close** when the installation is finished.

You can confirm that the BranchCache service is running by checking for it in the **services.msc**. It should be enabled and its startup type set as **Automatic**.

File Servers

Enabling BranchCache for file servers is a bit more involved than it is for the Web and BITS application servers. You need to do the following:

- Install the BranchCache for network files role on the file server
- You then enable BranchCache on file shares (either all shares on the servers or a subset of those shares)

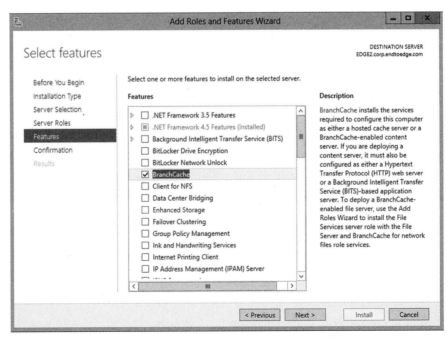

FIGURE 12.2 Install BranchCache. (For color version of this figure, the reader is referred to the online version of this chapter.)

When configuring BranchCache for file servers, there are three main steps:

- Configure new file servers
- Configure existing file servers
- Enable publication

There are two scenarios where you will find yourself installing BranchCache on a file server:

- You install BranchCache on a new server, that is not yet a file server
- You install BranchCache on a server that is already configured as a file server

New File Servers

To install BranchCache and file services on a new server that will take on the role of a file server, you can use either PowerShell or Server Manager to perform the configuration.

For PowerShell, use the lines:

```
Install-WindowsFeature FS-BranchCache -IncludeManagementTools

Restart-Computer
```

Also, we highly recommend that you enable data deduplication on all your file servers. To enable data dedupe, use the following PowerShell line:

```
Install-WindowsFeature FS-Data-Deduplication -IncludeManagementTools
```

If you want to use Server Manager to install BranchCache and data dedupe on this computer, perform the following steps:

1. In **Server Manager**, click **Manage** and then click **Add Roles and Features**. The **Add Roles and Features Wizard** opens.
2. On the **Before You Begin** page, click **Next**.
3. On the **Select Installation Type** page, make sure that **Role-based or feature-based installation** is selected and then click **Next**.
4. On the **Select destination server** page, make sure that the correct server is selected and then click **Next**.
5. On the **Select Server Roles** page, in the **Roles** section, note that the **File And Storage Services** role is already installed; click the arrow to the left of the role name to expand the selection of role services, and then click the arrow to the left of **File and iSCSI Services** to expand that section (Figure 12.3).
6. Put a checkmark in the check boxes for **File Server** and **BranchCache for Network Files**
7. On the **Select features** page, click **Next**.
8. On the **Confirm Installation Selections** page, review your selections and then click **Install**. The **Installation progress** pane is displayed during installation. When installation is complete, click **Close**.

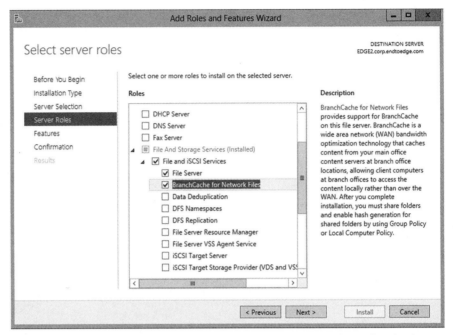

FIGURE 12.3 Installing file services. (For color version of this figure, the reader is referred to the online version of this chapter.)

Existing Files Servers

For existing file servers, the steps are basically the same except that when you run the Server Manager, you do not need to install the File Server Role again. As seen in Figure 12.3, the **File Server** option will have already been selected and all you need to do is put a checkmark in the **BranchCache for Network Files** checkbox (Figure 12.4).

Enable Hash Publication

For domain member computers, the most effective and efficient way to enable hash publication for "content information" on the BranchCache-enabled servers is to use Group Policy. This is the policy we will take in this chapter.

There are essentially four activities you will carry out to enable content information to be created for the files on your BranchCache-enabled servers:

- Create an OU that you put the BranchCache servers into
- Put the BranchCache file servers into the BranchCache OU
- Create a GPO that will contain the BranchCache hash publication settings
- Configure the BranchCache hash publication settings in the GPO

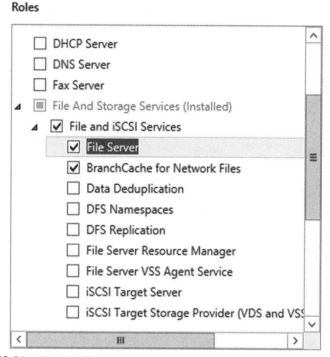

FIGURE 12.4 Installing roles. (For color version of this figure, the reader is referred to the online version of this chapter.)

Let us start by creating the OU for the BranchCache-enabled file servers:

1. On a computer where Active Directory Domain Services is installed, in the **Server Manager**, click **Tools** and then click **Active Directory Users and Computers** (Figure 12.5).
2. The **Active Directory Users and Computers** console opens. In the **Active Directory Users and Computers** console, right-click the domain to which you want to add an OU. For example, if your domain is named endtoedge.com, right-click **endtoedge.com**. Point to **New** and then click **Organizational Unit** (Figure 12.6).
3. The **New Object—Organizational Unit** dialog box opens. In the **New Object—Organizational Unit** dialog box, in **Name**, enter a name for the new OU. For example, if you want to name the OU BranchCache file servers, type **BC file servers** and then click **OK** (Figure 12.7).

With the OU in place, you can now put the file servers into this OU:

1. On a computer where Active Directory Domain Services is installed, in **Server Manager**, click **Tools** and then click **Active Directory Users and Computers**.
2. The **Active Directory Users and Computers** console opens. In the **Active Directory Users and Computers** console, locate the computer account

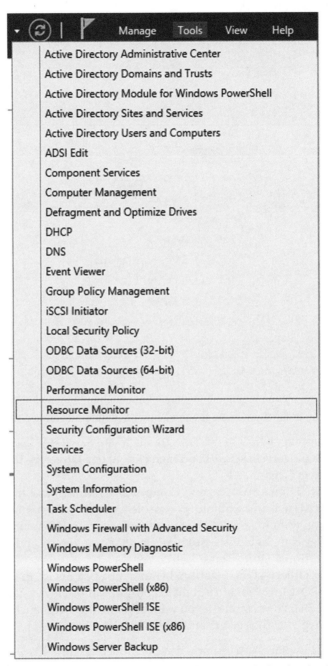

FIGURE 12.5 The Tools menu. (For color version of this figure, the reader is referred to the online version of this chapter.)

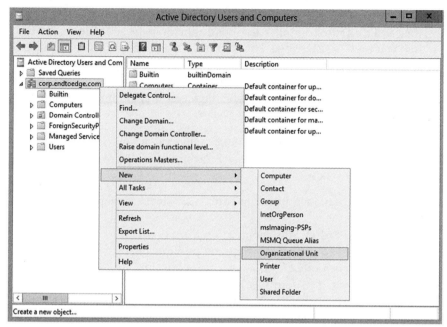

FIGURE 12.6 Create OU. (For color version of this figure, the reader is referred to the online version of this chapter.)

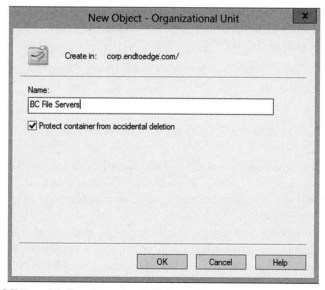

FIGURE 12.7 Name OU. (For color version of this figure, the reader is referred to the online version of this chapter.)

for a BranchCache file server, left-click to select the account, and then drag and drop the computer account on the BranchCache file servers OU that you previously created. For example, if you previously created an OU named **BranchCache file servers**, drag and drop the computer account on the **BranchCache file servers** OU.

3. Repeat step 2 for each BranchCache file server in the domain that you want to move to the OU.

Now you need to create the Group Policy Object that will contain the Group Policy settings that configure the BranchCache servers. Perform the following steps to create the GPO:

1. In the **Server Manager**, from the **Tools** menu, click **Group Policy Management**.
2. In the **Group Policy Management**, expand the path to the BranchCache file servers OU that you previously created. For example, if your forest is named endtoedge.com, your domain is named endtoedge.com, and your OU is named BC file servers, expand the following path: **Group Policy Management, Forest: endtoedge. com, Domains, endtoedge.com, BC file servers**. Right-click **BC file servers**, and then click **Create a GPO in this domain, and Link it here** (Figure 12.8).
3. The **New GPO** dialog box opens. In **Name**, type a name for the new Group Policy Object (GPO). For example, if you want to name the object BranchCache Hash Publication, type **BranchCache Hash Publication**. Click **OK** (Figure 12.9).

Finally, you need to configure the new Group Policy Object. Perform the following steps to configure the GPO (you must be a domain admin to carry out these steps):

1. Right-click the **BranchCache Hash Publication** GPO and click **Edit** (Figure 12.10).
2. The Group Policy Management Editor console opens. In the Group Policy Management Editor console, expand the following path: **Computer Configuration, Policies, Administrative Templates, Network, Lanman Server** (Figure 12.11).
3. In the Group Policy Management Editor console, click **Lanman Server**. In the details pane, double-click **Hash Publication for BranchCache**. The **Hash Publication for BranchCache** dialog box opens. In the **Hash Publication for BranchCache** dialog box, click **Enabled**. In **Options**, click **Allow hash publication for all shared folders** and then click one of the following:
   a. To enable hash publication for all shared folders for all file servers that you added to the OU, click **Allow hash publication for all shared folders**.

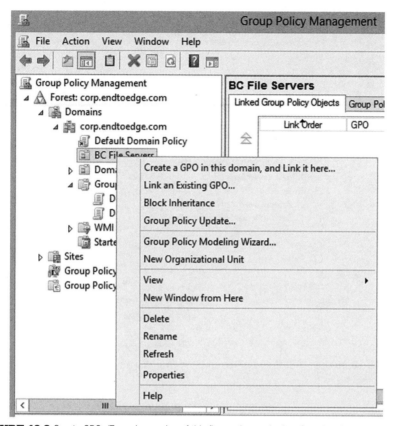

FIGURE 12.8 Create GPO. (For color version of this figure, the reader is referred to the online version of this chapter.)

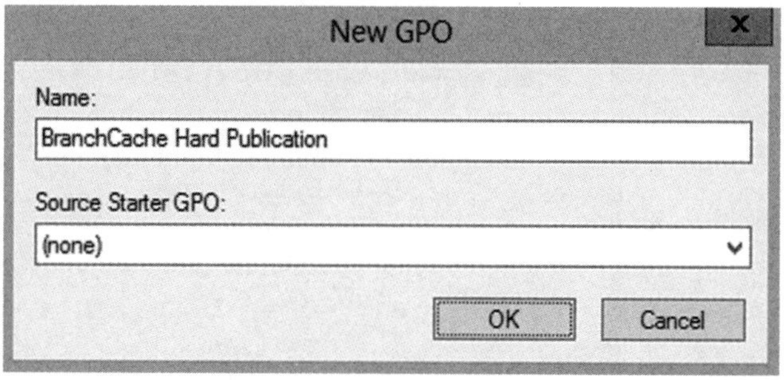

FIGURE 12.9 Name GPO. (For color version of this figure, the reader is referred to the online version of this chapter.)

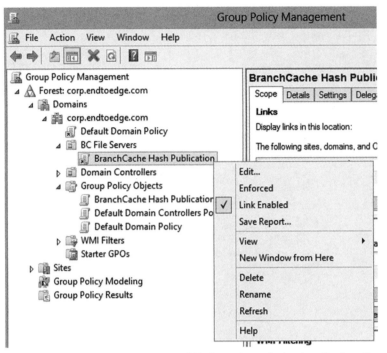

FIGURE 12.10 Open GPOs. (For color version of this figure, the reader is referred to the online version of this chapter.)

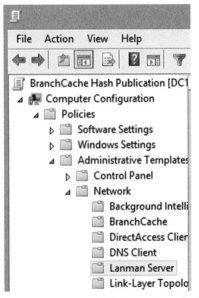

FIGURE 12.11 GPO settings. (For color version of this figure, the reader is referred to the online version of this chapter.)

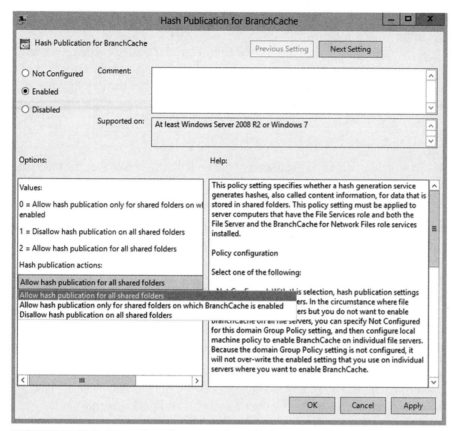

FIGURE 12.12 Enabling settings. (For color version of this figure, the reader is referred to the online version of this chapter.)

  b. To enable hash publication only for shared folders for which BranchCache is enabled, click **Allow hash publication only for shared folders on which BranchCache is enabled**.
  c. To disallow hash publication for all shared folders on the computer even if BranchCache is enabled on the file shares, click **Disallow hash publication on all shared folders** (Figure 12.12).
4. Click **OK**.

Hosted Cache Server Configuration

If you decide to go with the distributed cache mode, then you can skip this section. This section applies only if you plan on deploying hosted mode BranchCache servers.

1. Run the following command at a Windows PowerShell prompt to install the BranchCache feature on all machines that will act as a BranchCache server:

```
Install-WindowsFeature BranchCache -IncludeManagementTools
```

2. Configure the computer as a hosted cache server by using one of the following commands:
   - To configure a domain-joined computer as a hosted cache server, and to register a service connection point (SCP) in Active Directory for automatic hosted cache server discovery by client computers, enter the following command at the Windows PowerShell prompt, and then press ENTER.

```
Enable-BCHostedServer -RegisterSCP
```

3. To verify the correct configuration of the hosted cache server, type the following command at the Windows PowerShell prompt, and then press ENTER.

```
Get-BCStatus
```

The status show **HostedCacheServerIsEnabled** is **True**.

Preloading the Hosted Cache Servers

A common practice when dealing with caching servers of any type is to "preload" the cache. This improves the performance immediately for the branch office users and can reduce the overall bandwidth utilization, especially if you use out-of-band mechanisms to get the information to the branch office BranchCache servers. There are two steps here:

- Force the content servers to generate the "content information" (hashes) immediately
- Put the information on the content servers into packages that can be transferred to the BranchCache servers

Perform the following steps to accomplish these tasks:

1. Go to the content server containing the data you wish to preload and identify the folders and files you wish to load on the hosted cache servers.
2. Run an elevated PowerShell prompt. For each folder and file, run either the `Publish-BCFileContent` command or the `Publish-BCWebContent` command, depending on the type of content server, to trigger hash generation and to add data to a data package.
3. After all the data has been added to the data package, export it by using the `Export-BCCachePackage` command to create the data package file.
4. Move the data package file to the remote hosted cache servers by using your choice of file transfer technology. FTP, SMB, HTTP, DVD, and portable hard disks are all viable transports. Use an out-of-band mechanism to save bandwidth.
5. Import the data package file on the remote hosted cache servers by using the `Import-BCCachePackage` command.

For details on using the PowerShell commands in the above steps, please see http://technet.microsoft.com/en-us/library/hh848412.aspx.

Configure the Clients

We are in the home stretch! The final step is to configure the clients. The steps for client configuration include the following:

- Use Active Directory Group Policy to configure the client computers
- Confirm BranchCache client computer settings

First, create a new GPO and enter the settings to configure the BranchCache mode of operation:

1. On a domain controller, in **Server Manager**, click **Tools** and then click **Group Policy Management**.
2. In the **Group Policy Management** console, expand the following path: **Forest:** *endtoedge.com*, **Domains**, *entoedge.com*, **Group Policy Objects**, where *endtoedge.com* is the name of the domain where the BranchCache client computer accounts that you want to configure are located.
3. Right-click **Group Policy Objects** and then click **New**. The **New GPO** dialog box opens. In **Name**, enter the name for the new GPO. For example, enter **BranchCache Client Computers**. Click **OK**.
4. In the **Group Policy Management** console, make sure that **Group Policy Objects** is selected, and in the middle pane of the console, right-click the GPO the new GPO. Click **Edit**.
5. In the **Group Policy Management Editor** console, expand the following path: **Computer Configuration**, **Policies**, **Administrative Templates: Policy definitions (ADMX files) retrieved from the local computer**, **Network**, **BranchCache**.
6. Click **BranchCache** and then in the middle pane of the console, double-click **Turn on BranchCache**.
7. In the **Turn on BranchCache** dialog box, click **Enabled** and then click **OK**.
8. To enable BranchCache distributed cache mode, in the middle pain of the console, double-click **Set BranchCache Distributed Cache mode**.
9. In the **Set BranchCache Distributed Cache mode** dialog box, click **Enabled** and then click **OK**.
10. If you have one or more branch offices where you are deploying BranchCache in hosted cache mode, and you have deployed hosted cache servers in those offices, double-click **Enable Automatic Hosted Cache Discovery by Service Connection Point**.
11. In the **Enable Automatic Hosted Cache Discovery by Service Connection Point** dialog box, click **Enabled** and then click **OK**.

NOTE

When you enable both the **Set BranchCache Distributed Cache mode** and the **Enable Automatic Hosted Cache Discovery by Service Connection Point** policy settings, client computers operate in BranchCache distributed cache mode *unless they find a hosted cache server* in the branch office, at which point they operate in hosted cache mode.

Use the procedures below to configure firewall settings on client computers by using Group Policy. First, create the inbound traffic rules:

1. In the **Group Policy Management** console, expand the following path: **Forest**: *endtoedge.com*, **Domains**, *endtoedge.com*, **Group Policy Objects**, where *endtoedge.com* is the name of the domain where the BranchCache client computer accounts that you want to configure are located.

2. In the **Group Policy Management** console, make sure that **Group Policy Objects** is selected, and in the details' pane right-click the **BranchCache Client Computers** GPO that you created previously. For example, if you named your GPO **BranchCache Client Computers**, right-click **BranchCache Client Computers**. Click **Edit**.

3. In the **Group Policy Management Editor** console, expand the following path: **Computer Configuration**, **Policies**, **Windows Settings**, **Security Settings**, **Windows Firewall with Advanced Security**, **Windows Firewall with Advanced Security—LDAP...**, **Inbound Rules**.

4. Right-click **Inbound Rules** and then click **New Rule**.

5. The **New Inbound Rule Wizard** opens. In **Rule Type**, click **Predefined**, expand the list of choices, and then click **BranchCache—Content Retrieval (Uses HTTP)**. Click **Next**.

6. In **Predefined Rules**, click **Next**.

7. In **Action**, ensure that **Allow the connection** is selected and then click **Finish**. Note that you must select **Allow the connection** for the BranchCache client to be able to receive traffic on this port.

8. To create the WS-Discovery firewall exception, right-click **Inbound Rules** and then click **New Rule**. The **New Inbound Rule Wizard** opens.

9. In **Rule Type**, click **Predefined**, expand the list of choices, and then click **BranchCache—Peer Discovery (Uses WSD)**. Click **Next**.

10. In **Predefined Rules**, click **Next**.

11. In **Action**, ensure that **Allow the connection** is selected and then click **Finish**. You must select **Allow the connection** for the BranchCache client to be able to receive traffic on this port.

Finally, create the outbound traffic rules:

1. In the **Group Policy Management Editor** console, right-click **Outbound Rules** and then click **New Rule**. The New Outbound Rule Wizard opens.

2. In **Rule Type**, click **Predefined**, expand the list of choices, and then click **BranchCache—Content Retrieval (Uses HTTP)**. Click **Next**.

3. In **Predefined Rules**, click **Next**.

4. In **Action**, ensure that **Allow the connection** is selected and then click **Finish**. Note that you must select **Allow the connection** for the BranchCache client to be able to send traffic on this port.

5. To create the WS-Discovery firewall exception, again right-click **Outbound Rules** and then click **New Rule**. The New Outbound Rule Wizard opens.

6. In **Rule Type**, click **Predefined**, expand the list of choices, and then click **BranchCache—Peer Discovery (Uses WSD)**. Click **Next**.

7. In **Predefined Rules**, click **Next**.

8. In **Action**, ensure that **Allow the connection** is selected and then click **Finish**. Note that you must select **Allow the connection** for the BranchCache client to be able to send traffic on this port.

At this point, the clients and servers are configured. As is typical for deployments that depend on Group Policy, you will have to wait unless there is a complete Group Policy refresh for the clients and servers before everything starts working. If you do not want to wait, you can trigger a gpupdate using your favorite triggering mechanism.

ADMINISTRATOR'S PUNCH LIST

- Understand the current remote access landscape in order to make decisions that will impact your company while planning your remote access strategy.
- Plan the remote access protocol adoption by having security in mind since the conception of the project.
- Evaluate IPV6 adoption on your company; identify the opportunities and the challenges to move to this platform. Create a SWOT (Strengths, Weaknesses, Opportunities, and Threats) matrix before even start planning the migration to IPv6.
- Enumerate the devices that will need remote access to the company and what are the core scenarios of supportability.
- Plan DirectAccess coexistence with legacy platform and integration with existing technologies such as NAP.
- Plan DirectAccess topology to adjust to your company needs. Evaluate the requirements and plan any potential upgrade on the infrastructure that might enhance the overall security solution.
- Plan for high availability only if it is part of your remote access requirement.
- Evaluate potential migration for clients that are not using Windows 8 in order to take advantage of enhancements available in this new release.
- Plan for BranchCache placement and operation mode.

SUMMARY

In this chapter, we went through some of the details and new features included in DirectAccess and BranchCache. For DirectAccess, we spent a good deal of time talking about the challenges of remote access solutions and how DirectAccess meets most of them. Then we considered the new features included in Windows Server 2012 DirectAccess and how they answered the questions and solved the problems encountered with Windows and UAG DirectAccess. Finally, we took a quick look at Windows Server 2012 BranchCache and some security considerations around it, and then went through the steps on how to configure clients and servers in either a distributed or hosted BranchCache deployment. In the next chapter, we will look at how to configure DirectAccess in some traditional as well as some new scenarios.

DirectAccess Deployment Scenarios

CONTENTS

When it comes to remote access security solutions, it is hard to argue that there is a better solution than Microsoft DirectAccess. DirectAccess solves all the most important problems we have faced when it comes to providing a secure, transparent, and reliable connection for external users to access internal network resources. If you have not read Chapter 12 yet, you should. All the reasons for why we believe this is true are included in that chapter.

And that is where most of us start our trek with DirectAccess—with the promise of remote access nirvana. If your first taste of DirectAccess was with Windows Server 2008 R2, you probably felt like a kid who got to go to the circus with the intent of seeing the "naked lady." You saw the paintings of her outside the circus tent and you were really "excited" to finally see her in person—that was until you actually got into the tent and found out that the difference between your imagination and reality was significant. That is how you might have felt after you tried to get the Windows Server 2008 R2 DirectAccess solution to work. It sounded great, but there were so many limitations and so many complex, manual requirements that to say that you were disappointed and could not do justice to the feelings that you had.

Or maybe you started your DirectAccess journey with the UAG DirectAccess solution. If that was the case, you might have been more optimistic about the DirectAccess solution. The UAG DirectAccess wizard simplified the DirectAccess deployment (in comparison to the Windows Server 2008 R2 experience) and did much of the hard work required to get DirectAccess working. However, there was still a lot of background services that you needed to stand up, and there were some limitations and "gotcha's" that took some of the bang out of the DirectAccess buck and reduced what you considered a positive ROI.

Probably, the most difficult requirement to meet for DirectAccess before Windows Server 2012 was the fact that you needed to use two consecutive public IP addresses on the external interface of the DirectAccess server. Given that public IP addresses (at least public IPv4 IP addresses) are getting in short supply these days, it made this an onerous requirement, especially for smaller businesses. And for larger organizations, the problem was not necessarily access to the public addresses but instead the fact that the network security guys did not want the DirectAccess server to have public addresses.

Another problem for both small and large organizations is the fact that you needed to deploy your own PKI in order to deploy DirectAccess. It is funny to think of establishing a PKI as a problem in this day and age for businesses of any size, but the fact is that PKI's need to be designed well and need a lot of care and feeding. In spite of over a decade of strong advice that PKI is something that must be supported in the future, organizations of all sizes continue to drag their feet.

Microsoft, in spite of its strong support for PKI in an overall security solution, admits to the reality that PKIs are not going to be universal and that those who have not established one now are unlikely to establish one in the future and that there needs to be a way to accommodate these customers. That is why you will see an increasing number of Microsoft solutions enable "PKI-less" deployments. The Windows Server 2012 DirectAccess is one of those.

That brings us to the primary subject of this chapter, which is the simplified DirectAccess wizard—a brand new and highly anticipated feature in Windows Server 2012. This new wizard is aimed primarily at those organizations that are happy with a simplified deployment that introduces a few, but important to consider, limitations.

The simplified DirectAccess wizard is characterized by the following:

- **No requirements for a PKI**. The DirectAccess wizard will create a self-signed certificate that DirectAccess clients will trust when establishing a DirectAccess connection.
- **Support for a single NIC configuration**. In the past, you needed at least two NICs in the DirectAccess server. With the new simplified DirectAccess wizard, you can configure the DirectAccess server with a single NIC on the internal network. That said, you can still deploy with multiple NICs if you like.

- **Public IP addresses not required**. In contrast to the "full-blown" version of DirectAccess, the simplified DirectAccess configuration allows you to use private addresses on the DirectAccess server. This makes it possible to deploy the DirectAccess server behind a NAT device, such as a network firewall that also performs NAT.

- **Support for only IP-HTTPS**. In order to use alternate IPv6 transition protocols (such as Teredo), you need at least two addresses on the DirectAccess server so that the client could determine what type of NAT device it was behind. With the simplified DirectAccess server, you can use a single IP address on a single NIC that accepts the incoming DirectAccess client connection requests. Because of this, only the IP-HTTPS IPv6 transition protocol is supported.

- **Improved performance of IP-HTTPS connections**. One of the problems with the IP-HTTPS protocol in the past was the issue of double encryption and the processing overhead incurred because of this. With Windows Server 2012, the IP-HTTPS protocol uses SSL/TLS with NULL encryption. This allows for server authentication without having to deal with the overhead of SSL/TLS encryption. Credentials are secured inside an IPsec tunnel, so there are no security risks due to open exchange of credentials.

- **Network Location Server right on the box**. In a full-blown deployment of DirectAccess, you need to deploy at least one network location server on some server on the corporate network, and in most cases, multiple network location servers for fault tolerance and high availability. The Network Location Server is used by DirectAccess clients to determine whether or not they are currently located on the corporate network. When you run the simplified DirectAccess wizard, the wizard will configure the DirectAccess server as a Network Location Server. Clients will connect to the Network Location Server over a custom TCP port number, which is TCP port 62000.

- **No support for DirectAccess server arrays**. For high availability, you typically want to set up a DirectAccess server array, where you configure members of the array through a central policy that is applied to all array members. This is how it was done with the UAG DirectAccess solution. This option is not available in the simplified DirectAccess server solution. While you could use something similar to the high availability methods recommended for DirectAccess in Windows Server 2008 R2, it does not give you the same reliability.

- **Built-in NAT64/DNS64 support**. The Windows Server 2008 R2 DirectAccess server did not include a NAT64/DNS64 solution, so you had to configure the internal network to provide native IPv6 support. That support could include introducing an ISATAP server, but ISATAP really was not designed to be a long-term solution. The UAG DirectAccess solution included built-in support for ISATAP, but it also included a NAT64/DNS64 solution, so that you did not need IPv6 support on the corporate network. The simplified DirectAccess solution does not set up an ISATAP server on the DirectAccess server and instead completely relies on NAT64/DNS64 to enable DirectAccess client access to IPv4 only resources.

NOTE

Throughout this chapter, I refer to the "simplified DirectAccess solution" as being the DirectAccess deployment option that includes a single network interface and a single IP address on that inter-face. It is true that the simplified DirectAccess wizard will allow you to configure the DirectAccess server to be on the edge with multiple NICs. In that scenario, the wizard makes a number of deci-sions for you. I do not cover that scenario because in most cases involving multiple NICs and edge deployments (or even multiple NICs behind a NAT device), users will use the full-blown configura-tion wizard for enterprise deployments.

As you can see, the simplified setup is quite a bit different from the full-blown deployment of DirectAccess. For larger organizations, the major drawback is the lack of high availability built into the solution. There are workarounds, such as those you had to use with the Windows Server 2008 R2 solution, where you could have the DirectAccess servers configured as virtual machines and back-up DirectAccess servers could sit as cold stand-by servers. Not elegant, but it did work—even though it did not provide transparent failover.

THE SIMPLIFIED DIRECTACCESS SERVER TEST LAB

I am a big fan of the Test Lab Guides. Joe Davies and I came up with the idea of Test Lab Guides and now Microsoft makes Test Lab Guides for a large number of products and technologies. Test Lab Guides are great for learning about new technologies because they are all based on a common "Base Configuration" that you can snapshot and reuse; this speeds up your testing because you do not have to create custom labs each time you want to test a new product or technology. You build out the Base Configuration once and use it over and over again in multiple test scenarios.

Microsoft has prepared a number of Test Lab Guides for Windows Server 2012 and you can find a list of them at http://social.technet.microsoft.com/wiki/contents/articles/7807.windows-server-2012-test-lab-guides.aspx. There is even a Test Lab Guide listed on that page that shows you how to configure the simplified DirectAccess solution. However, there are some significant prob-lems with that guide that make it a worthwhile effort to write this chapter with a focus on the simplified DirectAccess wizard, as the simplified DirectAccess wizard Test Lab Guide does not really highlight the real values of the simpli-fied configuration.

Let me explain this is in more detail. I believe that the simplified DirectAccess wizard provides two major value propositions for small- and mid-sized businesses (and larger organizations too). Those are:

- The ability to deploy the solution behind a NAT device
- The ability to deploy the solution with a single network interface card

The problem with the Microsoft simplified DirectAccess Test Lab Guide is that it is based on the Base Configuration without making the changes required to make it a more realistic demonstration of the value of the simplified DirectAccess Wizard. The figure below shows the network configuration on which the Microsoft simplified DirectAccess configuration is based on. This is the pure Base Configuration that includes both the Corpnet and Internet subnets (Figure 13.1).

As you can see, the network topology in that Test Lab Guide is designed primarily to support the full-blown DirectAccess server deployment. You can see that there are two network interfaces on the DirectAccess server (EDGE1) and the external interface of EDGE1 has two public IP addresses. This seems to me to be completely against the spirit and philosophy of the simplified DirectAccess configuration.

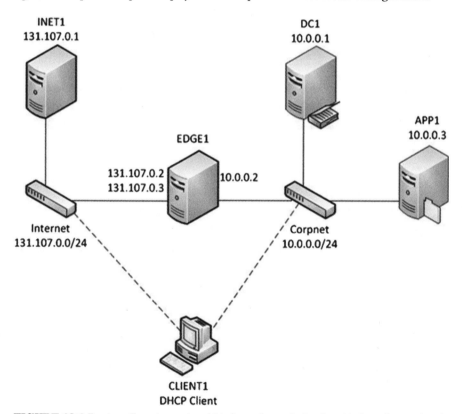

FIGURE 13.1 Topology. (For color version of this figure, the reader is referred to the online version of this chapter.)

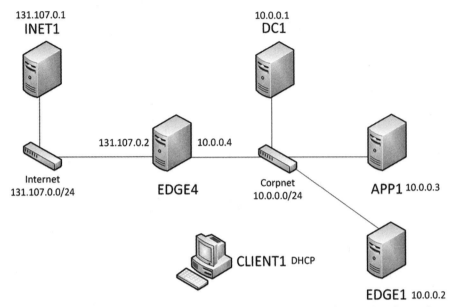

FIGURE 13.2 New topology. (For color version of this figure, the reader is referred to the online version of this chapter.)

Instead, there should be a NAT device of some kind in front of the DirectAccess server, and the DirectAccess server (EDGE1) should be reconfigured to have a single network interface card. The network topology of that configuration would look like what you see in the Figure 13.2.

NOTE

For details on how to configure Windows Server 2008 R2 as a reverse NAT server, please see my article on how to do this at http://www.windowsnetworking.com/articles-tutorials/windows-server-2008/Using-Windows-Server-2008-R2-Publish-Internal-Resources.html.

As you see in this figure, there is an "edge" device that is a NAT device (EDGE4). In this chapter, I used a Windows Server 2008 R2 computer as an RRAS NAT server that performs reverse NAT. The server was configured to forward all TCP 443 connections to the server to the IP address of EDGE1—which is **10.0.0.2** for the test lab in this chapter.

Another change you need to make to the base configuration in order to make this work is to configure the default gateway address in DHCP and on the individual servers to be the IP address on the internal interface of the RRAS NAT server (EDGE4), which is **10.0.0.4** in this test lab. The reason for this is that EDGE4 is now the gateway address to the Internet, and even EDGE1, which is the simplified, single NIC DirectAccess server, is configured to use EDGE4 as its default gateway. No worries, I guarantee that this will work—as you will see in the example worked out in this chapter.

With these minor changes to the Base Configuration, you will be able to get a full feel and realistic representation of the value and the operations of the simplified DirectAccess configuration.

In the test lab exercise for the simplified DirectAccess wizard, you will carry out the following steps:

- Create a security group that the DirectAccess client computers will be placed in
- Install the Unified Remote Access Server Role on EDGE1
- Run the Getting Started Wizard on EDGE1
- Setup and test CLIENT1 on both the Corpnet Subnet and the Internet Subnet

CREATE A SECURITY GROUP FOR DIRECTACCESS CLIENTS ON DC1

Group Policy is used to configure both the DirectAccess servers and the DirectAccess Clients. In order to take advantage of Group Policy, you can either use the default approach or create a custom Global Group in which you can place the machines that will be assigned the role of DirectAccess clients. The latter approach is the one that was used in previous version of DirectAccess. In Windows Server 2012, the DirectAccess wizard can take advantage of a WMI filter and assign the DirectAccess client settings to all machines that identify themselves as "laptop" computers.

Since we are using virtual machines in this lab, we will not be able to take advantage of the WMI filter approach. Therefore, we will need to create a Global Group for the DirectAccess clients and then place the computer account of CLIENT1 into this Global Group. In a production network, you might want to use the same approach or you may want to use the default setting that uses the WMI filter.

Perform the following steps on **DC1** to create a security group that you will use to assign the DirectAccess client Group Policy settings to:

1. On **DC1**, in the **Server Manager**, click **Tools** and then click **Active Directory Administrative Center** (Figure 13.3).
2. In the left pane of the console, click the arrow to expand **corp (local)**, and then click **Users** (Figure 13.4).
3. In the **Tasks** pane, click **New** and then click **Group** (Figure 13.5).

FIGURE 13.3 Tools menu. (For color version of this figure, the reader is referred to the online version of this chapter.)

FIGURE 13.4 Active Directory console. (For color version of this figure, the reader is referred to the online version of this chapter.)

FIGURE 13.5 Create new. (For color version of this figure, the reader is referred to the online version of this chapter.)

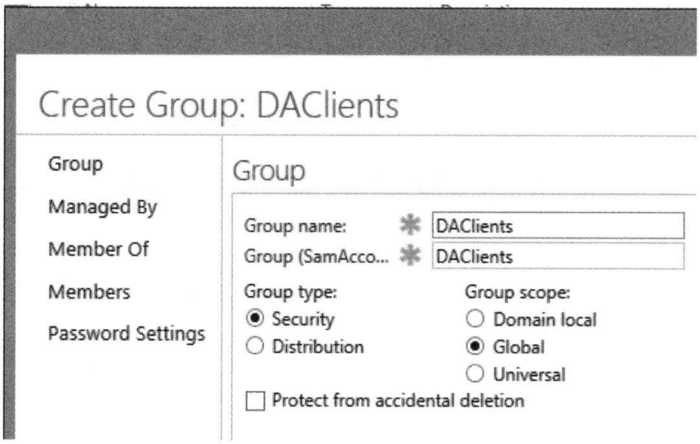

FIGURE 13.6 Security group. (For color version of this figure, the reader is referred to the online version of this chapter.)

4. In the **Create Group** dialog box, enter **DAClients** for **Group name**. Confirm that **Group type** is set to **Security** and that **Group scope** is set to **Global** (Figure 13.6).
5. Scroll down to access the **Members** section of the **Create Group** dialog box and click **Add**.
6. Click **Object Types**, put a checkmark in the **Computers** checkbox, and click **OK**.
7. Enter **CLIENT1** and then click **OK**.
8. Click **OK** to close the **Create Group** dialog box (Figure 13.7).
9. Close the **Active Directory Administrative Center**.

INSTALL THE UNIFIED REMOTE ACCESS SERVER ROLE ON EDGE1

Before you can run the simplified DirectAccess wizard on **EDGE1**, you need to install the Unified Remote Access Server Role. The wizard will provide you the option to install the remote access servers and the routing services. In this example, we will only install the remote access services; we will not install the routing services.

Perform the following steps to install this role:

1. In the **Server Manager**, click **Manage** and then click **Add roles and features** (Figure 13.8).
2. Click **Next** three times to get to the server role selection screen.
3. In the **Select Server Roles** dialog box, select **Remote Access**, click **Add Features** when prompted in the **Add Roles and Features Wizard** dialog box, and then click **Next** (Figure 13.9).

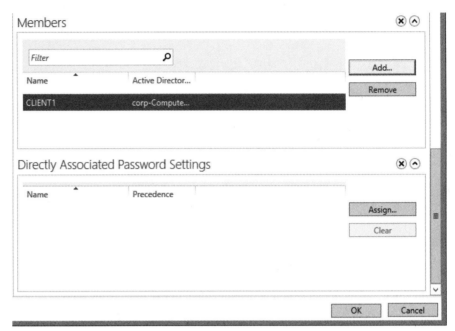

FIGURE 13.7 Select servers. (For color version of this figure, the reader is referred to the online version of this chapter.)

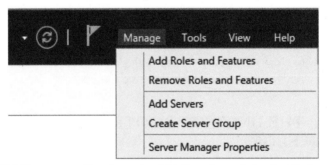

FIGURE 13.8 Manage menu. (For color version of this figure, the reader is referred to the online version of this chapter.)

4. Click **Next** five times to accept the defaults for features, remote access role services, and Web server role services. Note on the **Role Services** page, do not select the **Routing** option (Figure 13.10).

5. On the Confirmation screen, put a checkmark in the **Restart the destination server automatically if required** checkbox and then click **Yes** in the dialog box warning you that the server will automatically restart without any further warning. Click **Install** (Figure 13.11).

6. The server will automatically restart. Log on as **CORP\Administrator**. Wait for a few minutes for the installation to complete—the **Server Manager**

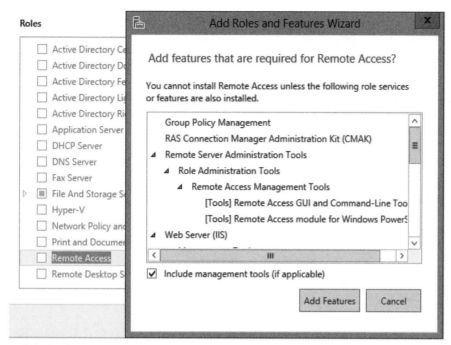

FIGURE 13.9 Adding features. (For color version of this figure, the reader is referred to the online version of this chapter.)

FIGURE 13.10 Roles. (For color version of this figure, the reader is referred to the online version of this chapter.)

will open first, and then the **Add Roles and Features** wizard will appear a few minutes after that and show you that the installation is continuing.

7. When installation completes, you will see the comment **Configuration required. Installation succeeded on EDGE1.corp.endtoedge.com**. Proceed to the next step.

RUN THE GETTING STARTED WIZARD ON EDGE1

After the Unified Remote Access Server role is installed on the DirectAccess server, you are ready to run the Getting Started Wizard. The Getting Started Wizard will provide you the options of installing either or both DirectAccess

To install the following roles, role services, or features on selected server, click Install.

☑ Restart the destination server automatically if required

Optional features (such as administration tools) might be displayed on this page because they have been selected automatically. If you do not want to install these optional features, click Previous to clear their check boxes.

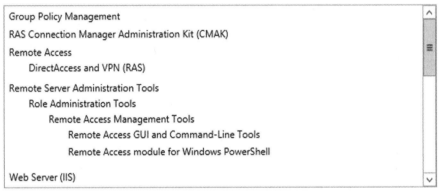

Group Policy Management

RAS Connection Manager Administration Kit (CMAK)

Remote Access

    DirectAccess and VPN (RAS)

Remote Server Administration Tools

    Role Administration Tools

        Remote Access Management Tools

            Remote Access GUI and Command-Line Tools

            Remote Access module for Windows PowerShell

Web Server (IIS)

FIGURE 13.11 Installing.

and traditional VPN services. It will also ask you what type of DirectAccess deployment you wish to have (behind a NAT device, multiple NICs, etc.).

Perform the following steps to run the Getting Started Wizard to install the simplified DirectAccess Server role:

1. On the **Add Roles and Features** page, click the **Open the Getting Started Wizard** link (Figure 13.12).
2. On the **Configure Remote Access** page, click **Deploy DirectAccess only**. Note that you have several options on this page:
   Deploy both DirectAccess and VPN (recommended)—This option enables you to configure the server as both a DirectAccess and traditional remote access client VPN server. This allows machines that are not able

Installation progress

DE:
EDGE1.c

Results

View installation progress

ⓘ Feature installation

Configuration required. Installation succeeded on EDGE1.corp.endtoedge.com.

Remote Access
    DirectAccess and VPN (RAS)
        Configure the role
        Open the Getting Started Wizard

FIGURE 13.12 Results. (For color version of this figure, the reader is referred to the online version of this chapter.)

to act as DirectAccess clients to connect to the corporate network using alternative means, such as SSTP VPN connections. It also configures the DirectAccess server to also allow these SSTP and L2TP/IPsec connections to the server, something that you could not do in previous versions of the Windows DirectAccess server.

Deploy DirectAccess only—If you select this option, the machine will be configured as a DirectAccess server only and it will not be able to accepting incoming VPN connections. We will select this option since we have covered the VPN functionality in another chapter in this book.

Deploy VPN only—If you select this option, the machine will be configured to only be a traditional remote access client VPN server and/or site to site VPN gateway. While it will not support DirectAccess connections, you can use it like you used the Windows Server 2008 R2 VPN server (Figure 13.13).

3. Verify that **Behind an edge device (with a single network adapter)** is selected as the network topology. Enter **edge1.endtoedge.com** as the public name to which remote access clients will connect. Click **Next**.

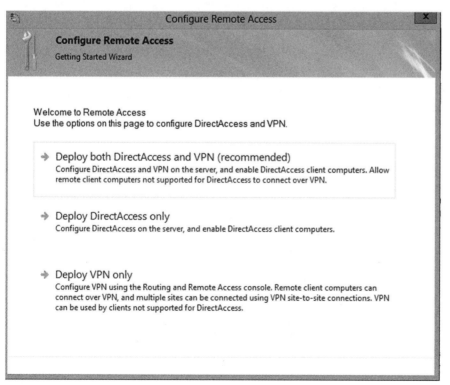

FIGURE 13.13 Scenarios. (For color version of this figure, the reader is referred to the online version of this chapter.)

Note that since we have only a single NIC in the EDGE1 computer, we select this option. Also, the Fully Qualified Domain Name you enter in the **Type the public name or IPv4 address used by clients to connect to the Remote Access server** is not necessarily the name of the DirectAccess server itself. As you can see in this example, it is actually the name that resolves on the external IP address of the RRAS NAT server (EDGE4). This is how you should set up your public DNS name when the DirectAccess is behind a NAT device. This name does not have to be the same as the name of the actual DirectAccess server located behind the NAT device (Figure 13.14).

NOTE

Recall our earlier discussion about how the Getting Started Wizard deploys DirectAccess to all laptops and notebook computers in the domain by applying a WMI filter to the client settings GPO. This default is not appropriate for our test lab demonstration. Since CLIENT1 is a member of the **DAClients** security group in Active Directory, you will need to perform the following steps to change the client security group setting for DirectAccess.

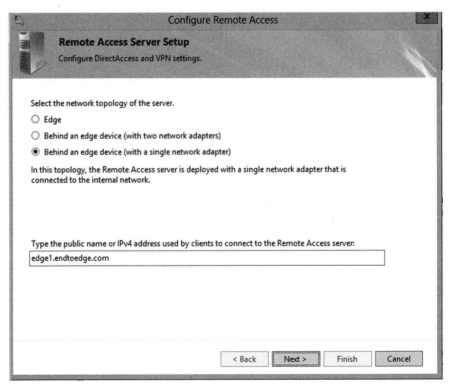

FIGURE 13.14 Topologies. (For color version of this figure, the reader is referred to the online version of this chapter.)

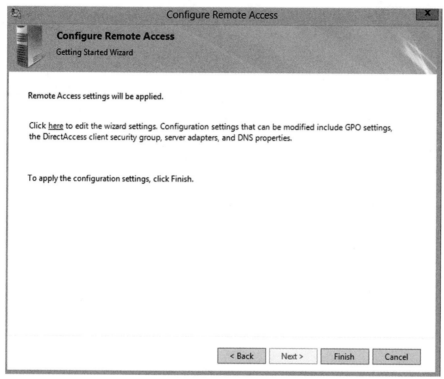

FIGURE 13.15 Wizard. (For color version of this figure, the reader is referred to the online version of this chapter.)

4. On the last page of the **Configure Remote Access Getting Started Wizard**, click the link (as seen in Figure 13.15) to edit the wizard settings.
5. In the Remote Access Review dialog box, next to **Remote Clients**, click the **Change** link (Figure 13.16).
6. On the **Select Groups** page, remove the checkmark from the **Enable DirectAccess for mobile computers only** checkbox.
7. Click **Domain Computers (CORP\Domain Computers)** and then click the **Remove** button.
8. Click **Add**, enter **DAClients**, and then click **OK** (Figure 13.17).
9. Click **Next**, and then click **Finish**. Note on this page that there are other options available. These include:
   Resources that validate connectivity to internal network—You can identify internal network resources that the DirectAccess clients can run connectivity tests against. Since we are using the simplified DirectAccess wizard in this example, there is no reason for you to do this.
   Helpdesk email address—Here, you can enter an email address that users can use to send email to the DirectAccess administrators. This

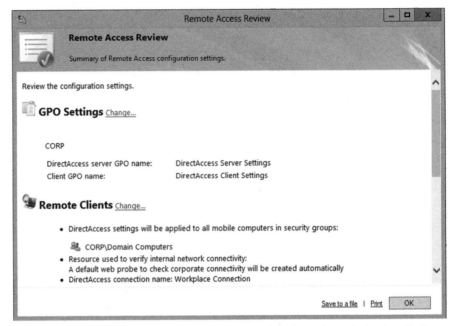

FIGURE 13.16 Remote client settings. (For color version of this figure, the reader is referred to the online version of this chapter.)

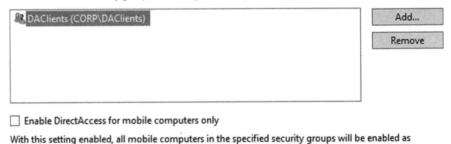

FIGURE 13.17 Groups. (For color version of this figure, the reader is referred to the online version of this chapter.)

information will be visible to the users if they check the properties of the DirectAccess network connection on their clients.

DirectAccess Connection Name—Here, you can enter a custom name for the DirectAccess client connection. A default name, **Workplace Connection**, is assigned to the DirectAccess connection but you can change this if you like. This is the name of the DirectAccess connection that users will use when they view their currently active network connections. We will see what this looks like later in this chapter (Figure 13.18).

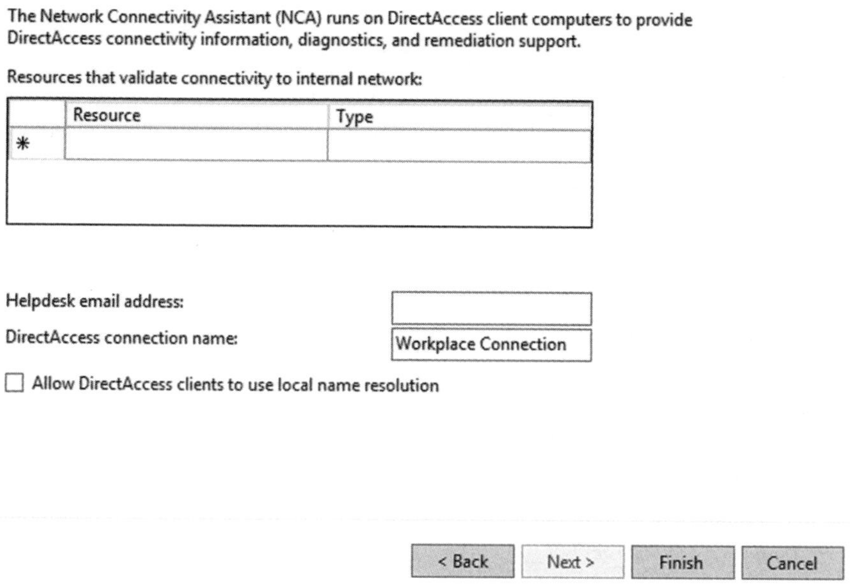

The Network Connectivity Assistant (NCA) runs on DirectAccess client computers to provide DirectAccess connectivity information, diagnostics, and remediation support.

Resources that validate connectivity to internal network:

	Resource	Type
*		

Helpdesk email address:

DirectAccess connection name:

Workplace Connection

☐ Allow DirectAccess clients to use local name resolution

[< Back] [Next >] [Finish] [Cancel]

FIGURE 13.18 NCA settings. (For color version of this figure, the reader is referred to the online version of this chapter.)

10. Click **OK** on the **Remote Access Review** page and then click **Finish**. Note that there are several key areas of information on this page. These include:
GPO Settings—The wizard will create a DirectAccess Server GPO with the name **DirectAccess Server Settings**. The wizard will create a client GPO name with the name **DirectAccess Client Settings**. You can review the settings of each of these GPOs by opening them in the Group Policy Editor.
Remote Clients—DirectAccess client machines are members of the **CORP\DAClients group.** The resource that will be used to determine corporate connectivity for the DirectAccess clients will be a default "Web probe" that the wizard will create. We will see the DNS entry for this Web probe later in this chapter. The DirectAccess connection name will be **Workplace Connection**.
Remote Access Server—The public name that DirectAccess clients will use to connect to the corporate network will be **edge1.endtoedge.com**. The NIC connected to the Internet via the reverse NAT server is named "Ethernet." This is the name of the single NIC on the DirectAccess server, which is EDGE1 in this lab scenario.
Infrastructure Servers—This section shows you the DNS suffix(es) that will define connections to the corporate network. In our lab example, all connections to corp.endtoedge.com should be directed to the internal network over the DirectAccess connection. In order to resolve names on the internal network, the DNS query requests will be sent to the **DNS Server**

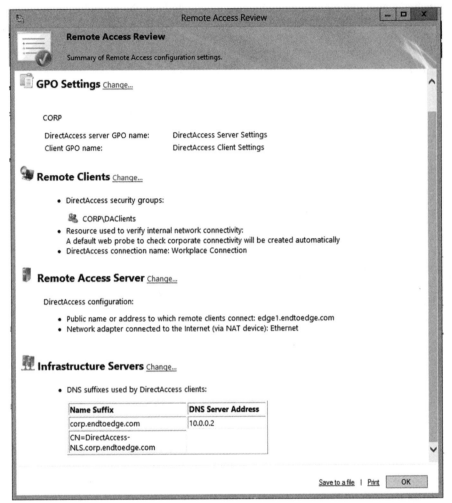

FIGURE 13.19 Review. (For color version of this figure, the reader is referred to the online version of this chapter.)

Address of **10.0.0.2**, which is the IP address of the DirectAccess server, EDGE1. Also note that the name of the Network Location Server is listed here, which in our current example is **DirectAccess-NLS.corp.endtoedge.com**. This name is automatically assigned to the DirectAccess server and registered in DNS when you use the simplified DirectAccess wizard (Figure 13.19).

11. The **Applying Getting Started Wizard Settings** page shows you all the activities that the wizard performs. When the wizard is complete, click **Close**. Wait a few moments for the **Getting Started Wizard** to close and for the **Remote Access Management Console** to open (Figure 13.20–13.24).

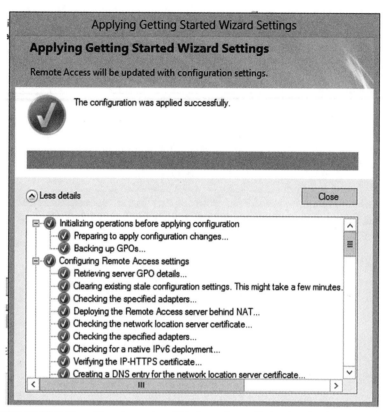

FIGURE 13.20 Settings. (For color version of this figure, the reader is referred to the online version of this chapter.)

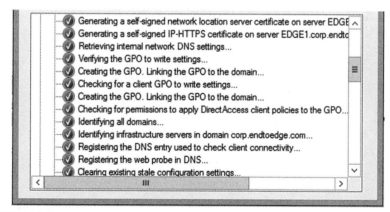

FIGURE 13.21 Settings. (For color version of this figure, the reader is referred to the online version of this chapter.)

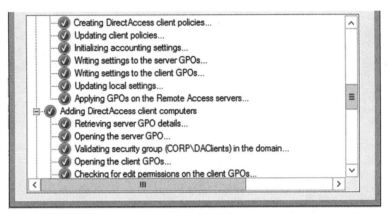

FIGURE 13.22 Settings. (For color version of this figure, the reader is referred to the online version of this chapter.)

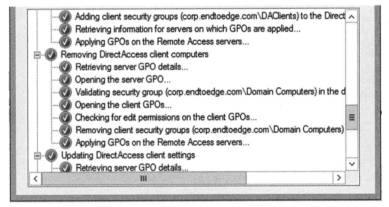

FIGURE 13.23 Settings. (For color version of this figure, the reader is referred to the online version of this chapter.)

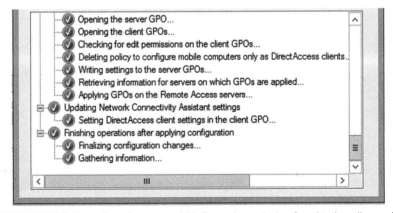

FIGURE 13.24 Settings. (For color version of this figure, the reader is referred to the online version of this chapter.)

12. In the console tree of the Remote Access Management console, select
Operations Status. Wait until the status of all monitors display as
"Working." From the Tasks pane under Monitoring, click **Refresh**
periodically to update the display. It is important that you click **Refresh**
a few times since it will appear that all the services are not yet online
when you first check the configuration.

NOTE

Since there is no PKI deployment in this test lab, the wizard will automatically provision self-signed
certificates for IP-HTTPS and the Network Location Server and will automatically enable Kerberos
proxy. The wizard will also enable NAT64 and DNS64 for protocol translation in the IPv4-only
environment.

For those of you who cannot see the graphics for what the wizard did during
the configuration process, the following list provides that information:

Initializing operations before applying configuration:

- Preparing to apply configuration changes
- Backing up GPOs

Configuring Remote Access settings:

- Retrieving server GPO details
- Clearing existing stale configuration settings. This might take a few
  minutes
- Checking the specified adapters
- Deploying the Remote Access server behind NAT
- Checking the network location server certificate
- Checking the specified adapters
- Checking for a native IPv6 deployment
- Verifying IP-HTTPS certificate
- Creating a DNS entry for the network location server certificate
- Generating a self-signed network location server certificate on server
  EDGE1. Corp.endtoedge.com
- Generating a self-signed IP-HTTPS certificate on server EDGE1.corp.
  endtoedge.com
- Retrieving internal network DNS settings
- Verifying the GPO to write settings
- Creating the GPO. Linking the GPO to the domain
- Checking for a client GPO to write settings
- Creating the GPO. Linking the GPO to the domain
- Checking for permissions to apply DirectAccess client policies to
  the GPO

- Identifying all domains
- Identifying infrastructure servers in domain corp.endtoedge.com
- Registering the DNS entry used to check client connectivity
- Registering the web probe in DNS
- Clearing existing stale configuration settings
- Creating DirectAccess client policies
- Updating client policies
- Initializing accounting settings
- Writing settings to the server GPOs
- Writing settings to the client GPOs
- Updating local settings
- Applying GPOs on the Remote Access servers

Adding DirectAccess client computers:

- Retrieving server GPO details
- Opening the server GPO
- Validating security Group (CORP/DAClients) in the domain
- Opening the client GPOs
- Checking for edit permissions on the client GPOs
- Adding client security groups (corp.endtoedge.com\DAClients to the DirectAccess client policy)
- Retrieving information for servers on which GPOs are applied

Removing DirectAccess client computers:

- Retrieving server GPO details
- Opening the server GPO
- Validating security group (corp.endtoedge.com\Domain Computers)
- Opening the client GPOs
- Checking for edit permissions of the client GPOs
- Removing client security groups (corp.endtoedge.com\Domain Computers)
- Applying GPOs on the Remote Access servers

Updating DirectAccess client settings:

- Retrieving server GPO details
- Opening the server GPO
- Opening the client GPOs
- Checking for edit permissions on the client GPOs
- Deleting policy to configure mobile computers only as DirectAccess clients
- Writing settings to the server GPOs
- Retrieving information for servers on which GPOs are applied
- Applying GPOs on the Remote Access Servers

Updating Network Connectivity Assistant settings:
- Setting DirectAccess client settings in the client GPO

Finishing operations after applying configuration:

- Finalizing configuration changes
- Gathering information

Now that the DirectAccess server is configured, we can take a look at some of the console screens that are available to you. When the wizard completes, it will open the Unified Remote Access console. When the console opens, click on the **OPERATIONS STATUS** node in the left pane of the console. In the middle pane of the console, you will see two sections:

- **Operations Status**—In the Operations Status section, you will see the components of the DirectAccess solution and their current status. It will be most likely that when you first view this section that many of the components will not be shown as **Working**. For that reason, it is important that you refresh the display a few times until you see all the components working.
- **Details**—In the Details section, you get more information about the current status of the component. If the component is working correctly, you will just see the comment **Working properly**. However, if there is a problem with any of the component, you may receive further information regarding why the component appears not to be working.

Figure 13.25 shows what the **OPERATIONS STATUS** page will look like when you complete the wizard.

Next, click on the **DASHBOARD** entry in the left pane of the console. Here, you see the following information:

- **Operations Status**—The information you see here is the same as the information you saw in the **OPERATIONS STATUS** node.
- **Configuration Status**—This section provides information on the last time the configuration was updated and whether or not the update was successful.
- **Remote Client Status**—This section provides information about remote DirectAccess client connections and provides information about **Total active clients**, **Total active DirectAccess clients**, **Total active VPN clients**, **Total cumulative connections**, **Total transferred data**, and **Maximum client connections**. There is also a link on this page that will take you to the **Remote Client Status page**. We will see what that looks like when we get CLIENT1 set up and connected to the network over a DirectAccess client connection (Figure 13.26).

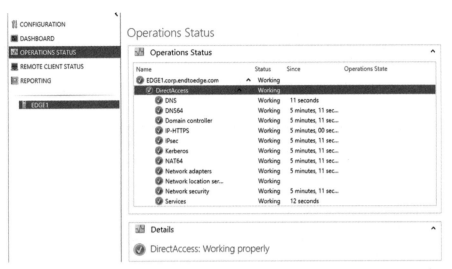

FIGURE 13.25 Operations. (For color version of this figure, the reader is referred to the online version of this chapter.)

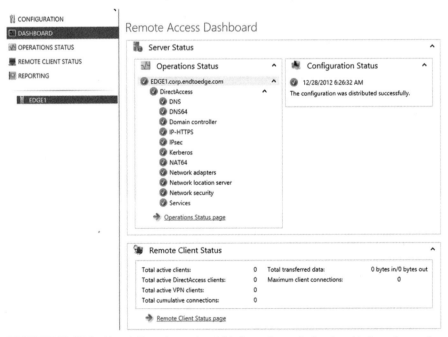

FIGURE 13.26 Dashboard. (For color version of this figure, the reader is referred to the online version of this chapter.)

Figure 13.27 shows the **Tasks** section in the console. Make sure that you make generous use of the **Refresh** option so that you can confirm that all services are up and running. You can also configure a **Refresh Interval** here too—but keep in mind that if you lower the refresh interval, performance of the server might be reduced.

A nice thing about the Unified Remote Access console is that it includes an integrated reporting feature. This is something completely new to the Windows remote access solution. In the past, you had to generate the reports yourself based on the type of record keeping your configure the RRAS server to use.

FIGURE 13.27

Monitoring. (For color version of this figure, the reader is referred to the online version of this chapter.)

Click on the **REPORTING** node in the left pane of the console. Notice in the middle pane that you receive the message **Inbox account must be configured before reporting can be used.** OK, no problem—go ahead and click the **Configure Accounting** link (Figure 13.28).

This will take you to the **Configure Accounting** dialog box. Here, you have a number of options:

- **Use RADIUS accounting**. Select this option if you want to store logs and generate reporting using a local (on-box) or remote RADIUS server. If you select this option, you will need to provide information about the RADIUS server.
- **Use inbox accounting**. Select this option if you want to store logs using the Windows Internal Database (WID) and generate reports on this server. This option is viable for single server deployments. For multiserver deployments, you will want to use a centralized accounting method, such as RADIUS. Windows Server 2012 includes a full RADIUS server option.
- **Accounting method**. Select from the drop-down box which accounting method you want to configure.
- **Store accounting logs for last**. Here, you configure how long you want the server to store accounting information.

FIGURE 13.28 Reporting. (For color version of this figure, the reader is referred to the online version of this chapter.)

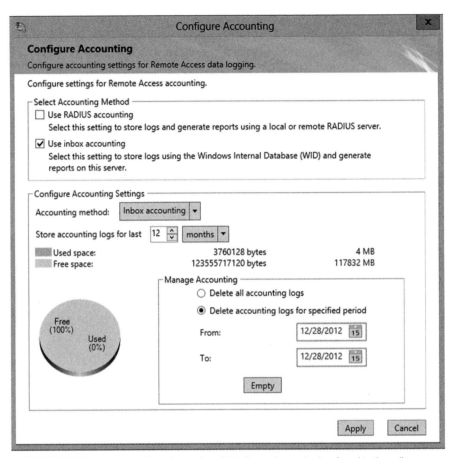

FIGURE 13.29 Accounting. (For color version of this figure, the reader is referred to the online version of this chapter.)

- **Delete all accounting logs**. Here, you can choose to delete all the log files, in the event you need to make space on the hard disk or just want to get rid of evidence ☺.
- **Delete accounting logs for a specified period**. If you have a policy to keep logs only for a specified amount of time, you can remove those you no longer need by setting the dates for the time to remove the log file entries (Figure 13.29).

After you make your selection, click the **Apply** button. That will bring up the **Configure Accounting** dialog box. Here, you can see what the wizard does when it configures the accounting feature (Figure 13.30).

If you are unable to see the graphic that shows what the wizard does, then you can see these activities in the following list:

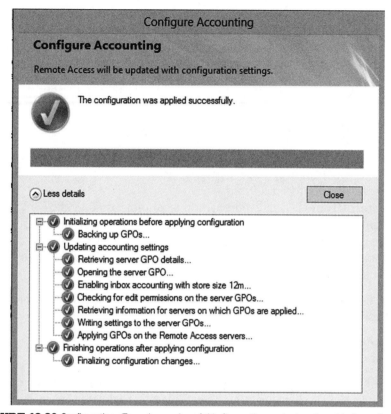

FIGURE 13.30 Configuration. (For color version of this figure, the reader is referred to the online version of this chapter.)

Initializing operations before applying configuration
- Backing up GPOs

Updating accounting settings

- Retrieving server GPO details
- Opening the server GPO
- Enabling inbox accounting with store size 12 m
- Checking for edit permissions on the server GPOs
- Retrieving information for servers on which GPOs are applied
- Writing settings to the server GPOs
- Applying GPOs on the Remote Access servers

Finishing operations after applying configuration
- Finalizing configuration changes

The Unified Remote Access console also has a reporting feature. Click the **Reporting** node in the left pane of the console. In the middle pane, you will see where you can enter a start date and an end date for the report. The report will give you the following information:

- **User name**. The name of the user who is connecting to a resource on a corporate network.
- **Host name**. The name of the DirectAccess client computer connecting to the resource on the corporate network.
- **ISP Address**. If the DirectAccess client is connecting from behind a NAT device, the IP address that the gateway uses to report the "source address" for the outbound connection.
- **Protocol/Tunnel**. The IPv6 transition technology used by the DirectAccess client to connect to the DirectAccess server. In the case of the simplified DirectAccess deployment, this will always be IP-HTTPS.
- **Duration**. The amount of time the client used when connection to the resource on the corporate network.

For each of the entries that appear in the report, there are two other sections that provide more details:

- Access Details
- Connection Details

We will see some examples of this report looks like after we connect the DirectAccess client to the DirectAccess server later in this chapter (Figure 13.31).

Click on the **REMOTE CLIENT STATUS** node in the left pane of the console. Here, you see a display very similar to what you see in the **REPORTING** node. The primary difference is that what you see here is in real time. The entries you see in this display are those for DirectAccess client that are currently connected to the DirectAccess server (Figure 13.32).

Now that we have had a short walk in the park around the Unified Remote Access console, let us get to setting up CLIENT1 and connecting CLIENT1 to the Internet so that it can act as a DirectAccess client.

SETUP AND TEST CLIENT1 FOR DIRECTACCESS CONNECTIVITY

Setup and configuration of CLIENT1 is easy—all you need to do is get the Group Policy settings applied to the client. Since CLIENT1 is already a member of the domain, all you need to do is get those Group Policy settings applied to

Remote Access Reporting

Start date: 12/28/2012 🗓 End date: 12/28/2012 🗓 Generate Report

Usage Report

User Name	Host Name	ISP Address	Protocol/Tunnel	Duration

Access Details ⌄

Protocol	Port	IP Address

Connection Details ⌄

Server Load Statistics ⌃

FIGURE 13.31 Reporting. (For color version of this figure, the reader is referred to the online version of this chapter.)

restart the computer. The reason for the restart is that the client will be part of the DAClients Security Group.

Perform the following steps to begin testing the client connectivity using DirectAccess:

1. Connect **CLIENT1** to the Corpnet subnet. Reboot **CLIENT1** while connected to the Corpnet subnet to update its security group membership and apply the DirectAccess client group policy settings.

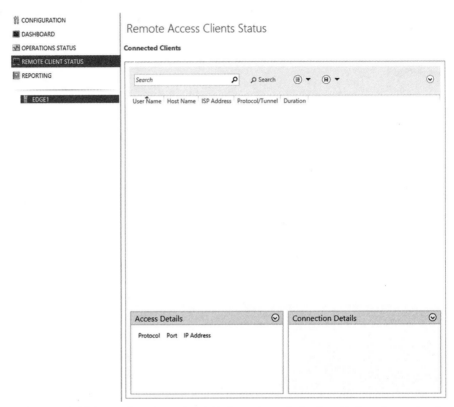

FIGURE 13.32 Clients. (For color version of this figure, the reader is referred to the online version of this chapter.)

2. From the **Start** screen, enter **PowerShell**, then right-click **Windows PowerShell**, and click **Run as administrator**.

3. In the PowerShell console, enter **Get-DnsClientNrptPolicy** and hit **ENTER**. The Name Resolution Policy Table (NRPT) entries for DirectAccess are displayed. Note that the NLS server exemption is displayed as DirectAccess-NLS.corp.contoso.com. The Getting Started wizard automatically created this DNS entry for the DirectAccess server and created a self-signed certificate so that the DirectAccess server can function as the Network Location Server. Recall that if a machine configured to be a DirectAccess client is able to connect to the Network Location Server using an HTTPS/SSL connection, then the client "assumes" that it is on the corporate network and does not begin to establish a DirectAccess connection to the DirectAccess server (Figure 13.33).

4. Enter **Get-NCSIPolicyConfiguration** and hit **ENTER**. The network connectivity status indicator settings deployed by the wizard are

```
PS C:\Users\administrator> Get-DnsClientNrptPolicy


Namespace                              : DirectAccess-NLS.corp.endtoedge.com
QueryPolicy                            :
SecureNameQueryFallback                :
DirectAccessIPsecCARestriction         :
DirectAccessProxyName                  :
DirectAccessDnsServers                 :
DirectAccessEnabled                    :
DirectAccessProxyType                  : UseDefault
DirectAccessQueryIPsecEncryption       :
DirectAccessQueryIPsecRequired         : False
NameServers                            :
DnsSecIPsecCARestriction               :
DnsSecQueryIPsecEncryption             :
DnsSecQueryIPsecRequired               : False
DnsSecValidationRequired               : False
NameEncoding                           : Utf8WithoutMapping

Namespace                              : .corp.endtoedge.com
QueryPolicy                            :
SecureNameQueryFallback                :
DirectAccessIPsecCARestriction         :
DirectAccessProxyName                  :
DirectAccessDnsServers                 : fd82:7ec8:76a4:3333::1
DirectAccessEnabled                    :
DirectAccessProxyType                  : NoProxy
DirectAccessQueryIPsecEncryption       :
DirectAccessQueryIPsecRequired         : False
NameServers                            :
DnsSecIPsecCARestriction               :
DnsSecQueryIPsecEncryption             :
DnsSecQueryIPsecRequired               : False
DnsSecValidationRequired               : False
NameEncoding                           : Utf8WithoutMapping
```

FIGURE 13.33 NRPT. (For color version of this figure, the reader is referred to the online version of this chapter.)

displayed. Note that the value of DomainLocationDeterminationURL is https://DirectAccess-NLS.corp.endtoedge.com:62000/insideoutside. Whenever this network location server URL is accessible, the client will determine that it is inside the corporate network and NRPT settings will not be applied. Note the alternate port number used for the SSL connection. This is required since we are colocating the IP-HTTPS server, which listens on TCP port 443 on the same machine as the Network Location Server. Since the DirectAccess server in this example has only a single IP address, both the IP-HTTPS listener and the Network Location Server cannot be listening on the same port and IP address. Hence, the alternate port number used by the Network Location Server (Figure 13.34).

5. Type **Get-DAConnectionStatus** and hit **ENTER**. Since the client can reach the network location server URL, the status will display as **ConnectedLocally** (Figure 13.35).

```
PS C:\Users\administrator> Get-NCSIPolicyConfiguration

Description                   : NCSI Configuration
CorporateDNSProbeHostAddress  : fd82:7ec8:76a4:7777::7f00:1
CorporateDNSProbeHostName     : directaccess-corpConnectivityHost.corp.endtoedge.com
CorporateSitePrefixList       : {fd82:7ec8:76a4:1::/64, fd82:7ec8:76a4:7777::/96, fd82:7ec8:76a4:1000::1/128,
                                fd82:7ec8:76a4:1000::2/128}
CorporateWebsiteProbeURL      : http://directaccess-WebProbeHost.corp.endtoedge.com
DomainLocationDeterminationURL : https://DirectAccess-NLS.corp.endtoedge.com:62000/insideoutside
```

FIGURE 13.34 Configuration. (For color version of this figure, the reader is referred to the online version of this chapter.)

```
PS C:\Users\administrator> Get-DAConnectionStatus

Status    : ConnectedLocally
Substatus : None
```

FIGURE 13.35 Not connected. (For color version of this figure, the reader is referred to the online version of this chapter.)

Now that we have confirmed that the DirectAccess client has received the Group Policy settings that enable it to be a DirectAccess client, we are ready to see if this thing actually works!

Perform the following steps to connect CLIENT1 to the Internet Subnet and trigger the DirectAccess connection:

1. Connect CLIENT1 to the Internet subnet. Once the network determination process completes, the network icon should indicate Internet access. You will notice that this icon showed no Internet connectivity when it was connected to the Corpnet subnet, since it was not able to connect to INET1. When it was moved to the Internet subnet, it was able to perform NCSI Internet connectivity detection and discovered that it was on the "Internet."

2. In the PowerShell window, type **Get-DAConnectionStatus** and hit **ENTER**. The status should show as **ConnectedRemotely**. Yay! This is the first indication that the DirectAccess connection is actually working—or at least that the connection was made to the DirectAccess server. We still need to find out if we can actually connect to resources on the Corpnet subnet (Figure 13.36).

```
PS C:\Users\administrator> Get-DAConnectionStatus

Status    : ConnectedRemotely
Substatus : None
```

FIGURE 13.36 Connected. (For color version of this figure, the reader is referred to the online version of this chapter.)

3. Click the network icon in the System tray. Note that **Workplace Connection** is listed as **Connected**. Recall that this is the default connection name provided by the DirectAccess wizard and that you could have changed it if you liked when you set up the DirectAccess server (Figure 13.37).

4. Right-click **Workplace Connection** and then click **Properties**. Note that Status shows as **Connected**. Also note here that if there was a problem with the DirectAccess connection, the user could click the **Collect Logs** button to get detailed information about the nature of the failure. Those logs could then be sent to the DirectAccess admin who can figure out what is wrong (Figure 13.38).

FIGURE 13.37 DA connection. (For color version of this figure, the reader is referred to the online version of this chapter.)

5. From the PowerShell prompt, enter **ping inet1. isp.example.com** and hit **ENTER** to verify Internet name resolution and connectivity. You should receive four replies from 131.107.0.1. If you do not, it might be because you did not enable ping requests to INET1 when you configured the Base Configuration. I have made that mistake before. Instead of going through the effort of enabling ping requests, just enter **arp –g** and see if you can see the MAC address of INET1. If you cannot, then that proves that you have network connectivity with INET1.

6. Enter **ping app1.corp.endtoedge.com** and hit **ENTER** to verify corporate intranet name resolution and connectivity. Note the format of the IPv6 address returned. Since there is no IPv6 deployed in the test lab, the dynamically created NAT64 address of APP1 is returned. The dynamically created prefix assigned by DirectAccess for NAT64 will be in the form fdxx:xxxx:xxxx:7777::/96. Remember, the DirectAccess client has no concept of IPv4 addresses and always uses IPv6 to communicate with corporate resources. It is only through the magic of NAT64/DNS64 that we are able to connect to the IPv4-only resources on the corporate network (Figure 13.39).

FIGURE 13.38 Client. (For color version of this figure, the reader is referred to the online version of this chapter.)

7. Click the Internet Explorer icon to launch IE. Verify that you can access the Websites on **http://inet1.isp.example.com** and **http://app1.corp. endtoedge.com** (Figure 13.40).

8. From the desktop taskbar, click the **Windows Explorer** icon.

9. In the address bar, type **\\app1\Files** and then press **ENTER**.

```
PS C:\Users\administrator> ping app1

Pinging app1.corp.endtoedge.com [fd82:7ec8:76a4:7777::a00:3] with 32 bytes of data:
Reply from fd82:7ec8:76a4:7777::a00:3: time=2ms
Reply from fd82:7ec8:76a4:7777::a00:3: time=1ms
Reply from fd82:7ec8:76a4:7777::a00:3: time=1ms
Reply from fd82:7ec8:76a4:7777::a00:3: time=3ms

Ping statistics for fd82:7ec8:76a4:7777::a00:3:
    Packets: Sent = 4, Received = 4, Lost = 0 (0% loss),
Approximate round trip times in milli-seconds:
    Minimum = 1ms, Maximum = 3ms, Average = 1ms
PS C:\Users\administrator>
```

FIGURE 13.39 It works! (For color version of this figure, the reader is referred to the online version of this chapter.)

FIGURE 13.40 Yay! (For color version of this figure, the reader is referred to the online version of this chapter.)

10. You should see a folder window with the contents of the **Files** shared folder (Figure 13.41).
11. In the **Files** shared folder window, double-click the **Example.txt** file. You should see the contents of the **Example.txt** file.
12. Close the **example.txt - Notepad** and the **Files** shared folder windows.
13. From the PowerShell window, type **Get-NetIPAddress** and then press **ENTER** to examine the client's IPv6 configuration. Note that the tunnel adapter iphttpsinterface is active with a valid IP-HTTPS address. CLIENT1 is using IP-HTTPS to tunnel IPv6 traffic to the EDGE1 server (Figure 13.42).

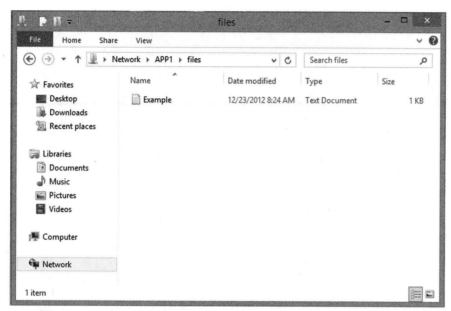

FIGURE 13.41 File. (For color version of this figure, the reader is referred to the online version of this chapter.)

14. Type **Get-NetIPHTTPSConfiguration** and hit ENTER. Examine the settings applied by group policy to direct the client to https://edge1. endtoedge.com:443/IPHTTPS (Figure 13.43).

15. Type **wf.msc** and then hit **ENTER** to launch the Windows Firewall with Advanced Security console. Expand **Monitoring**, then **Security Associations** to examine the IPsec SAs established. Note that the authentication methods used are Computer Kerberos and User Kerberos, and that no certificate-based authentication was needed to establish the single tunnel simplified connection security rule. The client leverages the Kerberos proxy automatically deployed by the DirectAccess wizard. Select **Connection Security Rules** in the console tree to examine the associated policies applied. Recall that in the previous versions of DirectAccess that the user authentication was NTLMv2—the Kerberos proxy enables to use Kerberos for both computer and user authentication now (Figure 13.44).

16. Close the **Windows Firewall with Advanced Security** console.

Now that we have established that the DirectAccess client connection actually works; let us take a look at some of the monitoring and reporting information that is available after the client is able to connect.

The first place to look at is the **REMOTE ACCESS CLIENT STATUS** node in the left pane of the console. When you click that node, you will see a list of the

```
PS C:\Users\administrator> Get-NetIPAddress

IPAddress           : fe80::4fc:696c:74c7:ddef%23
InterfaceIndex      : 23
InterfaceAlias      : iphttpsinterface
AddressFamily       : IPv6
Type                : Unicast
PrefixLength        : 64
PrefixOrigin        : WellKnown
SuffixOrigin        : Link
AddressState        : Preferred
ValidLifetime       : Infinite ([TimeSpan]::MaxValue)
PreferredLifetime   : Infinite ([TimeSpan]::MaxValue)
SkipAsSource        : False
PolicyStore         : ActiveStore

IPAddress           : fd82:7ec8:76a4:1000:9c33:a1d5:6489:3d1
InterfaceIndex      : 23
InterfaceAlias      : iphttpsinterface
AddressFamily       : IPv6
Type                : Unicast
PrefixLength        : 128
PrefixOrigin        : RouterAdvertisement
SuffixOrigin        : Random
AddressState        : Preferred
ValidLifetime       : 6.02:44:29
PreferredLifetime   : 6.02:44:29
SkipAsSource        : False
PolicyStore         : ActiveStore

IPAddress           : fd82:7ec8:76a4:1000:4fc:696c:74c7:ddef
InterfaceIndex      : 23
InterfaceAlias      : iphttpsinterface
AddressFamily       : IPv6
Type                : Unicast
PrefixLength        : 64
PrefixOrigin        : RouterAdvertisement
SuffixOrigin        : Link
AddressState        : Preferred
ValidLifetime       : 29.23:58:46
PreferredLifetime   : 6.23:58:46
SkipAsSource        : False
PolicyStore         : ActiveStore
```

FIGURE 13.42 IP address. (For color version of this figure, the reader is referred to the online version of this chapter.)

```
PS C:\Users\administrator> Get-NetIPHTTPSConfiguration

PolicyStore         : ActiveStore
ConfigurationType   : GroupPolicy
Profile             :
ProfileActivated    :
State               : Default
ServerURL           : https://edge1.endtoedge.com:443/IPHTTPS
Type                : Client
AuthMode            :
StrongCRLRequired   : False
```

FIGURE 13.43 Configuration. (For color version of this figure, the reader is referred to the online version of this chapter.)

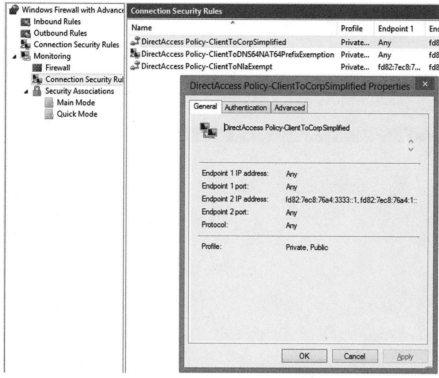

FIGURE 13.44 Connections. (For color version of this figure, the reader is referred to the online version of this chapter.)

DirectAccess clients that are currently connected to the DirectAccess server. As you can see in the figure below, you can see **CORP\CLIENT1$** is connected using the **IPHttps** protocol and that it had been connected for 19 s. Note that there is no user name associated with the connection yet, because the only connections the client has made to the network at this time is to a resource that only requires machine authentication. You can see more information about the connection in the **Connection Details** section in the lower right middle pane (Figure 13.45).

Let us see what happens after we run the DA server for a few days and then run a report. In this example, we will click on the **REPORTING** node and then set the start and end dates in the middle pane of the console. Then we will click the **Generate Report** link. It takes a few minutes to generate the report, with the time it takes based on how many days you include in the report range.

As you can see in the figure below, there is a lot of information included in the report. All entries in the log related to a DirectAccess client connection will be included in the report. You can see that there are entries that include both

Remote Access Clients Status

Connected Clients

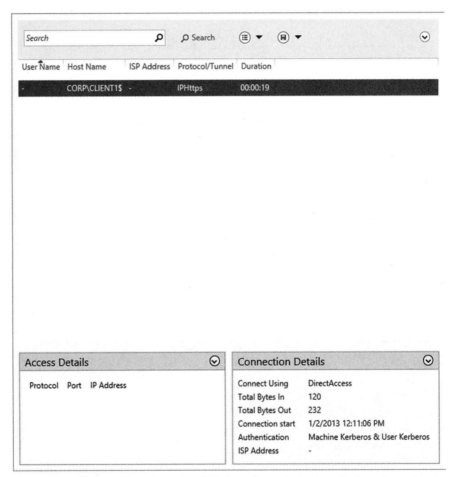

FIGURE 13.45 Status. (For color version of this figure, the reader is referred to the online version of this chapter.)

the user name and the computer name. In the **Access Details** section, you can see more details for the entry that you click on. This information includes the **Protocol**, **Port**, and **IP Address** of the network resource that the client is connected to. You can see in the figure that connecting to DC1 over TCP ports 445, 135, 49157, and 389. This looks like domain-related protocol activity, which makes sense since this is a connection to DC1. Note in the **Connection Details** section that no **ISP Address** is listed. The reason for this is that CLIENT1 is connected to the Internet subnet and is being assigned a public IP address.

Finally, notice the section at the bottom of the page, **Server Load Statistics**. Here, you get the following summary info for the period represented in the report:

- Total sessions
- Total DirectAccess sessions
- Total VPN sessions
- Average sessions per day
- Maximum concurrent sessions
- Total unique users
- Unique DirectAccess clients

You do need to be careful with these numbers, because in this example, there is only a single DirectAccess client machine, which is CLIENT1. So, why does the report indicate that there are *two* unique users? My assumption is that the report is considering both computer and user accounts as users. In that case, the two unique users are CLIENT1 and CORP\Administrator. The same may be true for **Unique DirectAccess Clients**, which the report indicates are 2 in number. However, CLIENT1 is the only DirectAccess client that has ever connected to the DirectAccess server, EDGE1. We have to wait for more comprehensive documentation on how reporting works with Windows Server 2012 DirectAccess before we rely too heavily on these summary numbers in the reports (Figure 13.46).

This brings us to the end of the first part of the chapter, where the focus has been on the simplified DirectAccess wizard and the configuration and end-user experience with this new deployment option. We wanted to make sure that this new deployment option got extra attention, since we suspect that this will likely be one of the most popular options, both for DirectAccess testing and pilot projects, and for actual deployment for small and mid-sized businesses. In the next section, we will take a look at what the new configuration experience is like with a more traditional DirectAccess deployment option.

OVERVIEW OF TRADITIONAL DIRECTACCESS SINGLE SERVER DEPLOYMENT

In this section of the chapter, we will take a look at the configuration experience for a more traditional deployment of DirectAccess. The configuration we will look at here is one that is very similar to the one we used to deploy using a single UAG DirectAccess server. This can be the foundation for other Windows Server 2012 DirectAccess scenarios, such as multiserver arrays and multisite configurations, as well as scenarios where you will want to deploy NAP access controls over DirectAccess clients.

We will not go through the entire configuration experience required to get the single server Windows Server 2012 DirectAccess server configuration working.

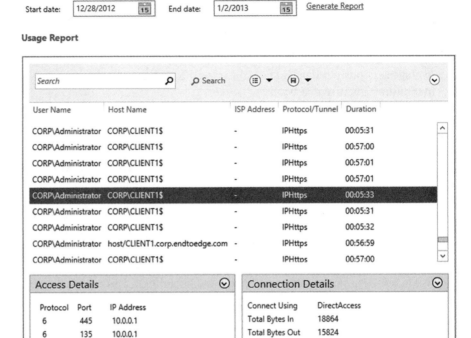

FIGURE 13.46 Reporting. (For color version of this figure, the reader is referred to the online version of this chapter.)

Instead, what we want to do is show you what the new wizard looks like and what configuration options are available to you. Unlike the simplified DirectAccess server configuration where a lot of the work is already done for you, in this deployment example, you have to do some background work. Some of this includes:

- Setting up a basic PKI to support IP-HTTPS, Network Location Server, and computer certificates
- Setting up a Network Location Server
- Creating certificate templates for certificates that will be assigned to DirectAccess clients and servers

- Creating certificate templates for the Network Location Server
- Creating Group Policy settings to allow IPv4 and IPv6 ping requests to domain member computers so that Teredo will work correctly

You can find the details on how to set up the entire test lab for this scenario at http://www.microsoft.com/en-us/download/details.aspx?id=29031. In this section, we will just walk through the DirectAccess configuration wizard for the nonsimple scenario so that you can see how it works and explain the important options to you.

Let us begin at the point after you have installed the Unified Remote Access role on this server.

1. From the **Server Manager**, click **Tools** and then click Remote **Access Management** (Figure 13.47).
2. In the **Remote Access Management** console, click **Run the Remote Access Setup Wizard**. Note that this takes us to a wizard that is different from the one we ran in the first part of this chapter. If you were to click on the **Run the Getting Started Wizard**, it would take you to the simplified remote access server wizard. Remember, the goal of the simplified wizard is to make things fast and easy—and most of the

FIGURE 13.47 Tools. (For color version of this figure, the reader is referred to the online version of this chapter.)

Remote Access Setup

Configure Remote Access, including DirectAccess and VPN.

 Configure Remote Access

DirectAccess & VPN settings have not yet been configured. Select one of the wizard options.

→ Run the Getting Started Wizard

Use this wizard to configure DirectAccess and VPN quickly, with default recommended settings.

→ Run the Remote Access Setup Wizard

Use this wizard to configure DirectAccess and VPN with custom settings.

 The Getting Started Wizard only appears the first time you run the Remote Access Management console. After running this wizard, click the Configuration node to edit DirectAccess and VPN settings using the Remote Access Setup Wizard.

FIGURE 13.48 Wizard. (For color version of this figure, the reader is referred to the online version of this chapter.)

decisions are made for you. Now we are going to see the wizard that allows you make your own decisions (Figure 13.48).

3. In the Configure Remote Access wizard, click **Deploy DirectAccess only**. This might look familiar, but the options you will see will be significantly different than what you saw earlier in this chapter (Figure 13.49).

4. In the middle pane of the console, under Step 1 Remote Clients, click **Configure** (Figure 13.50).

5. On the **Deployment Scenario** page of the Remote Client configuration wizard, you will need to make one of two decisions:

   Deploy full DirectAccess. This option enables you to allow DirectAccess clients to reach resources on the internal network and also allow for "manage out" functionality, where hosts on the corporate network will be able to initiate outgoing connections to DirectAccess clients.

   Deploy DirectAccess for remote management only. This option is used when you want to be able to initiate connections to DirectAccess clients from within the corporate network, but you do not want DirectAccess clients to be able to establish connections to any resource on the corporate network. This is useful if you want to make all DirectAccess client computers accessible to members of corporate IT or the help desk.

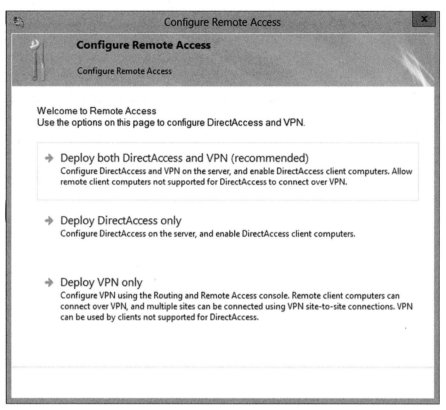

FIGURE 13.49 Remote Access. (For color version of this figure, the reader is referred to the online version of this chapter.)

We have found this option to be very popular among members of educational IT groups.

In this example, we will select the **Deploy full DirectAccess for client access and remote management** option and click **Next** (Figure 13.51).

6. On the **Select Groups** page of the DirectAccess client configuration wizard, you have several options:

Select one of more security groups containing client computers that will be enabled for DirectAccess. This is where you select the groups that contain the computer accounts that you will designate as DirectAccess clients. Typically, you will create this group before you run the DirectAccess wizard. You may already have established security groups that contain the machines that will become your DirectAccess clients; you can use those too. Just click the **Add** button to add those groups.

Enable DirectAccess for mobile computers only. If you want to make things easier, you can select this option to make only those machines

Step 1

FIGURE 13.50 VPN. (For color version of this figure, the reader is referred to the online version of this chapter.)

FIGURE 13.51 Scenarios. (For color version of this figure, the reader is referred to the online version of this chapter.)

that are seen as "mobile" computers DirectAccess clients. That way, you could use an established group like "Domain Computers" and then filter the settings so that only the mobile computers in that group receive the DirectAccess Group Policy configuration. How does the filter know if a machine is a mobile computer or not? If you are interested, check out this blog post from the Scripting Guy: http://blogs.technet.com/b/heyscriptingguy/archive/2004/09/21/how-can-i-determine-if-a-computer-is-a-laptop-or-a-desktop-machine.aspx.

Use force tunneling. By default, DirectAccess client computers on the Internet connect to resources on the corporate network by going through the DirectAccess tunnel(s) and access Internet content directly (meaning that connections to the Internet are not routed through the DirectAccess tunnel(s) and are sent directly to the destination servers). This default configuration is called "split tunneling." There is a lot of debate on whether split tunneling represents a security issue. It is our opinion that split tunneling does not represent a significant security issue and that what you lose from not enabling split tunneling does not make up for any theoretical or practical gains you would achieve by not enabling split tunneling. However, if you cannot enable split tunneling for any reason, then use the force tunneling option. Keep in mind that if you do require force tunneling, all traffic will go through the DirectAccess tunnels and you will have to provide a proxy mechanism that enables the DirectAccess clients Internet access. Also, the only protocol the DirectAccess client will be able to use will be the IP-HTTPS protocol, which although improved from the past, still requires more processing overhead than the other IPv6 transition protocols.

In this example do not enable either of these options and select the **DAClients** security group, which has the CLIENT1 computer account contained in it. Then click **Next** (Figure 13.52).

7. On the **Network Connectivity Assistant** page, you have the options:
Helpdesk e-mail address. Enter an address that will appear to users when they need to run diagnostics on their DirectAccess connections.

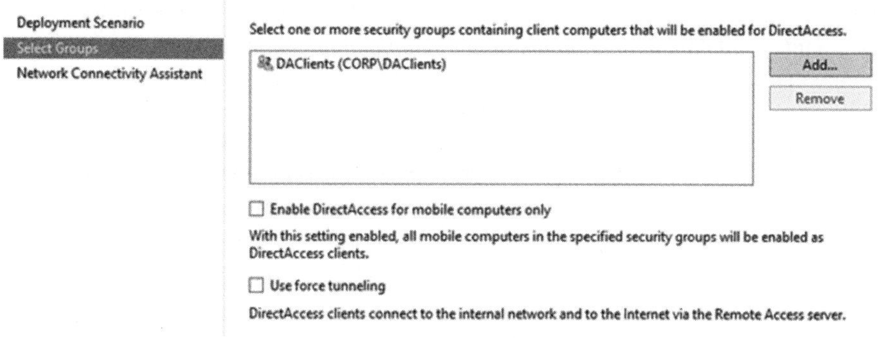

Deployment Scenario

Select Groups

Network Connectivity Assistant

Select one or more security groups containing client computers that will be enabled for DirectAccess.

DAClients (CORP\DAClients)

Add...

Remove

☐ Enable DirectAccess for mobile computers only

With this setting enabled, all mobile computers in the specified security groups will be enabled as DirectAccess clients.

☐ Use force tunneling

DirectAccess clients connect to the internal network and to the Internet via the Remote Access server.

FIGURE 13.52 Groups. (For color version of this figure, the reader is referred to the online version of this chapter.)

This will appear in the interface and the users will be able to click this address to e-mail diagnostic reports.

DirectAccess connection name. This is the name that will appear in the DirectAccess client interface.

Allow DirectAccess clients to use local name resolution. If you use this option, DirectAccess clients will be able to perform broadcast name resolution requests for names that are not resolvable over the DirectAccess connection. Some people consider this a potential security risk, as it does have the potential for exposing names of computers on your corporate network.

In this example, in the **Resources that validate connectivity to internal network** section, right-click on the >* cell and click **New** (Figure 13.53).

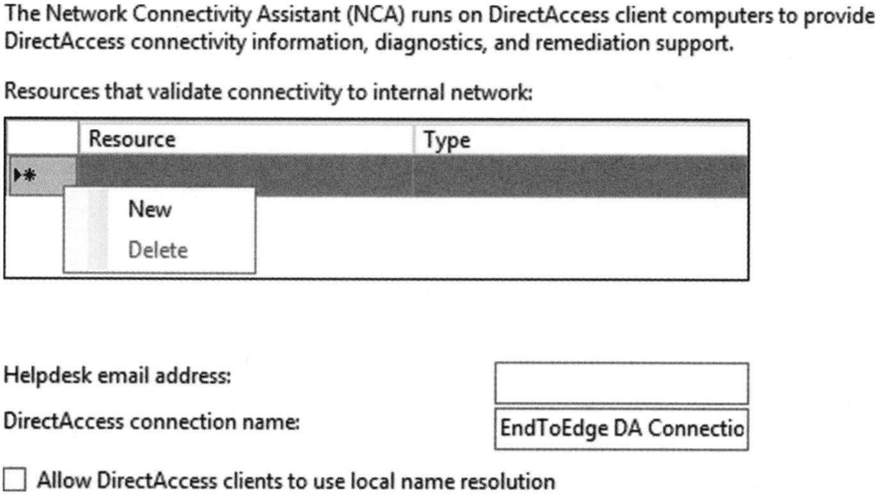

The Network Connectivity Assistant (NCA) runs on DirectAccess client computers to provide DirectAccess connectivity information, diagnostics, and remediation support.

Resources that validate connectivity to internal network:

	Resource	Type
▶*		
	New	
	Delete	

Helpdesk email address:

DirectAccess connection name:

EndToEdge DA Connectio

☐ Allow DirectAccess clients to use local name resolution

FIGURE 13.53 Internal resources. (For color version of this figure, the reader is referred to the online version of this chapter.)

8. This brings up the **Configure Corporate Resources for NCA** dialog box. Here, you can specify a corporate URL or FQDN that is always accessible to DirectAccess clients. In this example, click the down arrow where it says "PING." Notice that you have two choices: ping or HTTP. In this example, enter **dc1.corp.endtoedge.com** and click **Validate**. If that machine is accessible via an IPv6 address, the test will succeed. You could use a DC or some other key server on your network for this purpose. The goal here is that if the DirectAccess client cannot access the resource, the DirectAccess Connectivity Assistant will report that the DirectAccess connection has failed. Click **Add** (Figure 13.54).
9. Click **Finish** (Figure 13.55).
10. In the middle pane of the console, under Step 2 **DirectAccess Server**, click **Configure** (Figure 13.56).
11. On the **Network Topology** page, you have the options:
    Edge. Select this option if the DirectAccess server is an edge server and has two public IP addresses assigned to the external interface of the server. The server does not have to be on the actual edge of the network, but it must have two public IP addresses (and they must be consecutive addresses).
    Behind an edge device (with two network adapters). Select this option if you have a NAT device in front of the DirectAccess server. In this case, the DirectAccess server will need at least two network interfaces: an "external" (the one closest to the Internet) and an "internal" (the one closest to the corporate network). You will not need two public IP addresses—just one private address will work, because only the IP-HTTPS protocol will be available in this configuration.

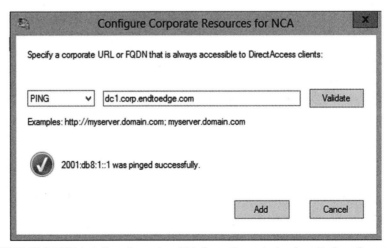

FIGURE 13.54 NCA test. (For color version of this figure, the reader is referred to the online version of this chapter.)

The Network Connectivity Assistant (NCA) runs on DirectAccess client computers to provide DirectAccess connectivity information, diagnostics, and remediation support.

Resources that validate connectivity to internal network:

	Resource	Type
	dc1.corp.endtoedge.com	PING
▶*		

Helpdesk email address:

DirectAccess connection name:

`EndToEdge DA Connectio`

☐ Allow DirectAccess clients to use local name resolution

< Back   Next >   Finish

FIGURE 13.55 NCA test. (For color version of this figure, the reader is referred to the online version of this chapter.)

Behind an edge device (with a single network adapter). This option is similar to the previous option, except that in this case the DirectAccess server has only a single NIC.

Type the public name or IPv4 address used by client to connect to the Remote Access server. This is a publicly resolvable name that DirectAccess clients on the Internet can use to reach the DirectAccess server. If there is a NAT device in front of the DirectAccess server, then this name will need to resolve to the IP address of the NAT device that is accepting the incoming requests. If there is no NAT device in front of the DirectAccess server, then it will be the primary IP address on the external interface of the DirectAccess server.

In this example, we will select the **Edge** option and enter the name **edge1.endtoedge.com** and click **Next** (Figure 13.57).

12. On the Network Adapters screen, wait for the wizard to populate the Internet and Corpnet interfaces. If the wizard does its job correctly, it will correctly identify the following:

Adapter connected to the external network. The name that appears is the name that you gave the NIC. For this reason, it is always a good idea

Step 2

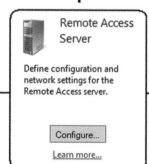

Remote Access Server

Define configuration and network settings for the Remote Access server.

Configure...

Learn more...

FIGURE 13.56 Remote Access Server. (For color version of this figure, the reader is referred to the online version of this chapter.)

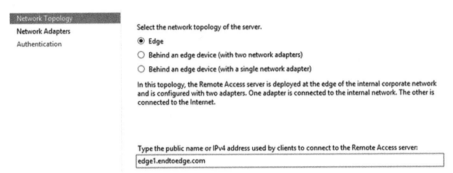

FIGURE 13.57 FQDN. (For color version of this figure, the reader is referred to the online version of this chapter.)

to rename the NICs in your DirectAccess servers so that it is easy for you to identify them. If you click the **Details** button, it will show you the IP addressing information associated with that NIC.

Adapter connected to the Internal network. Again, the name of the adapter appears, this time for the internal interface. Note that it identified the IPv6 address assigned to this NIC.

Select the certificate used to authenticate IP-HTTPS connections. When you click the **Browse** button, you will see a list of certificates that have been installed on the DirectAccess server. You would pick the one that you installed that was intended for use by the IP-HTTPS listener.

In this example, select the **edge1.endtoedge.com** certificate that we requested earlier from the custom certificate template that was created. Then click **Next** (Figure 13.58).

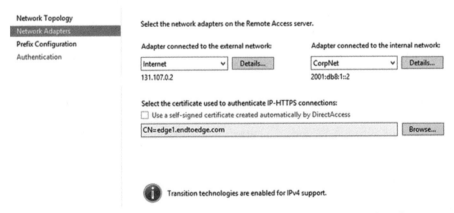

FIGURE 13.58 Certificates. (For color version of this figure, the reader is referred to the online version of this chapter.)

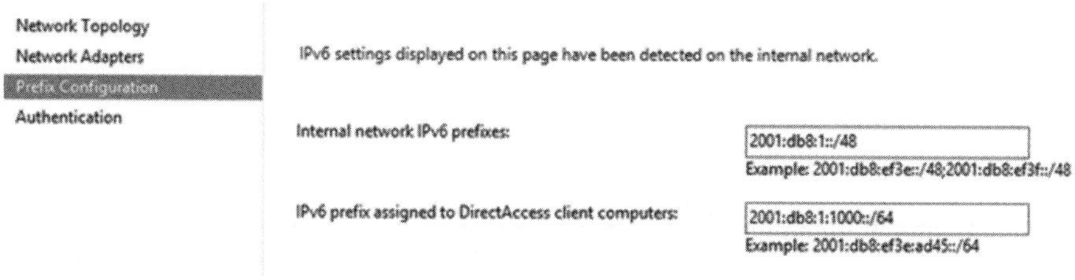

Network Topology
Network Adapters
Prefix Configuration
Authentication

IPv6 settings displayed on this page have been detected on the internal network.

Internal network IPv6 prefixes:

```
2001:db8:1::/48
```
Example: 2001:db8:ef3e::/48;2001:db8:ef3f::/48

IPv6 prefix assigned to DirectAccess client computers:

```
2001:db8:1:1000::/64
```
Example: 2001:db8:ef3e:ad45::/64

FIGURE 13.59 IP address prefix. (For color version of this figure, the reader is referred to the online version of this chapter.)

13. On the **Prefix Configuration** page, click **Next**. These numbers are derived from the IPv6 addresses that were already assigned to the computers on the intranet. You do not need an IPv6 infrastructure for this to work, but if you do have one in place already, the DirectAccess wizard will work with what you have (Figure 13.59).

14. There are several options available on the **Authentication** page:
Active Directory credentials. User needs to authenticate with the DirectAccess server. If you check this option, username and password will be used.
Two-factor authentication (smart card or one-time password (OTP)). If you require stronger authentication, you can require two-factor authentication. If you require two-factor authentication, the two options are smart card or one-time password (OTP) authentication.
Use OTP. If you choose the two-factor authentication option and you do not want to use smart cards but you do want to use OTP, then select this option.
Use computer certificates. DirectAccess client computers also need to be able to authenticate with the DirectAccess server. If you choose this option, computer certificate authentication will be used to authenticate the computer. If you do not choose this option, the Kerberos proxy will be used on the DirectAccess server to authenticate the computer. Obviously, this is more overhead when you have to deploy certificates and manage the PKI, but this is the better choice from an enterprise perspective and is less overhead on the DirectAccess server itself.
Enable Windows 7 client computers to connect via DirectAccess. Select this option if you want to support Windows 7 clients to connect to the DirectAccess server. You need to do this if you have Windows 7 clients, because the IP-HTTPS protocol is different for those clients and you need to make sure that the DirectAccess server is able to negotiate the correct protocol for these clients. Note that IP-HTTPS is available to both Windows 8 and Windows 7 clients, with the caveat that Windows

Step 3

Infrastructure Servers

Identify infrastructure servers accessed by DirectAccess clients before connecting to internal resources.

Configure...

Learn more...

FIGURE 13.61

Infrastructure servers. (For color version of this figure, the reader is referred to the online version of this chapter.)

7 clients do not have the ability to use NULL encryption. Enabling this option changes the way the IPsec tunnels are authenticated. In a pure Windows 8 deployment, the first tunnel is authenticated using Kerberos (via Kerberos proxy). Enabling the option to support Windows 7 clients reverts to the old UAG/DA method of using computer account/NTLM authentication for the first tunnel.

Enforce corporate compliance for DirectAccess clients with NAP. If you want to use NAP, enable this option. Unfortunately, the wizard will not set up your NAP infrastructure, so you have to have that all set up before you can use NAP with DirectAccess.

In this example, on the **Authentication** screen, select **Use computer certificates** and then click **Browse**. Select **corp-APP1-CA**, click **OK**, and then click **Finish** (Figure 13.60).

15. In the middle pane of the console, under Step 3 Infrastructure Servers, click **Configure** (Figure 13.61).

16. On the **Network Location Server** page, you have the option:

    The network location server is deployed on a remote Web server (recommended). When you choose this option, the DirectAccess server will look to another server to provide network location services to the DirectAccess clients. This is the recommended configuration, and you should deploy highly available, redundant network location servers throughout your organization. If you choose this option, you would enter the URL for the network location server and click **Validate** to confirm that the server is available on the network.

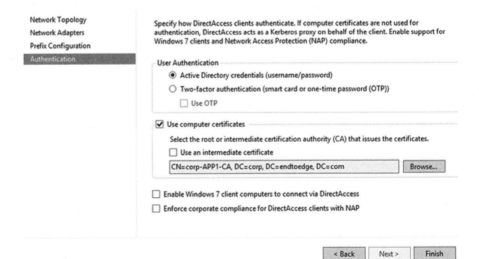

FIGURE 13.60 Certificates. (For color version of this figure, the reader is referred to the online version of this chapter.)

The network location server is deployed on the Remote Access server.
This option is similar to that we saw when we configured the simple
DirectAccess configuration. This is not a recommended configuration
because of the potential network and processing overhead you would
experience in larger deployments and the fact that it could represent a
single point of failure.

Use a self-signed certificate. If you choose this option, the DirectAccess
server will create a self-signed certificate. This is similar to what we saw
when we were working with the simplified DirectAccess configuration.
In this example, for the URL of the network location server, enter **https://
nls.corp.endtoedge.com** and then click **Validate**. Once connectivity to
the Network Location Server URL on APP1 is validated successfully, click
Next (Figure 13.62).

NOTE

For more information on Network Location Servers, please see my article "When Good Network
Location Servers Go Bad."

---

17. Click **Next** to view the **DNS** configuration page. On this page,
    you will see what DNS server address has been configured for the
    DirectAccess clients to use. In most cases, you will not need to
    edit these settings. Note that the address is the IPv6 address of the
    DirectAccess server itself. The reason for this is that this is the address

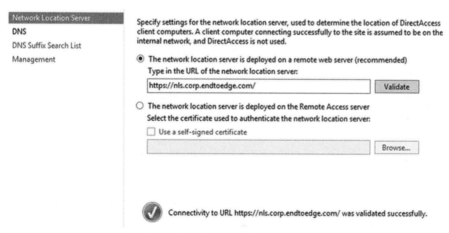

FIGURE 13.62 IP-HTTPS endpoint. (For color version of this figure, the reader is referred to the
online version of this chapter.)

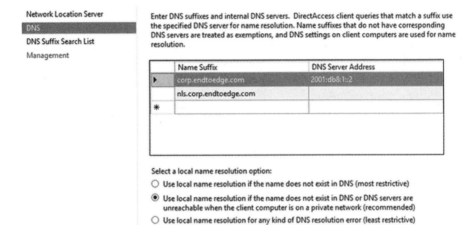

FIGURE 13.63 NLS. (For color version of this figure, the reader is referred to the online version of this chapter.)

that the DirectAccess clients will receive for their DNS server address to use when connecting to resources on the corporate network. In other words, the DirectAccess server is acting as a DNS proxy for the DirectAccess clients. The DirectAccess server always forward the DNS queries to DNS servers that it has configured on its internal interface. Click **Next** (Figure 13.63).

18. On the **DNS Suffix Search List** page, you can add suffixes to search for when short (unqualified or single-label host names) names are used by the DirectAccess client. This is similar to the DNS suffix search list you would assign to a NIC on a client computer. Since we do not have that same interface for the "DirectAccess interface," we can add the DNS suffix search list here and the DirectAccess client will devolve the queries in a similar fashion that it uses when using the DNS suffix search list on a physical interface. Make no changes here and click **Next** (Figure 13.64).

19. Management servers are computers that DirectAccess clients can reach through the infrastructure tunnel. That tunnel is set up for the intranet tunnel and opens before the user logs on to the computer. You typically will enter the names or IP addresses of management and infrastructure servers here—servers such as remediation, update, and systems management servers (such as System Center Configuration Manager). Note that even if you do not enter the names of System Center Configuration Manager servers here, they will be automatically included when the wizard completes. Do not make any changes here and click **Next** (Figure 13.65).

Network Location Server
DNS
DNS Suffix Search List
Management

Add additional suffixes to search for short unqualified name in multiple locations. If a query fails for a suffix, the other suffixes are appended to the name and the DNS query is repeated for the alternate FQDN.

☑ Configure DirectAccess clients with DNS client suffix search list

Detected domain suffixes:

Domain suffixes to use:

<Primary DNS suffix of client>
corp.endtoedge.com

Add ->

<- Remove

New Suffix: [　　　　　　　　] Add

ℹ The primary domain DNS suffix appears first in the list.

FIGURE 13.64 DNS suffix. (For color version of this figure, the reader is referred to the online version of this chapter.)

Network Location Server
DNS
DNS Suffix Search List
Management

Specify management servers used for DirectAccess client management. For example update and remediation servers.

Management servers:

	Management Servers (IP Address, IPv6 Prefix, FQDN)
*	

ℹ After you complete the wizard and apply the settings, the management servers list will be updated with automatically-discovered System Center Configuration Manager servers.

FIGURE 13.65 Management. (For color version of this figure, the reader is referred to the online version of this chapter.)

FIGURE 13.66
Application servers. (For color version of this figure, the reader is referred to the online version of this chapter.)

Step 4

Application Servers

Identify internal application servers requiring end-to-end authentication with DirectAccess clients.

Configure...

Learn more...

20. In the middle pane of the console, click **Configure** on **Step 4—Application Servers** (Figure 13.66).
21. On the **DirectAccess Application Server Setup** page, you have the following options:

   Do not extend authentication to application servers. This option allows DirectAccess clients to connect to corporate server without requiring them to authenticate to those servers.

   Extend authentication to selected application servers. This option requires that DirectAccess client authenticate with the servers that are part of a security group or groups that you select by clicking the **Add** button. These servers will require IPsec authentication with the

DirectAccess clients. When you choose this option, the DirectAccess clients need to be able to authenticate with the DirectAccess server and then will also need to be able to authenticate with the servers that are members of the group(s) you select. You will need to make sure that each of the servers in the group(s) has computer certificates so that end-to-end security works between them and the DirectAccess clients.

Allow access only to servers included in the security groups. If you select this option, not only will authentication be required when you connect to the machines in the security groups that are selected, but also the DirectAccess clients will only be able to connect to those machines. In other words, if the DirectAccess client is not required to authenticate to a server on the corporate network, the DirectAccess clients will not even be allowed to attempt a connection to the server. This is a very secure option and one that we highly recommend you consider in your deployments. Note that infrastructure servers do not need to be members of the selected security groups. So DNS, Active Directory, DirectAccess client management servers do not need to be part of the groups you select here.

Do not encrypt traffic. Use authentication only. This option enables you to take advantage of AuthIP so that you can use IPsec to authenticate with a server, but after the first packet of the connection is authenticated, the remainder of the communications is unencrypted. This scenario works for those who wish to continue to leverage their existing IDS/IPS solution. Of course, this is not as secure as the encrypted option, but it does reduce the processing overhead on both the DirectAccess clients and the destination servers.

In this example, we will click **Cancel** on this page (Figure 13.67).

22. At the bottom of the Remote Access Setup screen, click **Finish**.
23. In the Remote Access Review dialog, click **Apply** (Figure 13.68).
24. After the Remote Access Setup Wizard completes, click **Close**.
25. In the left pane of the console of the **Remote Access Management** console, select **Operations Status**. Wait until the status of all monitors display as "Working." In the Tasks pane under Monitoring, click **Refresh** periodically to update the display (Figure 13.69).

NOTE

There is a small bug in the DirectAccess configuration wizard which causes the status of Network adapters to be yellow instead of green. To ensure that the status of Network adapters shows as Working, open an elevated command prompt, type the following command and then press ENTER. After you run this command, refresh the Remote Access Dashboard and you will see all green.

---

netsh interface ipv6 add route 2001:db8:1::/48 publish=yes interface = "Corpnet"

DirectAccess Application Server Setup

Optionally configure authentication between DirectAccess clients and internal application servers.

By default, DirectAccess requires IPsec authentication and encryption between the DirectAccess client and server. In addition, you can optionally require end-to-end authentication and encryption between DirectAccess clients and selected internal application servers.

○ Do not extend authentication to application servers
◉ Extend authentication to selected application servers
Select the security groups containing the servers:

	Add...
	Remove

☐ Allow access only to servers included in the security groups

With this option enabled, clients can only access application servers in the specified security groups. Clients can still access infrastructure servers, including domain controllers, DNS servers, and servers used for DirectAccess client management.

☐ Do not encrypt traffic. Use authentication only

With this setting enabled, end-to-end traffic is authenticated but not encrypted. This option is less secure. Authentication without encryption is supported only for application servers running Windows Server 2008 R2 or a later operating system.

[Finish]   [Cancel]

FIGURE 13.67 Setup. (For color version of this figure, the reader is referred to the online version of this chapter.)

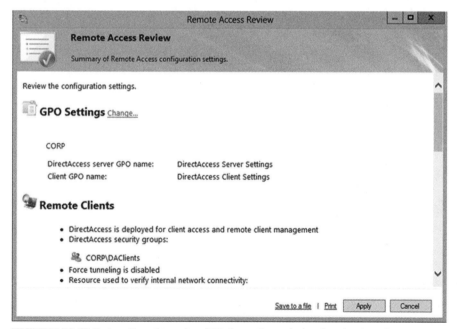

FIGURE 13.68 Review. (For color version of this figure, the reader is referred to the online version of this chapter.)

FIGURE 13.69 Dashboard. (For color version of this figure, the reader is referred to the online version of this chapter.)

ADMINISTRATOR'S PUNCH LIST

- The simplified DirectAccess wizard is targeted at small- and medium-sized businesses
- You can now deploy a DirectAccess server with a single NIC with a single private IP address
- The simplified DirectAccess wizard does not support complex enterprise scenarios
- When using a single NIC, only the IP-HTTPS protocol is available to DirectAccess clients
- When you add support for Windows 7 clients, the DirectAccess server will not use the Kerberos proxy

- If using Windows 8, remember that only Windows 8 Enterprise Edition is supported as a DirectAccess client
- The simplified DirectAccess wizard deploys the Network Location Server on the DirectAccess server
- If using a single NIC deployment with the simplified DirectAccess server, an ISATAP server will not be configured

SUMMARY

In this chapter, we went over a Test Lab Guide type configuration for the simplified, single NIC DirectAccess server. We saw that the simplified DirectAccess wizard made all the decisions for us and that we only needed to tell it a couple of pieces of network information to get a working solution. We also went over the "traditional" DirectAccess wizard and explained most of the options that are available to you and why you would pick any particular option.

CHAPTER 14

Protecting Legacy Remote Clients

CONTENTS

VIRTUAL PRIVATE NETWORKING WITH WINDOWS SERVER 2012

In today's business world, companies are spread out across the globe, with employees at all levels working from locations far from their home offices. Telecommuting team members are often situated in different cities, states, or even countries. For many years, Virtual Private Networking (VPN) has been the method of choice for connecting remote clients such as these to a local network. Unlike direct dedicated WAN links, it leverages the ubiquity of the Internet to create a cost-effective solution without sacrificing security and has virtually replaced the expensive leased lines that were originally used for the same purpose, especially in cases where the remote clients are a long distance from the corporate premises.

VPNs became popular not only because they are inexpensive to operate but also because they are fast and flexible. Remote workers can connect to the network through the VPN no matter where they are, from different client computers or portable devices. All they need is VPN client software (which is built into all modern Windows client operating systems) and the configuration information (including valid credentials, the name/address of the server to which they are connecting, and optionally, the protocol information) for making the connection.

On the server side, you need a computer that is set up as a Remote Access Services (RAS) server that is configured to allow incoming VPN connections. The RAS server can be dedicated to that task or RAS services can run on a server that performs additional tasks. Early VPNs required users to dial into the server using a modem and telephone line. Today, of course, VPNs are usually established over "always on" broadband Internet connections on the client's side.

Brief History of Windows VPN Protocols

Network administrators are familiar with the Windows Routing and Remote Access Service (RRAS) as the provider of both remote access and site-to-site VPN services. It has been around since Windows NT, where it was first called RAS. Windows NT 4.0 supported the Point-to-Point Tunneling Protocol (PPTP) for VPN connectivity. Windows 2000 added support for the Layer 2 Tunneling Protocol (L2TP), which provides better security with stronger encryption, but is more difficult to configure since high security deployment of L2TP requires a Public Key Infrastructure (PKI) for issuance of certificates.

With Windows Server 2008 and Windows Vista SP1, Microsoft added support for the Secure Socket Tunnel Protocol (SSTP), which functions similarly to other popular SSL VPNs. It provides a high level of security and is easy to configure. Let us take a closer look at each of the VPN protocols available for a Windows Server 2012 VPN Server.

Traditional PPTP VPN

PPTP is still supported by Windows Server 2012, although it is considered the least secure of all the supported VPN protocols. PPTP was developed by Microsoft, Ascend, 3Com, and other vendors to provide a secure remote access solution supported by Microsoft Dial-up Networking in Windows 95 OSR2, and defined by RFC 2637.[1] It uses the Point-to-Point Protocol (PPP) to authenticate the packets and Microsoft Point-to-Point Encryption (MPPE) to encrypt the PPP payload. MPPE is defined by RFC 3078.[2]

Vulnerabilities in the underlying protocols have led to the recommendation by Microsoft that PPTP VPNs be replaced by one of the more secure types. Tunneled traffic in a PPTP VPN can be authenticated by various means, including PAP, CHAP, MS-CHAPv1, MS-CHAPv2, or EAP/TLS. If a PPTP VPN is to be used, the most secure method is to use the Extensible Authentication Protocol/Transport Layer Security (EAP-TLS) for authentication. However, this requires a PKI for client and server certificates, which negates the primary advantage of PPTP as a VPN protocol: the simplicity of implementation.

If you do deploy a PPTP VPN, you would need to configure your edge firewall to allow PPTP communications from and to the external NIC on the VPN server. These communications typically use TCP port 1723; so, you will need to make sure your edge firewall allows traffic to and from that port, and you will also need to allow Generic Route Encapsulation (GRE) protocol 47.

L2TP/IPsec VPN

If you want to deploy a traditional VPN, L2TP is a more secure option than PPTP. Like PPTP, L2TP transmits PPP packets inside the tunnel. Because L2TP by itself only creates the tunnel, Microsoft's implementation uses IPsec to provide the

---

[1] *Point-to-Point Tunneling Protocol, Request for Comments 2637.* Network Working Group, The Internet Society (1999).

[2] *Microsoft Point-to-Point Encryption (MPPE) protocol, Request for Comments 3078.* Network Working Group, The Internet Society (2001).

authentication, integrity, and confidentiality for the packets. The L2TP/IPsec combination is defined in RFC 3193.[3] In this implementation, IPsec encapsulates the L2TP packets, which are hidden within the IPsec packet. Decryption occurs at the endpoint. IPsec can use a preshared key (PSK), which is a password/passphrase or digital certificate; the latter is the most secure method. Note that best security practices for deploying L2TP/IPsec include using a private CA rather than a public one.

As its name indicates, L2TP operates at Layer 2—the data link layer—of the OSI networking model. It uses UDP as the transport layer protocol. L2TP uses UDP port 1701 and UDP port 500. IP protocol 50 is used to allow IPsec ESP traffic to and from the VPN server.

SSTP VPN

SSTP was developed by Microsoft in response to the popularity of third-party SSL VPN solutions such as OpenVPN. Some networks, such as hotel networks, were blocking traditional VPN traffic to prevent traffic going over the network that has its IP address and other information hidden. Some countries with censorship laws were blocking VPN traffic to prevent communications that were not approved from getting out.

That is easy to do because the VPN technologies use specific ports that are not used by any other traffic; so, you can shut them off without affecting other Internet communications. The SSTP VPN gets around this because it uses the same port as secure Web traffic (HTTPS). Many Web services use HTTPS, so administrators are less likely to block it. By utilizing TCP Port 443, SSTP enables the packets to pass through most firewalls and proxies that block other types of VPN connections. The SSTP traffic can be either IPv4 or IPv6 traffic. Here is how it works, broken down into steps:

1. The SSTP client establishes a TCP connection with the SSTP server. The TCP port on the client is assigned dynamically. The VPN server uses TCP port 443.
2. The SSTP client sends an SSL Client-Hello message. This tells the server that the SSTP client wants to initiate an SSL session with the SSTP server.
3. The SSTP server sends its computer certificate to the SSTP client.
4. The SSTP client validates the server's computer certificate and negotiates the encryption method to be used for the SSL session. Then the client generates an SSL session key and encrypts it with the public key of the SSTP server's certificate. Finally, the client sends the encrypted SSL session key to the SSTP server.

---

[3] *Securing L2TP Using IPsec, Request for Comments 3193.* Network Working Group, The Internet Society (2001).

5. The SSTP server decrypts the encrypted SSL session key, using its own computer certificate's private key that is associated with the public key used by the client to encrypt the session key. After that point, the communications between the SSTP client and the SSTP server are encrypted with the negotiated encryption method, using the SSL session key.

6. The SSTP client next sends an HTTP over SSL request message to the SSTP server.

7. The SSTP client creates the SSTP tunnel between itself and the SSTP server.

8. The SSTP client establishes a PPP connection with the SSTP server. The negotiation of this connection includes authenticating the user's credentials with a PPP authentication method. The SSTP client and server also negotiate the configuration of settings for Internet Protocol version 4 (IPv4) or Internet Protocol version 6 (IPv6) traffic.

9. The SSTP client can now send IPv4 or IPv6 traffic over the PPP link, through the SSL tunnel.

SSTP is easy to configure and it is very secure since it uses strong encryption keys (2048 bit) and also uses authentication certificates. However, it does not work with Windows XP or Vista pre-SP1, so if you have older legacy clients, this is not a solution for them.

IPsec Tunnel Mode with IKEv2

Microsoft introduced another new VPN option in Windows Server 2008 R2 RRAS for Windows 7 clients. This is IPsec tunnel mode with Internet Key Exchange version 2 (IKEv2). This solves a common problem with VPN connections: the loss of the connection if Internet connectivity is temporarily interrupted. This was not much of a problem when most VPN clients were connecting from stable networks such as their home networks or a reliable hotel network where they were plugged in. However, with today's highly mobile wireless networks, it is all too common for the connection to drop when, for example, the client device is in a moving vehicle and travels from one wireless hot spot to another.

With earlier VPN implementations, this presented a problem for the user because he/she would have to manually reestablish the VPN connection. At best, this was an annoyance that detracted from the user experience. At worst, the user might be unable to reconnect and be without access to needed resources on the corporate network. IPsec tunnel mode with IKEv2 enables a feature called VPN Reconnect, by which the VPN automatically reconnects after such a drop, without any intervention or action on the part of the user.

Either EAP authentication or machine certificate authentication can be used with IPsec tunnel mode with IKEv2. If you use the former, a Network Policy Server (NPS) is required. With machine certificates, you do not need an NPS.

The RRAS Unified Server Role

In Windows Server 2008 R2, the configuration of RRAS VPNs was completely separate from DirectAccess (DA) configuration. You cannot run an RRAS server on the same Windows Server 2008 R2 edge server that serves as a DirectAccess server. This did not really make sense. DirectAccess, despite all of its benefits, has one big limitation. It only works with clients that:

- Are running Windows 7 Enterprise/Ultimate or Windows 8 Enterprise, and
- Are members of the Windows domain

Here is the problem: As of October 2012, Windows XP still had slightly over 36% of operating system market share, according to statistics published by NetMarketShare.[4] A healthy chunk of that includes businesses that had not yet migrated from Windows XP to a later version of Windows, even though extended support for XP will end in 2014. Many companies apparently plan to hang onto their XP machines until the very end. Those XP computers cannot be configured as DirectAccess clients.

But that is a temporary problem; eventually, the XP computers will be replaced by clients running more modern operating systems. However, in addition to these legacy clients, there are also Windows 7 client systems that need to connect to the corporate network but that, for whatever reasons, are not members of the domain. Thus, a significant number of network administrators are faced with managing remote access for both DirectAccess clients and clients that need another remote access solution.

It would seem to be more logical and convenient to combine the management tools for DA and RRAS. With Windows Server 2012, Microsoft went a step further than that and combined DA and RRAS into a new unified server role, which allows administrators to configure, manage, and monitor both the DirectAccess and VPN services together. Now DA and RRAS can coexist on the same server. This was made possible by the modification of IKEv2 policies and IPsec Denial of Service Protection (DoSP) in the following ways:

- Now IKEv2 policies allow IPv6 transition technology traffic.
- DoSP no longer drops all IPv4 packets, and IPv6 packets are not protected by IPsec as it did in the previous implementation.

Thanks to these changes, you no longer have to have two separate servers for running DA and RRAS and you do not have to switch back and forth between different interfaces to configure them. You can deploy and manage your RRAS VPNs (and DA) in one of two ways: through the graphical interface with the

---

[4] *Operating System Market Share*, NetMarketShare October 2012 http://www.netmarketshare.com/operating-system-market-share.aspx?qprid=10.

management console, or via the command line with PowerShell. Many organizations are now deploying Server Core installations to enhance performance and reduce the attack surface for network servers. You can install the RRAS Server role on a Server Core server.

Deploying a VPN Server on Windows Server 2012 via the GUI

Prior to deploying the VPN server(s) by which your legacy clients will connect to the network, you need to go through the planning process to determine the needs of those client computers, the operating system(s) they are running, and the level of security that is desired. Specifically, you need to answer the questions in the following checklist:

- Is the operating system configured correctly? The default service settings provide the properly configured starting point for enabling and configuring a VPN server on Windows Server 2012.
- Is the server properly secured? Legacy remote clients will be connecting to your corporate network through the VPN server; these clients can pose a threat to your network if the server is not properly secured.
- Does the server have two network interfaces? The server needs a NIC that connects to the Internet and a second NIC that connects to the corporate network. Ensure that the Internet connection has sufficient bandwidth to support the number of users that will be connecting through the server.
- Is Windows Firewall disabled on the server? When you configure RRAS, you will configure its basic firewall feature, which works in place of Windows Firewall.
- Will remote clients get their IP addresses via a DHCP server on your network or from the VPN server? If your DHCP server is on a different subnet from the VPN server, ensure that the router can relay DHCP messages.
- Will remote clients be authenticated by the VPN server or by a RADIUS server on your network?
- Do all users who will connect through the VPN have user accounts in Active Directory or on the VPN server?

This information is necessary to determine what VPN protocol(s) will be supported by your VPN server(s) and whether you will need a PKI with a certification authority. Once you have this information in hand, you will need to go through the following steps to deploy your VPN server(s):

1. Install the **Remote Access** server role on the server.
2. Install the **DirectAccess and VPN (RAS)** services on the server.
3. Install the Web Server (IIS) role, which is required in order to install Remote Access.

4. Configure the Remote Access VPN.
5. Configure packet filters in RRAS.
6. Configure your firewall to allow VPN traffic.
7. Install certificates for VPN connections.
8. Enable users to access the Remote Access VPN.

We will now walk through each of these steps in detail:

Install the Remote Access Server Role on the Server

To install the **Remote Access** server role on the Windows Server 2012 server, open the Server Manager from the taskbar button. You can configure a local or remote server. If you are configuring the local server, you can get started by selecting **Add Roles and Features** from the Server Manager Dashboard, as shown in Figure 14.1.

This will invoke the **Add Roles and Features Wizard,** which first displays an informational page instructing you to complete prerequisite tasks such as giving the administrator account a strong password, configuring network settings, and installing the latest security updates. You can select to skip this page in the future, as shown in Figure 14.2.

On the next page, you select whether you are configuring a single server to add roles, services, and features, or installing required roll services for a Virtual Desktop Infrastructure (VDI) to create a virtual machine-based or session-based desktop deployment. Select the first option, as shown in Figure 14.3.

On the next page of the wizard, select the server on which you want to install the **Remote Access** server role, from the list of servers in the server pool, as shown in Figure 14.4.

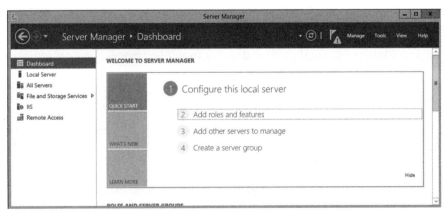

FIGURE 14.1 Add roles and features by configuring the server via the Server Manager Dashboard. (For color version of this figure, the reader is referred to the online version of this chapter.)

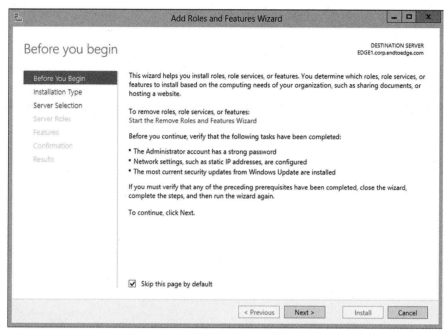

FIGURE 14.2 Begin the Add Roles and Features Wizard. (For color version of this figure, the reader is referred to the online version of this chapter.)

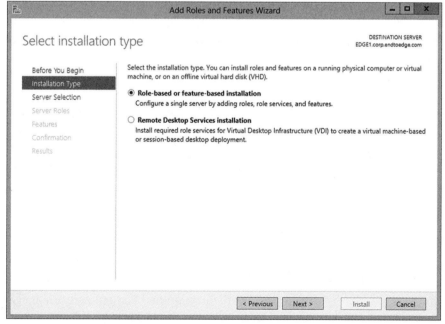

FIGURE 14.3 Select the installation type. (For color version of this figure, the reader is referred to the online version of this chapter.)

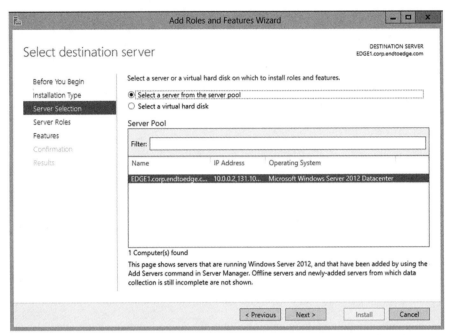

FIGURE 14.4 Select the server on which you want to install the Remote Access role. (For color version of this figure, the reader is referred to the online version of this chapter.)

In the next part of the wizard, you add the **Remote Access** server role (Figure 14.5).

You will be prompted to add features that are required for remote access, which include:

- RAS Connection Manager Administration Kit (CMAK)
- Remote Server Administration Tools (Role Administration Tools, Remote Access GUI and Command Line Tools, and Remote Access module for PowerShell)
- IIS Web Server, and
- Windows internal database

You cannot install Remote Access unless you agree to add these prerequisite features. The Remote Access and Web Server (IIS) checkboxes will then be checked.

On the next page of the wizard, you can install additional features on the server if you wish, as shown in Figure 14.6.

Install the DirectAccess and VPN (RAS) Services on the Server

The next page of the wizard explains the new unified Remote Access management console that combines management of DirectAccess and VPN functions, and briefly explains the different RRAS services (DirectAccess, VPN, and routing), as shown in Figure 14.7.

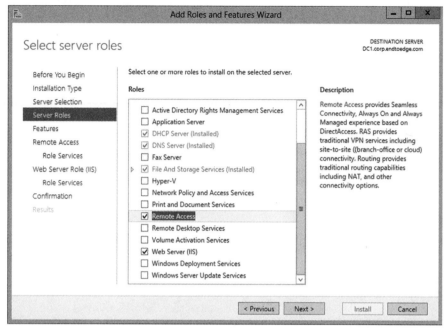

FIGURE 14.5 Select to install the Remote Access server role (IIS Web Server will also be installed). (For color version of this figure, the reader is referred to the online version of this chapter.)

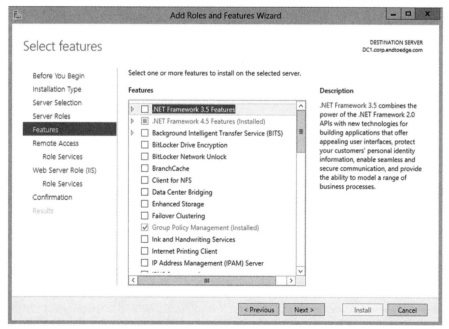

FIGURE 14.6 Install additional features if you wish. (For color version of this figure, the reader is referred to the online version of this chapter.)

FIGURE 14.7 Installing DirectAccess and RRAS VPN services. (For color version of this figure, the reader is referred to the online version of this chapter.)

On the **Role Services** page, you can select to install the RAS services (DirectAccess and VPN), the routing service, or both, as shown in Figure 14.8.

Install the Web Server (IIS) Role

On the next page of the wizard, you will find a brief explanation of the function of the Internet Information Services (IIS) Web Server that must be installed in order to install Remote Access, as well as information about the default installation of IIS, as shown in Figure 14.9.

The next page allows you to select the role services that you want to install for the IIS Web Server, with the default services already checked, as shown in Figure 14.10.

Finally, confirm the selections you made while going through the wizard and then click the **Install** button, as shown in Figure 14.11, to begin the installation. You can check the box to automatically restart the server or you can do it manually afterward.

NOTE

Be sure you have chosen to install the Remote Access Management tools. If you fail to install the tools, you will not be able to configure the Remote Access VPN as described in the section Configure the Remote Access VPN with the Getting Started Wizard. Instead, you will get a message that "Configuration failed for DirectAccess and VPN."

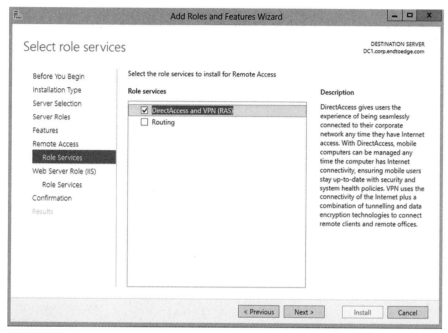

FIGURE 14.8 Selecting the role services. (For color version of this figure, the reader is referred to the online version of this chapter.)

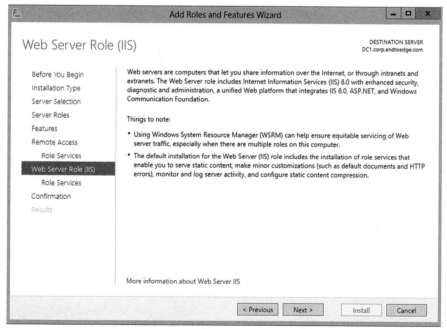

FIGURE 14.9 Understand the Web Server (IIS) role. (For color version of this figure, the reader is referred to the online version of this chapter.)

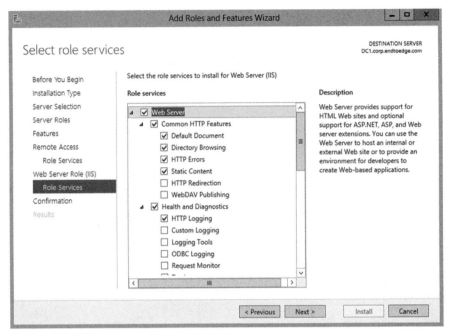

FIGURE 14.10 Select Web Server role services. (For color version of this figure, the reader is referred to the online version of this chapter.)

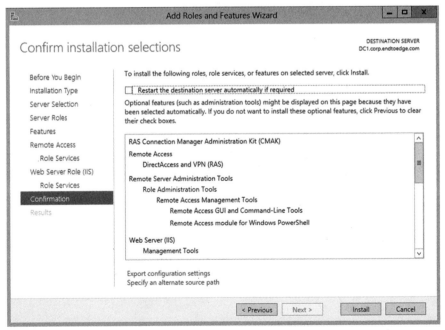

FIGURE 14.11 Confirm installation selection and begin the installation. (For color version of this figure, the reader is referred to the online version of this chapter.)

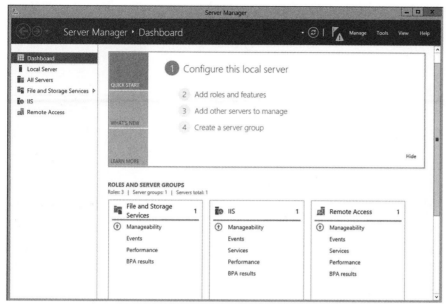

FIGURE 14.12 The Remote Access and Web Server (IIS) roles have been installed on this server. (For color version of this figure, the reader is referred to the online version of this chapter.)

After you have installed the Remote Access and IIS roles and restarted the server, they will show up in your **Roles and Server Groups** section of the Server Manager Dashboard, as shown in Figure 14.12.

Configure the Remote Access VPN with the Getting Started Wizard

When you double-click the **Remote Access** tile in the Roles and Server Groups, you will see a notification at the top of the **Server Manager** page that tells you that configuration is required for DirectAccess and VPN (RAS). Click the **More…** link at the right of the notification line, and in the **Task Details and Notifications** box, you see that "Post-deployment Configuration" is shown as a required task. Windows Server 2012 makes it easy for you, by providing a link to open the **Getting Started Wizard** from here, as shown in Figure 14.13.

NOTE

If you failed to install the Remote Access management tools in the previous step, when you click to open the Getting Started Wizard, you will get a popup dialog box that says: "File C:\Windows\system32\RAMgmtUI.exe cannot be located." At this point, you can go through the server role and features installation again and install the management tools at this time, as shown in Figure 14.14.

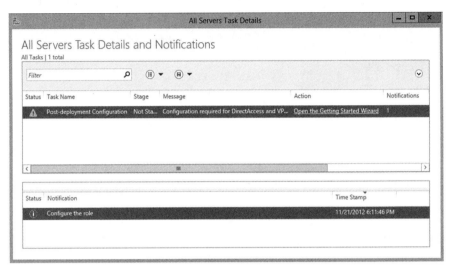

FIGURE 14.13 The Tasks Details box provides a link to open the Getting Started Wizard. (For color version of this figure, the reader is referred to the online version of this chapter.)

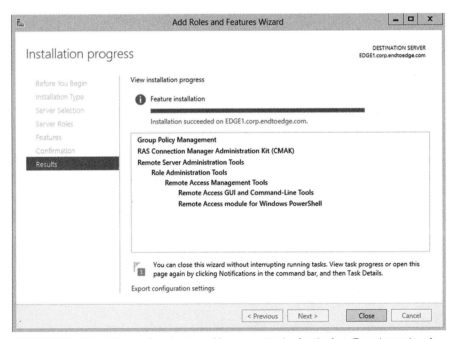

FIGURE 14.14 Installing the Remote Access Management tools after the fact. (For color version of this figure, the reader is referred to the online version of this chapter.)

When the Getting Started Wizard opens, you can configure Remote Access. On the first page of the wizard, you will first need to select the network topology of the server (edge, behind an edge device with two NICs, or behind an edge device with a single NIC). Then you need to enter the IP address (IPv4) or public name that will be used by the client computers to connect to the Remote Access server, as shown in Figure 14.15.

You can then accept the default settings, or you can edit some of the settings by clicking where indicated in the next page of the Getting Started wizard, as shown in Figure 14.16.

If you select to change some settings, the summary of your Remote Access configuration settings will be generated, divided into four groups:

- GPO settings
- Remote clients settings
- Remote Access server settings
- Infrastructure servers

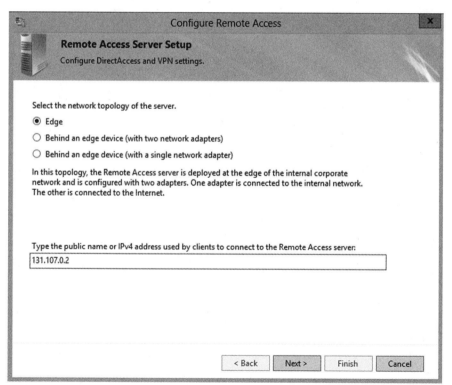

FIGURE 14.15 Select network topology and enter the name or address of the Remote Access server. (For color version of this figure, the reader is referred to the online version of this chapter.)

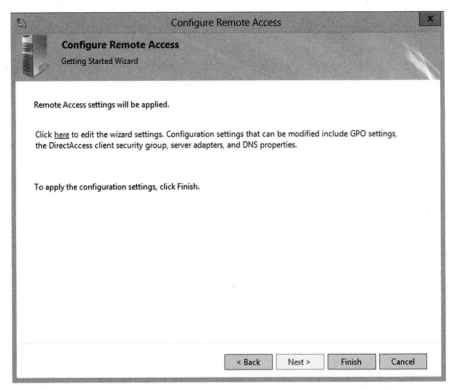

FIGURE 14.16 Click Finish to accept the defaults or select to edit the wizard settings. (For color version of this figure, the reader is referred to the online version of this chapter.)

Any of these can be modified by clicking the **Change** link next to its name. To make changes to the VPN server settings, click the **Change** link for **Remote Access Server,** as shown in Figure 14.17.

Next, click **VPN Configuration** in the left pane of the **Remote Access Server Setup** wizard. The first thing you will be able to configure is the IP address assignment method. You can have the VPN server assign IP addresses to VPN clients automatically via DHCP (this is the default) or you can have it assign addresses from a static address pool. You will need to enter the address ranges for pool if you choose this method, as shown in Figure 14.18.

On the second tab, you can configure how VPN clients are to be authenticated. The default method is to use Active Directory (Windows authentication), but if you have a RADIUS server, you can use RADIUS authentication instead, as shown in Figure 14.19.

When you have completed the configuration changes, click the **Finish** button. This will take you back to the **Remote Access Review** page. Note here that you can print the configuration settings or save them to a file. Then click **OK** to exit the review. Now click **Finish** on the Configure Remote Access Getting Started Wizard.

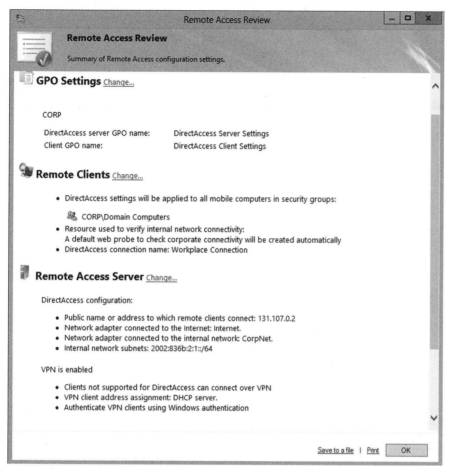

FIGURE 14.17 Modifying Remote Access settings. (For color version of this figure, the reader is referred to the online version of this chapter.)

The settings will be applied, and now the **All Servers Task Details** box will show the Post-deployment Configuration task status as "Complete."

Using the Remote Access Management Console

A tile representing the Remote Access Management tools will appear on the Windows Server 2012 Start screen, as shown in Figure 14.20.

You can also open the Remote Access Management console by typing **RAMgmtUI.exe** at the command line.

If you have not yet configured Remote Access, you can run the Getting Started Wizard or the Remote Access Setup Wizard from the RA Management console. You can see the RA Management console in Figure 14.21.

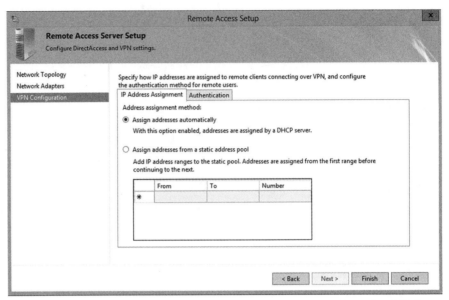

FIGURE 14.18 Configuring IP address assignment for the VPN server. (For color version of this figure, the reader is referred to the online version of this chapter.)

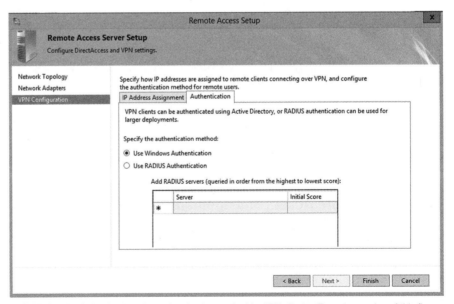

FIGURE 14.19 Configuring the authentication method for VPN clients. (For color version of this figure, the reader is referred to the online version of this chapter.)

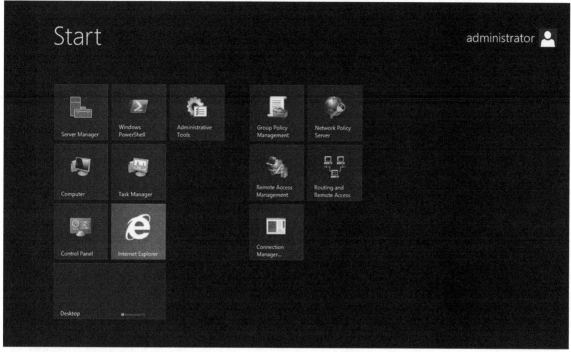

FIGURE 14.20 Remote Access management tools can be accessed from the Start Screen. (For color version of this figure, the reader is referred to the online version of this chapter.)

Running the Remote Access Setup Wizard

The Remote Access Setup wizard allows you to configure more customized settings for your remote access server, including the ability to deploy VPN only, if you do not want to run DirectAccess on this server. You also have the option of deploying DirectAccess only. The recommended setup is to deploy both VPN and DirectAccess, so that DA-capable computers can connect that way and legacy clients can connect via the VPN, as you can see in Figure 14.22.

The wizard will walk you through the steps involved in setting up clients, server, and other infrastructure components for your remote access deployment. There are four basic steps involved when you are deploying both DA and VPN:

1. Identify clients (if any) that will be enabled for DA.
2. Define the configuration and network settings for the Remote Access server.
3. Identify the infrastructure servers accessed by DA clients before connecting to internal resources.
4. Identify application servers requiring end-to-end authentication with DA clients.

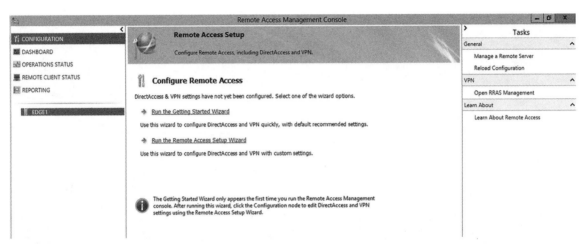

FIGURE 14.21 The Remote Access Management console. (For color version of this figure, the reader is referred to the online version of this chapter.)

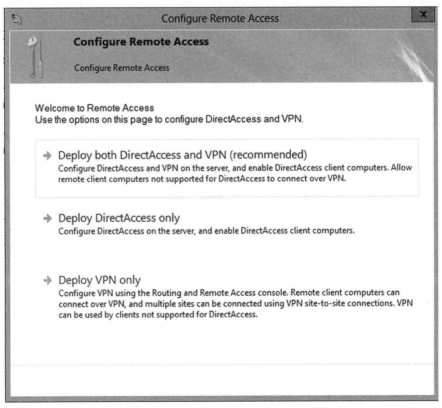

FIGURE 14.22 The Remote Access setup wizard allows you to deploy VPN, DirectAccess, or both. (For color version of this figure, the reader is referred to the online version of this chapter.)

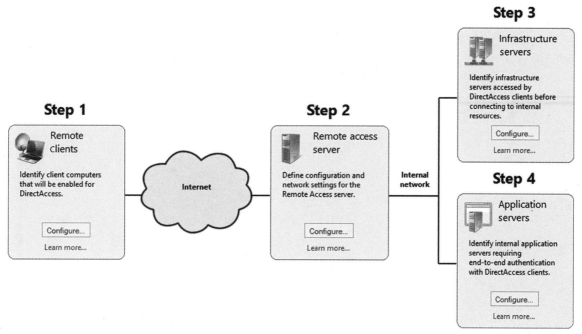

FIGURE 14.23 Steps for deploying VPN with DA (recommended setup). (For color version of this figure, the reader is referred to the online version of this chapter.)

These steps are illustrated in the graphic that appears in the Remote Access Management console, as shown in Figure 14.23.

Using the RRAS Console

When you select to deploy the VPN server only, the Routing and Remote Access console will appear. To set up RRAS, click the **Action** menu and then select **Configure and Enable Routing and Remote Access**, as shown in Figure 14.24.

This will open the Routing and Remote Access Server Wizard. After you click **Next** on the Welcome page, you will see the **Configuration** page where you can select which RRAS services you want to deploy on the RRAS server. You can enable remote access (dial-up or VPN), Network Address Translation (NAT), both VPN and NAT, a secure connection between two private networks (site-to-site VPN), or you can do a custom configuration to select any combination of these, as shown in Figure 14.25.

To set up a VPN server only, without NAT, select the first option and then you will choose **VPN** on the **Remote Access** page that offers the selections of VPN and/or Dial-up, as shown in Figure 14.26.

On the next page of the wizard, you will need to select the network interface that is connected to the Internet, and by default the box is checked to enable static packet filtering for better security. When packet filtering is enabled, only

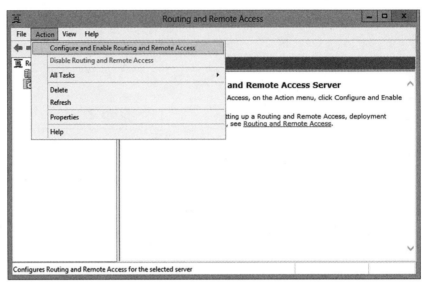

FIGURE 14.24 Configuring and enabling RRAS in the Routing and Remote Access console. (For color version of this figure, the reader is referred to the online version of this chapter.)

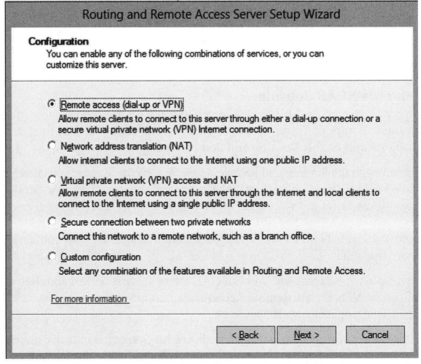

FIGURE 14.25 The Routing and Remote Access Server Setup Wizard Configuration page. (For color version of this figure, the reader is referred to the online version of this chapter.)

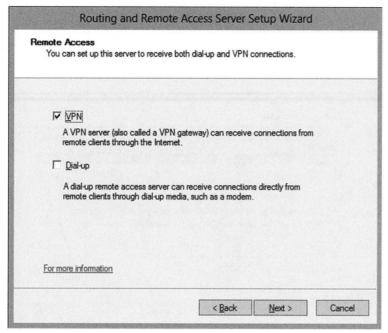

FIGURE 14.26 Setting up a VPN server only. (For color version of this figure, the reader is referred to the online version of this chapter.)

VPN traffic will be able to access the server through the selected interface. See the **VPN Connection** page of the wizard in Figure 14.27.

On the **IP Address Assignment** page of the wizard, you can choose whether you want to use a DHCP server to assign IP addresses to your VPN clients automatically or whether you want addresses to be assigned from a range or ranges of addresses in a static pool that you define, as shown in Figure 14.28.

The next step in the wizard is to set up the server to work with a RADIUS server if you have one on your network that you want to use for authentication; this is the common practice when managing multiple remote access servers. If you choose to do this, you will set up the VPN server to forward authentication requests to your RADIUS server. If not, the requests will be authenticated locally. See the **Managing Multiple Remote Access Servers** page of the wizard in Figure 14.29.

If you choose to use RADIUS for authentication of your VPN users, you will need to enter the information for your primary and alternate RADIUS servers and the password used to access the RADIUS servers, as shown in Figure 14.30.

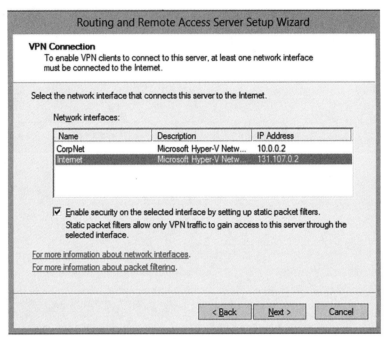

FIGURE 14.27 Selecting the NIC that connects the server to the Internet. (For color version of this figure, the reader is referred to the online version of this chapter.)

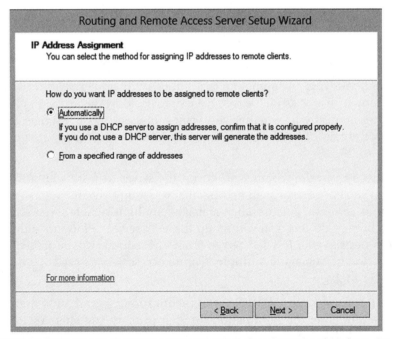

FIGURE 14.28 Defining the IP address assignment method. (For color version of this figure, the reader is referred to the online version of this chapter.)

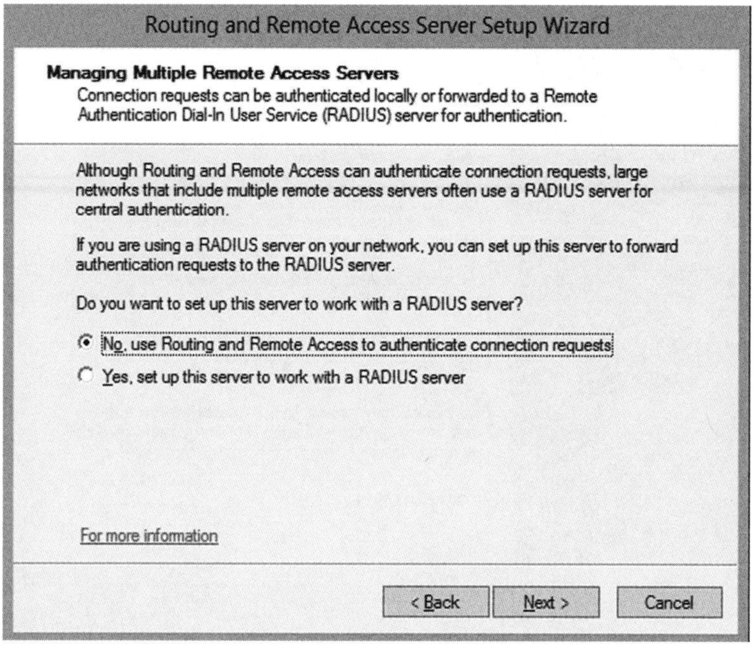

FIGURE 14.29 Defining how authentication requests will be handled. (For color version of this figure, the reader is referred to the online version of this chapter.)

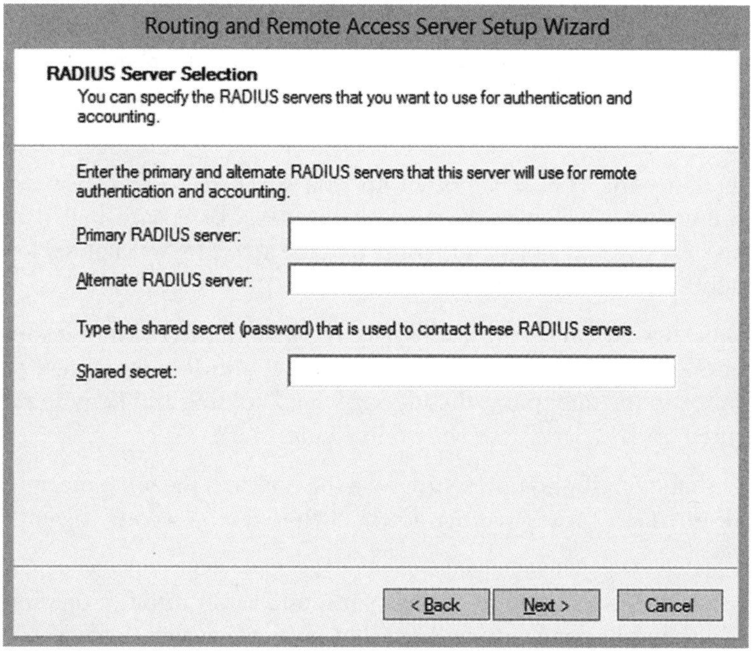

FIGURE 14.30 Setting up forwarding of authentication requests to a RADIUS server. (For color version of this figure, the reader is referred to the online version of this chapter.)

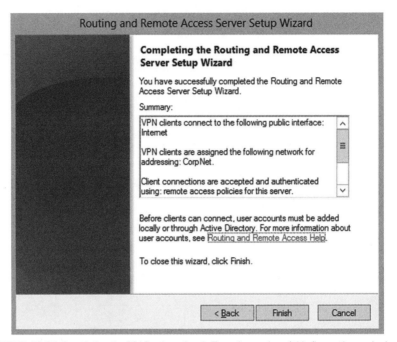

FIGURE 14.31 Completing the RRAS setup wizard. (For color version of this figure, the reader is referred to the online version of this chapter.)

When you have completed the information required by the Routing and Remote Access wizard, you will be shown a summary of your choices, as illustrated by Figure 14.31.

Note that after the VPN server is set up, you still have to add local accounts for the users who will connect through the VPN, or ensure that they have accounts in Active Directory, and ensure that the accounts are enabled for RRAS connections.

When you click **Finish** on the last page of the wizard, there will be a short wait while the RRAS service starts. Then the Routing and Remote Access console will display, in the right pane, the message that "Routing and Remote Access is Configured on This Server," as shown in Figure 14.32.

You can change configuration settings via the nodes in the left pane, including network interfaces, ports, remote access clients, remote access logging, IPv4, and IPv6.

If you click the **Ports** node in the left pane, and scroll through the ports displayed in the right pane, you will see that ports are available for SSTP, PPTP, L2TP, and IKEv2, as shown in Figure 14.33.

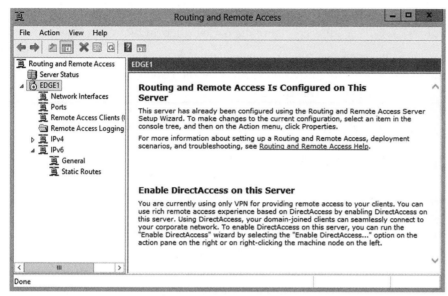

FIGURE 14.32 RRAS has been successfully configured on the server. (For color version of this figure, the reader is referred to the online version of this chapter.)

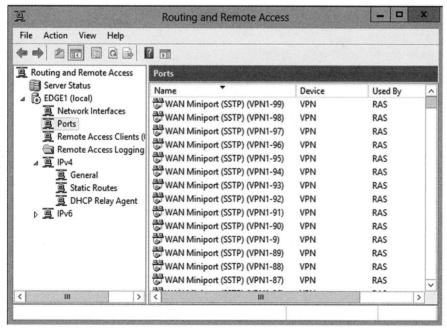

FIGURE 14.33 Ports available for SSTP, PPTP, L2TP, and IKEv2 connections. (For color version of this figure, the reader is referred to the online version of this chapter.)

Configure Packet Filters in RRAS

For an L2TP/IPsec VPN, configure the packet filters in RRAS as follows:

1. Open **Routing and Remote Access**.
2. In the console tree, expand the node for the VPN server, expand the node for IPv4, and click **General**.
3. In the details pane, click the interface on which you want to enable L2TP over IPSec filtering, scroll to the IP Address column, and write down the IP address assigned to the interface.
4. Right-click the interface, and then click **Properties**, as shown in Figure 14.34.

On the **General** tab, click the **Inbound Filters** button. Click **New** to create a new filter. For each of the following three new filters, set the filter action to drop all packets except those that meet the criteria below:

- Destination IP address of the VPN server's Internet interface, subnet mask of 255.255.255.255, and UDP destination port of 500. This filter allows Internet Key Exchange (IKE) traffic to the VPN server.
- Destination IP address of the VPN server's Internet interface, subnet mask of 255.255.255.255, and UDP destination port of 1701. This filter allows L2TP traffic from the VPN client to the VPN server.

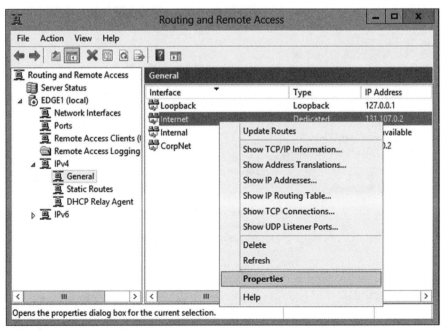

FIGURE 14.34 Configuring packet filters I RRAS. (For color version of this figure, the reader is referred to the online version of this chapter.)

- Destination IP address of the VPN server's Internet interface, subnet mask of 255.255.255.255, and UDP destination port of 4500. This filter allows IPSec network address translator traversal (NAT-T) traffic.

Go back to the **General** tab and click the **Outbound Filters** button. Configure the following output filters with the filter action set to drop all packets except those that meet the criteria below:

- Source IP address of the VPN server's Internet interface, subnet mask of 255.255.255.255, and UDP source port of 500. This filter allows IKE traffic from the VPN server.
- Source IP address of the VPN server's Internet interface, subnet mask of 255.255.255.255, and UDP source port of 1701. This filter allows L2TP traffic from the VPN server to the VPN client.
- Source IP address of the VPN server's Internet interface, subnet mask of 255.255.255.255, and UDP source port of 4500. This filter allows IPSec NAT-T traffic. Note that an IPSec NAT-T deployment for Windows that includes VPN servers that are located behind network address translators is not recommended.

Configure Your Firewall to Allow VPN Traffic

If your VPN server is in front of the firewall, you do not have to worry about the firewall configuration, but you need to ensure that you have packet filtering enabled on the VPN server so that only VPN traffic will be able to connect to the VPN server's external interface.

If the VPN server is behind the firewall, then you will need to configure filters on the firewall's Internet and perimeter interfaces to allow VPN traffic. First, configure the inbound packet filters on the Internet interface, to allow the following traffic:

- Destination IP address of the VPN server's perimeter network interface and UDP destination port of 500 (0×1F4) allows IKE traffic to the VPN server.
- Destination IP address of the VPN server's perimeter network interface and UDP destination port of 4500 (0×1194) allows IPSec NAT-T traffic to the VPN server.
- Destination IP address of the VPN server's perimeter network interface and IP Protocol ID of 50 (0×32) allows IPSec ESP traffic from the VPN client to the VPN server.

Next, configure the outbound packet filters on the firewall's Internet interface to allow the following traffic:

- Source IP address of the VPN server's perimeter network interface and UDP source port of 500 (0×1F4).
- Source IP address of the VPN server's perimeter network interface and UDP source port of 4500.

- Source IP address of the VPN server's perimeter network interface and IP Protocol ID of 50 (0×32).

Now configure the inbound packet filters on the firewall's perimeter interface to allow the following traffic:

- Source IP address of the VPN server's perimeter network interface and UDP source port of 500 (0×1F4).
- Source IP address of the VPN server's perimeter network interface and UDP source port of 4500.
- Source IP address of the VPN server's perimeter network interface and IP Protocol ID of 50 (0×32).

Finally, configure the outbound packet filters on the firewall's perimeter interface to allow the following traffic:

- Destination IP address of the VPN server's perimeter network interface and UDP destination port of 500 (0×1F4).
- Destination IP address of the VPN server's perimeter network interface and UDP destination port of 4500 (0×1194).
- Destination IP address of the VPN server's perimeter network interface and IP Protocol ID of 50 (0×32).

Install Certificates for VPN Connections

A public key infrastructure and certification authority are not required if you deploy a PPTP VPN, but this is not a recommended practice because of the security issues. Certificates are also not required if you select to use preshared key authentication for L2TP VPN connections, but again, this is a less secure method because the VPN server uses the same preshared key for all the connections. In addition to the security implications, preshared keys can cause problems when the key must be changed; in that instance, the key must be changed on all the clients, as well—either manually or by reissuing new Connection Manager profiles that have to be installed on all the client computers.

Utilizing a PKI to issue certificates for VPN connections is a much more secure option. The steps involved in creating the certificate infrastructure for L2TP/IPsec or SSTP connections require that you install a certificate in the Local Computer certificate store on the VPN server and install a user certificate in the Current User certificate store on each of the client computers. Certificates can be installed either via the Certificates MMC snap-in or via auto-enrollment, or by connecting the client to the certification authority's Web-based enrollment agent.

Installing and configuring certification authorities and creating a PKI are beyond the scope of this chapter, but you can find information and instructions in the TechNet Library.

Configure the Firewall to Block PPTP Connections

To prevent users from connecting via the less secure PPTP connections, you can configure the edge firewall to block PPTP. You can do this by blocking TCP port 1723 and GRE protocol ID 47. Another method is to set the number of PPTP ports to 0 in the RAS management console.

Enabling Users to Access the Remote Access VPN

The users who will connect to the corporate network through the Remote Access VPN must have user accounts on the VPN server or in the Active Directory domain. You must set the user account properties for each user to allow remote access connections by configuring the user account for Dial-in access.

To enable a domain user to connect to the VPN, in the Active Directory Users and Computers administrative tool, expand the node for the domain in the left pane and click **Users**. In the right pane, scroll down the list of users and find the user to whom you want to give permission to connect to the network through the VPN server. Right-click the user name and select **Properties**.

In the Properties dialog box, click the **Dial-in** tab. Under the **Network Access Permission** section, select either **Allow access** or (recommended) **Control access through NPS Policy** if you are setting up a Network Policy Server as we will discuss later in this chapter. This dialog box is shown in Figure 14.35.

Now, legacy remote clients and those Windows 7 and Windows 8 clients that are not members of the domain can connect to the network through the VPN, by using the built-in option to set up a dial-up or VPN connection to the workplace, as shown for a Vista client in Figure 14.36.

The Connect to a Workplace wizard will ask for the Internet address (public name or IP address) of the VPN server and the destination name, and then for the user's username, password, and (optionally) domain. When the connection has been created, the user will get notification that it is ready to use and have the option to "Connect now," as shown in Figure 14.37.

Afterward, the VPN connection that the user created will appear in the list of network selections on the **Connect to a Network** screen in the Network and Sharing Center. Its settings can be modified by right-clicking it and selecting **Properties.**

You may also want to create a Connection Manager profile for users to simplify client connection. A Connection Manager profile can be installed by the user from an executable file that you distribute via a flash drive or CD/DVD, through a network share, sent as an e-mail attachment, as a Web download, or through System Center or other software distribution system.

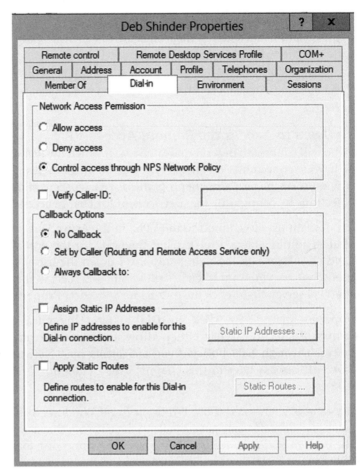

FIGURE 14.35 Configuring user accounts for dial-in access. (For color version of this figure, the reader is referred to the online version of this chapter.)

To create a Connection Manager profile, you run the Connection Manager Administration Kit (CMAK) wizard. The CMAK should have been installed as one of the features required for DirectAccess when you ran the Add Roles and Features wizard. If it is installed, you will find it in the Administrative Tools (which you can access from Start Screen), as shown in Figure 14.38.

Double-clicking it opens the CMAK wizard, which you can use to create the Connection Manager profiles. The steps involved in creating a connection profile include:

- Select the Target Operating System
- Create or Modify a Connection Profile
- Specify the Service Name and the File Name
- Specify a Realm Name

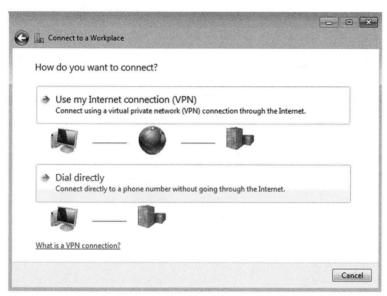

FIGURE 14.36 Setting up a VPN connection on the client. (For color version of this figure, the reader is referred to the online version of this chapter.)

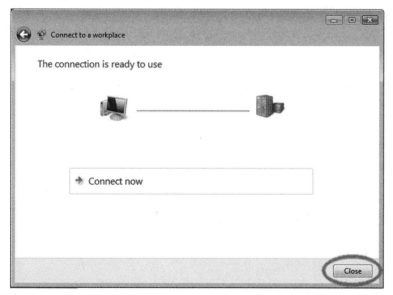

FIGURE 14.37 After the connection is created, the user can connect to the VPN server. (For color version of this figure, the reader is referred to the online version of this chapter.)

- Merge Information from Other Connection Profiles
- Add Support for VPN Connections
- Add a Custom Phone Book
- Configure Dial-up Networking Entries
- Specify Routing Table Updates

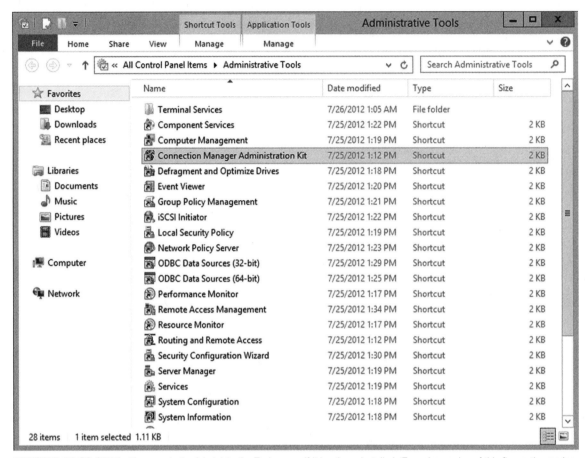

FIGURE 14.38 CMAK will appear in the Administrative Tools menu if it has been installed. (For color version of this figure, the reader is referred to the online version of this chapter.)

- Configure Proxy Settings for Internet Explorer
- Add Custom Actions
- Display Custom Bitmaps and Icons
- Customize the Notification Area Shortcut Menu
- Include a Custom Help File
- Display Custom Support Information
- Include Connection Manager Software with the Connection Profile
- Display a Custom License Agreement
- Install Additional Files with the Connection Profile
- Build the Connection Profile and its Installation Program
- Make Advanced Customizations
- Your Connection Profile is Complete and Ready to Distribute
- Troubleshoot the Connection Profile Build Process

Installing Remote Access Services on Windows Server 2012 via PowerShell

If you prefer to use the PowerShell command line interface to deploy your VPN server(s), open a Windows PowerShell session with administrative rights:

1. On the desktop, right-click Windows PowerShell on the taskbar or

On the Windows Start screen, right-click the **PowerShell** tile

2. Click **Run as Administrator** in the right context menu or on the app bar.

To install the **Remote Access** server role on the Windows Server 2012 server, you will need to use the Windows PowerShell cmdlet **Install-WindowsFeature RemoteAccess–includemanagementtools-restart**

NOTE

As discussed previously, it is essential that the management tools be installed or you would not be able to configure the Remote Access server.

When you run the cmdlet, you will get a message that Windows is collecting data, then notification of installation progress, and when it is done, you will see the results (Success=True) and the warning that you must restart the server to finish the installation process, as shown in Figure 14.39.

As you can see, with PowerShell, you can accomplish with a single cmdlet what took 11 pages of wizardry in the graphical interface.

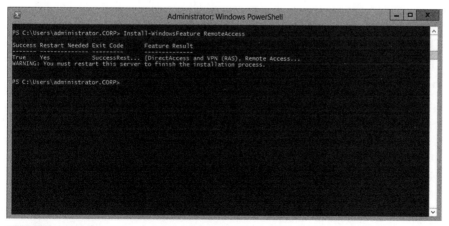

FIGURE 14.39 Remote Access feature was successfully installed via PowerShell. (For color version of this figure, the reader is referred to the online version of this chapter.)

There are a number of PowerShell cmdlets that can be used to manage VPN services, including the following:

- **Add-RemoteAccessRadius:** Adds a new external RADIUS server for VPN authentication.
- **Add-VpnIPAddressRange:** Adds a new IPv4 address range from which addresses can be assigned to VPN clients.
- **Disconnect-VpnUser:** Disconnects a VPN connection from a specific user or client computer.
- **Get-RemoteAccess:** Displays the configuration of the remote access VPN (and site-to-site VPN and DirectAccess if they are configured).
- **Get-RemoteAccessConnectionStatistics:** Displays statistics of the real-time currently active VPN connections for a specific period of time (and DA connections if it is configured).
- **Get-RemoteAccessConnectionStatisticsSummary:** Displays summary statistics of both real-time current connections and historical connections for a specific time duration.
- **Get-RemoteAccessRadius:** Displays a list of the RADIUS servers.
- **Get-RemoteAccessUserActivity:** Displays resources that have been accessed over the VPN (and DA, if configured) connections, both active and historical.
- **Set-RemoteAccess:** Modifies configuration common to DA and VPN (SSL certificate, internal interface, Internet interface).

These are just some of the cmdlets you can use to manage the Remote Access VPN server services; for a full list of all the available cmdlets, use the cmdlet: **Get-Command–Module RemoteAccess**.

You can also get more detailed information about specific cmdlets by using the cmdlet: **Get-Help < cmdlet name > - Detailed**.

DEPLOYING NETWORK ACCESS PROTECTION (NAP) THROUGH NETWORK POLICY AND ACCESS SERVICES

If you are coming to Windows Server 2012 from Windows Server 2003, when you think of RADIUS in Windows, you probably think of Internet Authentication Service (IAS). That changed in Windows Server 2008 when IAS was replaced by NPS—the Network Policy Server. The NPS is part of a larger framework: Microsoft's Network Policy and Access Services. The Network Policy and Access Services include the following role services:

- Network Policy Server (NPS)
- Health Registration Authority (HRA)' Host Credential Authorization Protocol (HCAP)

So, in addition to deploying RADIUS servers, this is the server role through which you deploy Network Access Protection (NAP) in Windows Server 2012. A new feature in Windows Server 2012 is the ability to use PowerShell to install and configure the Network Policy Server.

Note, too, that in Windows Server 2008/2008 R2, the RRAS service role was included in the Network Policy and Access services. That is no longer true; in Windows Server 2012, the RRAS role service is part of the **Remote Access** server role, as we saw earlier in the chapter.

NAP enforces health policies on a number of connection types, including IPsec-protected communications, IEEE 802.1X-authenticated communications, and terminal services gateway connections. In this chapter, we will be looking at NAP primarily as an enforcement mechanism for remote legacy clients connecting via a VPN.

NAP Overview

NAP utilizes a number of components on the server and client to allow administrators much greater control over which computers are allowed to connect to the network, and specifically to prevent systems that may be at risk—such as those that do not have up-to-date security patches, are not running antivirus software and antimalware software with current definitions, do not have an active host firewall, etc.—from connecting to the network and potentially putting other systems at risk as well.

NAP can be used with legacy clients running Windows XP SP3 and above; these operating systems support the NAP Agent that is the component on the client that collects and manages health information. When the NAP Agent service is installed and running, the client can communicate its health status to the NAP servers.

Health status information is based on the state of the client's configuration and can include such factors as the firewall status, antivirus signature status, and status of service packs and security updates. The health information that the client sends to the NAP server is called a statement of health or SoH. The server evaluates this information based on the policies and settings that have been configured.

How NAP Protects the Network

NAP is Microsoft's implementation of Network Access Control (NAC), a "health" enforcement solution. In the context of protecting remote legacy clients and protecting the network from health "issues" that they may bring to the network, it checks the identity of each remote client and determines whether it is in compliance with the organization's health policies. It uses this information, along with Active Directory group membership, to determine whether and at what level of access the client will be allowed to connect to the corporate network. Clients that are out of compliance with the policies can be brought into compliance through NAP's mechanisms.

NAP does this through a flexible process that performs a network health analysis, verifies the effectiveness of existing security policies, helps you to identify risks by creating a health profile for the network, and thus improves the overall health of the network by enforcing compliance with your network health policies and restricting the access of remote client computers that are not in compliance.

Understanding NAP Concepts and Components

The Network Policy Server is the core component of a NAP deployment. It is used to manage network access through the VPN server, RADIUS servers, and other points of access to the network. Depending on your network environment, you may deploy multiple NPS servers. An NPS can be a RADIUS server, a RADIUS proxy, or a NAP policy server. In this chapter, we are most interested in this third role. The NAP server is where you configure the NAP policies and settings such as health policies, SHVs, and remediation server groups. Remediation servers are the servers to which noncompliant clients are allowed to connect in order to update their configurations so as to become compliant, after which they can be reevaluated and allowed to connect to other network resources.

Note that the NPS works in conjunction with other components—the System Health Agents (SHAs) and System Health Validators (SHVs). The SHA that is built into Windows Vista and Windows 7 operating systems is called the Windows Security Health Agent (WSHA), which works with the Windows Security Center on the client computer and the Windows Security Health Validator (WSHV). You can configure the WSHV settings to report on the host firewall, virus protection, spyware protection, automatic updating status, and security updates installed. Third-party vendors can use the NAP API to create SHAs and SHVs for their software products (for example, third-party antivirus programs). For more information about the WSHV, see the document *Windows Security Health Validator* in the TechNet Library.[5]

The Health Registration Authority (HRA) is another server-side component of NAP that is used in IPsec enforcement and is installed on a computer that is running NPS and IIS. These services must be installed on the HRA computer. When you install Network Policy and Access Services server role, the HRA administrative tool will be installed on the NPS

---

[5] Network Policy Server: *Windows Security Health Validator*. TechNet Library: http://technet.microsoft.com/en-us/library/cc731260.aspx.

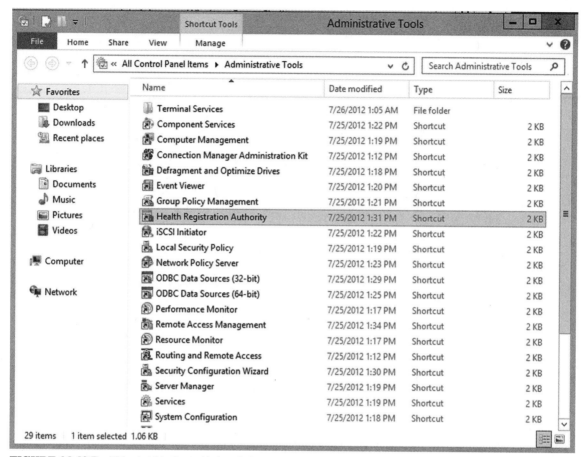

FIGURE 14.40 The HRA administrative tool is installed when you install the NPS role service. (For color version of this figure, the reader is referred to the online version of this chapter.)

server, as you can see in Figure 14.40. Likewise, if you install HRA, NPS is automatically installed.

The HRA approves the issuance of health certificates to NAP clients. There are X.509 certificates that are issued by an Active Directory certification authority (CA). A CA that issues health certificates is known as a NAP CA. To get a health certificate from the NAP CA, the client must submit a SoH to the HRA. IIS is used to provide the interface by which the clients contact the HRA to request a health certificate.

Deploying NAP on Windows Server 2012

To deploy NAP on Windows Server 2012, you need to install the Network Policy and Access Services role with the Network Policy Server role service. You can do this in one of the two ways: by using Server Manager to install NPS via the graphical user interface, or by using PowerShell to install NPS via the command line.

Note before attempting installation that if there is a manually configured static IPv6toIPv4 address on the computer, NPS may fail to install correctly. You should disable the IPv6 configuration before attempting to install NPS. Here is how:

1. On the Windows Server 2012 Start Screen, type **Network.**
2. In the right Search pane, select **Settings.**
3. Click the **View Network Connections** option in the list.
4. Right-click the network connection for your local network and select **Properties.**
5. On the **Networking** tab, uncheck the check box for **Internet Protocol version 6 (TCP/IPv6).**
6. Click **OK.**

Using Server Manager to Install and Manage the Network Policy Server

To install the NPS role service in Windows Server 2012 via the graphical interface, first open Server Manager from the desktop taskbar or the **Server Manager** tile on the Start Screen, and perform the following steps:

1. In Server Manager, click **Manage** and click **Add Roles and Features.**
2. On the **Before you begin** page, click **Next.**
3. On the **Select Installation Type** page, click **Role/Feature Based Install** and then click **Next.**
4. On the **Select destination server** page, click **Select a server from the server pool**, click the names of the servers where you want to install NPS, and then click **Next.**
5. On the **Select Server Roles** page, click **Network Policy and Access Services** and then click **Next** three times.
6. On the **Select role services** page, click **Network Policy Server**, and in the **Add Roles and Features Wizard** dialog box, verify that **Include management tools (if applicable)** is selected.
7. Click **Add Features** and then click **Next.**
8. On the **Confirm installation selections** page, click **Install.**
9. On the **Installation Results** page, verify that the installation was successful and then click **Close.**

Using PowerShell to Install and Manage Network Policy Server

To install the NPS role service in Windows Server 2012 using PowerShell, you first need to right-click the PowerShell icon on the taskbar and select **Run as**

administrator in order to open a PowerShell session with administrative privileges. Then perform the following steps:

1. Load the Server Manager module by typing: **Import-Module Servermanager**
2. Next, install the NPS role service by typing: **Install-WindowsFeature–name napas-policy-server–includemanagementtools**

NOTE

This will also install the DHCP server role.

---

3. When the role service has been successfully installed, PowerShell will report Success=True and the Feature Result will show Network Policy and Access Services, as shown in Figure 14.41.

Configuring the Network Policy Server

You can configure the NAP server with three different types of policies:

- **Connection Request Policies** that use connections and settings to authenticate client requests to access the network. These policies also control where the authentication will be performed. You must have a connection request policy for each NAP enforcement method.
- **Network Policies** that use conditions, settings, and constraints to determine the level of access that will be authorized for a client that attempts to connect to the network. You need at least two network policies to deploy NAP: one for client computers that are found to be compliant with your health policies and one for those clients that are out of compliance.
- **Health Policies** that specify which System Health Validators (SHVs) are to be evaluated and how they are to be used to evaluate health status. You have to enable at least one SHV for each health policy.

FIGURE 14.41 The NPS role has been successfully installed. (For color version of this figure, the reader is referred to the online version of this chapter.)

When creating network policies, you need to keep in mind that a client request can match one connection policy and one network policy. It cannot match multiple policies of a type, so when a match is made, none of the other policies will be applied. That means the order of processing policies is important. The source of the request is also used in determining the order for evaluation.

If there are policies that specify a source, requests sent from a matching source are only evaluated against these policies. If none of the policies specify a source that matches, clients try to match policies with the **Unspecified** source. If there are multiple policies with the same source that matches the client source, the policy that is highest in the processing order is used (and if it fails, the NPS goes down the list of policies in the processing order until it finds a policy that matches). For more information on types of polices and policy design principles, see the *NAP Health Policy Servers* document in the *NAP Infrastructure Overview* in the TechNet Library.[6]

To configure NSP with a network policy, use the New Network Policy wizard on the NPS server. On the NPS server, open the Network Policy Server administrative tool from the Administrative Tools menu. In the left pane, expand the **Policies** node and click **Network Policies**. Right-click and select **New** to start the New Network Policy Wizard, as shown in Figure 14.42.

Similarly, you can create a new connection request policy or a new health policy by right-clicking the **Connection Request Policy** or **Health Policies** node and selecting **New**.

Configuring VPN Servers with NPS

The steps involved in configuring VPN servers with NPS are as follows:

1. Install and configure your VPN servers as discussed in the first part of this chapter.
2. Decide what authentication method is to be used.
3. Install the NPS role on the NPS server.
4. Autoenroll a server certificate to the NPS server(s) or purchase a server certificate (for PEAP-MS-CHAP v2 authentication).
5. For EAP-TLS or PEAP-TLS without smart cards, autoenroll user and/ or computer certificates to domain users and client computers that are domain members.
6. Configure your VPN servers as RADIUS clients in NPS.
7. Create an Active Directory user group for users who will be allowed to connect via the VPN servers.
8. Configure network policies for VPN services in NPS.

---

[6] INAP Infrastructure Overview: *NAP Health Policy Servers*. TechNet Library http://technet.microsoft. com/en-us/library/dd125305(v=ws.10).aspx.

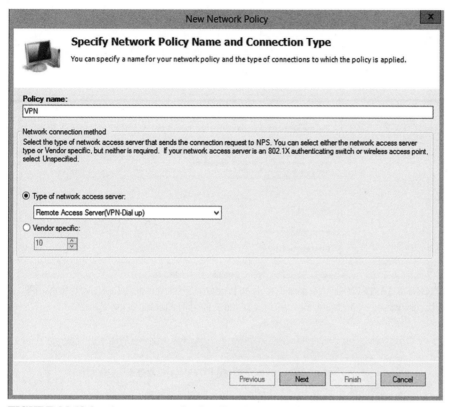

FIGURE 14.42 Creating a new network policy. (For color version of this figure, the reader is referred to the online version of this chapter.)

To create the connection request and network policies that you need in order to deploy VPN servers as RADIUS clients to the NPS server, you can use the **New Dial-up or Virtual Private Network Connections** wizard. Open the NPS console from the Administrative Tools menu on the server where you have installed the Network Policy Server role service. Click the **NPS (Local)** top level node in the left pane and follow these steps:

1. Under **Standard Configuration,** in the drop-down box, select **RADIUS server for Dial-up or VPN Connections,** as shown in Figure 14.43.
2. Click **Configure VPN or Dial-Up.**
3. In the wizard, select **Virtual Private Network (VPN) Connections** under the **Type of connections** section, as shown in Figure 14.44.

Provide text to be part of the name for each of the policies the wizard creates or accept the default and click **Next.**

4. On the **Specify Dial-Up or VPN Server** page, the local computer will be automatically added as a RADIUS client to the NPS server if it is running RRAS as a VPN server. You can add remote VPN servers by clicking the **Add** button.

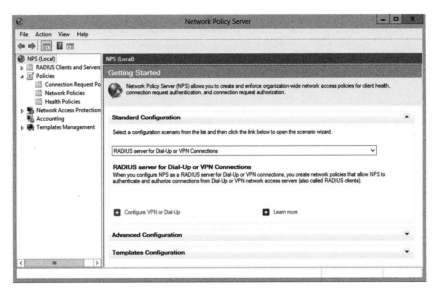

FIGURE 14.43 Creating the policies required to deploy VPN servers as RADIUS clients to the NPS. (For color version of this figure, the reader is referred to the online version of this chapter.)

FIGURE 14.44 Selecting the connections type (VPN). (For color version of this figure, the reader is referred to the online version of this chapter.)

FIGURE 14.45 Configuring the authentication method(s). (For color version of this figure, the reader is referred to the online version of this chapter.)

5. On the **Configure Authentication Methods** page, select the protocol(s) you want to use for authentication, as shown in Figure 14.45.
6. On the **Specify User Groups** page, you can select the groups to which the policy will apply by clicking the **Add** button. If you do not select any groups, the policy will apply to all users.
7. On the **Specify IP Filters** page, you can configure IPv4 and IPv6 input and output filters for the RRAS VPN server.
8. On the **Specify Encryption Settings** page, you can select the encryption strength to be used for MPPE (40-bit, 56-bit, and/or 128-bit). By default, all the three are selected, as shown in Figure 14.46.
9. On the **Specify Realm Name** page, you can specify a realm name to replace the domain name in user credentials. This is the name that your ISP uses to forward requests. This is an optional field.
10. On the **Completing New Dial-Up or Virtual Private Network Connections and RADIUS clients** page (the last page of the wizard), you

FIGURE 14.46 Specifying encryption settings. (For color version of this figure, the reader is referred to the online version of this chapter.)

can click **Configuration Details to review** your configuration choices. This will open the configuration details in your default Web browser, as shown in Figure 14.47.

11. Click **Finish** in the wizard to create the policies. They will now show up in the **Connection Request Policies** and **Network Policies** nodes in the Network Policy Server console, as shown in Figure 14.48.

Configuring the HRA

You can configure the authentication requirements, certification authority, and request policy for the HRA:

■ **Authentication requirements:** You can either restrict the issuance of health certificates to authenticated domain users or you can allow anonymous users to obtain health certificates. If you allow both, two separate Web sites will be created, one for requests by domain users and one for requests by anonymous users. You can enable SSL so that

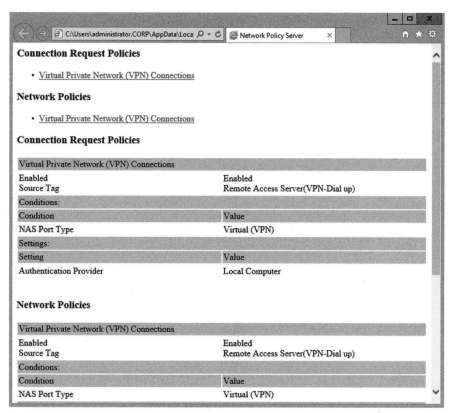

FIGURE 14.47 Viewing configuration details in the browser. (For color version of this figure, the reader is referred to the online version of this chapter.)

clients communicating with the Web sites must use a secure (https://) URL. The IIS server will need an SSL certificate in the local computer certificate store or the current user certificate store, to be used for server authentication.

- **Certification Authority:** You must configure the HRA with at least one NAP CA. You can add or delete CAs and change their order from the HRA console's **Certification Authority** node. You can use either a standalone CA or an enterprise CA.
- **Request Policy:** The request policy settings define how the HRA communicates with clients, specifically the cryptographic policy elements that include asymmetric key algorithms, hash key algorithms, cryptographic service providers, and transport policy. You can use the default request policy setting that negotiates a mutually acceptable encryption mechanism, and this is usually the best practice unless you are certain your modified settings will work properly.

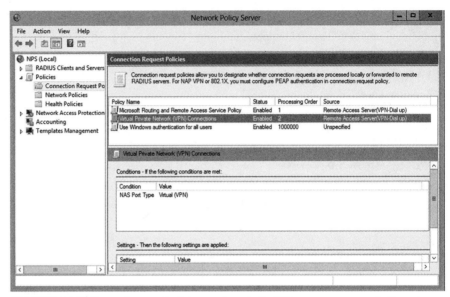

FIGURE 14.48 The newly created policies are shown in the NPS management console. (For color version of this figure, the reader is referred to the online version of this chapter.)

Configuring Client Computers

Microsoft recommends, as part of its practices, that client computers be configured automatically. NAP-capable client computers (those Windows XP SP3 and above systems on which the NAP Agent software is installed and running) can be configured automatically by importing NAP configuration files into Group Policy.

You can configure NAP client settings in one of the three ways:

- **NAP Client Configuration Console** gives you a graphical UI for configuring the NAP client settings.
- **Netsh** gives you a way to configure NAP client settings from the command line.
- **Group Policy Management Console** allows you to configure NAP client settings in Group Policy on clients that are domain members.

You can save NAP client settings in a configuration file that you can then apply to other computers. To import a configuration file, type **NAPCLCFG.MSC** at the command line or in the **Run** box to open the **NAP Client Configuration Console**. Right-click the top level node, **NAP Client Configuration (Local Computer)** in the left pane, and select **Import**, as shown in Figure 14.49.

Navigate to the location where the file is stored, type the file name for the configuration file, and select **Open**.

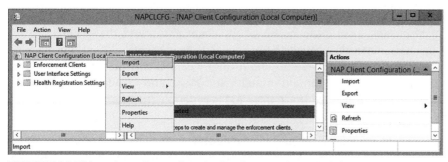

FIGURE 14.49 Importing a client configuration file. (For color version of this figure, the reader is referred to the online version of this chapter.)

Alternatively, you can type **netsh nap client import filename = <file name>**

You need to be a member of the local Administrators group on the computer to import a configuration file by either of these methods.

You must enable at least one NAP enforcement client on the client computers. The six NAP enforcement client types are:

■ DCHP
■ IPsec
■ Remote Desktop Gateway
■ EAP
■ Remote Access
■ Wireless EAP over LAN

Your VPN clients need to be enabled as Remote Access clients; so, health policies will be enforced when they attempt to access the network through the NAP-enabled VPN server. The NAP enforcement clients are enabled and disabled through the **NAP Client Configuration Console** or the **netsh** command. You need to be a local Administrator to enable or disable enforcement clients. To enable the Remote Access enforcement client through the console, click the **Enforcement Clients** node in the left pane. In the middle pane, right-click **Remote Access Quarantine Enforcement Client** and click **Enable**.

To enable the Remote Access enforcement client at the command line, type: **netsh nap client set enforcement ID = 79618 ADMIN–"ENABLE"**.

SUMMARY

Protecting remote legacy clients—and just as important, protecting your network from remote legacy clients that need to connect to it—tends to be a complex, multiforked strategy that involves the combination of multiple security mechanisms. In this chapter, we have focused on the deployment of a VPN server through Windows Server 2012 RRAS, and ways to secure those VPN connections and ensure the health of the client computers that connect to the corporate network through them. This is a good solution for Windows Vista or Windows XP client systems and for nonlegacy clients that are not members of the domain. For domain-joined Windows 7 and Windows 8 computers, DirectAccess (discussed in Chapter 13) is generally the more secure solution.

As part of our discussion regarding security issues surrounding remote legacy clients, we talked about how the deployment of a Network Policy Server for the implementation of Network Access Protection can offer an additional protective mechanism. NPS/NAP is a complicated technology and we only touched on the basics of its deployment in this chapter. There are many minute details involved in the full deployment of NAP, and specific configurations are dependent on the configuration of your network infrastructure. Network Policy and Access Services in Windows Server 2012 could easily consume an entire book; thus, there are many aspects of NAP deployment that are beyond the scope of this chapter. We did not discuss firewall configuration issues affecting NPS clients and servers, the NPS templates, registration of the NPS server in Active Directory Domain Services, certificate requirements, and deployment for PEAP and EAP, and many other configuration options for the NPS. For more information regarding those topics, be sure to check out the detailed documentation in the Network Policy and Access Services section of the Microsoft TechNet library.[7]

---

[7] *Network Policy and Access Services*, TechNet Library http://technet.microsoft.com/en-us/library/cc753220.aspx.

Cloud Security

CONTENTS

CHAPTER POINTS

- General Considerations for Cloud Security (SaaS)
- General Considerations for Cloud Security (IaaS)
- Building a Private Cloud with Windows Server 2012

GENERAL CONSIDERATIONS FOR CLOUD SECURITY (SaaS)

Many companies are considering moving their business to a model where they can offload the maintenance of their services to the cloud provider. The overall idea of not having to deal with software upgrade, hardware refresh, and other maintenance-related issues sounds just too good to be true. That is where the core concern comes into discussion: are we really secured when we moved to the cloud?

The fact of the matter is that there are many myths[1] out there related to cloud computing security. This is true mainly in the SaaS model because the company that is contracting the server and moving their business to be fully clouded based will lose access to physical resources (Oh dear, I cannot hug my server anymore!). Get over it! This idea that you must physically have it in order to protect it is not sustainable and should not be the core reason for you to avoid or embark on this cloud migration.[2]

IMPORTANT

we recommend you to use the Cloud Alliance (CSA) Cloud Control Matrix to understand what cloud vendors should be doing to protect their infrastructure and also to perform an assessment of the overall security risk for cloud provider. You can download this matrix from https://cloudsecurityalliance.org/research/ccm/.

When discussing the cloud options with the cloud provider, it is important to understand their offering based on the following security principals:

- IIA (Integration, Identity, and Access)
  - How this cloud platform does integrate with others vendors from the authentication and authorization perspective?
  - How the cloud provider does provide unintentional access to my resources?
  - What are the mechanisms in place to federate identity?
- Privacy[3]
  - What are the methods that are in place to protect my data while in transit and at-rest on the cloud provider datacenter? Is it using encryption?
  - From the privacy law perspective, how the cloud provider handles my data location? It will be possible that in a disaster recovery scenario that the data for my company have to resides outside of US?
  - Are my data replicated to another datacenter outside the United States?
  - Will my data be released to the government?
- Isolation
  - How isolation between tenants on the cloud is done?
  - Is my data inspected during the traffic within the datacenter?
  - Is it encrypted while in transit within the datacenter?

---

[1] You can find some myths documented in this chapter http://www.wired.com/insights/2012/03/cloud-security/.

[2] Some tangible reasons to migrate to a public cloud (SaaS based) can be found here http://blogs.technet.com/b/yuridiogenes/archive/2011/10/28/the-path-to-the-public-cloud.aspx.

[3] Beware of some risks involving privacy on the cloud by reading this chapter http://www.computerworld.com/s/article/9128636/Report_cites_potential_privacy_gotchas_in_cloud_computing.

- Integrity
  - How the cloud provider protects their assets, including software from malicious threats?
  - Does the software that will be used on the cloud was developed to be cloud-based software and did it use any type of SDL (Security Development Lifecycle)[4] approach during the development?
  - Does the cloud provider have any threat modeling for their core infrastructure?
  - What about hiring process? Who will handle my data?
- Incident Response & Forensics
  - How cloud provider handles incident response?
  - If my company needs access to audit logs in order to perform a forensics investigation how to obtain the data?
  - Can I install third party software to perform further investigation?
- Physical Security
  - What certifications the cloud provider's datacenter has?
  - Where is my data located[5]?
  - What are the physical security[6] practices in place to protect my data?

Those core security components of the cloud provider infrastructure as well as policy and certifications are the tip of the iceberg from the validation perspective. One of the most vital documents to be carefully validated during this negotiation is the SLA (Service Level Agreement). You must be diligent to carefully read every single clause and verify if it meets your company needs. The uptime of the service may vary according to the cloud provider and the "package" that you are about to subscribe. Review each and every aspect of the SLA and the overall security cloud infrastructure strategy[7] of the cloud provider and remember: do not be intimidated by the sales talk, you make the final decision when you are comfortable and confident with the answers.

NOTE

Some vendors will provide a Q&A about their own cloud computing infrastructure. Here, an example of security questions that are answered by Microsoft TwC http://www.microsoft.com/about/twc/en/us/cloud/faq.aspx.

---

[4] A very important video from Tim Rains about SDL in the cloud can be found at http://www.microsoft.com/en-us/showcase/details.aspx?uuid=dc92e8fa-75a5-48a3-a1cf-4263ce7fd155.

[5] A good example of how a datacenter looks like can be found in this video http://blogs.technet.com/b/yuridiogenes/archive/2011/07/26/where-is-my-data.aspx.

[6] Tim Rains cover some aspects of Physical Security in a Cloud environment in this video http://www.microsoft.com/en-us/showcase/details.aspx?uuid=3280cc50-de82-403d-b05d-dd8706cf3331.

[7] Microsoft has a paper describing their cloud infrastructure security that can be downloaded from http://cdn.globalfoundationservices.com/documents/WP_Securing_Microsoft_Cloud_Infrastructure.pdf.

Cloud Security Readiness Tool

Microsoft recently released a tool based on the CSA Cloud Matrix that aims to assist companies to realize the potential benefits in moving to the cloud. For this book, we will use the scenario of EndtoEdge.com to go over some rationale behind this tool and demonstrate how it works.

The first step is to access the tool, which is available at https://roianalyst.alinean.com/msft/AutoLogin.do?d=563612287085088525; once you access this tool, you have fill the company profile as shown in Figure 15.1.

The second part of the screen is to answer 27 questions (that was the number by the time we wrote this chapter). These questions are very important to reflect how mature the company is from the security perspective and must they all be answered. Once you finish answering all the questions, you will see the option to download the report as shown in Figure 15.2.

The report will show the control objective, the current state, the recommendation, and the advantage of moving to a SaaS solution as shown in Figure 15.3.

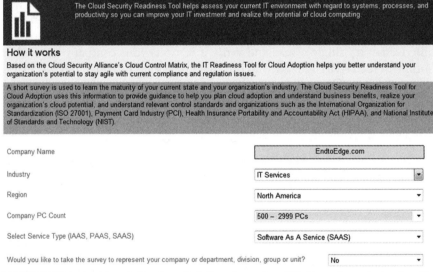

FIGURE 15.1 Cloud Security Readiness Tool. (For color version of this figure, the reader is referred to the online version of this chapter.)

FIGURE 15.2 Initial output. (For color version of this figure, the reader is referred to the online version of this chapter.)

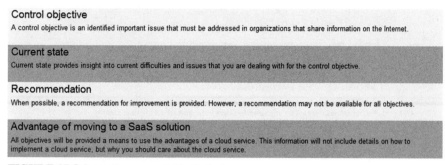

FIGURE 15.3 Suggestions generated by the tool.

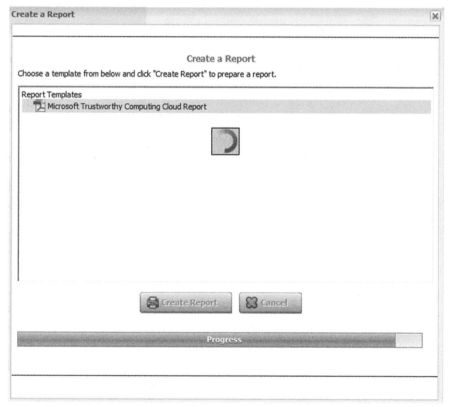

FIGURE 15.4 Generating the report in PDF. (For color version of this figure, the reader is referred to the online version of this chapter.)

Once you create the report, it will ask you to register with basic information (name, company, and e-mail) and it will start generating the PDF report as shown in Figure 15.4.

The report will contain very detail explanation of each section and the rationale for the option. The report for EndtoEdge.com had 60 pages going through each item and giving not only the current state (based on the answers that we gave)

EndtoEdge.com's Considerations

Security policies and procedures

Current State

No formal security policies or procedures have been created. Information security policies may be inconsistent or unclear, which can leave critical information such as your customer's data vulnerable. Your assets are at risk of unauthorized disclosure, alteration, or loss.

Recommendation

Adopting an information security management system (ISMS) that conforms to industry best practices for information security, as defined by ISO/IEC 27001-2005or other standards.

Advantage of moving to a SaaS service

A SaaS cloud solution would provide an improvement to your information security management practices.

An ISMS is a set of policies that govern information security for an organization. ISO/IEC 27001-2005 provides a model for creating, implementing, and maintaining an ISMS. SaaS service providers will typically implement centrally managed information security plans that conform to industry best practices regarding security, privacy, and risk; and are integrated with asset management, physical security, and access control policies. Regular audits help ensure effectiveness and conformance. A customer version of the provider's ISMS may be made available to qualifying customers and prospective customers on request.

FIGURE 15.5 Recommendations are based on the answers that were given. (For color version of this figure, the reader is referred to the online version of this chapter.)

but also the recommendation for each area and the advantage in moving to a SaaS model. Figure 15.5 brings an example of the first section of this report.

The report presented by Cloud Security Readiness Tool should assist your organization not only to realize the potential benefits of moving to a SaaS model but also to identify where your organization stands in the present moment related to security practices and industry standards.[8]

NOTE

For a deeper discussing around Cloud Security, we recommend you to read the book Securing the Cloud by Vic (J.R.) Winkler, also published by Syngrees. For more information about this book, read http://syngress.com/information-security-and-system-administrators/Securing-the-Cloud/.

---

[8] By the time we were writing this chapter, it was announced that Cloud Security Alliance recommended the Microsoft Cloud Security Readiness Tool as a simple way to evaluate IT potential and learn how to Adopt Cloud Services. You can read more about this announced here https://cloudsecurityalliance.org/csa-news/csa-recommends-cloud-security-readiness-tool/.

GENERAL CONSIDERATIONS FOR CLOUD SECURITY (IaaS)

Infrastructure as a Service (IaaS) is one of the three cloud service models. The aim of Infrastructure as a Service solution is to provide the core infrastructure that consumers of the cloud service would need to run operating systems without the consumer of the service need to worry about the core networking, compute and storage elements of the infrastructure. The service provider deals with those problems, and the consumer of the service only needs to worry about running an operating system and applications on the operating system they choose.

You can host an IaaS solution on-premises or in a hosted data center. They both have in common the fact that you control the entire stack. IaaS provides a core infrastructure that can grow your organization's business. IaaS involves virtualizing, abstracting, and automating the enterprise architecture and helps you move toward an IT as a service model. This may result in cost savings due to better utilization of hardware and increased faster time to market for consumers of your cloud service and through the ability to provide self-service access to enterprise infrastructure to application owners.

Many people are concerned with the use of public cloud Infrastructure as a Service solutions because by its very nature. Infrastructure as a Service uses a shared resource model, which organizations may be at odds with other organizations that are using the same infrastructure. While that might be true, you can also see the same phenomenon in a private cloud IaaS deployment. Whether public or private, isolation at each layer is critical. This isolation of virtual machines from one another is also required for Private Cloud IaaS solutions, as data held by one department or individual should not be made available to all tenants in the common IaaS Private Cloud infrastructure. In terms of security requirements, IaaS must implement security effectively at the level of the host, virtual machine, compute, memory, network, and storage.

In the following sections, we will talk about important security considerations and core Windows Server 2012 technologies that you can use to improve the security of your Hyper-V-based virtualization infrastructure for private cloud IaaS.

Network Security

When designing network connectivity for a secure IaaS cloud infrastructure, there are a number of security issues that you need to consider as they apply to current physical network infrastructure.

The first thing you should consider is a network vulnerability assessment (NVA) of your current network infrastructure. You should evaluate your

Table 15.1 Security Tasks

Task	Example
Detect and document vulnerabilities	■ Description: Switches located in the datacenter do not have the latest firmware. This may make them vulnerable to various network level attacks
Assign risk levels to discovered vulnerabilities	■ Risk Level: Severe, moderate, or low ■ Reason: Provide the reason why the network level attack you identified is severe, moderate or low
Follow on up identified vulnerabilities and determine if remediation has been completed	■ Description: Two months ago, the network vulnerability assessment (NVA) Report 00001 detected a specific network vulnerability (you would note the specific vulnerability). The problem was fixed/not fixed ■ Action: Note problem is resolved or escalate the problem to upper management to address this issue immediately

current position by evaluating every network access and control point, which includes routers and switches. The following table provides you with a framework that you can use to perform your network vulnerability assessment (Table 15.1).

Attackers typically look for network devices with outdated firmware or those that are poorly configure, or configured to use default value. In addition to the vulnerabilities that are resolved by applying security updates from the device vendor, you will need to consider other potential security issues, such as those caused by poor administration practices. Some of these include not changing weak default installation settings (such as a device-specific default password) and lack of network access controls.

You will also need to consider the following common network threats when thinking about network for a private cloud IaaS infrastructure:

- Sniffing
- Spoofing
- Session hijacking
- Denial of service

As a private cloud IaaS infrastructure administrator, you must be aware of threats that can compromise the network infrastructure. For more information about these common threats, please see Advanced Network Security at http://www.microsoft.com/learning/en/us/book.aspx?ID=6788&locale=en-us.

After you address the issues with the current network infrastructure, you will be ready to plan how you extend this level of security to the virtual network. Security considerations while designing and planning the cloud infrastructure should also include

- Network access control
- Network bandwidth control
- Network availability.

Network Access Control

One key network security issue is that of network access control. You want to make sure that when you are working with a shared infrastructure that tenants are not able to communicate with each other and that they are never able to impact the core cloud infrastructure over the network. In order to do this, you need built-in mechanisms that allow you to block and allow traffic as needed to maintain this level of isolation.

We typically think of several traffic profiles when working in a cloud IaaS environment:

- Tenant traffic
- Cluster/CSV traffic
- Management traffic
- Storage traffic

Each of these data flows needs to be isolated from each other to maintain the integrity of the IaaS cloud infrastructure.

Windows Server 2012 supports Hyper-V port ACLs that are controlled by the Hyper-V virtual switch. These ACLs enable you to create fine-grained rules that you can use to either allow or deny traffic destined to or from a virtual machine's virtual NIC. Port ACLs can be defined by IP address, IP address prefix or subnet mask, or the MAC address of the incoming or outgoing packets.

Since Port ACLs are a port property of the Hyper-V virtual switch, when a virtual machine live migrates to another host, the need to ACLs moves with the virtual machine. Although it is technically possible to provide multitenancy isolation by using only ACLs, the challenge is managing and keeping all ACLs updated on all machines that are participating in the IaaS cloud infrastructure. For this reason, you will need a fabric controller such as System Center Virtual Machine Manager to handle Port ACL mappings for all the nodes in the failover cluster that hosts the IaaS cloud infrastructure.

For more information about port ACLs in Hyper-V, see Hyper-V Virtual Switch Overview at http://technet.microsoft.com/library/hh831823.aspx.

Table 15.2 Access Control Plan

Issue	Description
Security goals	Defines the resources that you are protecting and the level of network security that is required. For example, Live Migration traffic contains workload data and therefore you might want to consider using IPsec for that traffic profile
Security risks	Enumerates the types of security hazards that affect your IaaS cloud infrastructure. These include ricks that pose threats and how significant these threats are. Also consider the different security risks that you might encounter for each of the traffic profiles
Security strategies	Describes the general security strategies necessary to meet the threats and mitigate the risks. The strategies that you define will then turn into your security tactics, which will be enumerated in your security policy
Security policy	Defines and enforces your security strategy both the tenant network and the IaaS cloud infrastructure network
Information security strategies	Defines how you plan to implement information security solutions. You may or may not want to enforce such policies on the tenants of the IaaS infrastructure, but you definitely want to define these for the cloud infrastructure itself
Administrative policies	Documents policies for delegation of administrative tasks and monitoring of audit logs to detect suspicious activity

You will want to develop a network access control strategy that describes the approach you decide to use to secure the IaaS cloud infrastructure. A typical network access control plan might include considerations listed in Table 15.2.

Network Bandwidth Control

Our team has documented in Private Cloud Security Challenges, which is part of our Private Cloud Reference architecture that one of the concerns of a designer of an IaaS cloud infrastructure is that: "A rogue application, client, or DoS attack might destabilize the datacenter by requesting a large amount of resources. How do I balance the requirement that individual consumers/tenants have the perception of infinite capacity with the reality of limited shared resources?"

What you want to prevent is a situation where one or more of the tenants step on each other in terms of network access. A compromised tenant might be able to DoS the network by using some type of network flooding exploits. In this case, even though a single tenant is compromised, that single tenant could end up compromising the entire tenant network infrastructure because other tenants will no longer have their workloads accessible to client systems.

One way to address this concern is by controlling the network traffic by using bandwidth shaping or quality of service (QoS) technologies. QoS in Windows Server 2012 is designed to help manage network traffic on the physical network and on the virtual network, as there is both a Windows QoS and a Hyper-V virtual switch QoS. Policy-based QoS is designed to manage network bandwidth allocations on the physical network and can be leveraged by both the virtual machine tenants and the host systems that comprise the IaaS cloud infrastructure. In that way, you can get very granular in terms of how you shape traffic at both the host and guest perspectives.

The use of policy-based QoS allows you to specify network bandwidth control based on the type of application, users, and computers. You can also use Policy-based QoS to help control bandwidth costs and negotiate service levels with bandwidth providers or departments (which would be represented as different tenants in the IaaS cloud infrastructure). Hyper-V QoS enables administrators of an IaaS cloud infrastructure to provide specific network performance values based on service-level agreements (SLAs) you set with your tenants. Most importantly, Hyper-V QoS also helps ensure that no tenant is impacted or compromised by other tenants on their shared infrastructure, since the tenant virtual machines can have their bandwidth limited by setting an absolute high limit or by allowing them a certain percentage of the total available bandwidth on the link.

QoS is also useful for making sure that all the infrastructure traffic profiles have the bandwidth they need. For example, you do not want the Live Migration traffic to step on the storage traffic and vice versa. Both these traffic profiles are high-throughput, low-latency traffic profiles, and thus they require QoS in order to operate effectively.

When designing security for your IaaS cloud infrastructure, consider developing a QoS plan that describes how to create a network fair share environment that incorporates both the IaaS cloud infrastructure and the tenants.

A typical QoS plan might include the following sections:

- SLA: Plan QoS policy-based on the tenants' SLA.
- IaaS cloud infrastructure QoS policy: determine absolutely min/ max bandwidth requirements for each infrastructure traffic profile or create percentage of bandwidth values that can be assigned to each infrastructure traffic profile.
- Network utilization: Put together a plan to measure the bandwidth utilization for each of the infrastructure and tenant traffic profiles. Then adjust QoS policies so that they are in line with your objective findings.

You have the ability to apply policies on a per tenant basis. You do this by creating multiple virtual NICs in Hyper-V and specify QoS[9] on each virtual NIC individually. An example on how to establish QoS per virtual NIC is shown below:

New-NetQosPolicy—Name "NIC Name Description"—NICName— MinBandwidthWeightAction 20.

Network Scalability and Performance

At first glance, you might not consider scalability and performance key factors in private cloud IaaS infrastructure security. But when you think about the Availability in the Confidentiality, Integrity, and Availability (CIA) information security model, you begin to realize that without the infrastructure components in place to meet your scalability and performance needs, and then your overall security posture is negatively affected.

These issues are especially important to consider when you think about private cloud IaaS infrastructure security. IaaS workloads, unlike traditional "siloed" datacenter workloads, are very unpredictable. You are providing a pool of network resources to consumers of the private cloud. Some of the consumers will have low bandwidth requirements, some moderate requirements, and some will have very heavy network bandwidth requirements. You need to maintain an SLA for all of these users and therefore will need to have a private cloud IaaS infrastructure in place that can scale to meet the needs of your anticipated workloads.

When considering the cloud IaaS network infrastructure, you should evaluate your current network to understand the port bandwidth usage and capabilities required at all layers. This includes the ability of the distribution and core tiers to provide higher-speed uplinks to aggregate traffic. This is especially important because as you consider placing members of the same cluster into different fault domains,[10] cloud infrastructure traffic is going to have to traverse top of rack switches and thus might represent a bottleneck in the system. Additional considerations include Ethernet broadcast boundaries and limitations, and spanning tree and/or other loop avoidance technologies should be considered because you have to deal with the Ethernet implications not only of the host operating systems but also of the hundreds or thousands or even tens of thousands of virtual machines that are connected to the same private cloud IaaS network infrastructure.

In order to improve overall performance per Ethernet broadcast domain, physical separation of the segments should also be considered. Make sure that the

---

[9] For more information about Policy-based QoS, see Quality of Service (QoS) Overview at http://technet.microsoft.com/library/hh831679.aspx.
[10] You can read more about the concept of Fault Domain at http://social.technet.microsoft.com/wiki/contents/articles/4346.private-cloud-principles-patterns-and-concepts.aspx.

host servers that support the guest virtual machines utilize different network segments by either using separate physical adapters for each traffic profile, or by using VLAN tagging or virtual NICs.

Although physical separation of the traffic can be a business requirement, there are viable scenarios for which this is not the case, and the primary business requirement is to reduce overall cost while maintaining logical isolation between tenants. When business requirements lead you to the most cost-effective planning decision, you can converge all the datacenter networks into basically two networks: physically or logically isolated:

- A cloud infrastructure network that carries all the storage, live migration, clustering, and management traffic flows.
- A tenant network that carries all of the virtual machine tenant-generated traffic.

The cloud infrastructure network traffic is typically handled by a NIC team that consists of two or more teamed NICs. This NIC team should include 10 Gbps NICs so that high bandwidth, low-latency traffic like Live Migration and Cluster/CSV traffic can move over this network without hitting significant bandwidth. Remember that Windows Server 2012 supports NIC teaming right out of the box and NIC teaming not only provides high availability for the NICs but also provides for bandwidth aggregation.

The tenant network can include a team of either 1 or 10 Gbps NICs. The choice should be made based on what your projected network requirements might be for the tenant network. The 1 Gbps NICs certainly are more cost-effective, and it is true that you can team up to 32 of these NICs to give you an aggregate bandwidth of up to 32 Gbps (although due to the NIC Teaming algorithm you will not always see this in practice). The problem is that most private cloud IaaS infrastructure networks are fairly dense, and so it is going to be hard to get the number of PCI slots per server that you need to support this kind of configuration. That makes the 10 Gbps option more attractive, but the problem here is that these modern NICs cost about $500 at the time that we are writing this and therefore adds significantly to the cost per server in the private cloud IaaS infrastructure.

This means that you will need to be very mindful of the number of virtual machines and the max amount of bandwidth you want to supply each virtual machine per server. You also want to be able to give yourself plenty of extra room because if you ever need to fail over a fault domain, or worse, if you reach maximum decay,[11] a failed fault domain, and an upgrade domain in action—you will want to be able to support all the virtual machines that will need to be moved

---

[11] You can read more about the concept of Maximum Decay at http://social.technet.microsoft.com/wiki/contents/articles/4346.private-cloud-principles-patterns-and-concepts.aspx.

Table 15.3 Network Technologies

Network Technology	Advantages	Disadvantages
10 GB Ethernet	High performance Support hardware-offloaded QoS through Datacenter Bridging Remote DMA (RDMA) available, also known as SMB Direct	Physical switch ports more expensive NICs more expensive
InfiniBand (32 and 56 GB)	Very high performance, very low latency RDMA supported (for SMB 3.0 file access)	Takes special skills to manage Overall solution is more expensive
1 GB Ethernet	May be enough for non-network intensive workloads Very low cost	Limited scalability

into the servers held in reserve capacity. It is likely that these servers in reserve capacity are going to have higher VM density than the servers they were migrated from, so you need to take those networking requirements into consideration.

When choosing the networking hardware for your cloud infrastructure, consider the network infrastructure options in Table 15.3.

You can use remote methods for management of the network infrastructure through Windows PowerShell or RDP to support the cloud infrastructure network. Remote access and administration methods can be used by management systems to automate complex or error prone configuration activities. For example, adding a VLAN to a distributed set of access-tier switches can be automated to avoid the potential for human error. This is one example of how you would take advantage of the cloud fabric management system to help insure optimal network uptime.

Compute Security

In a private cloud IaaS infrastructure, there are two primary areas to consider when it comes to compute security. These areas are

- Compute security from the guest perspective
- Compute security from the host perspective

Guest Compute Security

In a private cloud IaaS cloud infrastructure, the Hyper-V guests will be managed by the tenant networks. That is to say, the tenant administrators will need to access their workloads through the tenant network, and not through the infrastructure network. This transfers the bulk of the security responsibilities to the tenant administrators; however, as a cloud provider, it is important to consider establishing security considerations or policies that you can apply to all the tenants in the private cloud IaaS infrastructure. Some important policies that you might include are

- **Updating virtual machines before they are deployed in the private cloud infrastructure:** Since virtual machines are easier to move around and quicker to deploy than physical machines, there is a greater risk that a virtual machine that is not fully updated or patched might be deployed before it is introduced into the private cloud IaaS infrastructure. Make it a requirement that tenant administrators update their machines with the latest security updates before deploying them to the private cloud IaaS infrastructure.
- **Integration services:** Require tenants to enable integration services to ensure accuracy of timestamps. Accuracy of timestamps is critical because you need to be able to relay on this information to accurate interpret log entries from disparate resources. These log entries are important for computer forensics and compliance. Integration services ensure that time is synchronized between virtual machines, and the management operating system is correct. This also means that you need to have a common time keeping mechanism for all the host systems in the private cloud IaaS infrastructure.
- **Role-based access control (RBAC):** Require that tenants use RBAC to reduce the number of guests that have administrative privileges in the tenant's virtual machine. Just like in noncloud infrastructures, the higher the number of administrators that have full control of the server, the higher the number of possibilities that some security flaw will result from misconfiguration.

IMPORTANT

For general guidelines about protecting the private cloud IaaS infrastructure, consider using the National Institute of Standards and Technology (NIST) **Guide to Security for Full Virtualization Technologies** at http://csrc.nist.gov/publications/nistpubs/800-125/SP800-125-final.pdf.

Host Compute Security

Adding the Hyper-V role in Windows Server 2012 increases the attack surface of the server. To determine the attack surface of this role, you might consider identifying the following:

- **Installed files:** Identify the files that are installed as part of the Hyper-V role.
- **Installed services:** Identify the services that are installed as part of the Hyper-V role.
- **Firewall rules:** Identify the firewall rules that are installed or enabled as a part of the Hyper-V role.

After you identify these, you can take action to mitigate potential threats on each attack surface by reviewing the following security best practices:

- **Do not run any applications on the host operating system:** By keeping the management operating system free of applications, you will need fewer updates to the management operating system. This is also an effective way to reduce the overall attack surface of the host operating system.
- **Consider limiting or avoiding virtual machine administrator permissions on the host operating system:** In a cloud infrastructure, the principle of least privilege is crucial. Consider giving administrators of a virtual machine (sometimes called department administrators or tenant administrators) the minimum permissions required. Use role-based access control to specify access control in terms of the cloud infrastructure and its tenants.
- **Consider using a dedicated network adapter for the host operating system:** Consider using a dedicated network adapter for managing the server running Hyper-V. Try to avoid exposing it to untrusted network traffic. Try to avoid allowing virtual machines to use this network adapter. Use one or more different dedicated network adapters for virtual machine networking. This allows you to apply different levels of network security policy and configuration for your virtual machines.
- **Consider hardening the Hyper-V host:** To reduce attack surface, use the Hyper-V Security Compliance Template that is available with Security Compliance Manager 3.0. For more information about the Security Compliance Manager, see Microsoft Security Compliance Manager.
- **Consider enabling Secure Boot on the Hyper-V host**: It is important to mitigate the potential for malware to gain access to the system even before the operating system is loaded. This also helps to mitigate potential downtime for the tenants connected to the Hyper-V server. For more information, see Secure Boot Overview.
- **Consider limiting the scope of antivirus scanning.** When installing antivirus software in the management operating system, consider configuring any real-time scanning components to exclude the directories where virtual machine files are stored, as well as the Hyper-V related process. If you do not create these exclusion rules, you might encounter errors when creating and starting virtual machines.

BUILDING A PRIVATE CLOUD WITH WINDOWS SERVER 2012

Microsoft developed Windows Server 2012 to be a cloud OS,[12] but how easy really is to deploy a cloud infrastructure with this OS? Well, one of the main projects that Tom Shinder and I (Yuri Diogenes) worked in 2012 was the documentation of some keys scenarios to deploy a cloud infrastructure with Windows

---

[12] Some core cloud OS principles can be found it here http://blogs.technet.com/b/serverandtools/archive/2012/09/04/the-cloud-os-becomes-reality-windows-server-2012-now-available.aspx.

Server 2012. Working together with Windows Server product team, we were able to identify three major scenarios and how to design the cloud infrastructure for those scenarios. The result of this work can be found on the documents below:

- Designing your cloud infrastructure http://technet.microsoft.com/en-us/library/hh831630.aspx
- Building Your Cloud Infrastructure: Non-Converged Data Center Configuration http://technet.microsoft.com/en-us/library/hh831559.aspx
- Building Your Cloud Infrastructure: Converged Data Center with File Server Storage http://technet.microsoft.com/en-us/library/hh831738.aspx
- Building Your Cloud Infrastructure: Converged Data Center without Dedicated Storage Nodes http://technet.microsoft.com/en-us/library/hh831829.aspx

At TechEd North America 2012, there were some key presentations that you should watch it that also cover these scenarios in more details. The presentations are

- Architecting Private Clouds Using Windows Server 2012. http://channel9.msdn.com/Events/TechEd/NorthAmerica/2012/WSV329
- Understanding and Deploying Hosted Private Cloud: Concepts and Implementation. http://channel9.msdn.com/Events/TechEd/NorthAmerica/2012/WSV320
- Building Hosted Public and Private Clouds Using Windows Server 2012. http://channel9.msdn.com/Events/TechEd/NorthAmerica/2012/WSV301

Having all these materials can definitely assist you deploying your Private Cloud using Windows Server 2012. However, a different scenario that can leverage the same core infrastructure previously mentioned and enhance the overall security by reducing the attack surface is the installation of Windows Server 2012 using Server Core. Many OEM vendors are building solutions (appliance[13] based) with Server Core to take advantage of the Windows Server 2012 robustness and cloud features while reducing the footprint and services in use. The first step is to install Windows Server 2012 Server Core, which is the default installation option in Windows Server 2012. The steps below describe this initial installation process:

1. Start your Server with Windows Server 2012 DVD (or USB) on the drive and review the initial setup window as shown in Figure 15.6. Select the appropriate options and click **Next**.
2. Click **Install Now** on the second window.
3. On the operating system selection window, select **Datacenter** (Server Core Installation) and click **Next**.

---

[13] Read the Configuration Lockdown for a Server Appliance for more information about this http://msdn.microsoft.com/en-us/library/ff770035(v=winembedded.60).aspx.

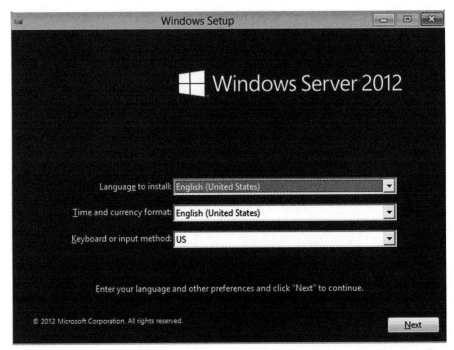

FIGURE 15.6 Windows Server 2012 installer. (For color version of this figure, the reader is referred to the online version of this chapter.)

4. Read the license terms, select the option **I accept the license terms**, and click **Next**.
5. Select the second option as shown in Figure 15.7.
6. Select the drive that you want to install Windows and click **Next**.
7. The installation will start as shown in Figure 15.8.
8. Once this part is finished, the server will restart, and once it comes back, you should see the prompt window, which means that the system is ready.

Once the Server is installed, you can automate the installation process of some core elements that are necessary for a cloud infrastructure in Windows Server 2012. Some of these keys elements are

- Networking (NIC Teaming, QoS, DCB, etc.)
- Failover Clustering
- Hyper-V
- Storage Spaces
- Disk Management (including MPIO)
- Server Management
- Active Directory

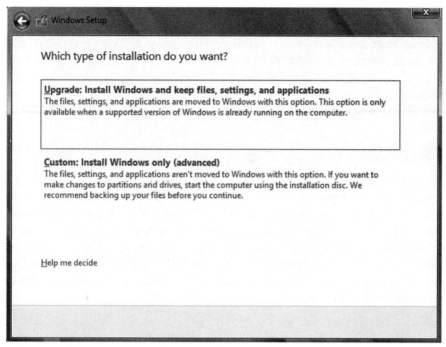

FIGURE 15.7 Selecting the type of installation. (For color version of this figure, the reader is referred to the online version of this chapter.)

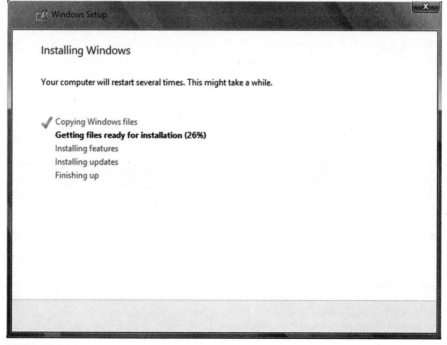

FIGURE 15.8 Installation in progress. (For color version of this figure, the reader is referred to the online version of this chapter.)

All these components can be configured and managed using PowerShell. Josh Adams, from Microsoft, wrote a table and published at TechNet Gallery[14] that brings the steps to configure each one of those components using PowerShell. If you are going to use SMB shares for Hyper-V storage in your cloud infrastructure, you can also automate the configuration process by using another PowerShell script created by Josh Adams.[15]

SUMMARY

In this chapter, we aimed at providing you an overview with some specific insights into how you can bolster your cloud security. In the first part of this chapter, we took a look at how you can evaluate security for your public cloud Software as Service solutions. In the second part of this chapter, we took a look at some of the important considerations you need to ponder when dealing with private cloud IaaS infrastructure security. We then rounded out the chapter with a discussion of resource available to you so that you can begin to build out your own private cloud.

---

[14] Download the table from http://gallery.technet.microsoft.com/Windows-Server-2012-IaaS-e4533522/file/68253/1/Windows%20Server%202012%20IaaS%20Build%20Tables.docm.

[15] Download this script from http://gallery.technet.microsoft.com/SMB-Share-Configuration-4a36272a.

Index

Note: Page numbers followed by *f* indicate figures and *t* indicate tables.

511